Socratic Logic

Other books by Peter Kreeft from St. Augustine's Press

The Philosophy of Jesus
Jesus-Shock
The Sea Within: Waves and the Meaning of All Things
I Surf, Therefore I Am
If Einstein Had Been a Surfer
An Ocean Full of Angels

Other books from St. Augustine's Press and Dumb Ox Books

James V. Schall, S.J., *The Regensburg Lecture*
William of Ockham, *Ockham's Theory of Terms: Part I of the* Summa Logicae, M. Loux, trans.
William of Ockham, *Ockham's Theory of Propositions: Part II of the* Summa Logicae, A.J. Freddoso & H. Schuurmann, trans.
Plato, *The Symposium of Plato: The Shelley Translation*, P. S. Shelley, trans.
Aristotle, *Aristotle – On Poetics*, S. Benardete & M. Davis, trans.
Aristotle, *Physics, Or Natural Hearing*, G. Coughlin, trans.
St. Augustine, *On Order [De Ordine]*, S. Borruso, trans.
St. Augustine, *The St. Augustine LifeGuide*, S. Borruso, ed.
Thomas Aquinas, *Commentary on Aristotle's Nicomachean Ethics*
Thomas Aquinas, *Commentary on Aristotle's De Anima*
Thomas Aquinas, *Commentary on Aristotle's Metaphysics*
Thomas Aquinas, *Commentary on Aristotle's Physics*
Thomas Aquinas, *Commentary on Aristotle's Posterior Analytics*, R. Berquist, trans.
Thomas Aquinas, *Commentary on the Epistle to the Hebrews*, C. Baer, trans.
Thomas Aquinas, *Commentary on St. Paul's Epistles to Timothy, Titus, and Philemon*, C. Baer, trans.
Thomas Aquinas, *Disputed Questions on Virtue*, R. McInerny, trans.
Henry of Ghent, *Henry of Ghent's* Summa of Ordinary Questions: Article One: On the Possibility of Human Knowledge, R.J. Teske, S.J., trans.
John of St. Thomas, *Introduction to the Summa Theologiae of Thomas Aquinas*, R. McInerny, trans.
Servais Pinckaers, O.P., *Morality: The Catholic View*, M. Sherwin, O.P., trans.

Socratic Logic
Edition 3.1

by Peter Kreeft

Edited by Trent Dougherty

A LOGIC TEXT USING
SOCRATIC METHOD,
PLATONIC QUESTIONS, &
ARISTOTELIAN PRINCIPLES

Modeling Socrates as the ideal teacher for the beginner
and Socratic method as the ideal method

Introducing philosophical issues along with logic
by being philosophical about logic and logical about philosophy

Presenting a complete system of classical Aristotelian logic,
the logic of ordinary language and of the four language arts,
reading, writing, listening, and speaking

ST AUGUSTINE'S PRESS
South Bend, Indiana

Manufactured in the United States of America

5 6 7   24 23 22 21 20

Library of Congress Cataloging in Publication Data
Kreeft, Peter.
Socratic logic:
a logic text using Socratic method, Platonic questions & Aristotelian
principles / by Peter Kreeft; edited by Trent Dougherty. – Ed. 3.1.
p. cm.
Previously published: 3rd ed. c2008.
Includes bibliographical references and index.
ISBN 978-1-58731-808-5 (hardcover: alk. paper) 1. Logic.
I. Dougherty, Trent. II. Title.
BC108.K67 2010
160 – dc22   2010032937

∞ The paper used in this publication meets the minimum requirements
of the American National Standard for Information Sciences – Permanence
of Paper for Printed Materials, ANSI Z39.48-1984.

ST. AUGUSTINE'S PRESS
www.staugustine.net

Contents

*   "P" = "philosophical"; "B" = "basic." See p. 13, last paragraph.

Preface

This book is a dinosaur.

Once upon a time in Middle-Earth, two things were different: (1) most students learned "the old logic," and (2) they could think, read, write, organize, and argue much better than they can today. If you believe these two things are not connected, you probably believe storks bring babies.

It is time to turn back the clock. Contrary to the cliché, you *can* turn back the clock, and you should, whenever it is keeping bad time. (I learned that, and thousands of other very logical paradoxes, from G.K. Chesterton, the 20th century Socrates.)

As I write this, it is the last Sunday of October, and we have just turned back our clocks from daylight saving time to standard time. This is a parable for what I am convinced we must do in logic. The prevailing symbolic/mathematical logic is a logic that a computer can do; it is artificial, like daylight saving time. It is very useful where there is already much intelligence (in the minds of geniuses, especially in science), just as daylight saving time is very useful in the summer when there is a plenitude of sunlight. But as the sunlight of clear thinking, writing, reading, and debating decreases in our society, it is time to make progress by turning back the clock from "daylight saving time" to real time, real language, real people, and the real world. The old Socratic-Platonic-Aristotelian logic is simply more effective than the new symbolic logic in helping ordinary people in dealing with those four precious things.

This text differs from nearly all other logic texts in print in the three ways suggested by the subtitle. It does this by apprenticing itself to the first three great philosophers in history, Socrates, Plato, and Aristotle. (Do we have better ones today?)

(1) No other logic text explicitly sets out to train little Socrateses.

(2) No other logic text in print is so explicitly philosophical in a classical, Platonic way.

(3) And only two or three other, shorter, formal logic texts bypass mathematical and symbolic logic for the "Aristotelian" logic of real people,

real inquiry, and real conversations. (The only other alternative to symbolic logic available today is "*informal* logic" or "rhetoric." This is useful, but less exact and less philosophical.)

Introduction

Section 1. What good is logic?

This section will give you 13 good reasons why you should study logic.[1]

1. Order. You may be wondering, "What can I do with logic?" The answer is that logic can do something with you. **Logic builds the mental habit of thinking in an orderly way.** A course in logic will do this for you even if you forget every detail in it (which you won't, by the way), just as learning Latin will make you more habitually aware of the structure of language even if you forget every particular Latin word and rule.

No course is more practical than logic, for no matter what you are thinking *about*, you are *thinking*, and logic orders and clarifies your thinking. No matter what your thought's *content*, it will be clearer when it has a more logical *form*. The principles of thinking logically can be applied to *all* thinking and to every field.

Logic studies the forms or structures of thought. Thought has form and structure too, just as the material universe does. Thought is not like a blank screen, that receives its form only from the world that appears on it, as a movie screen receives a movie. This book will show you the basic forms (structures) and the basic laws (rules) of thought, just as a course in physics or chemistry shows you the basic forms and laws of matter.

2. Power. Logic has power: the power of proof and thus persuasion. Any power can be either rightly used or abused. This power of logic is rightly used to win the truth and defeat error; it is wrongly used to win the argument and defeat

---

1   Making *numbered lists* like this is the first and simplest way we learn to order "the buzzing, blooming confusion" that is our world. Children, "primitive" peoples, and David Letterman love to make lists. Thus we find "twelve-step programs," "the Ten Commandments," "the Seven Wonders of the World," "the Five Pillars of Islam," "the Four Noble Truths," and "the Three Things More Miserable Than a Wet Chicken." To make a list is to classify many things under one general category, and at the same time to distinguish these things by assigning them different numbers.

your opponent. Argument is to truth as fishing is to fish, or war to peace, or courtship to marriage.

The power of logic comes from the fact that it is the science and art of argument. In the words of an old logic text, "Logick hath its name from *logos ratio*, because it is an Art which teacheth to Reason and Discourse." Thus beginneth Thomas Good's 1677 *A Brief English Tract of Logick*.

"Dialecticke, otherwise called Logicke, is an arte which teacheth to dispute well." This is the first sentence of a 1574 book, *Logicke*, by Peter Ramus Martyr.

Logic is so powerful that it can be dangerous to life. Socrates, the father of philosophy and the model for this book, was literally martyred for being logical – by the city of Athens, the ancient world's most famous and "civilized" democracy. The *Apology*, Socrates' "swan song," is his defense of philosophizing, of his life of logical inquiry. It is one of the greatest speeches ever made. No one should be allowed to die without reading it.[2]

Whether you use logic for right or wrong ends, it is a powerful tool. No matter what your thought's end or goal or purpose may be, it will attain that end more effectively if it is clearer and more logical. Even if you want to do something with logic rather than let logic do something with you – even if you want to deceive others, or "snow" them, or toy with them – you need to know logic in order to be a successful sophist. You must be a real logician even to be a fake one.

3. Reading. Logic will help you with all your other courses, for **logic will help you to read any book more clearly and effectively**. And you are always going to be reading books; books are the single most effective technological invention in the history of education. On the basis of over 40 years of full time college teaching of almost 20,000 students at 20 different schools, I am convinced that one of the reasons for the steep decline in students' reading ability is the decline in the teaching of traditional logic.

Mortimer Adler's classic *How to Read a Book* is based on the traditional common-sense logic of the "three acts of the mind" that you will learn in this book. If I were a college president, I would require every incoming freshman to read Adler's book and pass a test on it before taking other courses. (The most important points of that book are summarized in this book on p. 355.)

4. Writing. Logic will also help you to *write* more clearly and effectively, for clear writing and clear thinking are a "package deal": the presence or absence of either one brings the presence or absence of the other. Muddled writing fosters muddled thinking, and muddled thinking fosters muddled writing. Clear writing fosters clear thinking, and clear thinking fosters clear writing.

---

2   See *Philosophy 101 by Socrates: An Introduction to Philosophy via Plato's "Apology"* by Peter Kreeft (Ignatius Press, 2002).

Common sense expects this, and scientific studies confirm it. Writing skills have declined dramatically in the 40 years or so since symbolic logic has replaced Aristotelian logic, and I am convinced this is no coincidence.

There is nothing more effective than traditional logic in training you to be a clear, effective, and careful writer. It is simply impossible to *communicate* clearly and effectively without *thinking* clearly and effectively. And that means logic.

5. Happiness. In a small but significant way, **logic can even help you attain happiness.**

We all seek happiness all the time because no matter what else we seek, we seek it because we think it will be a means to happiness, or a part of happiness, either for ourselves or for those we love. And no one seeks happiness for any other end; no one says he wants to be happy in order to be rich, or wise, or healthy. But we seek riches, or wisdom, or health, in order to be happier.

How can logic help us to attain happiness? Here is a very logical answer to that question:

(1) When we attain what we desire, we are happy.
(2) And whatever we desire, whether Heaven or a hamburger, it is more likely that we will attain it if we think more clearly.
(3) And logic helps us to think more clearly.
(4) Therefore logic helps us to be happy.

No other things that make us happy are contradicted or threatened by logic, though many people think they are:

Beauty, for instance. There is nothing illogical about the beauty of a sunset, or a storm, or a baby.

Take heroism, or even holiness. What's *illogical* about being very, very good?

Even fantasy is not illogical. In fact, according to the greatest master of this art, J.R.R. Tolkien, "Fantasy is a rational, not an irrational, activity . . . creative fantasy is founded upon the hard recognition that things are so in the world as it appears under the sun; on a recognition of fact, but not a slavery to it. So upon logic was founded the nonsense that displays itself in the tales and rhymes of Lewis Carroll. If men really could not distinguish between frogs and men, fairy-stories about frog-kings would not have arisen." ("On Fairy-Stories") The reference to Lewis Carroll (the author of *Alice in Wonderland*) is particularly telling. Lewis Carroll was a pseudonym or pen name for Rev. Charles Lutwidge Dodgson, an Oxford mathematician who wrote a textbook in logic. In fact, he was working on volume two when he died.

6. Religious faith. All religions require faith. Is logic the ally or enemy of faith?

Even religion, though it goes *beyond* logic, cannot go *against* it; if it did, it would literally be unbelievable. Some wit defined "faith" as "believing what you know isn't true." But we simply *cannot* believe an idea to be true that we know has been proved to be false by a valid logical proof.

It is true that faith goes beyond what can be proved by logical reasoning alone. That is why believing in any religion is a free personal choice, and some make that choice while others do not, while logical reasoning is equally compelling for all. However, **logic can aid faith** in at least three ways. (And thus, if faith significantly increases human happiness, as most psychologists believe, it logically follows that logic can significantly increase happiness.)

First, logic can often *clarify* what is believed, and define it.

Second, logic can deduce the necessary *consequences* of the belief, and apply it to difficult situations. For instance, it can show that if it is true, as the Bible says, that "God works *all* things together for good for those who love Him" (Romans 8:28), then it *must* also be true that even seemingly terrible things like pain, death, and martyrdom will work together for good; and this can put these terrible things in a new light and give us a motive for enduring them with hope.

Third, even if logical arguments cannot *prove* all that faith believes, they can give firmer *reasons* for faith than feeling, desire, mood, fashion, family or social pressure, conformity, or inertia. For instance, if you believe the idea mentioned above, that "all things work together for good for those who love God," simply because you feel good today, you will probably stop believing it tomorrow when you feel miserable; or if you believe it only because your friends or family do, you will probably stop believing it when you are away from your friends or family. But if you have logical grounds for believing this, even though those grounds are not a compelling proof, they can keep your faith more firmly anchored during storms of changing feelings, fashions, friends, etc.

How could there be logical grounds for such a belief as this (that "all things work together for good") that seems to contradict common sense and experience? Some logical grounds might be the following: this conclusion can be logically deduced from four premises which are much easier to believe: (1) that God exists, (2) that God is the Creator of the universe and thus all-powerful, (3) that God is the source of all goodness and thus all-good, and (4) that God is the source of all design and order in the universe and thus all-wise. A God who is all-powerful is in control of everything He created; a God who is all-good wills only good to everything He created; and a God who is all-wise knows what is ultimately for the best for everyone and everything He created. So to deny that all things are foreseen and allowed by God for the ultimate good of those He loves, i.e. wills goodness to, is to deny either God's existence, power, goodness, or wisdom. In a logical argument, you cannot deny the conclusion without denying a premise, and you cannot admit the premises without admitting the conclusion. The logical chains of argument can thus bind our minds, and through them also even our feelings (to a certain degree), to God and to hope and to happiness.

And if these four more basic premises of God's existence, power, goodness, and wisdom are questioned, logic may also help to establish *them* by further reasonable arguments (e.g. the traditional arguments for the existence of God); and perhaps logic can give good grounds for the premises of *those* arguments too.

The point is not that logic can *prove* religious beliefs – that would dispense with the need for faith – but that it can *strengthen* them (and thus also the happiness that goes with them). And if it does not – if clear, honest, logical thinking leads you to *dis*believe something you used to believe, like Santa Claus – then that is progress too, for truth should trump even happiness. If we are honest and sane, we want not just any happiness, but true happiness.

7. Wisdom. "Philosophy" means "the love of wisdom." Although logic alone cannot make you wise, it can help. For **logic is one of philosophy's main instruments**. Logic is to philosophy what telescopes are to astronomy or microscopes to biology or math to physics. You can't be very good at physics if you're very bad at math, and you can't be very good at philosophy if you're very bad at logic.

8. Democracy. There are even crucial **social and political reasons for studying logic**. As a best-selling modern logic text says, "the success of democracy depends, in the end, on the reliability of the judgments we citizens make, and hence upon our capacity and determination to weigh arguments and evidence rationally." As Thomas Jefferson said, "In a republican nation, whose citizens are to be led by reason and persuasion and not by force, the art of reasoning becomes of the first importance." (Copi & Cohen, *Logic*, 10th edition, Prentice-Hall, 1998).

9. Defining logic's limits. Does logic have limits? Yes, but **we need logic to recognize and define logic's limits**.

Logic has severe limits. We need much more than logic even in our thinking. For instance, we need intuition too. But logic helps us to recognize this distinction.

In our lives, logical arguments are always embedded in a human context that is interpersonal, emotional, intuitive, and assumed rather than proved; and this colors the proper interpretation of a logical argument. For instance, in 1637 Descartes said "I think, therefore I am"; 370 years later, a bumper sticker says "I bitch, therefore I am." The logical form of both arguments is the same, but the contexts are radically different. Descartes was seriously trying to refute skepticism (the belief that we cannot be certain of anything) by a purely theoretical argument, while the bumper sticker was making a joke. We laugh at it because we intuitively understand that it means "Don't complain at my bitching; bitching makes me feel more 'real,' more alive." Logical thinking alone cannot know this, but it *can* know what its limits are: it can distinguish what it can understand from what it can't (non-logical factors such as humor and feeling and intuition).

10. Testing authority. We need authority as well as logic. But **we need logic to test our authorities**.

We need authorities because no individual can discover everything autonomously. We all do in fact rely on the human community, and therefore on the authority of others – parents, teachers, textbooks, "experts," friends, history, and tradition – for a surprisingly large portion of what we know – perhaps up to 99%, if it can be quantified. And that is another reason we need logic: we need to have *good reasons* for believing our authorities, for in the end it is you the individual who must decide which authorities to trust. It is obviously foolish to buy from every peddler of ideas that knocks on your mind's door. In fact, it is impossible, because they often contradict each other.

11. Recognizing contradictions. One of the things you will learn in this course is exactly what contradiction means, how to recognize it, and what to do with it. **Logic teaches us which ideas contradict each other.** If we are confused about that, we will be either too exclusive (that is, we will think beliefs logically exclude each other when they do not) or too inclusive (that is, we will believe two things that cannot both be true).

When we consider two different ideas which seem to contradict each other, we need to know three things:

(1) First of all, we need to know exactly what each one *means*. Only then can we know whether they really contradict each other or not.
(2) And if they do, we need to know which one is *true* and which is *false*.
(3) And we do this by finding *reasons* why one idea is true and another is false.

These are the "three acts of the mind": understanding a meaning, judging what is true, and reasoning. These are the three parts of logic which you will learn in this course.

12. Certainty. Logic has "outer limits"; there are many things it can't give you. But **logic has no "inner limits"**: like math, it never breaks down. Just as 2 plus 2 are unfailingly 4, so if A is B and B is C, then A is unfailingly C. Logic is timeless and unchangeable. It is *certain*. It is not certain that the sun will rise tomorrow (it is only very, very probable). But it is certain that it either will or won't. And it is certain that if it's true that it will, then it's false that it won't.

In our fast-moving world, much of what we learn goes quickly out of date. "He who weds the spirit of the times quickly becomes a widower," says G.K. Chesterton. But logic never becomes obsolete. The principles of logic are timelessly true.

Our *discovery* of these principles, of course, changes and progresses through history. Aristotle knew more logic than Homer and we know more than Aristotle, as Einstein knew more physics than Newton and Newton knew more than Aristotle.

Our *formulations* of these changeless logical principles also change. This book is clearer and easier to read than Aristotle's *Organon* 2350 years ago, but it teaches the same essential principles.

Our *applications* of the timeless principles of logic to changing things are also changing. The principles of logic apply to many different and changing things, but the principles themselves are unchanging and rigid. They wouldn't work unless they were rigid. When we hear a word like "rigid" or "inflexible," we usually experience an automatic ("knee-jerk") negative reaction. But a moment's reflection should show us that, though *people* should not usually be rigid and inflexible, *principles* have to be. They wouldn't *work* unless they were rigid. Unless the yardstick is rigid, you cannot use it to measure the non-rigid, changing things in the world, like the height of a growing child. Trying to measure our rapidly and confusingly changing world by a "flexible" and changing logic instead of an inflexible one is like trying to measure a squirming alligator with a squirming snake.

13. Truth. Our last reason for studying logic is the simplest and most important of all. It is that **logic helps us to find truth, and truth is its own end**: it is worth knowing for its own sake.

Logic *helps* us to find truth, though it is not *sufficient* of itself to find truth. It helps us especially (1) by demanding that we define our terms so that we understand what we mean, and (2) by demanding that we give good reasons, arguments, proofs.

These are the two main roads to truth, as you will see more clearly when you read Chapter II, on the three "acts of the mind": understanding, judging, and reasoning. Truth is found only in "the second act of the mind," judging – e.g. the judgment that "all men are mortal." But two *paths* to truth are "the first act of the mind" (e.g. understanding the meaning of the terms "men" and "mortal") and "the third act of the mind" (e.g. reasoning that "since all men have animal bodies, and whatever has an animal body is mortal, therefore all men are mortal"). These are the two main ways logic helps us to find truth.

Truth is worth knowing just for the sake of knowing it because truth fulfills and perfects our minds, which are part of our very essence, our deep, distinctively human core, our very selves. Truth is to our minds what food is to our bodies.

Aristotle pointed out, twenty-four centuries ago, that there are three reasons for pursuing truth and three corresponding kinds of "sciences" (in the older, broader sense of the word "sciences," namely "rational explanations through causes"). He called the three kinds of sciences (1) "productive sciences," (2) "practical sciences," and (3) "theoretical sciences." Each pursues truth for a different end:

(1) We want to know about the world so that we can change it, improve it, and make things out of it (like rubber, or roads, or rockets, or robots).

This is what Aristotle called "*productive science*," since its end is to produce things. We call it "technology," after the Greek word *techné*, which means approximately "know-how," knowing how to make or fix or improve some material thing in the world. "Productive sciences" include things as diverse as engineering, surgery, auto repair, cooking, and cosmetics.

(2) We also want to know about ourselves so that we can change and improve our own lives, our behavior, our activities. Aristotle called this "*practical science*," knowledge in practice, in action. "Practical sciences" include ethics and politics as well as knowing how to do things as diverse as economics, singing, and surfing.

(3) But most of all, we want to know simply in order to know, i.e. to become larger on the inside, as it were, to "expand our consciousness." Sciences that pursue this end Aristotle called "*theoretical sciences*," from the Greek word *theoria*, which means "looking" or "contemplating." ("Theoretical" does not necessarily mean "uncertain" or "merely hypothetical.") Theoretical sciences include such diverse things as physics, biology, theology, mathematics, astronomy, and philosophy. These all have practical *applications* and uses, but they are first of all aimed at simply knowing and understanding the truth, even if there is no practical application of it.

Many people today think that theoretical sciences are the least important because they are not practical. But Aristotle argued that the theoretical sciences were the most important for the same reason that practical sciences were more important than productive sciences: because their "payoff" is more intimate, their reward closer to home. For they improve our very selves, while practical sciences improve our actions and lives, and productive sciences improve our world. All three are important, but just as our lives are more intimate to us than our external world, so our very selves are even more intimate to us than our lives, our deeds, and certainly more intimate and more important to us than the material things in our world. As a very famous and very practical philosopher argued twenty centuries ago, "What does it profit a man to gain the whole world but lose his own self?" (Mark 8:36)

The original meaning of a "liberal arts" education was this: the study of the truth for its own sake, not only for the sake of what you can do with it or what you can make with it. The term "liberal arts" comes from Aristotle: he said that just as a man is called "free" when he exists for his own sake and a "slave" when he exists for the sake of another man, so these studies are called "free" ("liberal" or liberating) because they exist for their own sake and not for the sake of anything else.

Logic will prove very useful to you in many ways, but its most important use is simply to help you to see more clearly what is true and what is false.

Logic alone will not *tell* you what is true. It will only *aid* you in discovering truth. You also need experience, to get your premises; logic can then draw your conclusions. Logic will tell you that if all leprechauns are elves and all hobbits are leprechauns, then it necessarily follows that all hobbits are elves; but logic will not tell you whether all leprechauns are elves, or even whether there are any leprechauns. (I once asked my very Irish neighbor whether she believes in leprechauns and she answered, "Of course not. But they exist all the same, mind you." Perhaps the Irish should write their own logic textbook.)

To have logical clarity and consistency is admirable. But to have *only* logical clarity and consistency is pitiful. In fact, it is a mark of insanity, as G.K. Chesterton pointed out:

> "If you argue with a madman, it is extremely probable that you will get the worst of it; for in many ways his mind moves all the quicker for not being delayed by the things that go with good judgment. He is not hampered by a sense of humour or charity, or by the dumb certainties of experience. . . . Indeed, the common phrase for insanity is in this respect a misleading one. The madman is not the man who has lost his reason. The madman is the man who has lost everything except his reason . . . if a man says that he is the rightful King of England, it is no complete answer to say that the existing authorities call him mad; for if he were King of England that might be the wisest thing for the existing authorities to do. Or if a man says that he is Jesus Christ, it is no answer to tell him that the world denies his divinity; for the world denied Christ's . . . his mind moves in a perfect but narrow circle. A small circle is quite as infinite as a large circle; but, though it is quite as infinite, it is not so large. In the same way the insane explanation is quite as complete as the sane one, but it is not so large. . . . 'So you are the Creator and Redeemer of the world: but what a small world it must be! What a little heaven you must inhabit, with angels no bigger than butterflies! How sad it must be to be God; and an inadequate God! Is there really no life fuller and no love more marvelous than yours? . . . How much happier you would be, how much more of you there would be, if the hammer of a higher God could smash your small cosmos, scattering the stars like spangles, and leave you in the open, free like other men to look up as well as down!'. . . Curing a madman is not arguing with a philosopher; it is casting out a devil." (*Orthodoxy*)

(Especially for Teachers)

Section 2. Seventeen ways this book is different

There are literally hundreds of logic texts in print, and thousands more out of print. Why one more? How is this one different? How is it better?

1. It's simple. It's better for most students because it's *not* the best, i.e. the most advanced, sophisticated, state-of-the-art text. Most beginning students need a simpler, easier, *basic* logic text, just as most new computer owners would love to have a simple, "dumb," obedient computer that they can master and use quickly and easily instead of one with so many "bells and whistles" that by the time you master it, it's obsolete. But no one makes a "dumb" computer; the geniuses who make them are too proud to serve us "dummies."

Well, I'm not. This is a "dumb" logic book: it's for beginners.

For instance, its most basic points (which are summarized in Section 4 of this Introduction, "All of logic in two pages") are repeated so often that even the slowest and most confused students should not lose their way and lose hope.

2. It's user-friendly. It is for two kinds of users: it is a classroom text for teachers and also a "do-it-yourself" text for individuals.

The fact that it is simple enough for an intelligent "do-it-yourselfer" does not mean it is less useful for a teacher as a classroom text – unless obscure classroom texts are more useful than clear and simple ones.

3. It's practical. It covers topics in proportion to probable student use. E.g. it devotes more space than usual to topics like (1) Socratic method, (2) interpreting ordinary language and translating it into logical form, (3) *constructing* effective syllogisms, (4) material fallacies, (5) diagramming long arguments simply, and (6) smoking out hidden premises, because these are some of the logical skills we need and use the most outside a logic class.

Logic is like praying, fishing, or learning a language: you learn by doing. Much of the work is in the will, not the mind: in resolution and persistence and dogged honesty. Actually *practicing* a few basic logical principles will make you a far more effective arguer, evaluator, researcher, and writer than knowing ten times more and practicing it less. Most logic students learn too much, not too little; instead of learning what they need to use, they learn what they neither need nor use. That is why this book contains many exercises on basics, and only a very introductory treatment of non-basics.

When we actually argue, obeying a few basic rules well is much more rare, more difficult, and more adequate than we usually think. Just imagine for a moment how some of the arguments you have heard or read would have been different if both sides had only obeyed this one elementary principle:

> Don't ignore your opponent's arguments and counter with your own; don't just sit there waiting for your "turn" to attack. You must also defend by finding a logical fallacy, a false premise, or an ambiguous term in every single one of your opponent's arguments.

Practical usefulness is the main reason for preferring classical Socratic, Aristotelian logic to modern symbolic logic, even if the latter may be more theoretically adequate. It is like the difference between Einsteinian physics and

Newtonian physics, with its basic laws of motion and its principles of simple machines. Though Einstein is theoretically superior, Newton is still much more practical for beginners. I think I have never found anyone except a professional philosopher who actually used symbolic logic in actual conversation or debate.

4. It's linguistic. It emphasizes the use and understanding of ordinary language. E.g. it devotes considerable time to translating ordinary language into logical form (and it uses the logical form closest to ordinary language) because this is a skill teachers usually assume, but students usually lack (probably because of the decline in the teaching of grammar). I find today's students much more confused by language, and less by mathematical symbols, than previous generations. They are the digital generation, not the verbal. They need to re-learn the logic of language, for thought can no more escape words than fish can escape water.

There is of course a need for new and specialized forms of mathematical logic too, but this need is being well supplied, while the more basic need for the more basic logic is *not* being well supplied.

5. It's readable. Its linguistic style is popular, personal, informal, light, and sometimes even humorous.

6. It's traditional. Its master is Aristotle, "the master of common sense," the man whose philosophy has become as embedded in the Western tradition as Confucius's became embedded in the Chinese.

Aristotle's master was Plato. "All of Western philosophy is a series of footnotes to Plato," said Whitehead. In *The Last Battle*, C. S. Lewis has the old professor say, "It's all in Plato, all in Plato: bless me, what *do* they teach them at these schools?" Lewis says of his own thought: "To lose what I owe to Plato and Aristotle would be like the amputation of a limb" (*Rehabilitations*, "The Idea of an English School.").

Plato's master was Socrates, the most interesting philosopher who ever lived, and the father of the application of logic to philosophical questions. When Aristotle wrote the world's first logic text, he was reflecting on what Socrates had already done, defining the principles of Socrates' practice. Thus our title, "Socratic Logic."

This book is also traditional in the sense that it uses many classic examples from history and the Great Books. A side benefit is thus the student's exposure to these many "nuggets" of traditional wisdom, any one of which may some day enable him to win a large amount of money on a quiz show somewhere down in Plato's cave.

Since tradition (i.e. all of human history up until the present) has been much more religious than the present, many of the examples are about religious questions. There are at least five advantages to this. (1) Religious questions are intrinsically interesting. Only a fascinatingly dull mind is more fascinated with questions about life insurance rates than with questions about life after death. (2) They are not only subjectively interesting but objectively, intrinsically important, whether they are to be answered affirmatively or negatively. Religion is either humanity's most important wisdom or its most important illusion. (3) They are by nature not culturally and temporally relative, like most questions of politics and ideology, but universally human. (4) They are close to philosophical questions, and lead naturally into them. (5) And they are difficult, challenging, and mysterious.

Believers *or* nonbelievers in any religion should be able to use this book with profit. It makes no religious or antireligious *assumptions*.

7. It's commonsensical. Logic is like psychoanalysis in that it does not impose anything upon you from outside but only clarifies what is already present in you. Good logic never contradicts common sense, if we mean by "common sense" not something the polls determine (that's only "fashionable opinions") but something naturally and innately present in every mind. The American philosopher C.I. Lewis wrote that "everyone knows the distinction of cogent reasoning from fallacy. The study of logic appeals to no criterion not already present in the learner's mind."[3] *If any principle in this book ever seems to contradict what you know by innate common sense, something is wrong with that principle.* This is one of the main reasons for preferring traditional Aristotelian logic to the more fashionable modern symbolic logic. Aristotelian logic is far closer to common sense; that is why it is far easier to apply and use in ordinary conversations.

We all have used logic already, unconsciously, many times every day. Even animals do that. Chrysippus, a Stoic philosopher of the 3rd century, watched a dog chasing a rabbit come to a fork in the road; the dog sniffed at two of the three paths and then ran down the third without taking the time to sniff at it. Even the dog instinctively used logic to catch a real-world rabbit! He used a disjunctive syllogism: Either the rabbit took road A or road B or road C; not A or B; therefore C.

In one of Molière's comedies, Monsieur Jourdain suddenly discovers, to his amazement, that he has been speaking in prose all his life. You have been thinking and speaking in "logic" all your life. This course helps you to "know thyself."

---

3   Interestingly, Christian apologist C.S. Lewis was once confused with C.*I*. Lewis, who went on to be an important developer of symbolic logic. When C.*S*. Lewis saw a review of *The Principles of Symbolic Logic* which attributed the work to him, he wrote to his father: "I am writing back to tell them that they have got rather muddled. Symbolic Logic forsooth!" (*Letters*, 25 May 1919).

8. It's philosophical, both in its applications and in its foundations. Of all the applications of logic, philosophy is the most (subjectively) interesting and the most (objectively) important. Philosophy asks the Big Questions.

This book exposes students to the ideas of the great philosophers all along the way by frequent quotations from them in its exercises, and ends with a series of chapters which use logic to introduce the fundamental questions of metaphysics, philosophical theology, cosmology, ethics, anthropology, and epistemology. It prepares students for reading Great Books, not "Dick and Jane."

Philosophy is not only an *application* of logic, but logic also has philosophical *foundations*. Logic is not always philosophically neutral. Different kinds of logic sometimes imply or presuppose importantly different philosophical positions. (See Section 3, p. 15.)

This book's philosophy is Aristotelian realism. It dares to take a philosophical stand on controversial issues like truth, and certainty, and universals. (It affirms all three, by the way.) This stand is neither ideological nor religious but commonsensical and traditional; but precisely because it is commonsensical and traditional, it is counter-cultural and controversial in today's philosophical marketplace.

9. It's constructive. It teaches how to make good arguments as well as how to refute bad ones, and such constructive lessons as how to use the Socratic method, how to write a good essay, how to read a book, how to organize an outline, how to debate, and how to argue logically with difficult people. For some mysterious reason these practical arts are usually neglected in logic books.

10. It's clearly divided. There are 89 sections, or mini-chapters, in the 16 chapters of the book, but most of them are very short. Each section teaches only one basic point. This enhances clarity for the beginning student. Some logic textbooks try to teach too many things in a single section, and the result is confusion. This book does only one thing at a time.

The sections are determined by content, not by length. Since there is only one basic point per section, and since some points are easier than others, some sections are much shorter than others. (Why not? Why should quantity determine quality? Why should the accidental determine the essential?)

11. It's flexible. The division into so many sections gives the teacher the option to select a "mix and match" of sections in many different ways, depending on the emphasis desired.

There are four kinds of sections: basic logic, advanced logic, practical applications, and philosophical logic. The Table of Contents marks the basic sections "(B)", marks the philosophical sections "(P)", and puts the practical application sections in Chapter 15. This allows the book to be used in at least ten different ways, ranging from the very short to the very long:

(1) the bare basics only
(2) the basic sections plus the philosophical sections
(3) the basic sections plus the more advanced sections in logic
(4) the basic sections plus the practical application sections
(5) the basic sections plus any two of these three additions
(6) all of the book
(7) all or some of it supplemented by a text in symbolic logic
(8) all or some of it supplemented by a text in inductive logic
(9) all or some of it supplemented by a text in rhetoric or informal logic
(10) all or some of it supplemented by readings in and applications to the great philosophers

The first option should take about half a semester, (2) through (6) a whole semester, and (7) through (10) up to two semesters. In a one-semester, 14-week, one-class-a-week course, you can combine any or all of the following chapters into single-class lessons: (1) the Introduction and chapter 1; (2) chapters 6 and 7; (3) chapters 8 and 9; (4) chapters 10 and 11; (5) chapters 15 and 16.

12. It's short. The first few options above give you a short, basic, no-frills, no-fat logic text.

13. It's selective. It emphasizes a relatively small number of "big ideas" that the student will always need and use and remember, rather than the usual logic text's many "bells and whistles" that students will rarely use.

14. It's innovative where it needs to be. It includes some specific things most other logic texts do not, such as:

☆ a clear distinction between six quite different kinds of induction
☆ a unique explanation of the Square of Opposition that is much cleaner and simpler than any other
☆ a simple, streamlined solution to the problem of existential import
☆ an overview of the difference between the two logics and its philosophical significance
☆ practical advice on Socratic method, Socratic debates, and writing Socratic dialogues
☆ many interfacings with philosophy
☆ practical applications of logic to writing and debating
☆ an expanded list of material fallacies (49) divided into seven categories. (This is the most complete list of material fallacies I know of, except for two books entirely devoted to fallacies, *Fallacy; The Counterfeit of Argument* by Fernside & Holther [Englewood Cliffs, N.J.: Prentice-

Hall, 1959], which lists 51, and *Historians' Fallacies* by David H. Fischer [New York: Harper & Row, 1979], which lists 112.)

15. It's interactive. It includes many exercises, because this is how a logic course "takes" in students' minds and lives. It is more effective to master a few important principles, by much practice, than to be exposed to so many principles and so little practice that you cannot remember and apply the principles after the course is over. We remember general principles only by particular experiences in applying them. (This "practical empiricism" is part of the Aristotelian heritage behind the book.)

A suggestion for teachers: Instead of lecturing on the text, which would probably be only rehashing it, let it teach itself, but leave plenty of time for student questions on it.

A suggested class format: (1) first, discuss all student questions about the pages that were assigned, including exercises; (2) then, a short quiz (weekly or even daily); (3) then go over the correct answers to the quiz, so students can immediately learn from their mistakes; (4) then introduce the next assignment.

One more suggestion: If there are not enough questions, and only a small number of students, require at least two *written* questions from each student at the very beginning of each class, for you to answer (or have other students answer).

16. It's holistic. It emphasizes the whole, the "big picture," the structure and outline of the whole of logic. It repeatedly situates each topic within the "three acts of the mind" overview of the course, so that the student has a sense of where everything fits, and does not feel lost. (Teachers tend to underestimate this need for a continual orientation check, and how much confidence it gives the confused student.)

17. It's classroom-tested, based on the experience of teaching many kinds of logic in many kinds of ways to many kinds of students at many levels of intelligence and background at many kinds of schools over many years.

Section 3. The two logics (P)

(This section can be omitted without losing anything you will need later on in the book. It's here both to satisfy the advanced student's curiosity and to sell the approach of this book to prospective teachers who may question its emphasis on Aristotelian rather than symbolic logic, by justifying this choice philosophically.)

Almost four hundred years before Christ, Aristotle wrote the world's first logic textbook. Actually it was six short books, which collectively came to be known as the *Organon*, or "instrument." From then until 1913, when Bertrand Russell and Alfred North Whitehead published *Principia Mathematica*, the first classic of mathematical or symbolic logic, all students learned Aristotelian logic, the logic taught in this book.

The only other "new logic" for twenty-four centuries was an improvement on the principles of *inductive* logic by Francis Bacon's *Novum Organum* ("New Organon"), in the 17th century, and another by John Stuart Mill, in the 19th century.

(Inductive reasoning could be very roughly and inadequately defined as reasoning from concrete particular instances, known by experience, while deduction reasons from general principles. Induction yields only probability, while deduction yields certainty. "Socrates, Plato and Aristotle are mortal, therefore probably all men are mortal" is an example of inductive reasoning; "All men are mortal, and Socrates is a man, therefore Socrates is mortal" is an example of deductive reasoning.)

Today nearly all logic textbooks use the new mathematical, or symbolic, logic as a kind of new language system for deductive logic. (It is not a new *logic*; logical principles are unchangeable, like the principles of algebra. It is more like changing from Roman numerals to Arabic numerals.) There are at least three reasons *for* this change:

(1) The first and most important one is that the new logic really is superior to the old in efficiency for expressing many long and complex arguments, as Arabic numerals are to Roman numerals, or a digital computer to an analog computer, or writing in shorthand to writing in longhand.

However, longhand is superior to shorthand in other ways: e.g. it has more beauty and elegance, it is intelligible to more people, and it gives a more personal touch. That is why most people prefer longhand most of the time – as most beginners prefer simpler computers (or even pens). It is somewhat similar in logic: most people "argue in longhand," i.e. ordinary language; and Aristotelian logic stays close to ordinary language. That is why Aristotelian logic is more practical for beginners.

Even though symbolic language is superior in sophistication, it depends on commonsense logic as its foundation and root. Thus you will have a firmer foundation for all advanced logics if you first master this most basic logic. Strong roots are the key to healthy branches and leaves for any tree. Any farmer knows that the way to get better fruit is to tend the roots, not the fruits. (This is only an analogy. Analogies do not *prove* anything – that is a common fallacy – they only illuminate and illustrate. But it is an illuminating analogy.)

Modern symbolic logic is *mathematical* logic. "Modern symbolic logic has been developed primarily by mathematicians with mathematical applications in mind." This from one of its defenders, not one of its critics (Henry C. Bayerly, in *A Primer of Logic*. N.Y.: Harper & Row, 1973, p.4).

Mathematics is a wonderful invention for saving time and empowering science, but it is not very useful in most ordinary conversations, especially philosophical conversations. The more important the subject matter, the less relevant mathematics seems. Its forte is quantity, not quality. Mathematics is the only totally clear, utterly unambiguous language in the world; yet it cannot say anything very interesting about anything very important. Compare the exercises in a symbolic logic text with those in this text. How many are taken from the Great Books? How many are from conversations you could have had in real life?

(2) A second reason for the popularity of symbolic logic is probably its more scientific and exact form. The very artificiality of its language is a plus for its defenders. But it is a minus for ordinary people. In fact, Ludwig Wittgenstein, probably the most influential philosophical logician of the 20th century, admitted, in *Philosophical Investigations*, that "because of the basic differences between natural and artificial languages, often such translations [between natural-language sentences and artificial symbolic language] are not even possible in principle." "Many logicians now agree that the methods of symbolic logic are of little practical usefulness in dealing with much reasoning encountered in real-life situations" (Stephen N. Thomas, *Practical Reasoning in Natural Language*, Prentice-Hall, 1973).

– And in philosophy! "However helpful symbolic logic may be as a tool of the . . . sciences, it is [relatively] useless as a tool of philosophy. Philosophy aims at insight into principles and into the relationship of conclusions to the principles from which they are derived. Symbolic logic, however, does not aim at giving such insight" (Andrew Bachhuber, *Introduction to Logic* (New York: Appleton-Century Crofts, 1957), p. 318).

(3) But there is a third reason for the popularity of symbolic logic among philosophers, which is more substantial, for it involves a very important difference in philosophical belief. The old, Aristotelian logic was often scorned by 20th century philosophers because it rests on two commonsensical but unfashionable philosophical presuppositions. The technical names for them are "epistemological realism" and "metaphysical realism." These two positions were held by the vast majority of all philosophers for over 2000 years (roughly, from Socrates to the 18th century) and are still held by most ordinary people today, since they seem so commonsensical, but they were *not* held by many of the influential philosophers of the past three centuries.

(The following summary should not scare off beginners; it is much more abstract and theoretical than most of the rest of this book.)

The first of these two presuppositions, "epistemological realism," is the belief that the object of human reason, when reason is working naturally and rightly, is objective reality as it really is; that human reason can know objective reality, and can sometimes know it with certainty; that when we say "two apples plus two apples must always be four apples," or that "apples grow on trees," we are saying something true about the universe, not just about how we think or about how we choose to use symbols and words. Today many philosophers are skeptical of this belief, and call it naïve, largely because of two 18th century "Enlightenment" philosophers, Hume and Kant.

Hume inherited from his predecessor Locke the fatal assumption that the immediate object of human knowledge is our own ideas rather than objective reality. Locke naïvely assumed that we could know that these ideas "corresponded" to objective reality, somewhat like photographs; but it is difficult to see how we can be sure any photograph accurately corresponds to the real object of which it is a photograph if the only things we can ever know directly are photographs and not real objects. Hume drew the logical conclusion of skepticism from Locke's premise.

Once he limited the objects of knowledge to our own ideas, Hume then distinguished two kinds of propositions expressing these ideas: what he called "matters of fact" and "relations of ideas."

What Hume called "relations of ideas" are essentially what Kant later called "analytic propositions" and what logicians now call "tautologies": propositions that are true by definition, true only because their predicate merely repeats all or part of their subject (e.g. "Trees are trees" or "Unicorns are not non-unicorns" or "Unmarried men are men").

What Hume called "matters of fact" are essentially what Kant called "synthetic propositions," propositions whose predicate adds some new information to the subject (like "No Englishman is 25 feet tall" or "Some trees never shed their leaves"); and these "matters of fact," according to Hume, could be known only by sense observation. Thus they were always particular (e.g. "These two men are bald") rather than universal (e.g. "*All* men are mortal"), for we do not *sense* universals (like "all men"), only particulars (like "these two men").

Common sense says that we can be certain of some universal truths, e.g., that all men are mortal, and therefore that Socrates is mortal because he is a man. But according to Hume we cannot be certain of universal truths like "all men are mortal" because the only way we can come to know them is by generalizing from particular sense experiences (this man is mortal, and that man is mortal, etc.); and we cannot sense all men, only some, so our generalization can only be probable. Hume argued that particular facts deduced from these only-probable general principles could never be known or predicted with certainty. If it is only probably true that all men are mortal, then it is only probably true that Socrates is mortal. The fact that we have seen the sun rise millions of times does not prove that it will necessarily rise tomorrow.

Hume's "bottom line" conclusion from this analysis is skepticism: there is no certain knowledge of objective reality ("matters of fact"), only of our own ideas ("relations of ideas"). We have only *probable* knowledge of objective reality. Even scientific knowledge, Hume thought, was only probable, not certain, because science assumes the principle of causality, and this principle, according to Hume, is only a subjective association of ideas in our minds. Because we have seen a "constant conjunction" of birds and eggs, because we have seen eggs follow birds so often, we naturally assume that the bird is the *cause* of the egg. But we do not *see* causality itself, the causal relation itself between the bird and the egg. And we certainly do not *see* (with our eyes) the universal "principle of causality." So Hume concluded that we do not really have the knowledge of objective reality that we naturally think we have. We must be skeptics, if we are only Humean beings.

Kant accepted most of Hume's analysis but said, in effect, "I Kant accept your skeptical conclusion." He avoided this conclusion by claiming that human knowledge does not fail to do its job because its job is not to *conform* to objective reality (or "things-in-themselves," as he called it), i.e. to correspond to it or copy it. Rather, knowledge *constructs* or *forms* reality as an artist constructs or forms a work of art. The knowing subject determines the known object rather than vice versa. Human knowledge does its job very well, but its job is not to *learn* what is, but to *make* what is, to form it and structure it and impose meanings on it. (Kant distinguished three such levels of imposed meanings: the two "forms of apperception": time and space; twelve abstract logical "categories" such as causality, necessity, and relation; and the three "ideas of pure reason": God, self, and world.) Thus the world of experience is formed by our knowing it rather than our knowledge being formed by the world. Kant called this idea his "Copernican Revolution in philosophy." It is sometimes called "epistemological idealism" or "Kantian idealism," to distinguish it from epistemological realism.

("Epistemology" is that division of philosophy which studies human knowing. The term "epistemological idealism" is sometimes is used in a different way, to mean the belief that ideas rather than objective reality are the objects of our knowledge; in *that* sense, Locke and Hume are epistemological idealists too. But if we use "epistemological idealism" to mean the belief that the human idea (or knowing, or consciousness) determines its object rather than being determined by it, then Kant is the first epistemological idealist.)

The "bottom line" for logic is that if you agree with either Hume or Kant, logic becomes the mere manipulation of our symbols, not the principles for a true orderly knowledge of an ordered world. For instance, according to epistemological idealism, general "categories" like "relation" or "quality" or "cause" or "time" are only mental classifications we make, not real features of the world that we discover.

In such a logic, "genus" and "species" mean something very different than in Aristotelian logic: they mean only any larger class and smaller sub-class that we mentally construct. But for Aristotle a "genus" is the general or common part of a thing's real essential nature (e.g. "animal" is man's *genus*), and a "species" is the whole essence (e.g. "rational animal" is man's *species*). (See Chapter III, Sections 2 and 3.)

Another place where modern symbolic logic merely manipulates mental symbols while traditional Aristotelian logic expresses insight into objective reality is the interpretation of a conditional (or "hypothetical") proposition such as

"If it rains, I will get wet." Aristotelian logic, like common sense, interprets this proposition as an insight into real causality: the rain causes me to get wet. I am predicting the effect from the cause. But symbolic logic does not allow this commonsensical, realistic interpretation. It is skeptical of the "naïve" assumption of epistemological realism, that we can know real things like real causality; and this produces the radically anti-commonsensical (or, as they say so euphemistically, "counter-intuitive") "problem of material implication" (see page 23).

Besides epistemological realism, Aristotelian logic also implicitly assumes metaphysical realism. (Metaphysics is that division of philosophy which investigates what reality is; epistemology is that division of philosophy which investigates what knowing is.) Epistemological realism contends that the object of intelligence is reality. Metaphysical realism contends that reality is intelligible; that it includes a real order; that when we say "man is a rational animal," e.g., we are not imposing an order on a reality that is really random or chaotic or unknowable; that we are expressing our *discovery* of order, not our *creation* of order; that "categories" like "man" or "animal" or "thing" or "attribute" are taken from reality into our language and thought, not imposed on reality from our language and thought.

Metaphysical realism naturally goes with epistemological realism. Technically, metaphysical realism is the belief that universal concepts correspond to reality; that things really have common natures; that "universals" such as "human nature" are real and that we can know them.

There are two forms of metaphysical realism: Plato thought that these universals were real *things* in themselves, while Aristotle thought, more commonsensically, that they were real *aspects* of things which we mentally abstracted from things. (See Chapter II, Section 3, "The Problem of Universals.")

The opposite of realism is "nominalism," the belief that universals are only man-made *nomini* (names). William of Ockham (1285–1349) is the philosopher who is usually credited (or debited) with being the founder of nominalism.

Aristotelian logic assumes both epistemological realism and metaphysical realism because it begins with the "first act of the mind," the act of understanding a universal, or a nature, or an essence (such as the nature of "apple" or "man"). These universals, or essences, are known by concepts and expressed by what logic calls "terms." Then two of these universal terms are related as subjects and predicates of propositions (e.g. "Apples are fruits," or "Man is mortal").

"Aristotle never intended his logic to be a merely formal calculus [like mathematics]. He tied logic to his ontology [metaphysics]: thinking in concepts presupposes that the world is formed of stable species" (J. Lenoble, *La notion de l'expérience*, Paris, 1930, p. 35).

Symbolic logic is a set of symbols and rules for manipulating them, without needing to know their meaning and content, or their relationship to the real world, their "truth" in the traditional, commonsensical sense of "truth." A computer can do symbolic logic. It is quantitative (digital), not qualitative. It is reducible to mathematics.

The new logic is sometimes called "propositional logic" as well as "mathematical logic" or "symbolic logic" because it *begins with propositions, not terms*. For terms (like "man" or "apple") express universals, or essences, or natures; and this implicitly assumes metaphysical realism (that universals are real) and epistemological realism (that we can know them as they really are).

Typically modern philosophers criticize this assumption as naïve, but it seems to me that this is a very reasonable assumption, and not naïve at all. Is it too naïve to assume that we know what an apple is? The new logic has no means of saying, and even prevents us from saying, *what* anything is!

And if we cease to say it, we will soon cease to think it, for there will be no holding-places in our language for the thought. Language is the house of thought, and homelessness is as life-threatening for thoughts as it is for people. If we should begin to speak and think only in nominalist terms, this would be a monumental historic change. It would reverse the evolutionary event by which man rose above the animal in gaining the ability to know abstract universals. It would be the mental equivalent of going naked on all fours, living in trees, and eating bugs and bananas. (Could monkeys have evolved by natural selection from nominalists?)

While it may be "extremist" to suggest it, such a mental "devolution" is not intrinsically impossible. And changes in logic are not wholly unrelated to it. Already, "internet logic," or the logic of spontaneous association by "keywords," is replacing "genus and species logic," or the logic of an ordered hierarchy of objectively real categories. To most modern minds, those last seven words sound almost as archaic as alchemy or feudalism. Many criticize them as ideologically dangerous. These critics dislike categories because they "feel that" (that phrase is a category confusion, by the way) classifications, and universal statements about classes such as "Hittites could not read Hebrew," constitute "prejudice," "judgmentalism," "oppression," or even "hate speech."

Logic and social change are not unrelated. Not only our logicians but also our society no longer thinks primarily about the fundamental metaphysical question, the question of *what things are*, the question of the nature of things. Instead, we think about how we feel about things, about how we can use them, how we see them behave, how they work, how we can change them, or how we can predict and control their behavior by technology. But all this does not raise us above the animal level in kind, only in degree. The higher animals too have feelings, and things to use, and sight, and action, and even a kind of technology of behavior prediction and control. For the art of hunting is an art of predicting and controlling the behavior of other animals. What do we have that no mere animal has? The thing that many modern philosophers vilify: abstraction. We have the power to abstract and understand universals. This is the thing traditional logic is founded on, and this is the thing symbolic logic ignores or denies.

Logic is deeply related to moral and ethical changes in both thought and practice. All previous societies had a strong, nearly universal, and rarely questioned consensus about at least some basic aspects of a "natural moral law," about what was "natural" and what was "unnatural." There may not have been a greater *obedience* to this law, but there was a much greater *knowledge* of it, or agreement about it. Today, especially in the realm of sex (by far the most radically changed area of human life in both belief and practice), our more "advanced" minds find the old language about "unnatural acts" not only "politically incorrect" but literally incomprehensible, because they no longer accept the legitimacy of the very question of the "nature" of a thing. Issues like homosexuality, contraception, masturbation, pedophilia, incest, divorce, adultery, abortion, and even bestiality are increasingly debated in other terms than the "nature" of sexuality, or the "nature" of femininity and masculinity. It is not an unthinkable suspicion that one of the most powerful forces driving the new logic is more social than philosophical, and more sexual than logical.

Symbolic logic naturally fosters *utilitarian ethics*, which is essentially an ethic of consequences. The fundamental principle of utilitarianism is that an act is good if its probable consequences result in "the greatest happiness for the greatest number" of people. It is an "if . . . then . . ." ethics of calculating consequences – essentially, "the end justifies the means" (though that formula is somewhat ambiguous). Symbolic logic fits this perfectly because it is essentially an "if . . . then . . ." logic, a calculation of logical consequences. Its basic unit is the proposition (p or q) and its basic judgment is "if p then q." In contrast, Aristotelian logic naturally fosters a "natural law ethic," an ethic of universal principles, based on the nature of things, especially the nature of man. For its basic unit is the term, a subject (S) or a predicate (P) *within* a proposition (p); and its basic judgment is "all S is P" – a statement of universal truth about the *nature* of S and P.

The very nature of reason itself is understood differently by the new symbolic logic than it was by the traditional Aristotelian logic. "Reason" used to mean essentially "all that distinguishes man from the beasts," including intuition, understanding, wisdom, moral conscience, and aesthetic appreciation, as well as calculation. "Reason" now usually means only the last of those powers. That is why many thinkers today who seem at first quite sane in other ways actually believe that there is no fundamental difference between "natural intelligence" and "artificial intelligence" – in other words, you are nothing but a computer plus an ape. (Having met some of these people at MIT, I must admit that their self-description sometimes seems quite accurate.)

Aristotelian logic is not exact enough for the nominalistic mathematical logician, and it is too exact for the pop psychology subjectivist or New Age mystic. Out at sea there between Scylla and Charybdis, it reveals by contrast the double tragedy of modern thought in its alienation between form and matter, structure and content, validity and meaning. This alienated mind was described memorably by C.S. Lewis: "the two hemispheres of my brain stood in sharpest contrast. On the one hand, a glib and shallow rationalism. On the other, a many-islanded sea of myth and poetry. Nearly all that I loved, I believed subjective. Nearly all that was real, I thought grim and meaningless" (*Surprised by Joy*). Neither mathematical logic nor "experience" can heal this gap; but Aristotelian logic can. It is thought's soul and body together, yet not confused. Mathematical logic alone is abstract and "angelistic," and sense experience and feeling alone is concrete and "animalistic," but Aristotelian logic is a human instrument for human beings.

Aristotelian logic is also easier, simpler, and therefore time-saving. For example, in a logic text book misleadingly entitled *Practical Reasoning in Natural Language*, the author takes six full pages of symbolic logic to analyze a simple syllogism from Plato's *Republic* that proves that justice is not rightly defined as "telling the truth and paying back what is owed" because returning a weapon to a madman is *not* justice but it *is* telling the truth and paying back what is owed. (pp. 224–30). Another single syllogism of Hume's takes *eight* pages to analyze (pp. 278–86).

I have found that students who are well trained in Aristotelian logic are much better at arguing, and at understanding arguments, than students who are trained only in symbolic logic. For Aristotelian logic is the logic of the four most basic verbal communication arts: reading, writing, listening, and speaking. It is the logic of Socrates. If you want to be a Socrates, this is the logic you should begin with.

The old logic is like the old classic movies: strong on substance rather than sophistication. The new logic is like typically modern movies: strong on "special effects" but weak on substance (theme, character, plot); strong on the technological "bells and whistles" but weak on the human side. But logic should be a human instrument; logic was made for man, not man for logic.

The Problem of "Material Implication"

The following issue is quite abstract and difficult, though I shall try to make it as simple as possible. It is included because I believe it shows that "something is rotten in the state of Denmark" at the very heart of the new logic. (For a fuller treatment of the new logic see the Appendix, p. 364.)

Logic is most especially about reasoning, or inference: the process of thinking by which we draw conclusions from evidence, moving from one proposition to another. The proposition we begin with is called a "premise" and the proposition we move to, or infer, or reason to, is called a "conclusion."

The simplest and most straightforward kind of reasoning is to move from a true premise (or, more usually, from a number of true premises together) to a true conclusion. But we can also use *false* propositions in good reasoning. Since a false conclusion cannot be logically proved from true premises, we can know that if the conclusion is false then one of the premises must also be false, in a logically valid argument.

A logically valid argument is one in which the conclusion necessarily follows from its premises. In a logically valid argument, if the premises are true, then the conclusion must be true. In an invalid argument this is not so. "All men are mortal, and Socrates is a man, therefore Socrates is mortal" is a valid argument. "Dogs have four legs, and Lassie has four legs, therefore Lassie is a dog" is not a valid argument. The conclusion ("Lassie is a dog") may be true, but it has not been proved by this argument. It does not "follow" from the premises.

Now in Aristotelian logic, a true conclusion logically follows from, or is proved by, or is "implied" by, or is validly inferred from, only *some* premises and not others. The above argument about Lassie is *not* a valid argument according to Aristotelian logic. Its premises do not prove its conclusion. And common sense, or our innate logical sense, agrees. However, modern symbolic logic disagrees. One of its principles is that "if a statement is true, then that statement is implied by any statement whatever." Since it is true that Lassie is a dog, "dogs have four legs" implies that Lassie is a dog. In fact, "dogs do *not* have four legs" also implies that Lassie is a dog! Even false statements, even statements that are self-contradictory, like "Grass is not grass," validly imply any true conclusion in symbolic logic. And a second strange principle is that "if a statement is false, then it implies any statement whatever." "Dogs do not have four legs" implies that Lassie is a dog, and also that Lassie is not a dog, and that 2 plus 2 are 4, and that 2 plus 2 are not 4.

This principle is often called "the paradox of material implication." Ironically, "material implication" means exactly the opposite of what it seems to mean. It means that the matter, or content, of a statement is totally irrelevant to its logically implying or being implied by other statements. Common sense says that Lassie being a dog or not being a dog has nothing to do with 2+2 being 4 or not being 4, but that Lassie being a collie and collies being dogs does have something to do with Lassie being a dog. But not in the new logic, which departs from common sense here by totally sundering the rules for logical implication from the matter, or content, of the propositions involved. Thus, the paradox ought to be called "the paradox of *non*-material implication."

The paradox can be seen in the following imaginary conversation:

Logician: So, class, you see, if you begin with a false premise, anything follows.
Student: I just can't understand that.
Logician: Are you sure you don't understand that?
Student: If I understand that, I'm a monkey's uncle.
Logician: My point exactly. (Snickers.)
Student: What's so funny?

Logician: You just can't understand that.

The relationship between a premise and a conclusion is called "implication," and the process of reasoning from the premise to the conclusion is called "inference." In symbolic logic, the relation of implication is called "a truth-functional connective," which means that the only factor that makes the inference valid or invalid, the only thing that makes it true or false to say that the premise or premises validly imply the conclusion, is not at all dependent on the content or matter of any of those propositions, but only whether the premise or premises are true or false and whether the conclusion is true or false.

That last paragraph was cruelly abstract. Let's try to be a little more specific. In symbolic logic,

(1) If the premise or premises (let's just say "the premise" for short) are true and the conclusion is true, then the "if . . . then" proposition summarizing the implication is true. If p is true and q is true, then "if p then q" is true. So "if grass is green, then Mars is red" is true.

(2) If the premise is true and the conclusion is false, then the "if . . . then" proposition summarizing the implication is false. If p is true and q is false, then "if p then q" is false. So "if grass is green, then Mars is not red" is false.

(3) If the premise is false and the conclusion is true, then the "if . . . then" proposition summarizing the implication is true. If p is false and q is true, then "if p then q" is true. So "if grass is purple, then Mars is red" is true.

(4) If the premise is false and the conclusion is false, then the "if . . . then" proposition summarizing the implication is true. If p is false and q is false, then "if p then q" is true. So "if grass is purple, then Mars is purple" is also true!

In this logic, if the premise and the conclusion are both false, the premise implies the conclusion (this is #4), and if the premise is false and the conclusion is true, the premise also implies the conclusion (this is #3). So if the moon is blue, then the moon is red (#4); and if the moon is blue, then the moon is not blue (#3)! This may make some defensible sense mathematically, but it certainly does not make sense commonsensically, for it does not seem to make sense in the real world.

Logicians have an answer to the above charge, and the answer is perfectly tight and logically consistent. That is part of the problem! Consistency is not enough. Logic should be not just a mathematically consistent system but a human instrument for understanding reality, for dealing with real people and things and real arguments about the real world. That is the basic assumption of the old logic. If that assumption is naïve and uncritical, unfashionable and unintelligent – well, welcome to Logic for Dummies.

Section 4. All of logic in two pages: an overview (B)

This is one of the shortest and simplest sections in this book, but it is also one of the most important, for it is the foundation for everything else in logic. If you do not understand it clearly, you will be hopelessly confused later on. (It is explained in more detail in the next section, Section 5.)

The ancient philosophers defined Man as the "rational animal." To be human is (among other things) to reason, to give reasons for believing things to be true.

We can see common forms, or structures, in all human reasoning, no matter what the contents, or objects, that we reason about. Logic studies those structures.

The fundamental structure of all reasoning is the movement of the mind from *premises* to a *conclusion*. The conclusion is what you are trying to prove to be true; the premises are the reasons or evidence for the truth of the conclusion.

The two basic kinds of reasoning are *inductive* and *deductive*. Inductive reasoning reasons from particular premises (e.g. "I'm mortal" and "You're mortal" and "He's mortal" and "She's mortal"), usually to a more general or universal conclusion (e.g. "All men are mortal"). Deductive reasoning reasons from at least one general, or universal premise (e.g. "All men are mortal") usually to a more particular conclusion (e.g. "I am mortal"). Inductive reasoning yields only probability, not certainty. (It is not certain that all men are mortal merely on the basis that four men, or 4 million, are.) Deductive reasoning, when correct, yields certainty. (It is certain that if all men are mortal, and if I am a man, then I am mortal.)

A deductive argument succeeds in proving its conclusion to be true if and only if three conditions are met. These are **the three check points of any deductive argument.**

(1) First, *all the terms must be clear* and unambiguous. If a term is ambiguous, it should be defined, to make it clear. Otherwise, the two parties to the argument may think they are talking about the same thing when they are not.

(2) Second, *all the premises must be true.* You can (seem to) "prove" *anything* from false premises: e.g. "All Martians are infallible, and I am a Martian, therefore I am infallible."

(3) Third, *the argument must be logically valid.* That is, the conclusion must necessarily follow from the premises, so that *if* the premises are true, then the conclusion *must* be true.

(1) A "term" in logic is the subject or the predicate of a proposition (a declarative sentence). *Terms* are either *clear* or *unclear*. Terms cannot be either true or false. E.g. "mortal" is neither true nor false. The *proposition* "All men are mortal" is true, and the proposition "Some men are not mortal" is false.

(2) Propositions are declarative sentences. They are either *true* or *false*. "True," in commonsense usage, means "corresponding to reality," and "false" means the opposite. There is no one simple and infallible way of telling whether any proposition is true or false.

(3) There is, however, a fairly simple and truly infallible way of telling whether an argument is *valid* or *invalid*: the laws of logic, which you will learn in this book.

A deductive argument is logically valid if its conclusion necessarily follows from its premises, invalid if it does not. There are various forms of argument, and each form has its own inherent rules for validity.

All the rules for each form of argument are natural to that form of argument and to the human mind. If at any point in this book you think that any of its logical laws contradict what you already implicitly know by innate common sense, please stop and check; for you must be misunderstanding either the laws of logic or what you think common sense tells you, for *logic does nothing more than make explicit the rules everyone knows innately by common sense*.

Arguments are made up of propositions (premises and a conclusion), and propositions are made up of terms (subject and predicate). Terms are either clear or unclear. Propositions (whether premises or the conclusion) are either true or false. Arguments are either logically valid or invalid. Only terms can be clear or unclear; only propositions can be true or false; only arguments can be logically valid or invalid.

So **the three questions you should habitually ask** of yourself when writing or speaking, and of others when you are reading or listening to them, are:

(1) Are the terms all clear and unambiguous?

(2) Are the premises all true?

(3) Is the reasoning all logically valid?

If the answer to all three of these questions is Yes, then the conclusion of the argument must be true.

So in order **to disagree with any conclusion, you must show that there is either (1) an ambiguous term, or (2) a false premise, or (3) a logical fallacy** in the argument such that the conclusion does not necessarily follow from the premises. (You will soon learn the rules for judging that.) If you cannot do any of these three things, then honesty demands that you admit that the conclusion has been proved to be true. (All this applies to deductive arguments only; inductive arguments do not claim certainty.)

Section 5. The three acts of the mind (B)

This section gives you the outline for all of logic. It is an expansion of the previous section (Section 4) and a summary of the rest of the book.

The basis for the science and art of logic is two facts: the fact that human beings think, and the fact that thought has a structure. That structure can be classified from various points of view and for various purposes. For instance, a physiologist or physician might distinguish brain activity of the autonomic nervous system (e.g. breathing) from activity of the frontal lobes (self-conscious thought). A moralist might distinguish thoughts that are voluntary, and under our control, from those that are involuntary, since we are responsible only for what is under our control. A Marxist would distinguish thoughts supposedly produced by a Capitalist system from those produced by a Communist system. But from the viewpoint of logic, we distinguish three kinds of thoughts, three "acts of the mind":

1. Simple apprehension
2. Judging
3. Reasoning

"Simple apprehension" is a technical term. It means basically "conceiving," "understanding," or "comprehending" one object of thought, one concept, such as 'mortal' or 'man' or 'triangle' or 'triangle with unequal angles.' Animals apparently cannot perform this act of understanding; if they can, they do not express it in words. Computers certainly cannot do this; a computer no more *understands* what you program into it than a library building understands the information in the books you put into it.

Judging is more complex than simple apprehension. Instead of just thinking one concept, like 'man,' it relates two concepts, like "man" and "mortal," to each other by predicating one term (the predicate) of the other (the subject) in judging that, e.g., "Man is mortal" or "Man is not a triangle."

As judging is more complex than simple apprehension, reasoning is more complex than judging. As judging moves from one act of simple apprehension (the subject) to another (the predicate), reasoning moves from two or more judgments (the premises, or assumptions) to another (the conclusion) in arguing that if the premises are true, then the conclusion must be true. E.g. "All men are mortal, and I am a man, therefore I am mortal," or "A man is not a triangle, and that is a triangle, therefore that is not a man."

The mental products produced in the mind by the three acts of the mind are:

1. Concepts (the products of conceiving)
2. Judgments (the products of judging)
3. Arguments (the products of reasoning, or arguing)

Distinguishing between the acts and their objects is not crucial for logic. What is crucial is distinguishing the three acts, and the three objects.

These three mental entities (concepts, judgments, and arguments) are expressed in logic as:

1. Terms
2. Propositions
3. Arguments (the most usual form of which is the **syllogism**)

They are expressed in language as:

1. Words or phrases (less than a complete sentence)
2. Declarative sentences
3. Paragraphs, or at least two or more declarative sentences connected by a word like 'therefore' which indicates an argument

Examples:

1. "Man"
2. "Socrates is a man."
3. "All men are mortal, and Socrates is a man, therefore Socrates is mortal."

(Logic does not deal with *interrogative sentences* (questions, like "What time is it?"), *imperative sentences* (commands or requests, like "Pass the mustard, please"), *exclamatory sentences* (like "Oh! Wow! What a hit!"), or *performative sentences* (like "I dub thee knight"), but only with declarative sentences, sentences that claim to state a truth.) Non-declarative sentences are not propositions.

The difference between *logic* and *language* is (1) that languages are manmade artifices and therefore (2) there are many languages that are different in place and time, while (1) logic is not made but discovered, and (2) there is only one logic. There is no "Chinese logic" or "American logic," no "19th century logic" or "20th century logic," or even "masculine logic" or "feminine logic," just logic. (What is often called "feminine logic" is intuition rather than logic: a formidable and invaluable power of the mind but not teachable by textbooks.) Like mathematics, logic is objective, universal, and unchangeable in its basic laws or principles. But the forms in which these unchangeable laws of logic are expressed are linguistic forms, and these forms are changing and varied.

A *term* has no structural parts. It is a basic unit of meaning, like the number one in math or like an atom in the old atomic theory (when they believed atoms were unsplittable and had no parts).

A *proposition* has two structural parts: the subject term and the predicate term. *The subject term is what you're talking about. The predicate term is what you say about the subject.* The word "subject" and "predicate" mean the same thing in logic as in grammar.

An *argument* has two structural parts: the premises and the conclusion. The premises are the propositions that are assumed. They are the reasons or evidence for the conclusion. The conclusion is the proposition that you are trying to prove.

For instance, in the classic example "All men are mortal, and I am a man, therefore I am mortal," the argument is everything inside the quotation marks. The two premises are (a) "All men are mortal" and (b) "I am a man." The conclusion is "I am mortal." The subject of the first premise is "men" and the predicate is "mortal;" the subject of the second premise is "I" and the predicate is "a man;" and the subject of the conclusion is "I" and the predicate is "mortal."

Structural parts of a term: none
Structural parts of a proposition: subject term & predicate term
Structural parts of an argument: premises & conclusion

We can think of the subject and predicate terms as two rooms which together make up one floor of a building (say, a town house). Each floor is a proposition. A syllogism is a building with three floors. The rooms are the parts of the floors, and the floors are the parts of the building.

Subject term	Predicate term	←	1st premise	⎫
Subject term	Predicate term	←	2nd premise	⎬ argument
Subject term	Predicate term	←	conclusion	⎭

These three logical entities answer three different questions, the three most fundamental questions we can ask about anything:

1. A *term* answers the question *what* it is.
2. A *proposition* answers the question *whether* it is.
3. An *argument* answers the question *why* it is.

1. "What are we talking about? "Man."
2. "What are we saying about it?" "That man *is* mortal."
3. "Why is it mortal?" "Because man is an animal, and all animals are mortal, therefore man is mortal."

Terms, propositions, and arguments reveal three different aspects of reality:

1. *Terms* reveal *essences* (*what* a thing is).
2. *Propositions* reveal *existence* (*whether* it is).
3. *Arguments* reveal *causes* (*why* it is).

This (above) is the theoretical basis for the practical art of logic. The practical art consists in discriminating between clear and unclear (ambiguous) terms, true and false propositions, and logically valid and invalid arguments.

Logic is a (practical) *art* as well as a (theoretical) *science*. Therefore it does not only tell us what *is* but also what *should* be; it not only *reveals* these three fundamental logical structures but also *judges* and tries to improve them. For all three can be either logically good or logically bad:

1. Terms are either *clear or unclear* (ambiguous).
2. Propositions are either *true or false*.
3. Arguments are either *valid or invalid*

You will be hopelessly confused for the rest of this book if you do not clearly understand this.

Terms are never true or false in themselves; the propositions they are in are true or false.
Terms are never valid or invalid. Only arguments are valid or invalid.
Terms are only either clear or unclear.

Propositions are never clear or unclear; the terms in them are clear or unclear.
Propositions are never valid or invalid in themselves; the arguments they are parts of are either valid or invalid.
Propositions are only either true or false.

Arguments are never clear or unclear; each of the terms in an argument is clear or unclear.
Arguments are never true or false. Each of the propositions in an argument is true or false.
Arguments are only either valid or invalid.

Most (but not all) of logic consists of deciding when arguments are valid. "Valid" is a technical term in logic. It does not mean just "acceptable." *An argument is logically valid when its conclusion necessarily follows from its premises.* That is, "if the premises are all true, then the conclusion must be true" – that is the definition of a valid argument. An invalid argument is one in which the conclusion does not necessarily follow even if the premises are true.

For instance, this argument is valid:

All men are mortal.
And I am a man.
Therefore I am mortal.

But this argument is not valid:

All men are mortal.
And all pigs are mortal.
Therefore all pigs are men.

It is invalid not just because the conclusion is false but because the conclusion does not follow from the premises. The following argument is also invalid, even though the conclusion (and also each premise) is true:

All men are mortal.
And Socrates is mortal.
Therefore Socrates is a man.

For this argument has the same logical form as the one above it; it merely replaces "pigs" with "Socrates."

An argument may have nothing but true propositions in it, yet be invalid. E.g.:

I exist.
And grass is green.
Therefore Antarctica is cold.

An argument may have false propositions in it and yet be logically valid. E.g.:

I am a cat.
And all cats are gods.
Therefore I am a god.

For if both those premises were true (that I am a cat and that all cats are gods) it would necessarily follow that I was a god.

An argument that has nothing but true propositions and also is logically valid is the only kind of argument that is worth anything, the only kind that convinces us that its conclusion is true, and the only kind that we can use to convince others that its conclusion is true.

If an argument has nothing but clear terms, true premises, and valid logic, its conclusion must be true. If any one or more of these three things is lacking, we do not know whether the conclusion is true or false. It is uncertain.

If the terms are	and the premises are	and the logic is	then the conclusion is
Clear	true	valid	true
Clear	true	invalid	uncertain
Clear	false	valid	uncertain
Clear	false	invalid	uncertain
Unclear	true	valid	uncertain
Unclear	true	invalid	uncertain
Unclear	false	valid	uncertain

(See also p. 194 for more on the relation between truth and validity.)

Logic gives us rules for deciding when an argument is valid or invalid. It also gives us ways of defining terms so as to make them clear and unambiguous. Unfortunately, logic cannot give us any one way to tell whether any proposition is true. There are many ways of finding truth: sensation, intuition, reasoning, experimentation, authority, experience, etc.

(By the way, "what is truth?" is a very easy question to answer, as we shall see in Chapter VI, Section 2. We all know what the word means: it means knowing or saying what is. Aristotle defined truth in words of one syllable: "If a man says of what is that it is, or of what is not that it is not, he speaks the truth; if he says of what is that it is not, or of what is not that it is, he does not speak the truth." Defining truth is easy, finding it is harder.)

Because there are three acts of the mind and three corresponding logical entities (terms, propositions, and arguments), there are three basic questions we should habitually ask in each of the four basic language arts of reading, writing, listening, and speaking. The more we habitually ask these three questions, of ourselves (when speaking or writing) and of others (when listening or reading), the more critical and logical our thinking is. The questions are:

1. What do you mean? (Define your terms.)
2. What's the point? (What's your conclusion?)
3. Why? (Prove it.)

When you want to make an unanswerable argument, you must be sure of three things:

1. Be sure your terms are clear.
2. Be sure your premises are true.
3. Be sure your logic is valid.

If you fulfill all three conditions, you have proved your conclusion.

If you want to answer someone else's argument, you must find in it one of the three following errors:

1. a term used ambiguously
2. a false premise
3. a logical fallacy, an invalid argument, a conclusion that does not necessarily follow from the premises

If you cannot find any one of these three, you must admit that the conclusion is true. For this is the power of logic: if the terms are unambiguous and the premises are true and the logic is valid, then the conclusion really *is* true and has been proved to be true.

	1ST ACT OF MIND	2ND ACT OF MIND	3RD ACT OF MIND
NAME OF ACT	Understanding	Judging	Reasoning
LOGICAL EXPRESSION	Term	Proposition	Argument (usually syllogism)
LINGUISTIC EXPRESSION	Word or Phrase	Declarative Sentence	Paragraph
EXAMPLE OF EACH	"Man," "Mortal"	"Socrates is a man."	All men are mortal. And Socrates is a man. Thus Socrates is mortal.
STRUCTURAL PARTS	None	Subject Term & Predicate Term	Premises and Conclusion
QUESTION ANSWERED	What it is	Whether it is	Why it is
ASPECT OF REALITY	Essence	Existence	Cause
GOOD WHEN	Clear or unambiguous	True	Valid
HOW ACHIEVED	Definition of terms	No one way	Rules of Logic
BAD WHEN	Unclear or ambiguous	False	Invalid
QUESTION TO HABITUALLY ASK	What do you mean? (Define your terms.)	What is your point? (State your conclusion.)	Why? (Prove it.)

Exercises

A. (easy) Identify each of the following as a term, a proposition, an argument, or none of the above.

1. Everyone
2. Everyone in America
3. Everyone in America and in the rest of the world as well
4. I think, therefore I am.
5. Are you mad?
6. You won't pass.
7. You won't pass because you haven't studied.
8. Don't take this logic course.
9. Please be quiet.
10. A falsity so obvious that it couldn't fool a child
11. God exists.
12. It ain't broke, so it don't gotta be fixed.
13. You're weird.
14. Everything in the kitchen sink except the sink itself
15. Ouch!

B. (harder) Use the chart on page 32 to tell whether the following statements are true or false. Assuming all terms are clear and unambiguous,

1. If an argument is logically valid, its conclusion must be true.
2. If an argument's conclusion is true, it must be logically valid.
3. If an argument's conclusion is not true, it cannot be logically valid.
4. If an argument's conclusion is not true, its premises cannot be true.
5. If an argument's premises are true and it is invalid, its conclusion must be false.
6. If an argument's premises are true and its conclusion is true, it must be valid.
7. If an argument's premises are true and its conclusion is false, it must be invalid.
8. If an argument's premises are true and it is valid, its conclusion must be true.

I: The First Act of the Mind: Understanding

Section 1. Understanding: the thing that distinguishes man from both beast and computer (P)

(This section is more philosophical than logical, but it is important because it fleshes out the positive alternative to nominalism and provides the essential philosophical foundation for Aristotelian logic.)

As we have already reported, a new species of human has appeared: one that does not know the difference between a human mind and a computer, between "natural intelligence" and "artificial intelligence." Some of these people even teach philosophy!

For centuries there have also been some people – many of them philosophers – who say they do not know what the difference is between a human being and an ape. After all, apes seem to reason quite well sometimes. If you put an ape in a pit with a dozen wooden crates, he might figure out how to get out by piling up the crates against a wall in the form of a stairway, whereas some humans would not figure that out.

But there is one simple, observable behavior that clearly distinguishes humans from both computers and animals: asking questions. Computers never question their programming (unless they have been programmed to do so); computers never disobey. They have no will, therefore no will to know. And animals, though curious, cannot ask formulated questions; their language is too primitive.

There is a story that Aristotle, after one of his lectures, was disappointed that his students had no questions afterwards, so he said, "My lecture was about levels of intelligence in the universe, and I distinguished three such levels: gods, men, and brutes. Men are distinguished from both gods and brutes by questioning, for the gods know too much to ask questions and the brutes know too little. So if you have no questions, shall I congratulate you for having risen to the level of the gods, or insult you for having sunk to the level of the brutes?"

Logic specializes in questioning. The three most basic questions humans ask are: What, Whether, and Why, i.e. What is it? Is it? and Why is it? These are dealt with in the three parts of logic.

The part that most clearly distinguishes humans from computers is the first: understanding a "what," an "essence," the nature of a thing. Computers understand *nothing*; they merely store, process, relate, and regurgitate data. You don't really think there is a little spirit somewhere inside your hand-held calculator, do you? But the world's most complex computer has nothing qualitatively more in it than that, only quantitatively more. An *amoeba* is closer to understanding than a computer, for it has some rudimentary sensation of feeling (e.g. it detects food).

A baby often goes around pointing to everything he[1] sees, asking "What's that?" The baby is a philosopher. "What's that" is philosophy's first question. (Look at any Socratic dialogue to see that.)

The act of understanding, or "simple apprehension" as it is technically called, produces in our minds a *concept*. (Sometimes we use the word "idea" as synonymous with "concept," but at other times we use the word "idea" more broadly, to include judgments and arguments as well as concepts.)

We do not merely understand *concepts*, we understand *reality* by means of concepts. Our concept of a house is our means of understanding the real house. The real house is physical, but our concept is not. The house is independent of our mind, but the concept of it is not: it is in our mind. If all we understood was our own concepts, we would not understand objective reality.

Concepts are amazing things. They can do what no material thing in the universe can do. They can transcend space and time. No body can be in two places

---

1   The use of the traditional inclusive generic pronoun "he" is a decision of language, not of gender justice. There are only six alternatives. (1) We could use the grammatically misleading and numerically incorrect "they." But when we say "one baby was healthier than the others because they didn't drink that milk," we do not know whether the antecedent of "they" is "one" or "others," so we don't know whether to give or take away the milk. Such language codes could be dangerous to baby's health. (2) Another alternative is the politically intrusive "in-your-face" generic "she," which I would probably use if I were an angry, politically intrusive, in-your-face woman, but I am not any of those things. (3) Changing "he" to "he or she" refutes itself in such comically clumsy and ugly revisions as the following: "What does it profit a man or woman if he or she gains the whole world but loses his or her own soul? Or what shall a man or woman give in exchange for his or her soul?" The answer is: he or she will give up his or her linguistic sanity. (4) We could also be both intrusive *and* clumsy by saying "she or he." (5) Or we could use the neuter "it," which is both dehumanizing and inaccurate. (6) Or we could combine all the linguistic garbage together and use "she or he or it," which, abbreviated, would sound like "sh . . . it."

    I believe in the equal intelligence and value of women, but not in the intelligence or value of "political correctness," linguistic ugliness, grammatical inaccuracy, conceptual confusion, or dehumanizing pronouns.

at the same time, but a concept can. Suppose someone asks you whether you think San Francisco or Boston is a more beautiful city. You understand the question, and you answer it. Your mind compared (and therefore was present to) two cities 3000 miles apart – at once! Your concepts did what your body cannot do.

Though your body is unimaginably tiny compared with the universe, your concept of the universe is greater than the universe! For if you understood the word "universe," your thought 'surrounded' the universe – the same universe that surrounds your body. You did that by having a *concept* of the universe.

Concepts have at least five characteristics that material things do not have. They are spiritual (or immaterial), abstract, universal, necessary, and unchanging.

1. **Concepts are spiritual (immaterial, non-material).** Compare the concept of an apple with an apple. The apple has size, weight, mass, color, kinetic energy, molecules, shape, and takes up space. The concept does not. It is "in" your mind, not your body. It is not in your brain, for your brain is part of your body. It has no size, so it cannot fit there. (If you say that it does have size, the size of an apple, then you must say that your brain must get as big as an elephant when you think of an elephant.) It has no weight, for when you stand on a scale and suddenly think the concept "tree," you do not gain the slightest amount of weight.

In contrast to the *concept* "apple," the *word* "apple" is just as physical as an apple. It takes up space on the page, and it is made of molecules. The spoken word also is made of molecules: wave-vibrations of sound of a certain size and shape. But between these two material things – the apple and the word "apple" – there is the concept. That is the only reason why we can use the word "apple" to mean the physical apple we eat. We use one physical thing (the word "apple") as a symbol of another physical thing (the apple we eat), and that mental act, or mental relation, that we set up, is not a third physical thing. It is a concept, and its *meaning* is the real apple even though its *being* is not the being of an apple. (It is not in space, has no molecules, etc.) The concept's *meaning* is "a physical fruit that grows on apple trees, has red or green skin, etc.," but the concept's *being* is not physical (material), but spiritual (immaterial).

Our having the concept of an apple is dependent on our having a physical body, of course: it is dependent both on the eye, which perceives the apple, and on the brain, which works whenever we have a concept. If we had never seen an apple, we would never have a concept of one, and if we had no brain we could not think the concept of an apple. But the concept is not just the physical apple or the visible word or even the sense image, which is somewhere between a physical and a spiritual thing. (We will see the difference between a concept and a sense image more clearly in the next few paragraphs.) The sense image is like a scouting report sent out by the intellect. The intellect is like a king who stays in a soul-castle and sends out scouts (the senses) to report to him what's going on in his kingdom. Or, to change the image, the intellect is like a paralytic in a wheelchair who directs a blind man where to push him. (In this image, the intellect is symbolized, paradoxically, by the physically sighted paralytic and the senses by the blind pusher.) The two are interdependent.

When a thing is known, it acquires a second existence, a mental existence; the *thing* becomes a *thought*. If familiarity did not dull us, we would find this utterly remarkable, unparalleled in all the universe. No galaxy, no physical energy, no cell, no animal can do this; only a mind can give a thing a second life.

Every language speaks of the human mind, or intellect, as doing something more than the (animal) senses do: as going "deeper" or "below the surface" or "penetrating" what is sensed, like an X-ray; as going beyond appearances to reality, beyond *seeing* to *understanding*. (Thus the irony in a blind poet or "seer" like Homer, John Milton, or Helen Keller "seeing" more than sighted people.) Only because we distinguish between appearance and reality do we ask questions. There would be no philosophy and no science without this distinction.

2. **Concepts are abstract.** The English word "abstract" comes from the Latin *abstraho*, "to draw *(traho)* from *(ab(s))*" or "to drag out of." Our mind extricates, or separates, something from something else. What is this something?

When we form a concept, we abstract one aspect of a concrete thing from all its other aspects – e.g. the size of a flower (when we measure it), or its color (when we paint it). No one can physically or chemically separate the size from the color, or either one from the whole flower; but anyone can do it mentally.

We can abstract, or mentally separate, adjectives from nouns. Animals simply perceive "green-grass," but even the most primitive men mentally distinguished the green from the grass; and this enabled them to imagine green skin, or red grass, even though they had never seen it. And once they imagined these things, they set about making them, e.g. by dying their skin green from the juice of grasses, or painting pictures of red grass with dye made from beet juice. (When he was two, my son made the thrilling discovery that he could make "purple doo-doo" by mixing up blue and red Play-Doh® in the shape of a hot dog.) Technology and art both flow from this human power of abstraction.

The most important act of abstraction is the one by which we abstract the essential from the accidental. By having a concept we can focus on the essence and abstract from the accidents. Some people are reluctant to do this. Their conversation is utterly concrete – and utterly boring. You want to scream at them, "Come to the point!" These people have few friends, for to have friends you must learn to abstract, i.e. select, set apart, or pick out, the things that interest both them and you. Abstraction fosters friendship – a concrete payoff!

Abstractions have received bad press in the modern world. Too bad. The next time you hear someone say "I'm a concrete, practical person, and I hate abstractions," remind them that babies are very concrete – and uncivilized.

Abstract ideas do not move us as much as concrete things do. Intellectuals, who live with abstractions, are often practically ineffective dreamers and rarely "movers and shakers" of men, because men will not usually live and die for abstractions that move only our mind – even stirring abstractions like "liberty, equality, fraternity" or "democracy" or "freedom" – but for concrete things that move their loves, like their families or their buddies next to them in the trenches.

3. **Concepts are universal.** Ask a child what he wants and he may answer, "Everything!" He has formed a universal concept. (Most concepts are only relatively universal, not absolutely universal like "everything" or "something" or "being.")

E.g. "tree" is a universal concept because it is a concept of not only that one tree in your yard, but of all trees. "Beauty" is a universal concept, and when we judge whether San Francisco or Boston is more beautiful, we judge both cities by the universal concept "beauty" (or "beautiful city").

The literal meaning of "universal" is "one with respect to many" (*unum versus alia*). This means that a concept, while remaining one – one essence, one meaning – nevertheless is true of many things, predicable (sayable) of many things, applicable to many things. This oak and that oak and that maple are all "trees." We can truly apply the concept "tree" to any and every possible and actual tree that ever was, is, or will be.

The concept signifies something common to many different things. This oak and that oak are different in size, and oaks and maples are different in shape of leaves and taste of sap, but all are trees. All share the same common essence, or essential nature. That is what we are seeking to know when we ask "*What* is that?"

Only the concept gets at this one-in-many, this common essence in many different things. It is not in sense perception that we see this universal. We perceive only individual men and women, who are either tall or short, either old or young, but "human being" is neither male nor female, neither tall nor short, neither old nor young. "Human nature" does not *look* male or female, tall or short, old or young. It does not "look" at all; it "means." Appearances are particular; but essences, or meanings, or the natures of things, are universal. You cannot touch them or feel them; you can only understand them. They are known by concepts.

4. **Relations between concepts are necessary.** Every tree *necessarily* has leaves; every triangle *necessarily* has three sides. A tree may or may not have *many* leaves, but it must have *leaves*. A triangle *has* to have three sides; that is dictated by its essence, which is grasped in the concept.

Thus we can be *certain* of relations between concepts, as we cannot be certain of material things. We can be certain that a triangle will have 180 degrees in its three angles, but we cannot be certain how tall a tree will be.

5. **Concepts are unchanging.** Two plus two can never become other than four, but two bunnies plus two bunnies can become more than four bunnies. The concept "blue" can never become not-blue, but the blue sky can become not-blue. The nature of a thing, which is known by a concept, is unchanging; but things, which are known by sense experience, are changing. Humans change; essential human nature does not.

The most important of these characteristics of concepts for philosophy is their universality. "Universal" means "one-in-many," or "one-something-in-many-diverse-somethings" ("uni-versa"), one nature or essence or form in many different concrete individuals. A single concept unifies many sense perceptions under one idea. With our senses we perceive houses of different shapes, sizes, and colors, but with our mind we understand the nature of all of them as "house." We see many individual houses and many parts of each house – the doors, roofs, windows, and porches – but we do not physically see the one nature of the house, the "houseness." It is only the understanding mind that brings all houses under the single concept "house." The concept makes what we see intelligible. It brings order out of chaos.

Without it, metaphysics would be impossible. Metaphysics is the most fundamental branch of philosophy; it is the study of being, or reality as such; the study of the laws or principles that are true universally of all being. The most universal concept of all is "being." Everything is some kind of being. Thus "being" is the most fundamental concept. Before we know more specifically what a thing is, we know that it is a being. There is nothing outside being.

The concept of being is implicit in every other concept. E.g. when we know what a house is, we know what a house *is*; we know its being, its essence, its reality, its substance.

The concept of being is like the genie in the bottle: once the bottle is opened it grows so large that it fills the whole sky.

This is crucial to logic as well as philosophy. For all of logic, really, is about two words, two very common yet very profound little words: "is" and "therefore." "Is" is the first word that relates two concepts to each other in a proposition (the subject and the predicate): "Man *is* mortal," or "A tomato *is* not a fruit." "Therefore" is the word that relates two or more propositions (the premises and the conclusion) in an argument: "All men are mortal, *therefore* none are immortal," or "Tomatoes are vegetables, and vegetables are not fruits, *therefore* tomatoes are not fruits."

Section 2. Concepts, terms, and words (P)

A *concept* exists only privately, in an individual mind; a *term* is in the public domain. A term expresses objectively what is known subjectively in a concept; a concept is a person's subjective knowledge of the meaning of a term.

A *word* (or group of words forming a phrase that is less than a complete sentence) is the linguistic expression of a term. The difference between a term and a word is the difference between what is common to all languages and what is different in different languages; for the same term, the same unit of meaning, is expressed in different words by different languages. Languages are man-made, conventional, and changeable. Terms are not. That is why it is possible to translate between different languages: because the same stable term, or unit of meaning, anchors many different words in many different languages. E.g. *"love," "caritas," "agape," "lieb," "amor,"* and *"amour"* are the same *term* in six different *words.*

A word is physical and sensible (to the eyes or the ears, or to the touch, in Braille). A concept is not. A term mediates between a concept and a word: insofar as it is a unit of meaning, it is not something made of matter or perceivable with the senses; insofar as it is expressed by a word, in any language, it *is* perceivable by the senses, like the word "word" in this sentence.

The difference between a term and a concept, and the difference between a term and a word, may be difficult to grasp, and it is not crucially important from a practical point of view for the logic student to understand it; but it *is* crucially important to understand the difference between a concept, a judgment, and an argument; or between a term, a proposition, and a syllogism; or between a word, a sentence, and a paragraph.

A term is the most simple and basic unit of meaning. A term is simply any word or group of words that denotes an object of thought. The English word "term" comes from the Latin "terminus," which means "end." A term is one of the two "ends" of a proposition, as the first and last points on a line are the two ends of the line; for a term is either the subject (the beginning) or the predicate (the end) of a proposition, when it is in a proposition. Whether a term is inside a proposition or not, a term is whatever *can* be used as the subject or the predicate of a proposition. "Apples" has the same meaning whether it is in the proposition "Apples are fruits" or whether it is outside the proposition and merely "apples." A term is simply any word or group of words that denotes one object of thought.

Terms are never either true or false. Only propositions are true or false. "Apple" is neither true nor false. The proposition "Apples are fruits" is true, and the propositions "Apples are vegetables" is false. Instead of being true or false, terms are unambiguous or ambiguous, clear or unclear. Propositions are ambiguous or unambiguous only insofar as their terms are ambiguous or unambiguous. You will learn how to change ambiguous terms into unambiguous terms in the chapter on *defining* terms.

Section 3. The "problem of universals" (P)

The fact that most terms are universal (predicable of many things) has given rise to one of the classic problems in the history of philosophy, the so-called "problem of universals." First raised by the ancient Greek logician Porphyry, the problem arises when we ask this question: What is there in reality that universal terms refer to – especially *abstract* universal terms like "beauty" or "humanity"? It is clear that concrete singular terms like "Socrates" or "the moon" refer to concrete individual entities that exist in a particular space and time; but where and when do we find beauty or humanity, as distinct from this beautiful thing or that human being?

We have said that terms express concepts, that concepts are universal, and that concepts refer to the *essences* or *natures* of things. Are these essences universal, like the concepts we have of them?

If they are not, then it seems that our concepts of them are not accurate, for they do not correspond to their objects. And in that case, our concepts would distort rather than reveal the true nature of things.

But are universals then real things? Is beauty real as well as beautiful things? Does humanity or human nature or the human species really *exist* in addition to the 6+ billion human beings that *have* the same essential human nature?

Plato thought they did. He called these universals "Forms" or "Ideas" – not ideas in minds but Ideas outside minds, objective Truths; not thoughts but the objects of thoughts. He believed there were two kinds of reality, two "worlds": a world of concrete, material individual things in space and time that we know by our bodily senses, and another world of immaterial universal Forms that we know with our minds through concepts.

The "two worlds theory" seems fantastic to common sense and an example of what one philosopher (Alfred North Whitehead) calls "the fallacy of misplaced concreteness," treating an abstracted aspect of a thing (its essential nature) as if it were another concrete thing. This theory of Plato's is sometimes called "Extreme Realism" because it claims that universals are "extremely real," so to speak – just as real as individual things, in fact *more* real since they are timeless and immortal and unchangeable. A beautiful face changes with age, but beauty does not.

The theory most totally opposed to Plato's is called Nominalism. The fourteenth century medieval philosopher William of Ockham is usually credited for inventing the theory, and modern philosophies such as Empiricism, Pragmatism, Marxism, and Positivism have embraced it and made it popular. Nominalism claims that universals are only names (*nomini*) that we use as a kind of shorthand. Instead of giving each individual tree a separate proper name, we group together, for our own convenience, under the one vague name "tree," all those things that resemble each other in certain ways (e.g. having trunks and branches and leaves). But in reality, all trees are different, not the same; not one-in-many ("uni-versal"), but only many.

Nominalism seems logically self-contradictory, for if all trees are different, how can it be true to call them all "trees"? The very sentence that says all trees are *not* really the same presupposes that they are! If universals are only our names for individuals that resemble each other in certain ways, those "certain ways" must be *really universal* (e.g. all have trunks, branches, and leaves); so we have eliminated one universal ("tree") only by appealing to three others ("trunk," "branches," and "leaves"). *Something* in trees must justify our use of a universal term "tree." What is this? Is it their "resemblance" or "similarity"? But they must resemble each other in *something*. What could this be but their nature, their essence, their treeness, what-trees-really-are?

Aristotle, as usual, takes a middle position between these two extremes, and his view accords best with common sense. His position was developed by the Arabic philosopher Avicenna and by St. Thomas Aquinas in the Middle Ages. It is called "Moderate Realism," and it holds that essences are objectively *real* (contrary to Nominalism) but not real *things* (contrary to Extreme Realism). They are the essential "forms" or natures of things. Forms exist in the world only in individual material things, but they exist in our minds as universal concepts when our minds abstract them from things. It is the very same nature (e.g. humanness) that exists in both states; otherwise our concept of it would not be accurate, would not be a concept of *it*, of what really is in the things. A universal form such as humanness exists in the world only individually, but the same form or nature exists in the mind universally, by "abstraction" from individuals.

So according to Aristotle the Nominalist is right to say that universality is only in the mind, not in things, but wrong to say that there is nothing in reality that is the object of universal concepts. And the Extreme Realist is right to affirm that universals are objectively real and not just names, but wrong to think they are "substances." (Aristotle's technical term for concrete individual things was "substances.") They are the "forms" of substances (e.g. the treeness of trees, the humanness of humans, the beauty of beautiful things, the redness of red things). Some are *essential* forms (like "humanness") which a thing must have in order to be what it is, others are *accidental* forms (like "redness") which a thing can gain or lose and still remain what it is, as when a tomato changes from green to red.

This apparently very technical, abstract, logical dispute has great practical consequences. If universals are more real than individuals, then individuals, and human individuals too, are not *primarily* important – a convenient philosophy for totalitarians! And if individual things are less real than universals, then the senses do not reveal anything very important, and only the few "brains" who can think very abstractly are wise. On the other hand, if universals are not real at all, then we have the even more radical consequence of skepticism: reality is an unknowable chaos, and all so-called universal truths are merely subjective and man-made, including all principles of science and ethics.

Section 4. The extension and comprehension of terms

Every term (and the concept it expresses) has both an *extension* and a *comprehension*.

The extension of a term is simply all the real things the term refers to – the "population" of the term, so to speak, in the world. E.g. the extension of "man" is the 6+ billion men who exist. Or, if "man" is taken exclusively instead of inclusively, then its extension is 3+ billion males.

The "comprehension" of a term means the term's inner meaning, as distinct from its external "population." The word "comprehension" here does not refer to our mind's act of comprehending, i.e. understanding, the term, but rather all the meaning that the term "comprehends" or includes within itself. E.g. the comprehension of "man" is "rational animal."

Sometimes the words "extension" and "*intension*" are used instead of "extension" and "comprehension." Do not confuse "intension," which is the objective meaning of a term, with "intention," which is the subjective motive of a person.

Another set of two words sometimes used to make the same distinction is "denotation" and "connotation." The denotation of a term is the real beings it refers to; the connotation is all the attributes or qualities or characteristics meant by it. However, "connotation" is sometimes used in a different and narrower sense, as meaning only those characteristics referred to *implicitly*, or "between the lines," as nuances or shades of meaning that are not explicitly part of the term's comprehension. "Con" means "with" and "notation" means "meaning," so literally, "connotation" means a "meaning-along-with."

Another set of two words sometimes used to make the same distinction is "meaning" (comprehension) and "reference" (extension). A term's "reference" is all the real things the term refers to. These two words are usually used to make the point that a term can have a meaning yet no reference at all, e.g. the term "unicorn."

The two aspects of terms:

QUALITATIVE	QUANTITATIVE
Comprehension	Extension
Intension	Extension
Connotation	Denotation
Meaning	Reference

The extension (or denotation or reference) of a term is quantitative. You can count all the individual beings the term refers to. The comprehension (or intension or connotation or meaning) of a term is qualitative, not quantitative. You cannot *count* a term's inner meaning.

Logical *divisions*, or outlines, analyze the *extension* of a term. Logical *definitions* analyze the *comprehension* of a term.

The Principle of Inverse Relation between Extension and Comprehension

Extension and comprehension usually *vary inversely*. ("Usually" because there are rare and technical exceptions.) As comprehension increases, extension decreases; as comprehension decreases, extension increases. When we add attributes to increase the comprehension of a term, we add to its meaning but decrease its reference. E.g. "animal" has more extension than "man," for there are only 6+ billion men but trillions of animals, including both rational animals (men) and irrational animals ("brutes"). But "animal" has less *comprehension* than "man," for "animal" means only "a living and sensing thing" while "man" means "a living and sensing thing with reason."

"Beer" has more comprehension than "drink," for it means "drink made from malt and hops." But "drink" has more extension than "beer," for that extension includes milk, water, wine, etc.

As terms become more abstract, they lose comprehension and gain extension.

Common misunderstandings come about from confusing comprehension with extension. E.g. when we judge that "males are taller than females," or "fish gotta swim, birds gotta fly," we are speaking of the comprehension of the subject term "males" or "fish," not the extension. Not all 3+ billion human males are taller than all 3+ billion human females, of course, but the *nature* of males is on average to be taller than females.

Another example: Aristotle's famous first line of his *Metaphysics*, "All men by nature desire to know," is not disproved by the fact that some men are in fact uncurious, lazy couch potatoes. Even the couch potato *by nature* desires to know; he is suppressing his nature at the moment by being hypnotized into thoughtless stupefaction by the boob tube.

Perhaps "boob tube hypnosis" is the reason why so many people today will immediately and thoughtlessly reject all "generalizations" like "men are more aggressive than women" as "stereotypes." They are confusing comprehension and extension. They are misinterpreting a statement about comprehension as if it were one about extension, and that is why they think that the fact that Mrs. X is more aggressive than Mr. X disproves the statement that "men are more aggressive than women." They cannot or will not rise to the original statement's level of abstraction and argue with it on its own level. The statement is not about all the individuals that have the nature of male and the nature of female, but about those *natures* in abstraction from the individuals that have them. Those who reject all generalizations because they can find some exceptions to them are thinking only on the concrete sense level of extension, not on the abstract conceptual level of comprehension; they are operating like cameras (sense experience) plus computers (calculating the quantities of extension), but not like human minds (understanding essences, natures, "whats").

The point is important enough philosophically to justify going through it again. When I say "all my books are paperbacks," I am not speaking of the *comprehension* of "book," only the extension; for there is nothing in the essential *nature* of a book that requires it to be a paperback. But when I say "all men are mortal," I am speaking of the comprehension of "man" and seeing "mortal" in it, for man *by nature* has an animal body and thus is subject to death. When I say "all my books are paperbacks," I am simply reporting on what my senses tell me about all the concrete individual books I own; and what makes that proposition true or false is not the essential nature of the things it refers to (i.e. books *qua* books, the essential nature of books), but something accidental, contingent, uncertain, and unpredictable. But when I say "all men are mortal," I am abstracting the essential nature of men from the individual men I have met and making a statement about its comprehension that is universal.

Universally and necessarily true statements like "all men are by nature mortal" are not tautologies. Tautologies are mere repetitions, like "x=x" or "x is either y or not y," or "whatever has legs and toes has toes." "Rational animals are animals" is a tautology; a computer can tell that it is self-evidently true. But "all men are mortal" is not a tautology; it requires insight into the comprehension of "man" to know that "all men are mortal" is necessarily true, and some people have that insight while others do not.

Computers do not have the power of insight. We need more than computer logic because we are more than computers. There are enough logics around for computers, and not enough for humans.

II: Terms

Section 1. Classifying terms

From the viewpoint of practical logic, the most important distinction between two kinds of terms is the distinction between ambiguous terms and unambiguous terms. However, there are also other distinctions between different kinds of terms. Terms are either

(1) unambiguous or ambiguous
(2) clear or unclear
(3) exact or vague
(4) univocal, analogical, or equivocal
(5) literal or metaphorical
(6) positive or negative
(7) simple or complex
(8) categoregmatic or syncategoregmatic
(9) universal, particular, or singular
(10) collective or divisive
(11) concrete or abstract
(12) absolute or relative

(1) Terms are either *unambiguous or ambiguous*. "Ambiguous" means "having more than one meaning." Strictly speaking, no term as such is ambiguous until it is *used* ambiguously. "Good" is not ambiguous when I use it in only one way – e.g. "A saint is a very good person" and "St. Francis was a very good person." But it becomes ambiguous when I use it with two different meanings – e.g. "That is a good axe" and "A murderer is not a good person" – for the bad murderer needs a good axe to do the bad deed of chopping off his victim's head.

If a term is used ambiguously, we are misled; we do not know what we are talking about. Worse, we think we do. Most ambiguity is hidden. We do not realize we are using terms ambiguously, unless we are deliberately trying to deceive or making a pun.

We will say more about ambiguity in the chapter on definitions. *Defining* a term is the way to heal the disease of ambiguity.

(2) Terms are either *clear or unclear*. Clarity is not quite the same as unambiguousness. A term is clear in the way light is clear: it "comes through" to the mind. Unambiguousness means a lack of confusion between two meanings. Unless a term is first of all clear, it cannot be either ambiguous or unambiguous. Until there is light, it cannot be either one color or two colors.

Whether a term is clear or not depends not only on the term but also on the mind that tries to think it. The term "quasar" is clear to those who know modern astronomy but not to those who do not.

René Descartes, often called "the father of modern philosophy," said that we could not be sure any proposition was true or false unless its terms were "clear and distinct (unambiguous)." "Clear and distinct ideas" was his criterion for certitude that any proposition is true. It is not a criterion of *truth*, for a proposition with ambiguous terms can still be true (e.g. "Life is good"). It is not even a *sufficient* criterion for certitude, for many uncertain and even false propositions can have clear and distinct terms. But it seems to be a *necessary* criterion for certitude, a minimum, a beginning.

(3) Terms are either *vague or exact*. Vague terms are not necessarily ambiguous *or* unclear. "Tall" is a vague term ("six feet tall" is an exact term) but "tall" is neither ambiguous nor unclear.

There is nothing necessarily wrong with a vague term. We often need vague terms rather than exact terms; they are very useful. For much of our knowledge is not exact, so the terms that express that knowledge rightly cannot be exact either. We often need a "fuzzy logic" in our terms.

But although there is room for "fuzzy logic" in *terms*, there is no room for "fuzzy logic" in propositions or arguments. Propositions are either true or false and arguments are either valid or invalid; and there is no third possibility and no fuzziness or sliding scale or matter of degree between true and false, or between valid and invalid.

However, we often cannot be *certain* whether a given proposition is true or false; and *that* dimension (namely, probability) can sometimes be "fuzzy." At other times, that dimension can be exact, as in statistics. In statistics, even inexactness can be exact: e.g. a "5% margin of error."

(4) Terms are either *univocal, equivocal, or analogical*. A univocal term has one and only one meaning. An equivocal term has two or more quite different and unrelated meanings. An analogical term has two or more meanings that are (a) partly the same and partly different, and (b) related to each other.

When I say "I ate two apples" and "You ate two hamburgers," I use "ate" and "two" univocally. When I say "The river has two banks" and "The town has two banks," I use "banks" equivocally, for there is no connection between a river bank and a money bank. When I say "The good man gave his good dog a good meal," I use "good" analogically, for there is at the same time a similarity and a difference between a good man, a good dog, and a good meal. All three are desirable, but a good man is wise and moral, a good dog is tame and affectionate, and a good meal is tasty and nourishing. But a good man is not tasty and nourishing, except to a cannibal; a good dog is not wise and moral, except in cartoons, and a good meal is not tame and affectionate, unless it's alive as you eat it.

Strictly speaking, a term is never univocal, equivocal, or analogical in itself; it is only *used* univocally, equivocally, or analogically. The phrases "bark of a dog" and "bark of a tree" use "bark" equivocally; the phrases "bark of an oak" and "bark of a maple" use "bark" univocally. (So do "bark of a hound" and "bark of a poodle.") "Healthy food" and "healthy exercise" use "health" univocally (for both mean something that causes health in a human body), but "a healthy climate," "a healthy body," and "a healthy sweat" uses "healthy" analogically, for a healthy climate is a *cause* of a healthy body, while a healthy sweat is an *effect* of a healthy body. 'Exercise' is an *action*, 'sweat' is a *substance*, 'climate' is neither.

One of the things computers cannot do is to understand and use analogies. One of the things philosophers and poets do especially well is to understand and use analogies. See also "arguments by analogy," p. 329.

Exercises: Classify each of the underlined terms as univocal, equivocal, or analogical.
1. I <u>love</u> ice cream and I <u>love</u> you too.
2. To murder is <u>evil</u>, and to be murdered is also <u>evil</u>.
3. A <u>litter</u> of pups was living in the street in the middle of a pile of <u>litter</u>.
4. <u>Two</u> customers paid <u>two</u> hundred dollars each for <u>two</u> chairs <u>two</u> days ago.
5. After I <u>digest</u> this logic course, I'm going to <u>digest</u> my dinner.
6. Macbeth <u>murdered</u> Banquo, but he didn't <u>murder</u> the English language as you do.
7. Water is heavier than <u>air</u>, and the <u>air</u> is very fresh today.
8. I will <u>air</u> my opinions after I <u>air</u> this room.
9. The candidate who is <u>running</u> for governor was <u>running</u> after a bus.
10. With my <u>hands</u> I changed the <u>hands</u> of the clock.
11. Poetry is an <u>art</u>, and painting is also an <u>art</u>.
12. "Death is a great <u>change</u>, and it would be no surprise if a man were unprepared for it." "Nonsense! Throughout his life man has experienced <u>change</u> of many kinds every day."
13. Christian: "We call God the <u>Father</u> and Jesus his <u>Son</u>."
    Muslim: "For a <u>father</u> to have a <u>son</u>, he must first have a <u>wife</u>. Who is God's <u>wife</u>?"
    Christian: "God has no <u>wife</u>."
    Muslim: "Then God has no <u>son</u>."
    (Which of the three underlined words is used univocally by both sides here? Which is not?)

14. "Christians believe God is three persons." "Then he must be triplets. Three persons make triplets."
15. "Buddhists seek Enlightenment. Only a few attain it." "Oh, 'the Enlightenment' – we Westerners went through that once, back in the 18th century." "What are you two talking about? Enlightenment happens every morning when the sun rises."
16. "I have to change the change I gave you for your dollar; I made a mistake."

(5) Terms are either *literal* or *metaphorical*. A *metaphor* is not the same as an *analogy*. When I call my dog an "affectionate" dog, I am using an analogy; for the dog shows some but not all of the signs of the kind of human love we call "affection," and we think the dog feels some but not all of the same emotions feel when we are affectionate to other human beings. But even though I am using the term "affectionate" analogically rather than univocally, I am using it literally, not metaphorically. But when Jesus calls wily King Herod a "fox" or St. Peter a "rock" or God a "good shepherd," he is using metaphors. The word "good" in "good shepherd" is not metaphorical but analogical (for "good God," "good man," "good dog," "good meal," and "good shepherd" are all *good* in different ways). But the word "shepherd" is metaphorical, for God is not literally a man with sheep at all. A metaphor is literally false; an analogy is not.

(6) Terms are *positive or negative*. It is usually easy to tell the difference between a positive term and a negative term simply by looking for a negative syllable at the beginning, like "un-" or "non-" or "in-." But this is not always so. Some terms that begin with these syllables are not negative, like "underwear" or "interference." And some terms have an essentially negative meaning without a negative syllable, like "absence" or "blindness" or "evil." Some words are both positive and negative at the same time, like "inconvenience," which means a (negative) absence of convenience but also a (positive) presence of trouble.

(7) Terms are *simple or complex*. A single object of thought, like "apple," is a simple term; two or more objects of thought which could be either together or apart, like "green apple," constitute a complex term. No matter how long or complex it is, if it is not a complete sentence, it is only a term. "Everything in the kitchen sink except the kitchen sink itself, including all the garbage from last night's steak dinner for four and all the dirty forks, knives, and spoons" is still only one complex term. As a term, the whole complex phrase in quotes can be the subject of a proposition with a predicate such as "can be thrown away."

(8) Terms are *categoregmatic or syncategoregmatic*. A categoregmatic term can stand by itself as a unit of meaning, like "apple" or "green" and thus can be a subject or predicate. A syncategoregmatic term (mainly articles, prepositions, and conjunctions, like "the" or "on" or "when") cannot. In the strict sense, a

syncategoregmatic term is not a term at all, only a word, because it cannot be a subject or a predicate. In another sense, it is a term because it has a definite meaning, though one that is totally relative to another word. There is no such thing as "the," only "the *something*," e.g. "the apple." But there is such a thing as "apple."

(The term "syncategoregmatic term" will probably be less practically useful to you for doing logic than for doing a vocabulary "snow job.")

(9) Terms are *universal, particular, or singular.* A universal term designates all members of a class of things, as in "*all men* are mortal." A particular term designates some members of a class, as in "*some men* are blind." A singular term designates only one member, as in "*Socrates* is dead."

When we get to propositions and arguments, this distinction among terms will be the one we will be using the most.

There are other words besides "all" that indicate that the subject of a proposition is being used universally, such as "*every*," "*each*," "*no*," "*none*," "*never*," "*always*." And other words besides "some" indicate that it is particular, such as "*a few*," "*few*," "*not all*," "*sometimes*," "*occasionally*," "*seldom*."

In ordinary language (as distinct from logical form, which we will learn soon) we often imply rather than state whether we are using a term universally or particularly. "Triangles have three sides" means "*All* triangles have three sides"; but "Vacations are disappointing" means "*Some* vacations are disappointing." When there is no word like "all" or "some" before the subject of a proposition to indicate whether the subject term is universal or particular, a good rule is to interpret it as universal if the predicate belongs to the subject by nature, i.e. by the nature of the subject, and to interpret it as particular if not. E.g. "men" is universal in "men are mortal" because mortality belongs to the essence or nature of man, but "men" is particular in "men are unreliable" because "unreliable" does not belong to the essence of man. (See "indesignate propositions" on p. 154.)

Exercise: Tell whether the subject of each of the following propositions is universal, particular, or singular.

1. Only a few planes came back.
2. The whole air force failed.
3. Several planes crashed.
4. The pilot brought no parachute.
5. Nobody could have survived.
6. Every plane with two engines had trouble.
7. Without exception everyone experienced multiple troubles.
8. Some pilots did not pass any of their tests at all.
9. None of those planes was in the air for the last two weeks.

(10) Terms designating groups of things are used either *collectively or divisively*. When I use a term collectively, I mean the group as a whole; when I use a term divisively, I mean each individual member of the group. A collective term refers to a number of individuals looked at as a single group, like the soldiers in an army or the crew of a ship.

Only terms designating groups can be either collective or divisive. Which of the two it is, is determined by use, by how the term is used in a sentence. For instance, "library" is used collectively in the sentence "This library is composed of ten thousand books," but the same term is used divisively in the sentence "This town has three libraries." When I say "this class is the smartest logic class I've ever taught," I use "class" collectively, because I don't mean that every single member of the class is smart, only that the class as a whole is. But when I say "all men are mortal," I use "men" divisively because I mean that every single man is mortal, not just that the species *homo sapiens*, or humanity, is mortal as a species.

Exercise: Tell whether each underlined term is used collectively or divisively.
   1. That is a tall pile of bricks.
   2. The trees on Holly Hill make a fine sight.
   3. None of my philosophy courses is easy.
   4. The marbles in this bag weigh five pounds.
   5. Men have a soul.
   6. The United Nations decided to censure Israel yesterday.
   7. Mankind survives by the skin of its teeth.
   8. Native Americans are disappearing, and you are a Native American, therefore you are disappearing.
   9. The Cubs have lost for over 80 years in a row, and Sosa is a Cub, therefore Sosa has lost for over 80 years in a row.

(11) Terms are *concrete or abstract*. "Concrete" does not necessarily mean something you can touch or see, and "abstract" does not necessarily mean something you cannot touch or see. Terms that mean physical things can be either concrete or abstract: "red" and "hard" are concrete, while "redness" and "hardness" are abstract. Terms that mean nonphysical things can also be either concrete or abstract: "equal" and "spirit" are concrete, while "equality" and "spirituality" are abstract. An abstract term is the expression of a mental act of "abstracting," in which we have "abstracted" or mentally "taken-out" some aspect or quality from a real thing and placed that quality itself before the mind. Whenever we make an adjective into a noun, it becomes abstract: "hot" becomes "heat" and "true" becomes "truth." Whenever we add "ness" to an adjective, it becomes abstract: "dry" becomes "dryness" and "kind" becomes "kindness."

(12) Terms are *absolute or relative*. "Absolute" comes from *"ab-solutus,"* which is Latin for "loosed-from." What is absolute is thought of as loosed from

connection or relationship with something else. By contrast, what is relative cannot be thought without relation or reference to something else.

"Father," "higher," "king," "shepherd," and "winner" are relative terms. "Father" means "father-*of*-a-child." "Higher" means "higher-*than*-something-lower." "King" means "king-*over*-some-kingdom." "Shepherd" means "herder-*of*-sheep." "Winner" means "winner-*of*-a-contest" or "winner-*over*-someone-else" (the "loser").

"Man," "mortal," "ball," "triangle," and "grass" are absolute terms because they do not require the kind of additions and qualifications given in the previous paragraph. The concept "winner" is a relative term because it is meaningless without the concept of a game or a loser. "Winner" means "winner over a loser" or "winner of a game." But the concept "man" is still meaningful even if you do not think the concept "mother" or "air," even though no man can physically come to be without a mother or survive without air. Mankind is in reality *physically dependent* on mothers and air, but the *concept* "man" is not *logically relative* to the concept "mother" or "air."

Exercises: Explain and resolve the ambiguities in the following (see also pp. 71–73):

1. The end of a thing is its purpose and perfection, and death is the end of life, therefore death is life's purpose and perfection.
2. Cancer is made of human cells, and whatever is made of human cells is human, and what is human should not be killed, so cancer should not be killed.
3. *Innuendo* is an Italian suppository.
4. Condemned prisoner to judge: "But I don't *feel* guilty."
5. Condemned prisoner to judge: "You're a bad man, judge; you're terribly judgmental."
6. Condemned prisoner to judge: "You're supposed to do justice, judge. But you've just done a bad thing, and a bad thing can't be just, because justice is a good thing, not a bad thing." "What bad thing have I done?" "You've lowered my self-esteem in declaring me guilty. Self-esteem is good, and you've taken away something good, so you're bad. You should be punished instead of me."
7. There shouldn't be laws against drugs, because the people who use drugs don't believe there should be laws against them, and that means the country doesn't have consensus about it, and laws should reflect the people's consensus.
8. Philosophy is a kind of love – the love of wisdom. Therefore philosophy teachers who accept salaries are mercenary lovers. They're intellectual prostitutes; they sell their love for money.
9. Antigravity should be easy. We disobey all kinds of laws, even the law of non-contradiction, so we should be able to disobey the law of gravity.

10. How can we claim to define ambiguity? It can't be done, because to define anything is to take its ambiguity away. But if you take the ambiguity away from ambiguity, it won't be ambiguity any more.

Section 2. Categories (B)

To order and classify things in our mind is to put them into categories or general classes of things. One of the most important disputes in philosophy is about whether all categories are simply inventions of the human mind for the sake of convenience or whether they are based on objective reality. Are they merely "conventional" or are they "natural"? E.g. are animals really different from plants and also from human beings, or is that just the way we think? As we saw in the section on the "problem of universals," this is the dispute between metaphysical realism and nominalism.

Obviously, *some* categories are merely conventional; e.g. "those things that smell worse than a dead yak," or "all the students in the class with grades lower than 70." But the fact that we can identify these categories as conventional categories means that we are judging them as not being natural categories, and thus that we have in our mind the concept of the natural category. We may not be certain whether a given category is natural or conventional, but the very distinction presupposes that some categories are natural, i.e. based on the real nature of things.

If categories categorized only subjective thoughts and not objective things, then those (categorized) thoughts would not correspond to (uncategorized) things. Then we could never be sure of the objective truth of our judgments that used these categories. But all judgments use categories. So all our judgments would be like a dream, or a game. As G.K. Chesterton says, it is simply an "attack on thought" to say "that every separate thing is unique, and there are no categories at all . . . a man cannot open his mouth without contradicting it. Thus when Mr. Wells says (as he did somewhere), 'All chairs are quite different,' he utters not merely a misstatement, but a contradiction in terms. If all chairs were quite different, you could not call them 'all chairs.'" (*Orthodoxy)*

If reality is ordered and not chaotic, categories constitute one of its most basic kinds of order. We have seen that universals, or class concepts, can be arranged in a hierarchical order of extension and comprehension, and that as either extension or comprehension increases, the other decreases. This naturally leads to the question: what are the largest, most extensive, most general of all categories?

Aristotle came up with ten categories which he thought were the most fundamental, in the sense of the most broad, the most general, the most generic. These categories are called the *summa genera*, the general classes that are the greatest in extension. Everything real, Aristotle thought, must be in one of these ten categories:

"For there is (1) *substance*, in the common understanding of the term, such as man or horse; (2) *how much*, e.g. as being of two or three cubits; (3) *of what kind*, e.g. as being white or being grammatical; (4) being *related* to something, e.g. as double, half, or greater; (5) *where*, e.g. as being in the grove or market place; (6) *when*, e.g. as tomorrow or the day before yesterday; (7) having a *posture*, e.g. as one is reclining or standing; (8) to be *equipped*, e.g. as one is shod or armed; (9) to *act*, e.g. as a thing cuts or burns; (10) to *receive*, e.g. as a thing is cut or burned."

The traditional terms for the ten categories are:

1. substance (an individual thing or entity, not a kind of matter, like "salt")
2. quantity
3. quality
4. relation
5. place
6. time
7. posture (the internal order of a thing's parts)
8. possession
9. action
10. passion (being acted upon)

"Relation" seems to be more fundamental than Aristotle thought, and "posture" and "possession" less fundamental, but the rest of the list seems as fixed as the structure of language itself. For the parts of speech in language correspond to this list of categories: nouns and pronouns usually express substances, adjectives express qualities or quantities, prepositions and conjunctions express relations, verbs express actions or passions, and adverbs express times or places (or, more often, qualities or quantities of actions or passions).

Exercises: Identify the category of each categoregmatic term (see p. 50) in the following sentences:

1. In the square sat seven skinny soldiers stuck in the stocks at six o'clock.
2. Near the blasted heath at midnight, the three Weird Sisters stood, gleefully stirring the round, black witches' pot filled with three tiny broken frogs.
3. Politically proper Professor Pete, painted partly pink, proffered puzzling paradoxes of pop psychology, ponderously pontificating.
4. Pooping on pieces of pork in the park is proper performance for perky pelicans.
5. Sam was struck Saturday by scads of silver saliva spat by six scraggly singers sitting stupidly on solid seats simultaneously singing scary seven-syllable songs.
6. Categories are used to classify things.

7. *(H) Comment on the following passage (explain the last paragraph in different words):

And what did it profit me that when I was barely twenty years old there came into my hands, and I read and understood, alone and unaided, the book of Aristotle's Ten Categories – a book I had longed for as some great and divine work because the master who taught me Rhetoric at Carthage, and whom others held to be learned, mouthed its name with such evident pride? I compared notes with others, who admitted that they had scarcely managed to understand the book even with the most learned masters not merely lecturing upon it but making many diagrams in the dust; and they could not tell me anything of it that I had not discovered in reading it for myself. For it seemed to me clear enough what the book had to say of substances, like man, and of the accidents that are in substances, like the figure of a man, what sort of man he is, and of his stature, how many feet high, and of his family relationships, whose brother he is, or where he is placed, or when he was born, or whether he is standing or sitting or has his shoes on or is armed, or whether he is doing something or having something done to him – and all the other countless things that are to be put either in these nine categories of which I have given examples, or in the chief category of substance.

Not only did all this not profit me, it actually did me harm, in that I tried to understand You, my God, marvelous in Your simplicity and immutability, while imagining that whatsoever had being was to be found within these ten categories – as if You were a substance in which inhered Your own greatness of beauty, as they might inhere in a body. But in fact Your greatness and Your beauty are Yourself; whereas a body is not large and beautiful merely by being a body, because it would still be a body even if it were less large and less beautiful.

(St. Augustine, *Confessions* IV, 16)

Section 3. Predicables (B)

To "predicate" is to affirm or deny a predicate of a subject. E.g. the proposition "Blueberries are red" predicates "red" of "blueberries." The proposition "swallowing a whale is not easy" predicates "not easy" of "swallowing a whale."

There are five possible relationships that any predicate may have to its subject. A predicate may be a **genus, specific difference, species, property** or **accident** of its subject. These are called the five "predicables," or predicate possibilities, the five things a predicate can predicate of its subject.

The ten *categories* are a classification of (a) all terms, (b) absolutely, or

---

*   (H) designates an unusually hard exercise; (E) an unusually easy one.

simply, or in themselves, (c) whether they are in a proposition or not. But the five *predicables* are a classification of (a) only predicate terms, (b) relatively, in relation to their subjects, (c) in a proposition.

Symbolic logic has no room for the predicables because the predicables presuppose the forbidden idea of nature, or essence, or whatness. The five predicables are a classification of predicates based on the standard of how close the predicate comes to stating the essence of the subject:

(1) The **species** (not a *biological* species) states the whole essence of the subject. In the proposition "Man is a rational animal," "rational animal" is the *species* of "man." In the proposition "A triangle is a three-sided plane figure," "three-sided plane figure" is the *species* of "triangle." In the proposition "Democracy is government by the people," "government by the people" is the *species* of "democracy."

(2) The **genus** states the generic or general or common aspect of the essence of the subject. (This is to define "genus" in terms of comprehension; to define it in terms of extension, a genus is a more general class to which the subject essentially belongs.) "Animal" is a genus of "man." "Plane figure" is a genus of "triangle." "Government" is a genus of "democracy." Note that the genus is part of the species, i.e. part of the species' comprehension. (In modern logic we usually say a species is part of a genus because modern logic thinks in terms of extension rather than comprehension.)

(3) The **specific difference** states the specific, or differentiating, or proper aspect of the essence of the subject, the aspect of its essence that differentiates it from other members of the same genus. "Rational" is the specific difference of "man." "Three-sided" is the specific difference of "triangle." "By the people" is the specific difference of "democracy."

(4) A **property** or "proper accident" is any characteristic that is not the essence itself but "flows from" the essence, is caused by the essence, and therefore is always present in the subject *because* the essence is always present. A property is necessarily connected with the essence and therefore inseparable from it. "Able to speak," "able to laugh," and "mortal" are *properties* of "a man." "Having its three interior angles equal to two right angles" is a *property* of "triangle." "Able to change laws by popular consent" is a *property* of "democracy."

(5) An **accident** is any characteristic of the subject that is not essential (neither the essence nor necessarily present as "flowing from" or caused by the essence), and therefore can come and go, is sometimes present and sometimes not. "Bald" and "Athenian" are *accidents* of "man." "Equilateral" and "tiny" are *accidents* of "triangle." "Modern" and "bicameral" are *accidents* of "democracy." In ordinary language *any* attribute , essential or accidental, is often called a "property," but in logic "accidents" are *distinguished* from "properties."

A technical point about singular terms: the purists among Aristotelian logicians say that predicables are only relations between universal terms; more pragmatic logicians allow them to be applied also to singular terms like "Socrates" – e.g. "rational" is the specific difference of "Socrates" as well as the specific difference of "man." The theoretical dispute seems unimportant for purposes of practical logic.

A clarification regarding the two uses of the term "accident": The same word, "accident," is used in logic both for nine of the ten categories (all of them except "substance" are "accidents") and for one of the five predicables. Do not confuse categories with predicables; remember that the categories classify terms absolutely, in themselves, while the predicables classify terms relatively, as relations of a predicate to a subject in a proposition.

However, individuals cannot be predicate terms in strict logical form, since the predicate is some aspect of the nature of the subject, and individuals are not (universal) natures. They *have* natures. Thus, "The murderer is Lucretia" must be translated into "Lucretia is the murderer" before we can speak of a predicable relationship (here, accident). "Clark Kent is Superman" is not a proposition with a predicable relationship at all but an equation between two names. Here "is" is the same as "=" in math. That is *not* its usual meaning: see p. 140.

A clarification regarding the two uses of the terms "genus" and "species": The words "genus" and "species" are used in popular speech, and often in science, to mean any larger or smaller classes, relative to each other (a "genus" contains a "species" or subclass) and relative to the mind that classifies them. That is, these classes of things are thought of as mere conventional concepts that a mind arranges at will without reference to the essence or nature of anything, since "essence" and "nature" are philosophical concepts about which there is much confusion and skepticism today. But in Aristotelian logic, genus and species presuppose the notion of essence because they are relative to the essence of the subject of a proposition. They are relative not to the subjective will or purposes or interests of the classifier, but to the objective nature of the subject.

We can also speak of genus and species outside propositions. When we do this, we are usually treating genus and species in terms of extension (larger or smaller classes, classes and subclasses). We repeat, because the point can be confusing: in terms of comprehension, a genus is part of a species; in terms of extension, a species is part of a genus. In terms of the inner meaning of a term (comprehension), a genus (e.g. "animal") is part of the meaning of a species (e.g. "man," who is "the rational animal'). But in terms of the population designated by the term (extension), a species (e.g. "man") is part of a genus (e.g. "animal").

in terms of COMPREHENSION	in terms of EXTENSION
Genus is part of **species** The concept "animal," which is man's genus, is *part* of the concept "rational animal," which is man's species.	**Species** is part of **genus** The *class* "man" is only a *part* of the *class* "animal."

A clarification about two meanings of "essence": The word "essence" also has two meanings. (1) It could mean simply what a thing is, the whole nature of a thing. It is then contrasted with *existence* or with *activity* or with *appearance*. For instance, unicorns and cows both have an essence, but unicorns do not exist, while cows do. Cows act in certain ways (e.g. they make calves and give milk) because of their essence, their cowness. And cows may *appear* to be unappetizing but are *really* very tasty by their nature. (2) "Essence" can also have a more restricted meaning: the fundamental and unchangeable nature of a thing, as contrasted with its changeable accidents. For instance, a cow is not essentially a brown cow or a healthy cow, but it is essentially a mammal. It could become a white cow or a sick cow, but it could never become a reptile or a fish.

In this second, restricted meaning, essences are often hard to define exactly when it comes to things in nature like cows, as distinct from man-made objects like democracy or cathedrals or corkscrews. The reason is obvious: we designed democracy, cathedrals, and corkscrews, so we know clearly what their essence is. But we did not design cows. Presumably the Creator knows the essence of a cow as clearly as we know the essence of a corkscrew.

Yet we have *some* knowledge of the essence of a natural thing like a cow. If we didn't, we couldn't make the distinctions above – e.g. we are not surprised to see a change of health or color in a cow because we know that that does not change the essence of a cow; but we would be amazed to see a cow become a reptile or become a fish, because that would be a change of essence.

It is much easier to distinguish the essence of a thing in nature from its *accidents* than from its *properties*. Is mass the essence of matter and energy a property of matter, or is it the other way round? Is taking-up-space a property of matter? Is it a property of energy? Is three-sides the essence of a triangle and three-angles a property or is it the other way round? The chemical elements are distinguished by their atomic weights, not by their essence, because we simply do not know what it is in the essence of any element that determines it to have the atomic weight it has. We may not know *why* it is that water boils at 212 degrees Fahrenheit at sea level, but there must be *something* in the very nature of water that makes it do that, for all water does it and nothing else does. We know ourselves better than we know water, so we know what there is in us that accounts for our properties – it is our ability to understand that accounts for our ability to laugh, and to use language, and it is our ability to freely choose that accounts for our moral responsibility. But whether we know its essence or not, *a thing acts as it is* ("*operatio sequitur esse*"); its observable activity flows from its being, its nature, its essence. A cow does bovine things *because it is a cow*. What could be more commonsensical than that?

Even though it is no longer fashionable to do so in modern philosophy or modern logic, the human mind by nature (i.e. by its essence!) still meaningfully asks the question of the essence of anything. I remember our son at age 2 running around the house pointing to each object and demanding, "Wot dat? Wot dat?"

We have an intuitive, commonsensical knowledge of essences which is useful enough for everyday conversation, but not clear enough for scientific purposes. Because science cannot usefully deal with this implicit, everyday, intuitive, commonsense knowledge of essences, science has rightly put aside the notion and demanded more empirically verifiable and "operational" definitions of things. Things are defined by scientists in terms of what we can see them do, rather than in terms of what they are. Medieval science did not clearly take this useful step.

However, the mistake typically made by medieval science, in confusing common sense (which knows essences), with science (which does not), is still with us, but in its opposite form: where the medievals reduced science to common sense, we reduce common sense to science if we reject the notion of essences entirely. And since logic and philosophy (at least any logic and philosophy applicable to the humanities) are based on common sense rather than on the scientific method, it is a mistake to drop the commonsense notion of essences – and to drop from logic the doctrine of the predicables, which is built on it.

Because it has dropped the notion of essence and therefore has no doctrine of the predicables, modern logic has difficulty answering the question of the ancient skeptic Antisthenes, who claimed that every proposition was a self-contradiction because it asserts that *one thing*, the subject, *is another thing*, the predicate. He argued that on the basis of the law of non-contradiction, we should only say that S is S, not that S is P. In terms of modern logic, Antisthenes' argument is a dilemma: either the proposition is a mere tautology (if P is identical with S), or it will be self-contradictory (if P is not identical with S). E.g. Antisthenes argued, "How can you say a cloud is white? A cloud is one thing and whiteness another. To say that a cloud is white is saying a cloud is not a cloud. That is a contradiction." If you have understood the doctrine of the predicables above, you will be able to answer Antisthenes easily. But not by the law of non-contradiction alone, not by "computer logic" alone.

The "Tree of Porphyry": The ancient Greek logician Porphyry arranged the basic genera and species in the universe into a kind of upside down tree, as seen on page 61.

The Tree is useful for a number of things. For one thing, it helps us to see the inverse relationship between extension and comprehension. As you move down the tree, each successive branch has more comprehension (more properties) but less extension (fewer members). It also helps us to see the categories as the "summa genera," highest genera, most general classes. It gives us a metaphysical road map, a basic map of being. With this map, we at least know what continent we are on; without it, we are lost: we do not know where or even what we are.

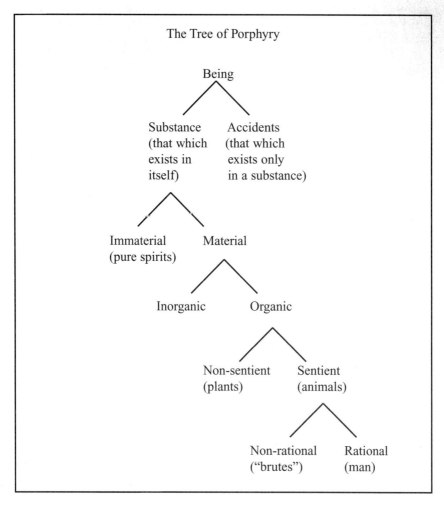

The Tree of Porphyry

Being

Substance
(that which
exists in
itself)

Accidents
(that which
exists only
in a substance)

Immaterial
(pure spirits)

Material

Inorganic

Organic

Non-sentient
(plants)

Sentient
(animals)

Non-rational
("brutes")

Rational
(man)

Exercises: Identify the predicable in each of the following propositions:
1. Regicide is murder of a king.
2. Regicide is murder.
3. Predicables are relations between terms.
4. Purple is a color.
5. Men are often hot-tempered.
6. To be human is to have a temper.
7. Justice is more profitable than injustice.
8. Justice is a virtue.
9. Justice gives to each his due.
10. Justice will improve your soul.
11. Justice was done to Socrates.

12. Biology is the science of living things.
13. Biology studies mammals.
14. Biology is hard for me.
15. Logic is an art.
16. Logic is a science.

Section 4. Division and outlining (B)

This is one of the simplest but also most practical sections. It is simplest because its rules are commonsensical. It is practical because the only alternative to outlining is confusion, whether in life or in writing. If we do not distinguish things (in the world) or points (in our thought or writing or speech), we confuse them; and if we confuse them, we are confused. To have a *clear* idea, the idea must also be *distinct*.

Modern minds often have a vague ideological aversion to distinctions; they think they are "discriminatory." In other words, they fail to distinguish three very different kinds of distinctions: (1) distinctions between thoughts, which are always helpful, (2) just and reasonable distinctions between things and people, such as distinguishing between medicines and poisons, or between students who pass and who fail, and (3) unjust and unreasonable distinctions between people, "discrimination" in the ideological sense, e.g. basing salaries on gender or race instead of performance.

Outlining is the most practical application of logical division. Like most teachers in the humanities, I have read tens of thousands of student essays and papers. No matter what the content of those papers, no matter what is said, those that are not outlined, or not clearly or intelligently outlined, always receive a lower grade than those that are.

We can (1) divide *terms* or we can (2) divide something more complex than terms: propositions, points, theses, or topics in a discourse, by *outlining* it. The two kinds of division have somewhat different rules.

Dividing terms

When we *divide* a term, we divide the *extension* of the term. When we define a terms, we define the comprehension of the term. (see page 43.) There are three rules: the division must be *exclusive, exhaustive*, and use only *one standard*.

1. **The division must be *exclusive***; i.e., the things divided must be really distinct, and not overlap.

Dividing political systems into monarchical, constitutional, and democratic violates this rule because a regime could be both monarchical and constitutional, as well as both democratic and constitutional.

Dividing regimes into totalitarian and democratic also violates this rule, for the two could overlap. You could have a totalitarian democracy. For totalitarianism and democracy are not two mutually exclusive answers to the same question, but answers to two different questions. Democracy is an answer to the question of sovereignty: who ultimately holds the power? Its answer is: the *demos*, the people at large, or the majority. Totalitarianism is an answer to the question of quantity: how much power, or power over how much of human life, especially private life, is there? Its answer is: total, unlimited power. *Brave New World* is a totalitarian democracy; so is Rousseau's idea of "the general will" as infallible (*vox populi, vox dei*: "The voice of the people is the voice of God").

Dividing attitudes into loving, hating, and indifferent also violates this rule because although love and hate both exclude indifference, they do not exclude each other. Though an attitude cannot be loving and indifferent at the same time, it can be loving and hating at the same time.

Dividing attitudes into amoral, moral, and hateful also violates this rule because an attitude of hatred toward evil – evil that harms persons – is quite moral. The division should be between the amoral, the moral, and the immoral.

One simple way of obeying this first rule is to divide in an "either/or" way, into only two subclasses, one of which negates the other. For instance, "loving and non-loving" are exclusive, while "loving and hating" are not. "Democratic and non-democratic" are exclusive, while "democratic and totalitarian" are not. Such a division is called *dichotomous* (literally, "cut in two").

2. **The division must be *exhaustive***; i.e., the divided parts should add up to a whole.

This rule must always be obeyed in dividing terms, but not always in outlining. Dividing the term "meat" into beef and lamb violates this rule because it omits pork. But we can divide "examples of healthy meats" *in an outline* into beef and lamb if we wish, omitting pork.

Dividing tools into hand tools and electrical tools is a non-exhaustive division, thus violates this rule, because it omits tools that use power sources such as gas or steam. Such non-exhaustive divisions are sometimes useful, though, because they often do exhaustively divide a *part* of the class, the part we are concerned with. For instance, in the above division, "tools" may be shorthand for "the tools at hand" or "the tools in my house" or "the tools I can afford," and electrical and hand tools may be the only two kinds of *those* tools.

Dividing the parts or aspects of a person into head and body violates this rule because it omits the soul or mind. Even dividing a person into body and soul might be said to omit the spirit, if spirit is distinguished from soul, as it sometimes (but not usually) is. But "head and body" *do* exhaustively divide a person's body, in the narrower sense of "body" as "what's below the head."

3. The division should have **only *one basis* or standard**. We should not divide people simultaneously by their race and by their intelligence, e.g., or books by their objective truth and their subjective appeal. One of the things we

should clearly divide and distinguish is the basis or standard by which we divide and distinguish.

Exercise: Evaluate the following divisions of terms and tell which, if any, of the three rules they violate:
1. women into blondes, brunettes, and redheads
2. men into bald and hirsute
3. parts of speech into nouns, verbs, adjectives, and adverbs
4. cats into tailless and those with tails
5. animals into reptiles, mammals, amphibians, marsupials, birds, and fish
6. regimes into popular and totalitarian
7. human acts into those that are morally good and those that cause pain
8. human beings into male and female
9. animals into rational animals ("men") and irrational animals ("brutes")
10. organisms into plants and animals
11. things ("substances") into physical things and spiritual things
12. reality into that which is real in itself and that which is real only relative to something else
13. beings into mental beings and objectively real beings
14. musical keys into major and minor
15. (H) "All Gaul is divided into three parts. The Belgians inhabit one part, the Aquitanians another, and those who call themselves Celts – in our language, Gauls – inhabit the third." (Julius Caesar)
16. (H) "Democracy has therefore two excesses to avoid: the spirit of inequality, which leads to aristocracy or monarchy, and the spirit of extreme equality, which leads to despotic power, as the latter is completed by conquest." (Montesquieu)
17. (H) "Let me ask you now: How would you arrange goods? Are there not some which we welcome for their own sakes, and independently of their consequences, as for example harmless pleasures and enjoyments, which delight us at the time though nothing follows from them?"
    "I agree in thinking that there is such a class," I replied.
    "Is there not also a second class of goods, such as knowledge, sight, health, which are desirable not only in themselves but also for their results?"
    "Certainly," I said
    "And would you not recognize a third class, such as gymnastic and the care of the sick, and the physician's art; also the various ways of money-making? These do us good but we regard them as disagreeable, and no one would choose them for their own sakes." (Plato, *Republic*, Book II)
18. (H) "Now order can be compared to reason in four ways. There is a certain order which reason does not make but only considers, such as the

order of natural things. There is another order which reason in carrying on its considerations makes in its own proper act, as when, for example, it orders its own concepts and the signs of these concepts in so far as these are significant sounds. There is a third order which reason makes in the operations of the will. There is a fourth order which reason makes in external things of which it is the cause, as for example in a chest or in a house." (St. Thomas Aquinas)

19. (H) "Before the end of the present century, unless something unforeseeable occurs, one of three possibilities will have been realized. These three are: I. The end of human life, perhaps of all life on our planet. II. A reversion to barbarism after a catastrophic diminution of the population of the globe. III. A unification of the world under a single government, possessing a monopoly of all the major weapons of war." (Bertrand Russell)

20. (H) Plato's division of states into (a) aristocratic (rule by "the best"), (b) timocratic (rule by "the brave"), (c) plutocratic (rule by the rich), (d) democratic (rule by the masses), and (e) despotic (rule by a tyrant)

21. (H) Aristotle's division of states into (a) monarchies, (b) despotisms, (c) aristocracies, (d) oligarchies, (e) democracies, and (f) anarchies (What are the bases for his division? How many bases does he use? Is this one division or two?)

22. (H) From the Catholic point of view there are thirteen religious options. First, there is Agnosticism, or Skepticism, which is the negative answer to the question: Is there any hope of finding the truth about religion? All twelve other options answer Yes. Second, there is Atheism, which is the negative answer to the question: Is there any kind of God, any ontologically superhuman mystery that justifies the fundamental religious attitude of piety? All eleven other options answer Yes. Third, there is Polytheism, which is the negative answer to the question: Is there an ultimate oneness to this mystery? All ten other options answer Yes. Fourth, there is Pantheism, which is the negative answer to the question: Is this mystery transcendent and distinct from the universe and human consciousness, rather than simply the sum total of all being, or another word for Everything, or that which everything really is? All nine other options answer Yes. Fifth, there is Vague Philosophical Theism, which is the negative answer to the question: Is this mystery a Person, an "I" who could say "I AM," rather than a Force or a Principle? All eight other options answer Yes. Sixth, there is Non-religious Philosophical Theism, which is the negative answer to the question: Did this "I AM" reveal Himself through prophets? All seven other options answer Yes, and stem from the Hebrew Bible. Seventh, there is Judaism, which is the negative answer to the question: Did this "I AM" send any prophet greater than Moses? All six other options answer Yes. Eighth, there is Islam, which is the negative

answer to the question: Is this greatest prophet Jesus rather than Muhammad? All five other options answer Yes. Ninth, there is Unitarianism, which is the negative answer to the question: Is Jesus a divine person as well as a human person, and is God three Persons rather than one? All four other options answer Yes. Tenth, there is Protestant Christianity, which is the negative answer to the question: Did this Jesus establish a single, visible, infallible Church with authority to teach in His name? All three other options answer Yes. Eleventh, there is Eastern Orthodox Christianity, which is the negative answer to the question: Is the Pope in Rome the present universal head of this Church? The two other options answer Yes. Twelfth, there is orthodox Catholicism, which is the negative answer to the question: May I pick and choose which teaching of the Church to believe and obey? The other option answers Yes, and this is the thirteenth option, which is "cafeteria Catholicism."

■ (1) Diagram this, (2) evaluate it, and (3) if you think you can, give an alternative classification of religions.

23. (H) Do the same for philosophies, political systems, or moral systems as #22, above, did for religions.

Outlining

The principles of outlining are like the principles of morality in that they are usually simple and easy to understand but hard to obey. They are not hard in themselves; we are just lazy! But their practice has a big payoff. Few things clarify and improve writing and thinking more. By far the most important rule about outlining is: JUST DO IT!

The basic rules are these:

1. Titles and subtitles are not parts of the outline but placed above it.

2. Use Roman numerals for main topics, capital letters for main subtopics, then Arabic numerals for sub-subtopics, then small letters, then Arabic numerals in parentheses, then small letters in parentheses.

3. For each number or letter there must be a topic. Each must stand on a line by itself. E.g. never write "AI" or "IA."

4. There must always be more than one subtopic under any topic. (No A without a B, no 1 without a 2.)

5. A subtopic must be placed under the main topic which it qualifies. This is the rule that gives many students the most trouble: distinguishing the relative rank of each point, deciding which are coordinate with which, and which are subordinate to which. This is an ability that is more intuitive than teachable; but it can be greatly improved by practice, and cannot be greatly improved without practice.

6. Subtopics are indented, so that all numbers or letters of the same kind come directly under each other vertically.

7. Begin each topic with a capital letter, even if they are not complete sentences.

8. Do not include Introduction or Conclusion as points within the outline.

Outlining is *not* simply putting numbers and letters in order before sentences or before headings. They must be in *logical order* and *logical subordination.*

Students usually dislike outlining because they find it mechanical and inflexible. But when we construct any work of art with a complex structure, whether a garage or a symphony, there is simply no comparison between having a plan or outline and not having one.

III: Material Fallacies

First, we must distinguish material fallacies, which are covered in this chapter, from formal fallacies, which are covered later. Formal fallacies are mistakes in reasoning, errors in the operation of the third act of the mind. For instance, "Some men are mortal, and some mortals are fish, therefore some men are fish" commits a formal fallacy. "Some men are fish" does not logically follow from the two premises that "some men are mortal" and "some mortals are fish," even though both the premises are true. There is no ambiguity or wrong use of terms in this argument, only bad reasoning. We will learn the rules of good logical reasoning in the third section of this book, which covers the third act of the mind.

Material fallacies, on the other hand, are treated here, in the section of the book which covers the first act of the mind, because they are mistakes in understanding the meaning or use of terms, errors in the operation of the first act of the mind. These material fallacies are found in the course of an argument, so they are called "fallacies," or mistakes in reasoning; but they are not mistakes in the logical *form* but mistakes in the content or *matter* or meaning.

Most of the errors and misunderstandings that plague our conversation and argumentation come from a loose use of language rather than from formal fallacies. Formally fallacious arguments don't deceive us as often as materially fallacious arguments do. Therefore we have made this section, on material fallacies, longer than it is in most logic texts. Most logic texts do not do this because they specialize in what they do best: the clear, black-or-white formal fallacies, as distinct from the more messy and intuitive material fallacies. But the topics in a practical text should be determined not by the topic's clarity but by its practicality, i.e. by human need and use.

How many material fallacies are there? There is an exact number of formal fallacies, but no exact number of material fallacies, because they often overlap, because the list can always be added to, and because they can be classified in different ways. Most logic texts list only a dozen or two; we list 49, because the more we know, the more we can avoid. Like sins, fallacies are easier to avoid if they are labeled. "It would be a very good thing if every trick could receive some short and obviously appropriate name, so that when a man used this or that particular trick, he could at once be reproved for it" (Arthur Schopenhauer, *The Art of Controversy*).

Students have more legitimate arguments about the right answers to test questions on the material fallacies than on any other topic in logic, since the fallacies often overlap and in some cases more than one fallacy is present. It is less important to distinguish them from each other than to distinguish them from good reasoning, less important to "get the answer right" to the question "Which fallacy is present here?" than simply to be aware of them and on the watch for them. This is why we do not include a set of exercises after this section.

For each of the 49 fallacies, we will give (1) a definition, (2) an explanation, and (3) some typical examples of it.

Here is a systematic outline of the 49 fallacies, grouped under seven different kinds, each of which happens to have seven major fallacies under it; and in each of the seven kinds, **the most important and most common fallacy is placed first.**

Many have Latin names. This is not a reason for panic or attacks on history or Western civilization. Knowing a few Latin terms does not make you a snob or a showoff.

Section 1. Fallacies of language

1A, **Equivocation**

Equivocation is the simplest and most common of all the material fallacies. It means simply that the same term is used in two or more different senses in the course of an argument.

Fallacies, in the logical sense, occur only in *arguments*. In ordinary language the word "fallacy" is often used for any kind of mistake, but in logic a fallacy is a mistake in argument. A fallacious argument is one that seems to prove its conclusion but does not, for one of two reasons: material (the use of terms) or formal (the reasoning process). Almost any terms, except numbers, have the potential to be used equivocally. But no term *is* equivocal in itself; a term is only *used* equivocally. This happens when it changes its meaning in the course of an argument.

Concepts are not equivocal, only *terms* (i.e. the *words* that express them). To have a concept in your mind is to know what it means. If your mind holds two meanings, it holds two concepts, not one. But you may be using only one term to express the two concepts. E.g. you may use the term "pen" to express both the concept "ink writing instrument" and also the concept "pig enclosure." But the two concepts are clear and distinct: the first concept is just what it is and nothing else; and the second concept is just what it is and nothing else. The disease of equivocation is in the term, not the concept.

When two people use the same word in two different senses, they are said to be "**quibbling**" over the term. We remove the quibble by exposing the double identity of the term, i.e. by showing how the same *term* (word or phrase) expresses two different *concepts*. "Quibbling" usually means *deliberate* equivocation: e.g. "Since 'automobile' means 'self-mover,' locomotives must be automobiles." Or "Mom told us not to go swimming right after lunch, but I'm not swimming; I'm on a bodyboard."

To expose the equivocation or double identity of the equivocal term, use these two steps:

(1) **First identify the word or phrase that shifts its meaning.**

(2) **Then identify the two different meanings by using two different words or phrases.**

The golden rule here is: **To unmake an ambiguity, make a distinction**. Medieval "Scholastic" philosophy was famous for making many distinctions. People today tend to think of this as artificial and overdone; but that is because, with one exception, people today do not like to take the time and care to think clearly and exactly. The one exception is in the sciences – and it is no coincidence that science is the most spectacular success story of modern civilization.

Making distinctions is *not* the vice of **verbalism** or "getting hung up on words." It is exactly the opposite: it is the way to *avoid* "getting hung up on words," being victimized by words. The reason we make distinctions (and also definitions [Chapter V]) is because we insist on going *beyond* unclear words to clear concepts.

A term used analogically, a term used metaphorically, or a term used vaguely ("fuzzily") is not necessarily one used equivocally. (See above, page 48 on analogy and fuzziness. And for a very clear account of metaphor, see *Practical Logic* by Monroe Beardsley [Prentice-Hall, 1950], ch. 4.)

Many jokes, and all puns, depend on equivocation.

Exercises: Explain and remove the ambiguity in the following examples of equivocation by using the two-step procedure on page 71. NB: some of these are single propositions rather than arguments; in this case, identify two possible meanings for the potentially equivocal terms.

1. (E) Only men are rational, and women are not men, therefore women are not rational.
2. (H) Those who are the most hungry, eat the most. Those who eat the least, are the most hungry. Therefore those who eat the least, eat the most.
3. All laws require lawgivers, and the laws of nature are laws, therefore the laws of nature require a lawgiver.
4. Like most ten year olds, Sam was bored with church services. He overheard his parents worrying about this: his father said, "I'm afraid Sam is just about bored to death in church." Being very literal, this worried Sam. Later that day, Sam asked his minister who were all those names on the church's war memorial plaque. The minister replied that they were "all the people that died in the service." Sam asked, "Was it the morning service or the evening service?" (Find *two* ambiguous terms here.)
5. (H) The more you study, the more you learn. The more you learn, the more you know. The more you know, the more you forget. The more you forget, the less you remember. The less you remember, the less you know. So why study?
6. "Who's on first?" (from the famous Abbot and Costello routine)
7. A logician, walking past a library at 6 A.M., heard a man call out from one of the windows, "Help! I've been locked inside here all night by mistake!" The logician replied with this argument: "The sign says that no one can be

in the library all night. You are someone. Therefore you have not been in the library all night." And he walked away.

8. G.K. Chesterton, visiting New York City for the first time, saw two women screaming at each other from the windows of their 4th floor apartments, which were directly across a narrow alley from each other. He commented, "Those women will never agree because they are arguing from different premises."

9. (E) "What is the highest form of animal life?" "The giraffe."

10. (E) "Your argument is sound. In fact, it's nothing but sound."

11. A Russian-English language translator computer was tested by being given this sentence, "The spirit is willing, but the flesh is weak," to translate into Russian, and then back into English. It came out: "The vodka is agreeable but the meat is too tender."

12. Foreign language teacher informing a student that he had failed a test on pronunciation: "I will now pronounce your sentence."

13. "Oh, I am very fond of children," said the Giant to Jack.

14. "He cares for her."

15. (E) "I couldn't work for NASA because safety regulations demand that some missions be aborted, and I don't believe in abortion."

16. (E) "The English don't drive on the right side of the road. Therefore they drive on the wrong side."

17. The 9th-century philosopher John the Scot Eriugena was sitting at dinner with the rude, racist, and very drunken king Charles the Bald, who said to him, in a feeble attempt at humor, "Tell me, John, what separates a Scot from a sot?" The philosopher answered, "Only the width of the table, Sire." (What word's ambiguity is the point of John's riposte?)

18. "Why do you love violence?" "Because I am pious." "That's ridiculous." "No, that's logical. To be like what God is, is to be Godlike, and what God is, is love, therefore to love is Godlike. To be Godlike is to be pious, therefore he who loves is pious. He who loves violence, loves, therefore he who loves violence is pious. I love violence. Therefore I am pious."

19. (H) "If you move, you're dead. If you're dead, you can't move. Therefore if you move, you can't move." (Which word is equivocal here? Hint: unpack the contractions.)

20. (H) President Clinton, responding to a question from a prosecutor who was investigating whether he had engaged in illegal activities: "That depends on what you mean by 'is.'" Could this be a reasonable, intelligent, and honest answer? Can "is" be equivocal?

21. (H) "Evil makes you think; thinking makes you wise; being wise is good; therefore evil makes you good."

22. (H) "Nothing is more expensive than diamonds. But paper is more expensive than nothing. Therefore paper is more expensive than diamonds."

1B, **Amphiboly**

An "amphiboly" is not an ambiguous *word* (or phrase) but ambiguous *syntax* (word order or grammatical structure). Simple puns are based on equivocation; slightly longer "language jokes" are usually based on amphiboly, e.g.: What word is pronounced incorrectly by nearly all English people? Answer: the word "incorrectly."

Here is an example of amphiboly that is not a joke, just an ambiguity: "Aristotle the peripatetic (i.e. the 'walker') taught his students walking." There are two ambiguities here. First, who was walking, Aristotle or his students? Second, did he teach them the art of walking or did he teach them something else while he was walking?

The 18th century philosopher Berkeley was trying to prove his conclusion that *esse est percipi*, "to be is to be perceived," i.e. that there is no "material world," no objective reality independent of perception or awareness, whether mental or sensory. He used this argument: "Is it not a great contradiction to think a thing exists when you do not think it?" The ambiguity here comes from the fact that the adverbial phrase "when you do not think it" can modify either the verb "think" or the verb "exists." Only the first interpretation is "a great contradiction," for it means "to think . . . when you do not think." But the second is no contradiction, for it means "to believe the following idea: that a thing will not stop existing when I stop thinking about it."

Most of Jay Leno's "headlines" are examples of amphiboly. The *New Yorker* magazine used to collect humorous amphibolies, or (as they used to be called) malapropisms (after Mrs. Malaprop, a character in an old comedy). E.g.

(1) "WENCH FOR SALE, complete with rope. For further information call 3081." (advertisement in the Fairmont *West Virginian*, reprinted in *The New Yorker* 3/6/54, p. 104)

(2) "SUMMER RENTAL: 5-room house with wood paneling plus small guest and garage in rear." (advertisement in Princeton *Town Topics*, reprinted in *The New Yorker* 6/12/54)

(3) "It won't be a real New England clam chowder unless you put your heart into it." (New England *Homestead*, reprinted in *The New Yorker* 6/12/54)

(4) "Although slightly hazy around the city this afternoon, weather bureau officials claimed that no fog was imminent." (Hartford *Times*, reprinted in *The New Yorker* 5/15/54)

(5) "GUEST FOR LUNCH ONE WAY TO SOLVE EATING PROBLEM" (headline in the Providence *Bulletin*, reprinted in *The New Yorker* 5/8/54)

(6) "I shall lose no time in reading your manuscript." (Samuel Johnson)

(7) "Sir: I have your manuscript before me. I am sitting in the smallest room in my house. Soon I shall have your manuscript behind me." (Samuel Johnson) (If you don't get it, ask yourself what is the smallest room in your house.)

(8) Alice: "Would you – be very good enough – to stop a minute – just to get – one's breath again?" White King: "I'm *good* enough, only I'm not *strong*

enough. You see, a minute goes by so fearfully quick. You might as well try to stop a Bandersnatch." (Lewis Carroll)

(9) "The duke yet lives that Henry shall depose." (Shakespeare, *Henry VI*, Part II, Act I, scene 4)

(10) "Would you rather a cannibal ate you or a shark?"

(11) (title of article in student newspaper): "How To Cook Yourself"

(12) (TV commercial): "Drive this 4x4 fully loaded."

(13) (Advertisement): "Dogs bathed, fleas removed and returned to your house for $40"

(14) "And the skies are not cloudy all day." ("Home on the Range")

(15) "Most men love cigars more than their wives."

(16) (newspaper advertisement): "For Sale: Antique desk suitable for lady with curved legs and large drawers, also mahogany chest." (reprinted in the *Journal of the American Medical Association*, 9/19/53)

(17) "The cook opened the oven stuffed with sausages."

(18) "George, you are being selfish and rude to your sister in calling her stupid. Tell her you're sorry." "O.K., Mom. Hey, Sis, I'm sorry you're stupid."

(19) "I'm not myself today." "I see you have revoked the Law of Non-contradiction."

Exercise: Expose the ambiguity in each of the above examples by the two steps on p. 71.

1C, Accent

Here the ambiguity comes from voice inflection, ironic or sarcastic tone, or even facial expression, or innuendo. (If you don't know what "innuendo" means, look it up. Every literate person should have – and, more importantly, use – a dictionary.) Accent and amphiboly are the two fallacies that are almost always humorous, usually ironic, and often sarcastic.

Notice, in the following two examples, how the same sentence can have many significantly different meanings by implication if different words are emphasized:

"*I* do not choose to run at this time." (But perhaps *he* will.)

"I do *not* choose to run at this time." (no ambiguity)

"I do not *choose* to run at this time." (But I can be forced.)

"I do not choose to *run* at this time." (But I can be drafted.)

"I do not choose to run at *this* time." (But I may do it tomorrow.)

Another, similar example:

"*We* don't have to tell the whole truth, you know." (But others do.)

"We *don't* have to tell the whole truth, you know." (You only think we do.)

"We don't *have* to tell the whole truth, you know." (It's optional.)

"We don't have to *tell* the whole truth, you know." (But we should know it.)
"We don't have to tell the *whole* truth, you know." (Half truths are OK.)
"We don't have to tell the whole *truth*, you know." (Tell myths or evasions instead.)
"We don't have to tell the whole truth, *you* know." (But no one else does.)

More examples of ambiguity by accent:

(1) Aristotle was a good *logician*. (but not a good physicist)

(2) "Mr. Benchley, that whiskey you are drinking is a slow poison." Robert Benchley: "That's O.K., I'm in no hurry."

(3) John Austin, the prestigious English logician, was explaining to a Sidney Morgenbesser, a skeptical New Yorker, that in the English language a double negative could mean something positive but a double positive could not mean something negative. He concluded, "You understand that, don't you?" Morgenbesser replied sarcastically, "Yeah, yeah."

(4) The old King James Bible used italics for words that were not literally in the original Hebrew or Greek text but had to be added to make sense in English. But italics in English usually means emphasis. Thus the ambiguity of the following: "And he said, 'Saddle me an ass.' And they saddled *him*." (The humor depends on two fallacies: accent, and equivocation on the word "ass.")

(5) A famous example of accent by sarcasm or irony is Marc Antony's funeral oration in "Julius Caesar." It is also a sarcastic undermining of the argument from authority, the authority of Brutus as an honorable man:

> Come I to speak in Caesar's funeral.
> He was my friend, faithful and just to me;
> But Brutus says he was ambitious;
> And Brutus is an honorable man . . .
> He hath brought many captives home to Rome,
> Whose ransoms did the general coffers fill;
> Did this in Caesar seem ambitious?
> When that the poor have cried, Caesar hath wept:
> Ambition should be made of sterner stuff.
> Yet Brutus says he was ambitious;
> And Brutus is an honorable man.

1D, Slanting

Slanting is sometimes called the fallacy of the "**question-begging epithet**" because it is really a form of "begging the question" (fallacy 4C, below) in a single word. "Begging the question" means assuming what you're supposed to prove, and the use of "slanted" language "begs the question" by telling you whether to like or dislike the thing the word describes. Instead of *proving* that the thing it describes is good or bad, it *assumes* its value or disvalue in the very description of it – e.g. calling an idea "up-to-date" or "wild," "traditional" or "stagnant," "flexible" or "fickle." This is equivocation or double meaning because it both describes and evaluates at once, in a single word. It both *denotes* a fact and *connotes* an evaluating attitude toward the fact. That is why it is classified under the heading of fallacies of equivocation.

The most obvious and egregious examples of slanting are in **propaganda** (which has been defined by a famous punster as the proper mate for a proper goose). But slanting can also be done negatively, by omitting relevant information, and by selecting only favorable, or only unfavorable, data. This form of slanting is much subtler and harder to detect. The old U.S.S.R.'s official newspaper *Pravda* was full of blatant propaganda; but even ("even"?) American newspapers habitually slant by omission, sometimes as part of deliberate editorial policy, e.g. by giving candidates of its favored political party more coverage, and the opposing candidates less, and reversing this when it comes to scandals or accusations. Newspapers also have linguistic policies on divisive issues like abortion: one paper will label the two sides "pro-choice" and "anti-choice," another paper will label the same sides "pro-abortion" and "anti-abortion," and a third paper will label them "pro-life" and "anti-life." For papers of the Left, there *are* no "left-wing extremists," and for papers of the Right, there are no "right-wing extremists." What the Left calls "centrist" the Right calls "left-wing" and what the Right calls "centrist" the Left calls "right wing."

One of the most common forms of slanting is the *euphemism*: the Holocaust was called "the final solution to the Jewish problem," and the slaughter of civilians in war is called "collateral damage." Slavery was defended by some such linguistic indirection as the following: "Since a gradation of human enterprise is necessary for the optimal functioning of human society, there must be a lowest position on the spectrum; and since this position is odious to the majority of humankind, it is necessary to enforce its occupation by establishing appropriate civil structures to protect it."

The above was written by an obscure legal writer; but the following was written by one of the most famous judges in American history: "We have seen more than once that the public welfare may call upon the best citizens for their lives. It would be strange if it could not call upon those who already sap the strength of the state for these lesser sacrifices, often not felt to be such by those concerned, in order to prevent our being swamped with incompetence. It is better for all the world if instead of waiting to execute degenerate offspring for crime or to let them starve for their imbecility, society can prevent those who are manifestly unfit from continuing their kind. The principle that sustains compulsory vaccination is broad enough to cover cutting of the Fallopian tubes" (Justice Oliver Wendell Holmes, U.S. Supreme Court, upholding the Virginia Compulsory Sterilization Law, 1927 [274 US 200]).

A long list could be made of slanted adjectives. Each of the following sets of three terms means the same thing, but with three different connotations:

"I am firm, you are stubborn, he is pigheaded." (Bertrand Russell)

"I am open-minded, you are flexible, he is a waffler."

"I am righteously indignant, you are annoyed, he is whining."

"I am a public servant, you are a government official, he is a bureaucrat."

The reader is invited to add many more examples. For example, Benjamin Disraeli distinguished "lies, damned lies, and statistics."

Here is a famous "slanted" passage by a famous philosopher, David Hume: "If we take into our hand any volume, or divinity of school metaphysics, for instance, let us ask: *Does it contain any abstract reasoning concerning quantity or number?* No. *Does it contain any experimental reasoning concerning matter of fact and existence?* No. Commit it then to the flames, for it can contain nothing but sophistry and illusion" (David Hume, *Enquiry Concerning Human Understanding*, XII, 3).

Hume may be exaggerating here for rhetorical effect, but if what he says is true, most of the history of philosophy, including most of the thinking of Socrates, Plato, and Aristotle, is "sophistry and illusion" because it is neither mathematical nor empirical. Hume's critique is also an example of a self-contradiction (fallacy # D6), for his statement about philosophical statements being meaningless ("sophistry and illusion") is itself a philosophical statement. And if all statements that are neither mathematical nor empirical are meaningless, then that very statement (that all statements that are neither mathematical nor empirical are meaningless) is meaningless, because it is neither mathematical nor empirical. It therefore deserves only to be "committed to the flames."

1E, Slogans

There is no fallacy in a slogan as such, but in its use as a substitute for argument. E.g., "I'm pro-life." "Why?" "Because of that bumper sticker: 'A Child, Not a Choice.'" "Well, I'm pro-choice." "Why?" "Because of that bumper sticker: 'Every Woman's Right To Choose.'"

Or: "Why are you voting for the incumbent?" "You know the saying: 'Don't change horses in the middle of the stream.' And 'If it ain't broke, don't fix it.'" "Why are you voting for his opponent?" "Because I believe in Progress. I'm progressive."

Almost any expression can become a slogan when it is used to produce a thoughtless knee-jerk reaction of agreement or disagreement simply on the basis of the familiarity of the words rather than on the basis of reason. The words function like the logo of the local football team.

1F, Hyperbole

"Hyperbole" means "exaggeration." This is routinely done by "media hype." For instance, note every occurrence of the word "crisis" in your daily newspaper. How may are really crises and how many are only "a tempest in a teapot"? Do the same with the word "shocking." Surely it is highly ironic that this word is used more and more as Americans find less and less to be shocked at.

Another form of hyperbole is the "absurd extension" of the other speaker's claim. Children often do this:

"You need to clean up your room." "Oh, so you want me to be your slave."

"You shouldn't drink so much." "You're always harping on that." (A wimpy once-a-month reminder becomes "harping.")

"You can't stay out all night. You're only sixteen." "My life is ruined. I'm a prisoner in my own home forever."

"Oh, so you're against pornography. You must be against freedom of speech."

"Absurd extension" must be distinguished from the legitimate form of argument called "reduction to absurdity," or *reductio ad absurdum*, which consists in proving that if you accept a certain proposition as a premise, that premise necessarily leads to a conclusion which is "absurd," i.e. one which everybody knows is false, and therefore the premise cannot be accepted. It is *not* fallacious to argue that "If p were true, then q would be true. But q is not true, for it is absurd. Therefore p is not true." One of the two premises of this argument may be *false* – it may be false that q follows p, or that q is absurd – but there is no formal or material *fallacy* in the argument.

1G, "Straw Man"

The "straw man" fallacy consists in refuting an unfairly weak, stupid, or ridiculous version of your opponent's idea (either his *conclusion* or his *argument*) instead of the more reasonable idea he actually holds. You first set up a "straw man," or scarecrow, then knock it down, since a straw man is easy to knock down.

One of the rules of medieval debate was designed to block "straw man" arguments: you must first state your opponent's idea in your own words (to be sure you understand the idea instead of just parroting the words), to his satisfaction, before you go on to refute it.

Even great philosophers often fall into the "straw man" fallacy. E.g. the optimist may "refute" the pessimist by noting that "not *everything*" is bad, and the pessimist may "refute" the optimist by noting that "not *everything* is good." Rationalists have "refuted" empiricists by noting that man is not merely a clever animal, the eye is not merely a camera, and the brain is not merely a computer. Only an extreme empiricist would hold that. And empiricists have "refuted" rationalists by noting that man is not a god or an angel and that babies are not born with innate ideas. Only an extreme rationalist would hold that. E.g. there is a story that the poet Shelley, converted to Platonic rationalism by reading Plato's dialogues, rushed out of his house onto London Bridge, snatched the first baby he saw from its mother's arms, and demanded of it an account of all the innate ideas it had been born with. Alas, the baby only cried.

That great paragon of common sense, Samuel Johnson, according to his biographer Boswell, "refuted" Berkeley's philosophical claim that so-called material things were really ideas (i.e., that matter does not exist independent of, or outside of, mind) by kicking a stone, and saying "Thus I refute Berkeley." (But Berkeley did not say that we could not kick stones.)

Section 2. Fallacies of diversion

The next group of seven fallacies are fallacies of distraction or diversion – ways of diverting attention away from the argument, the point, the issue. Instead of an *argumentum ad rem* ("argument to the point" or "argument addressed to the real thing"), we have *argumentum ad* seven other things with Latin names: personality, authority, threat, pity, shame, popularity, or ignorance.

Fallacies of *equivocation* look with double vision, so to speak, at a set of words and see two different things, confusing two meanings. Fallacies of *diversion*, in contrast, turn our attention away from the facts, from reality, to something else. They are diversionary tactics, as in battle.

2A, *Ad hominem*

The most common of these fallacies of diversion is the *argumentum ad hominem* (or simply "ad hominem" for short), which means an "argument addressed to the person" (or the personality) instead of to the issue. In other words, a personal attack, attacking the person instead of attacking the issue.

"**Poisoning the Well**" is the direct attack on the trustworthiness of the person making a statement instead of addressing the statement, e.g.: "How can you believe anything he says? He . . ." The fallacy does not consist in criticizing the person's character or reliability; that is certainly a relevant consideration, and it would be a fallacy to *suppress* it, or any other relevant evidence. The fallacy consists in *substituting* the personal attack for facing the person's argument or truth-claim, using it as a "reason" for *not* looking at the facts or reasons.

"Poisoning the Well" usually (but not always) involves another fallacy also, viz. slanting or name-calling *within* the attack on the person's character, the use of "question-begging epithets" or insulting labels instead of facts and reasons for doubting his reliability. If you believe your opponent's character or reliability is questionable, it is legitimate to say so, but *reasons* must be given for that belief too, not just *insults*.

"*Tu quoque*" (literally, "you too") consists of accusing your critic of the same thing your critic accuses you of, rather than defending yourself against the criticism. "I've just proved that you're a liar. Refute my argument." "Well, you're just as much a liar as I am." Perhaps he is, but that does not refute his argument.

The most common form of *ad hominem* today is "**the genetic fallacy**," which consists in "refuting" an idea by showing some suspicious *psychological* *origin* of it. There is nothing wrong with looking at an idea's psychological origin, but this is the task of the psychologist, not the logician. The "genetic fallacy" is a fallacy not because it is psychological but because it is a confusion, and an extremely common one, between logic and psychology. It is a confusion between the two fundamental meanings of the word "because." "Because" can mean (1) a *cause* of an effect, or it can mean (2) a *reason* or premise or evidence for a conclusion. If it means (1) a cause, then in turn that cause can be either (1a) an external, objective, physical cause of a physical effect, like heavy objects falling down because of gravity, or paper towels absorbing water because of their capillary action; or (1b) an internal, subjective, psychological cause of a belief, like believing in Santa Claus because it makes you happy, or fearing large black dogs because one bit you once when you were a child "The genetic fallacy" consists in substituting (1b) for (2), substituting a personal *motive* for a logical *reason* – e.g. "you believe that only because you've never grown up" or "you just can't admit I'm right because you're jealous of my intelligence" or "Your conclusion is false because you don't understand my feelings."

The Freudian emphasis on the subconscious has made this fallacy popular today. E.g. it is often thought that monarchists believed in God because they subconsciously wanted the universe to be hierarchical in order to justify their hierarchical society. But it is just as "reasonable" to argue that egalitarians opt for atheism for the same "reason" in reverse.

Arguments about gender issues frequently use this fallacy: "You say that just because you're a man." "And you deny it just because you're a woman." The two suspicions cancel each other out, and the real argument, the *argumentum ad rem*, can then begin. (But it rarely does.)

No matter how egregious the psychological origins of a belief may be, the logic of the argument for it is independent of the psychology. If Einstein had been a vicious Nazi and had discovered the Theory of Relativity only in order to give Hitler the atom bomb to kill his enemies and conquer the world, that would not prove that E does not equal MC^2.

If the genetic fallacy were not a fallacy, we would have to reject our model for the benzene molecule because it came from its founder's dream of a snake eating its own tail.

Examples of *ad hominem*:

(1) (*Tu Quoque*): Judge: "You have just been convicted of petty larceny." Prisoner: "Your honor, I just looked up your salary; you get $200,000 a year. If I'm a thief, you're a bigger one."

(2) (*Tu Quoque*): "St. Augustine led a wild life himself as a youth, so what right does he have to tell us we should be saints?"

(3) "Your preaching is worthless." "Why?" "Because you don't you practice what you preach."

(4) Modern version of the above: "Papa, don't preach." ("Madonna") (Note that this is also self-contradictory: preaching against preaching.)

(5) "O.J. Simpson was innocent because Mark Fuhrman, the cop who gathered the evidence, was proved to be a racist, which means that we cannot believe his claim that the DNA evidence proves O.J.'s guilt."

(6) "How could you possibly counsel married couples? You've never been married."

(7) "What do you know? You're only a teenager."

(8) "What do you know? You're not a teenager."

2B, *Ad verecundiam*

"*Ad verecundiam*" means "the appeal to reverence," i.e. reverence for authority. The fallacy is the *illegitimate* appeal to authority, or the appeal to illegitimate authority. Appeal to authority is not in itself fallacious. For "authority" does not mean "might" but "right." In fact, most of what we know, we have learned by trusting authorities: first of all our parents, then our teachers and textbooks. No one can learn everything first-hand; most of what we know comes to us second-hand, with many other human links in the chain.

G.K. Chesterton satirizes the uncritical refusal to accept *anything* on authority in the first sentence of his autobiography: "Bowing down in blind credulity, as is my custom, before mere authority, and the tradition of the elders, superstitiously swallowing a story I could not test at the time by experiment or private judgment, I am firmly of the opinion that I was born on the 29th of May, 1874, on Campden Hill, Kensington, and baptized according to the formularies of the Church of England in the little church of St. George opposite the large Waterworks that dominated that ridge."

However, humans are fallible, and therefore, according to the medieval maxim, "the argument from (human) authority is the weakest of all arguments." As we grow, we question our authorities and test them by reason and try to learn more and more on our own (though no one ever gets to the point where he no longer needs to rely on any authorities at all).

The appeal to authority becomes fallacious when the authority is (1) **irrelevant** (e.g. when a movie star is taken as an authority on science, or a priest on how to make a lot of money); or (2) **unreliable** (e.g. the "National Enquirer" or "Pravda"); or (3) **unnecessary**, since there is an argument from reason instead that is easy, clear, and readily available; or (4) when the appeal is **dogmatic**, i.e. closed rather than open, claiming certainty rather than probability; when men are treated as gods; or (5) when the appeal is **uncritical**, when there is no good reason why this authority should be trusted. This latter form includes such forms as the **"snow job,"** the **"appeal to the expert,"** and the **"appeal to Big Names."**

Examples: (Which, if any, of the five errors above does each of the following commit?)

(1) "The doctrine of Aristotle is the supreme truth, because his intellect was the limit of the human intellect. It is therefore rightly said that he was created

and given to us by divine providence so that we might know all that can be known" (Muslim philosopher Averroes, quoted by Etienne Gilson in *History of Christian Philosophy in the Middle Ages*, p. 220). (This was *not* the typical medieval attitude toward Aristotle!)

(2) "There must be something to astrology; my mother swears by it."

(3) "Ho Chi Minh was not a tyrant." "How do you know that?" "Jane Fonda said so."

(4) "According to 75% of all convicted felons, the American justice system is unjust."

(5) "Euclid said that the square on the hypotenuse of a right triangle is equal in area to the sum of the squares on the other two sides, so it must be true."

(6) "It must be true; I got it right from my philosophy professor."

(7) "Don't touch that!" "Why not?" "It's hot. It burns. It hurts." "How do you know? Did you try it? Did you get a boo-boo on it?" "No, but Mommy said so."

(8) "Evolution is probably true because nearly all scientists believe it."

(9) "Mary was assumed into Heaven." "How do you know?" "The Church says so."

(10) "Allah hates the aggressor." "How do you know what Allah thinks?" "It's in the *Qur'an*."

(11) "There probably are billions and billions of extraterrestrial life forms. Carl Sagan says so."

2C, *Ad baculum*

This is the appeal to force ("*baculum*" means "stick"), i.e. to fear (the fear of force) instead of reason.

The "other side of the coin," or correlative, of the appeal to fear is the appeal to desire. This has not yet received a separate technical name; yet the thought that "It's true because I want it to be true" is perhaps the commonest fallacy of all. Freud would certainly say so. (Is that an *argumentum ad verecundiam*?)

Examples:

(1) "Of course there's a real Santa Claus, but he doesn't bring presents to children who don't believe in him."

(2) "Before you answer, remember who pays your salary."

(3) Chairman of the Board: "All those in favor of my proposal, say 'I agree;' all those opposed, say 'I resign.'"

(4) "Thomas, if you could only see your way clear to agree with King Henry's theology, you would be Chancellor of England for life."

(5) "If you just *can't* agree with the reasonableness of company policy on this issue, you *can* start looking for another job."

(6) "It is reasonable to believe in God because if you believe in God, you have your best chance to be rewarded with Heaven. If you do not, you have a good chance to be punished with Hell." (Is "Pascal's Wager" a fallacy?)

(7) "If you adopted the belief that everywhere is Heaven, even here, and everyone is God, even you, you would be blissfully happy and free from fear. For what is there to fear in Heaven, and what does God have to be afraid of?"

(8) (Advisors to their campaigning politician): "The best argument we know for changing your mind on this controversial issue is the polls, which tell us that your constituents will not re-elect you unless you agree with them about it."

2D, *Ad misericordiam*

The fallacy of "*ad misericordiam*," or "appeal to pity" is the perversion of something that is perfectly legitimate in itself, just as is the "appeal to authority." Pity is usually a good thing, often appropriate and sometimes necessary; but it cannot be a substitute for argument.

The commonest form of this fallacy in teachers' experience is students' attempt to "buy" higher grades or more time to complete late assignments, because of the supposed suffering that they experienced either before the test or assignment ("Give me an A even though I scored a 70% on your test because I studied terribly hard all night") or afterwards ("If you flunk me, my parents will be devastated. They sacrificed all their savings on my tuition.").

Examples:

(1) "I do not think that when *you* have to look at the painful, lingering death of someone you love, you will still believe that euthanasia is morally wrong." (But the moral question is not whether such a death is painful and pitiable but whether it is man or God who has authority over man's life. In the words of the title of a pro-euthanasia movie, "Whose Life Is It, Anyway?" Pity no more *refutes* the traditional religious answer to that question than it *proves* it.)

(2) "If you don't commit adultery with me, I will despair and kill myself."

(3) "If you have tears, prepare to shed them now." (Mark Antony, in Shakespeare's "Julius Caesar")

(4) "Officer, I don't deserve a speeding ticket: my dog just died, my mother-in-law moved in, and my tax return is being audited!"

2E, *Ad ignominiam*

This is the "appeal to shame." Shame, like fear and pity, is another emotion that is often appropriate but never a valid substitute for a reason. To believe or disbelieve an idea, or to choose to do or not do a deed, only because you do not want to experience shame, is to substitute emotion for reason, and that is clearly just as unreasonable as substituting reason for emotion.

Shame itself is not a fallacy; but deciding what to do or say by appealing only to shame is a logical fallacy because it is a diversion from objective truth, facts, and evidence. For shame is subjective, or intersubjective; it is dependent on other people's minds: we feel shame only when others see or know us. E.g.

we are not ashamed to be naked in the shower, but in the street. Shame is essentially social and relative to social expectations, which change with time, place, and culture. What is shameful in one society is not shameful in another. Guilt, by contrast, we can feel when we are alone, and it is relative not to other people's feelings but to our own beliefs about moral rightness, or what we think we truly ought to do. So an appeal to guilt can be quite rational. It can also be irrational, of course, if the guilt is pathological, overdone, or inappropriate.

Examples of the "appeal to shame":

(1) "You're going to talk to teenagers about *chastity*? You'll be a laughing stock. They'll call you a Puritan behind your back, and a weirdo. Prepare for a big blush."

(2) "What? You're going to be a *lawyer*? Is it because you want people to tell jokes on you?"

(3) "There is nothing to feel guilt for except guilt feelings."

(4) St. Augustine said he stole some pears with some friends at the age of 16 because "Someone said, 'Let's do it,' and I was ashamed to be ashamed."

(5) "What! You still have heroes? In this day and age? You're the only person I know who will admit that. Don't you feel like a naïve little kid?"

2F, *Ad populum*

This fallacy is especially popular today, in what some sociologists call an "other-directed" age, when the need for acceptance by others is felt so strongly; it is the fallacy of believing or doing something only because it is popular, or getting someone else to believe or do something only because other people do. It is called the "appeal to the populace," or the "appeal to the masses," but sometimes the appeal is only to a select group of people, by implying "I'm one of your kind; trust me." This is sometimes called "**snob appeal**," and usually is negative rather than positive, e.g. "Can anything good come out of Nazareth?" (John 1:46)

As with the other fallacies in this group, the fallacy consists not in the feeling itself (the desire to be accepted), but in appealing to it instead of to reason, as a diversion from facts and evidence.

Examples:

(1) "I am no orator, as Brutus is; but as you know me all, a plain blunt man.
. . . For I have neither wit, nor words, nor worth,/ Action, nor utterance, nor the power of speech,/ To stir men's blood; I only speak right on." (Mark Antony in Shakespeare, "Julius Caesar" III, 2)

(2) ("**The Big Lie**") "The magnitude of a lie always contains a certain factor of credibility, since the great mass of the people . . . , in view of the primitive simplicity of their minds, more easily fall a victim to a big lie than a little one, since they themselves lie in little things, but would be ashamed of lies that were too big. Such a falsehood will never enter their heads." (Adolf Hitler, *Mein Kampf*) "The Big Lie" appeals to this process of unconscious reasoning: "If

most of 'my kind of people' believe an idea that seems absurd, the idea must be true, for people like me would never fall for *that* big a lie."

(3) "Capital punishment can't be wrong; 75% of the people support it."

(4) "If you let this man go, you are no friend of Caesar's." (John 19:12) (This is a good example of a fallacy that can be classified in more than one way; it is also an *argumentum ad baculum.*)

(5) "Forty million Frenchmen can't be wrong."

(6) "In Philadelphia, nearly everybody reads the *Bulletin.*" (Philadelphia *Bulletin* ad)

(7) "Evil spirits? Who believes in *that* today?"

(8) "The notion of timeless truth is based on an outmoded Greek metaphysics that we moderns have rejected."

2G. *Ad Ignorantiam*

The "appeal to ignorance" consists in arguing that an idea must be true because we do not know that it is not. It is a fallacy because ignorance can never be a premise or reason. Premises must express knowledge-claims. Nothing logically follows from nothing, i.e. from no-knowledge.

Examples:

(1) "He can't prove he earned that money, so he must have stolen it."

(2) "Aristotle? Never heard of him. So he can't be important."

(3) "We know of no natural cause that could have produced that effect. So it must have been a miracle."

(4) "How could there be a war going on? I haven't seen any evidence of it."

(5) "God must exist because I've never seen any proof that he doesn't."

Section 3. Fallacies of oversimplification

3A, *Dicto Simpliciter*

We now move to seven fallacies of oversimplification. The most obvious and direct of these is called "*dicto simpliciter*," which means saying something too simply, absolutely, or unqualifiedly; that is, applying a general principle to a special case without the needed qualification. It consists in ignoring the facts about the special case that requires the principle to be qualified.

Examples:

(1) Man is a rational animal. Therefore even an idiot can pass a logic course.

(2) "According to the Greek saying, water is best (*ariston to hudor*). So I'll swap you some water for those diamonds and you'll come out ahead."

(3) "*Dicto simpliciter* is a fallacy. Therefore don't read this logic textbook; it's too simple. It gives you only basics."

(4) "Man has been progressively more lenient, first to citizens, then to slaves, then to animals, and then (presumably) to plants. I think it wrong to sit on a man; soon, I shall think it wrong to sit on a horse; eventually (I suppose) I shall think it wrong to sit on a chair." (G.K. Chesterton, *Orthodoxy*)

3B, Special Case

This is exactly the reverse of *dicto simpliciter*: *Dicto simpliciter* argues that something is true simply, therefore it is true in some special case. "Special case" argues that something is true in some special case, therefore it is true simply. Both fallacies ignore the specialness of the special case.

The saying "the exception proves the rule" is a (rather sloppy and misleading) way of refuting this fallacy. What that saying really means is not, literally, that an exception like "some triangles are not three-sided" proves the rule that "all triangles are three-sided," or that "this man is ten feet tall" proves the truth of the rule that "no man is ten feet tall." That would be absurd and self-contradictory. What it means is that the exception or special case *presupposes* the rule. If there is no rule, there can be no exceptions to it. Most rules are generalizations that are only usually true, and admit exceptions or special cases; e.g. "It's wrong to take another man's property against his will," which is *not* true when the other man is about to commit suicide with his own gun. "Boston gets more snow than Charlotte, North Carolina" is true only 99 years out of 100, but not always.

Examples:

(1) "The Vatican allowed a convent of nuns in Italy who knew they were about to be raped by Nazi soldiers to take birth control pills to protect them from getting pregnant. Therefore the Church doesn't really think contraception is wrong."

(2) "There are a lot of idiots who can't pass a logic course. Therefore man is not rational."

(3) "Why don't you get under the covers and go to sleep? What are you doing?" "I'm making lizard check." "Do you do that often?" "I've done it every night for forty years." "Why?" "When I was a kid in Boy Scout camp, somebody put a lizard in my bed, and it bit me. I want to catch the next lizard before that happens again."

(4) "If women ran the world, we'd have fewer wars." "Oh yeah? Lizzie Borden was a multiple axe murderer. That goes to show you how aggressive women are."

3C, Composition

This fallacy consists in arguing from the part to the whole, ignoring the fact that what is true of the part is not necessarily true of the whole.

It can be done with either groups or single things. "This member of the Professor's logic class is smart, therefore that must be a smart class" does it for a group. "That chapter was fascinating. The whole book must be fascinating too" does it for a thing.

Examples:

(1) Mark Twain said to his minister, "I enjoyed your service this morning. I welcomed it like an old friend. I have, you know, a book at home containing every word of it."

"You have not," the minister protested.

"I have so."

"Well, you send that book to me. I'd like to see it."

"I'll send it," promised Twain. The next day, he sent the minister an unabridged dictionary.

(2) Texas has more millionaires than any other state, therefore Texas is the richest state.

(3) Every one of the actors in this movie is great, so it must be a great movie.

(4) "An arrow that appears to be in flight must really be at rest, for when a thing occupies a space equal to itself, it is at rest. Since the arrow never occupies a space greater or smaller than itself, it is always at rest. Since the arrow is at rest at each moment of flight, it can never move." (Zeno the Eleatic) (Math majors should explain how the infinitesimal calculus answers Zeno's puzzle.)

(5) "There's a bug on this blade of grass." "My goodness, you certainly have a buggy lawn."

3D, Division

This is the reverse of Composition; it consists in arguing from whole to part, ignoring the fact that what is true of the whole is not always true of the part.

It too can be done either with single things ("That book is fascinating, therefore each chapter must be") or with groups ("That class is smart, and he's a member of it, therefore he must be smart").

Examples:

(1) If ten glasses of wine per meal is harmful to health, then one glass of wine per meal must also be harmful to health, for it cannot be that many good things make one bad thing.

(2) Irishmen are scattered all over the world. Pat is an Irishman. Therefore Pat is scattered all over the world.

(3) "A frugal shepherd will buy only black sheep, not white sheep." "I did not know that. Why is that so?" "Because white sheep eat more than black sheep." "I did not know that either. Why is that so?" "Why, it's obvious. White sheep eat more than black sheep because there *are* more white sheep than black sheep."

(4) "Muslims are moving into France. He is a Muslim. Therefore he must be moving into France."

(5) We ought to use missionaries as foreign relations experts, because anyone who has gone to every nation on earth would make a good foreign relations expert, and missionaries have gone to every nation on earth.

(6) The average American male now has a life expectancy of 75 years. We're all average American males, so we will all live for 75 years.

(7) Asians score higher than Americans in math. She is Asian and I am American. Therefore she must score higher than I do in math.

(8) He'll make a great president; he comes from a good family.

(9) All the works of Shakespeare cannot be read in a single day. "Macbeth" is one of the works of Shakespeare. Therefore "Macbeth" cannot be read in a single day.

(10) The people of Ethiopia are suffering from famine, and Clement is one of the people of Ethiopia, therefore Clement must be suffering from famine.

(11) "All these fish weigh four hundred pounds." "You must have caught nothing but sharks."

3E, **The Black and White Fallacy**

This is similar to *dicto simpliciter* but the fallacy here consists in not allowing for *gradations* or means between extremes; *dicto simpliciter* consisted in not allowing for exceptions to a simple rule. There are blacks and whites, but there are also grays. Not everything is an "either-or." The fallacy here consists in arguing "it is not this one extreme, therefore it must be the opposite extreme."

Examples:

(1) "Do you hate me?" "No." "How wonderful! You love me!"

(2) "If the arrow moves, it must move either where it is or where it isn't. But it cannot move where it is; it simply *is* where it is. Nor can it move where it isn't, because it cannot move where it does not exist. Therefore it cannot move." (Zeno the Eleatic)

(3) "Why did you beat me up?" "Hey, shut your mouth. You're lucky we didn't kill ya."

(4) "No man is perfect, therefore all men are wicked."

(5) "Few men are wicked, therefore most men are innocent."

(6) God was seeking a man to be His mouthpiece, or prophet, to mankind. He first interviewed a philosopher, and asked, "I need a man who knows himself, to be my prophet. So tell me, what are you? What is man?" The philosopher replied, "Man is sweetness and light. Man is truth, goodness, and beauty. Man is a fragment of the divine mirror." God interrupted, "Don't call me, I'll call you," and went off to interview a barbarian warrior. He asked the same question, and the barbarian said, "Man is an animal. Man is a wolf, a shark, a bear. Man is a

set of teeth ready to chew and destroy." "Thanks," interrupted God, "Don't call me, I'll call you." Then he interviewed Abraham, and asked the same question, and Abraham replied, "Oh, God, don't ask me. I don't know what man is. I look into myself and sometimes I see light and sometimes darkness, sometimes an angel and sometimes an animal. In fact I seem to be a whole zoo of animals, some tame and some wild." "You shall be my prophet," said God. (God does not commit the black or white fallacy.)

3F, Quoting Out of Context

The meaning of this fallacy is quite clear from its name. It comes in two main forms: the context that is ignored can be either literary or real. In the literary form, it is simply the text before and after the quoted part that is the context ignored. In the other form, it is the real, lived situation surrounding the spoken words. What is ignored are relevant facts such as who the speaker was addressing, the relationship between the two, what issue they were discussing, and what else was said.

"Fundamentalists" are famous for quoting scripture out of context. The term "Fundamentalism" in its proper sense is theological, not logical; it arose in early 20th century Protestant theology as a reaction to "Liberalism" or "Modernism," which denied the supernatural and the miraculous; and "Fundamentalism" as first coined and defined by the scholarly Princeton theologian Benjamin Warfield meant simply belief in five fundamental miracles of traditional Christianity such as Christ's bodily Resurrection. But the popular meaning of the term nowadays has broadened to mean any simple-minded literalism, especially in interpreting the Bible, including insensitivity to symbolic language and quoting "proof texts" out of the textual context that would have significantly changed their meaning. If this were done consistently, it would produce absurdities such as the idea that the Bible teaches, in Ecclesiastes, that "all is vanity" (Eccl. 1:3; 12:7) and even that we should hang ourselves, for it says both that "Judas went and hanged himself" (Matthew 27:5) and "Go and do thou likewise." (Luke 10:37).

Theological arguments about "justification" which oppose Paul's teaching that "we are justified by faith" (Romans 3:28) to James's statement that "by works a man is justified and not by faith alone" (James 2:24) ignore the context of the two different problems the two writers were addressing: Paul was attacking legalism and James was attacking antinomianism.

Mystics, like lovers and poets, often "stretch" language in trying to describe the nearly-indescribable; and their language should not be interpreted without sensitivity to this context. For instance, when a mystic says, "I looked into myself and saw nothing but God," he is not claiming that he is literally God, any more than when a lover poetically addresses his beloved as "my whole life," he means it literally and biologically.

Some of the most egregious examples of quoting out of context consist simply in dropping the quotation marks or a phrase like "he said," thus making it seem as if the writer approves a quotation he really disapproves. For instance, Thomas Aquinas begins each "article" of the *Summa Theologica* by summarizing objections to the thesis he will defend; and students (and sometimes even scholars) sometimes quote these objections as if they were Aquinas's own position.

Some other examples of the fallacy of quoting out of context:

(1) "Kennedy said, 'Ask not what your country can do for you; ask what you can do for your country.' Therefore he must have been against federal public health care."

(2) "I am the Great Truth-Teller. No one can make me tell a lie." "I can. Watch me. Tell me, is it bad to lie?" "Yes." "So I should avoid it?" "Yes." "In order to avoid it, I must know what it is, right?" "Of course." "But I am confused about what it is to tell a lie. Please teach me." "How?" "I learn best by examples. So give me an example." "All right. I am a Martian." "Aha! The Great Truth-Teller has told a lie."

(3) "Milton wrote, 'Better to reign in Hell than serve in Heaven.' So he must have agreed with the Devil."

(4) "The manager is a thief. He told his baserunner to steal whenever he could."

(5) "Shakespeare was a nihilist. He wrote, 'Life's but a walking shadow, a poor player that struts and frets his hour upon the stage and then is heard no more. It is a tale told by an idiot, full of sound and fury, signifying nothing.'"

3G, **Stereotyping**

Like the fallacy *dicto simpliciter*, stereotyping makes no room for the exception.

Stereotypes are not the same as archetypes. Stereotypes are artificial, socially-fabricated, and changeable. Archetypes are givens in the "collective unconscious." "Women are weak and inferior" is a stereotype; "the sea is a woman" is an archetype. "The Jewish mother" is a stereotype; "Mother Earth" is an archetype. G.I. Joe is a stereotype; Ares, or Mars, the god of war, is an archetype.

Not all generalizations are stereotypes. In fact, one of the most misused stereotypes in modern discourse is that of the stereotype, for it is fashionable to call every generalization a stereotype.

Here are some real examples of stereotypes:

"You're tall; you must play basketball."

"You're Black; you must dance well."

"You're a man; you must throw your socks on the floor."

"You're a woman; you must get bad PMS."

"You're an American; you must be rich."

"You're fat; you must be happy."
"You're a cannibal; you must be primitive." (The movie "The Silence of the Lambs" shredded that stereotype.)

Section 4. Fallacies of argumentation

We now turn to seven fallacies in the course of arguing that could be called fallacies of logical strategy. They are analogous to bad military strategies. They too are material fallacies rather than formal fallacies, but they are close to formal fallacies, and it may be difficult to distinguish them from formal fallacies at this point in the course since we have not yet studied formal fallacies. We could distinguish the two kinds of fallacies this way: a computer could infallibly detect formal fallacies but not material fallacies. Formal fallacies are fallacies in logical form, e.g. in the relationship or the placement of the terms, rather than the meaning or use of the terms and propositions.

4A, *Non sequitur*

This is the master fallacy of this group of seven and by far the commonest one. In fact, it is so common that I once had a rubber stamp made up to save time in commenting on student papers and tests; the stamp said, "This is a *non sequitur*. (Look it up.)" (I also had two other rubber stamps that I got a lot of use out of. One said, "Please answer the question asked rather than another of your own devising," and one said simply "grammatically unintelligible." I found these were three of the commonest problems in essay tests and papers.)

"*Non sequitur*" means "it does not follow." The conclusion simply does not logically follow from the premises or reasons or evidence given. Of course, *every* invalid argument is a *non sequitur*, since that is what "an invalid argument" means: an argument in which the conclusion does not logically, necessarily, follow from the premises; an argument in which it is possible that the premises be true yet the conclusion false. But this specific fallacy of *non sequitur* is a material fallacy, not a formal one. It depends on the content of the propositions, not the logical form. E.g.

The sky is blue.
The sea is blue.
Therefore the sky is the sea.

is a formal fallacy. But

Grass is green.
I feel depressed today.
Therefore the grass is to blame for my depression.

is a *non sequitur*.

All courthouses are buildings.
Therefore all buildings are courthouses.

is a formal fallacy. But

I hate courthouses.
Therefore you will lose your case in court today.

is a *non sequitur*.

C.S. Lewis illustrates *non sequitur*, in satirizing the supposedly scientific atheism of the "Enlightenment" (the "Landlord" in the following conversation symbolizes God):

"But how do you *know* there is no Landlord?"

"Christopher Columbus, Galileo, the earth is round, invention of printing, gunpowder!" exclaimed Mr. Enlightenment in such a loud voice that the pony shied.

"I beg your pardon," said John.

"Eh?" said Mr. Enlightenment.

"I don't quite understand," said John.

"Why, it's as plain as a pikestaff," said the other. "Your people in Puritania believe in the Landlord because they have not had the benefits of a scientific training. For example, now, I dare say it would be news to you to hear that the earth was round – round as an orange, my lad!"

Well, I don't know that it would," said John, feeling a little disappointed. "My father always said it was round."

"No, no, my dear boy," said Mr. Enlightenment, 'You must have misunderstood him. It is well known that everyone in Puritania thinks the earth flat. It is not likely that I should be mistaken on such a point. Indeed, it is out of the question. Then again, there is the paleontological evidence."

"What's that?"

"Why, they tell you in Puritania that the Landlord made all these roads. But that is quite impossible, for old people can remember the time when the roads were not nearly so good as they are now, and what is more, scientists have found all over the country traces of *old* roads running in quite different directions. The inference is obvious."

John said nothing.

"I said," repeated Mr. Enlightenment, "that the inference was obvious."

"Oh, yes, yes, of course," said John hastily, turning a little red. (*Pilgrim's Regress*)

4B, *Ignoratio elenchi*

This fallacy is usually called the fallacy of **"irrelevant conclusion"** or the fallacy of "false refutation." It means literally "ignorance of the chain" – that is, the chain of reasoning. It consists in giving reasons that prove a different conclusion than the one the argument purports to prove. The premises, like a misdirected arrow, hit another target than the one aimed at. You could thus also call this the fallacy of **"missing the point."** It could be called a form of *non sequitur*.

For example, it may be argued that socialized medicine is necessary because many poor people die due to lack of adequate basic medical care. The premise is true, and certainly proves *something* in the area of social needs, but it does not prove that socialized medicine is necessary or even useful to attain this end. Neville Chamberlain argued for England's appeasement of Hitler on the grounds that peace was preferable to war. The premise is true, but did not support his conclusion; in fact, his appeasement encouraged Hitler to go to war.

4C, Begging the Question

"Begging the question" means *assuming what you set out to prove*, smuggling the conclusion back into the premises, usually under different words. This is a very common fallacy, and even great philosophers occasionally commit it. For instance, Descartes's famous *"cogito ergo sum"* ("I think, therefore I am") is really an example of begging the question. For what he wants to *prove* is that he exists, that there is an "I"; but he *assumes* that there exists this "I" behind the thinking and puts it into his premise. This is not clear in Latin, where the "I" is not separate from the verb; but it is clear in English, or in French (*"je pense, donc je suis"*), and Descartes quickly amended his argument, changing it from a syllogism to a single supposedly self-evident proposition ("I think," *or* "I am").

  . Some other examples:

(1) Moliere's doctor, asked "Why does opium make one sleepy," answered, "Because it possesses dormative [sleep-inducing] virtue [power]."

(2) "The accused will be given a fair trial before he is hanged."

(3) "Since everything that God wills is just for the very reason that He wills it, the terrible fate of the non-elect does not violate the principle of justice." (John Calvin)

(4) Mr. & Mrs. Strange were very proud of their son, for he was extremely intelligent, but he had one very strange belief: he believed he was dead. No kind of argument would convince him that he was not. Finally, after unsuccessfully visiting many psychiatrists, they found one who guaranteed to cure him, but it would cost $200,000 and four years. Having tried everything else in vain, they agreed. The psychiatrist demanded that the boy go through four years of medical school. After he graduated, he came to the psychiatrist's office for one last session. The psychiatrist asked, "Now that you have graduated from medical

school with straight A's, and learned everything that anyone else learned there, tell me this: Do dead men bleed?" "No," he answered. "Are you sure?" "Yes." "Good. Now watch –" and he took a pin and pricked the boy's hand. "What do you see?" "I'm bleeding," said the boy. "Yes. So what is your logical conclusion?" "Doctor, you are a genius! You have taught me that I was wrong all my life! Dead men do bleed after all."

(5) "Good sense is, of all things among men, the most equally distributed; for everyone thinks himself so abundantly provided with it that even those who are the most difficult to satisfy in everything else do not usually desire a larger measure of this quality than they already possess. Since it is unlikely that all men should err in such a matter, we may take it as assured . . ." (René Descartes, *Discourse on Method*)

(6) "You can't help believing in free will, you're predestined to think that way."

4D, Complex Question

This fallacy consists of asking a question which cannot be answered without "begging" another question. You're "damned if you do and damned if you don't." The classic example is: "Have you stopped beating your wife?" Whether you answer Yes or No, you implicitly admit that you have beaten your wife.

A question often has a hidden assumption. E.g. "Who made God?" assumes that God has been made (an assumption only a pagan believes); and the question "what happened before time began?" assumes that there was time before time (which is logically self-contradictory).

Usually, a complex question has a personal agenda, e.g.:

(1) "Do you think we should keep having these useless meetings or not?"

(2) "How could it be a good idea to reject my good idea? That's self-contradictory."

(3) "Are you more hopelessly stupid today than yesterday, or not?"

4E, Arguing in a Circle

This fallacy consists in using a conclusion to justify a premise after having used that premise to justify that conclusion. Thus it is really another version of begging the question, assuming what you are supposed to prove (namely, the conclusion) – but this time not just assuming it but also using it as a premise to prove your other proposition.

Examples:

(1) "All the precepts of the Qur'an are true."
    "Why?"
    "Because they are the word of Allah."

"How do you know they are the word of Allah?"

"Because the Prophet Muhammad says so."

"How do you know Muhammad tells the truth?"

"Because he is Allah's prophet, and Allah's prophet cannot lie."

"How do you know Muhammad is Allah's prophet?"

"The Qur'an says so."

(2) "Why are you studying so hard?"

"To pass this test."

"Why do you want to pass this test?"

"To pass the course."

"Why do you want to pass the course?"

"To graduate with a high grade point average."

"Why do you want to graduate with a high grade point average?"

"To get a good job."

"Why do you want a good job?"

"To make money."

"Why do you want to make money?"

"To raise a family and have kids."

"Why do you want to raise a family and have kids?"

"So that they can go to college and be successful."

"What will make them successful in college?"

"Studying hard for their tests."

(3) "There is a story of a sane person being by mistake shut up in the wards of a lunatic asylum, and when he pleaded his cause to some strangers visiting the establishment, the only remark he elicited in answer was, 'How naturally he talks! You would think he was in his senses.'" (John Henry Newman, *Apologia pro vita sua*, ch. 1)

(4) "The world must be well-ordered."

"Why?"

"Because it is the work of divine wisdom."

"How do you know it is the work of divine wisdom?"

"How can you doubt divine wisdom? Look how well His world is ordered."

(5) Descartes proved the existence of God from the clear and distinct idea of God that he found in his mind; for that idea was the idea of a being containing all conceivable perfections; and real, objective existence is one conceivable perfection. He then argued that he could trust all his clear and distinct ideas because God is no deceiver, and the Creator of the mind would not allow us to be deceived if we used our mind properly.

(6) "Somehow or other an extraordinary idea has arisen that the disbelievers in miracles consider them coldly and fairly, while believers in miracles accept them only in connection with some dogma. The fact is quite the other

way. The believers in miracles accept them (rightly or wrongly) because they have evidence for them. The disbelievers in miracles deny them (rightly or wrongly) because they have a doctrine against them. The open, obvious, democratic thing is to believe an old apple-woman when she bears testimony to a miracle, just as you believe an old apple-woman when she bears testimony to a murder. The plain, popular course is to trust the peasant's word about the ghost exactly as far as you trust the peasant's word about the landlord. . . . If I say, 'a peasant saw a ghost,' I am told, 'But peasants are so credulous.' If I ask, 'Why credulous?' the only answer is – that they see ghosts." (G.K. Chesterton)

4F, Contradictory Premises

The meaning of this fallacy is so obvious that nothing needs to be added to its name. It is, of course, usually camouflaged rather than clearly evident, as in the following examples, most of which are variations on the basic self-contradiction of using reason to attack reason. It is a surprisingly common fallacy among philosophers.

(1) "Our reason is capable of nothing but the creation of a universal confusion and universal doubt: it has no sooner built up a system than it shows you the means of knocking it down. It is a veritable Penelope, who unpicks during the night the tapestry that she has woven during the day. Accordingly, the best use that one can make of philosophical studies is to recognize that it is a way that leads astray." (Pierre Bayle)

(2) "My propositions are elucidatory in this way: he who understands me finally recognizes them as senseless, when he has climbed out through them. (He must so to speak throw away the ladder after he has climbed up on it.) He must surmount these propositions; then he sees the world rightly. Whereof one cannot speak, thereof one must be silent." (Ludwig Wittgenstein, *Tractatus*)

(3) "The only thing we have to fear is fear itself." (Franklin Roosevelt, First Inaugural Address)

(4) "The only thing to feel guilty about is feeling guilty."

(5) "I will not tolerate intolerance!"

(6) "You can't be dogmatic!"

(7) "There are absolutely no absolutes."

(8) "It is a universal truth that there are no universal truths."

(9) "We can know nothing."

(10) "All truths are culturally relative, despite the fact that no other culture outside our own believes that."

(11) "Words like 'should' and 'ought' are not permitted in these conversations."

(12) "Truth is subjective."

(13) "Truth changes."

(14) "There are only two kinds of people in the world: those who say there are only two kinds of people in the world and those who don't. And I'm in the second class." (Robert Benchley)

(15) "The trouble with people like you is that you're always stereotyping people like us."

(16) "One thing only do I know for certain and that is that man's judgments of value follow directly his wishes for happiness – that, accordingly, they are an attempt to support his illusions with arguments." (Sigmund Freud, *Civilization and Its Discontents*)

(17) "Why have you come to me, O seeker?"

"To hear your wisdom, O Enlightened One."

"What wisdom?"

"The wisdom of life. Tell me, what is life? What is the meaning of life?"

"Life is suffering. To live is to suffer."

"This is true wisdom, O Enlightened One. But can you also teach me how to escape suffering?"

"I can. If you desire to escape suffering, you must know its cause and cure."

"I await your wisdom, O Enlightened One. What is the cause of suffering?"

"The cause of suffering is desire."

"And what is its cure?"

"Its cure is the extinguishing of desire. For to take away the cause is to take away the effect."

"This is truly wisdom, O Enlightened One. And how can I attain this extinguishing?"

"Only by the Noble Eightfold Path."

"And is this path an easy one?"

"No, it is a very demanding one."

"And what will bring me success on this path, O Enlightened One?"

"What do you think?"

"I know not. Is it family connections, or fame, or money, or intelligence?"

"None of these will bring you success, O seeker."

"What will bring me success, then?"

"Only perseverance will bring you success on this path."

"But what is perseverance? Is it not great desire?"

(18) "Even if a fetus is a person, I still believe in abortion because I believe in every person's right to control her own body." (Do you see the self-contradiction there? If not, why not?)

(19) "It is useless to argue at all if all our conclusions are warped by our conditions. Nobody can correct anybody's bias if all mind is all bias. . . . The

man who represents all thought as an accident of environment is simply smashing and discrediting all his own thoughts – including that one. . . . When people begin to say that the material circumstances have alone created the moral circumstances, then they have prevented all possibility of serious change; for if my circumstances have made me wholly stupid, how can I be certain even that I am right in altering those circumstances?" (G.K. Chesterton)

(20) "A Socialist Government is one which in its nature does not tolerate any real opposition. For there the Government provides everything; and it is absurd to ask a Government to *provide* an opposition." (G.K. Chesterton)

(21) "The worship of will is the negation of will. To admire mere choice is to refuse to choose. If Mr. Bernard Shaw comes up to me and says, 'Will something,' that is tantamount to saying, 'I do not mind what you will,' and that is tantamount to saying, 'I have no will in the matter'. . . . He rebels against the law and tells us to will something or anything. But we have willed something. We have willed the law against which he rebels." (G.K. Chesterton)

(22) "They have invented a phrase, a phrase that is a black and white contradiction in two words – 'free love' – as if a lover ever had been, or ever could be, free. It is the nature of love to bind itself, and the institution of marriage merely paid the average man the compliment of taking him at his word." (G.K Chesterton)

4G, **False Assumption**

This fallacy is similar to "begging the question," but the false assumption is more covert. It is the basis for many jokes. E.g.:

(1) Two old men, Seth and Jed, lived next to each other in the Maine woods for fifty years without ever speaking to each other. Seth had often thought of breaking the ice, but he had always been afraid to go on Jed's property because of an enormous, fierce-looking dog that was always on Jed's porch. One day he called out, "Jed, kin I come into yer yard?" "Yep." "But Jed, if I come into yer yard, won't yer dog bite me?" "Nope." So Seth ventured into Jed's yard – and was promptly torn in pieces by the dog. "You said yer dog wouldn't bite me!" "That ain't my dog."

(2) A monk found another smoking while saying the Rosary. "Did the abbot give you permission to do that?" he asked. "Yes," replied the second monk. The first monk was upset. "Then why did the abbot say no to *me* when I asked him the same question?" "What did you ask him?" said the first monk. "I asked him if it was all right to smoke while I prayed." "Oh," said the second monk, "That explains it. I asked him if it was all right to pray while I smoked." (What is the hidden assumption of each question?)

(3) "Life is not a problem, so why are you asking for a solution?" (Alan Watts)

(4) "I can turn my bedroom light off and leap into bed before the room is

dark; yet my light switch is 20 feet away from my bed." "How do you do that?" "I wait till it's daytime."

(5) "When you sold me this parrot you told me it could repeat every word it heard." "That's right." "Well, I've been talking to it all day and it hasn't said a word yet. That's false advertising." "No it isn't. The parrot's deaf."

(6) The starship Enterprise has a crew of 300 humans, one non-human Klingon, and one half-human, half-Vulcan, Mr. Spock. If we call the Klingon human, how many humans do we have on the Enterprise? Answer: 300. Calling a Klingon human doesn't make it human.

Section 5. Inductive fallacies

(If you are not clear about the differences between deductive and inductive reasoning, first review this point on page 26.)

5A, Hasty Generalization

This is the commonest and simplest fallacy of induction, and it occurs in the commonest and simplest form of induction, the inference from some specific examples to a general principle. Mere examples never conclusively prove a general principle, of course; they only render it more probable as the examples are more numerous, more diverse, and more representative. So whether or not an inductive generalization is "hasty," and thus fallacious, is a matter of degree and a common-sense "judgment call."

Some examples of hasty generalization:

(1) "We went to three ball games this year and the home team lost each one. They're losers."

(2) "We went to three ball games this year and the home team lost each one. We're their jinx." (Here we have not a hasty generalization but a hasty causal induction.)

(3) "All the swans we've ever seen were white, so all swans must be white." ("All swans are white" was a classic logic textbook example of a universal proposition – until a species of black swan was discovered.)

(4) "Modern philosophers are all atheists. Look at Machiavelli and Hobbes and Hume and Mill and Russell and Marx and Nietzsche and Sartre."

5B, *Post Hoc*

The full name for this fallacy is "*post hoc ergo propter hoc*," which means "after this, therefore caused by this." It is a fallacy of causal induction (that form of induction which consists in reasoning to a cause), and it consists in inferring that one thing is the *cause* of another simply because the first thing is observed to occur *before* the second thing. The fact that A is observed to occur before B may be a clue, and it is reasonable to follow this clue further to determine whether A is the cause of B; but the mere temporal proximity is not a sufficient reason by itself for concluding that A is the cause of B. It may be, or it may not. It may be a mere coincidence, or it may be that A and B are both caused by a third thing, C, or it may be that B causes A.

Examples of post hoc:

(1) The rooster thinks his crowing brings up the sun each morning because each morning the sun rises shortly after he crows.

(2) "I ain't niver had a axydent cuz I allus cairy mah lucky rabbit's foot."

(3) "My doctor asked me whether I drank two hot scotches every night, and I answered him that I did, but only as a preventative of toothaches. I have never had a toothache." (Mark Twain)

(4) "Why are you putting all those little pieces of lemon around your yard?" "To keep the alligators away." "But there are no alligators within a thousand miles of here." "See? It works."

(5) "And the sailors said to one another, 'Come, let us cast lots, that we may know on whose account this evil (storm) has come upon us.' So they cast lots, and the lot fell upon Jonah." (Jonah 1:7)

5C, **Hypothesis Contrary to Fact**

This could be called the "if only" fallacy, for it consists in arguing that if only x were true, which it isn't, then y would be true. E.g. "if only you had studied harder, you would have passed this test." Perhaps so, but perhaps not. We cannot know what isn't, only what is.

It is a fallacy of *causal* induction because it claims to know that non-x is the *cause* of y. Since x does not exist, x is called "contrary to fact"; and since x is used as a hypothesis ("*if* x . . ."), it is a "hypothesis contrary to fact."

Here is a rather extreme but memorable example of hypothesis contrary to fact: If the Italians had believed in clocks, their trains would have run on time. If their trains had run on time, they would not have thought Mussolini was a god for his miracle of making the trains run on time. If they had not thought Mussolini was a god, they would never have let him become dictator. If he had not been dictator, Hitler would not have had him as his ally. If Hitler had not had him as his ally, he would not have had to bail him out when he invaded Greece and Yugoslavia. If he had not had to do that, Hitler could have invaded Russia earlier. If he had invaded Russia earlier, he would have conquered Russia. If he had conquered Russia, he could have fought a one-front war instead of a two-front war. If he had fought a one-front war, he could have invaded England. If he had invaded England, he would have conquered it. If he had conquered England, he would have ruled all Europe. If he had ruled all Europe, he would have ruled the world. If he had ruled the world, we would all have been brought up under Nazi propaganda and would have been Nazis. So the only reason we are not Nazis is because the Italians did not believe in clocks.

5D, **False Analogy**

Another form of induction is the argument from analogy. Analogies are extremely useful, even essential to human thinking. Analogies are comparisons between two things that are related or similar in some way; they are similes. Maps, for instance, are analogies to landscapes, and physical events (like a person entering a room) are analogies to nonphysical events (like an idea "entering" a mind).

Arguments from analogy are classified as inductive arguments because they begin with concrete, observed particulars rather than general principles. Analogies are rightly used to *suggest* or stimulate the mind to move from one of two similar things to the other, just as similes do, and also metaphors, which are implicit similes, without the word "like." Analogies also are rightly used to *illustrate* general principles (e.g. conceiving ideas is like conceiving babies). But analogies do not *prove* anything; and the fallacy of "false analogy" assumes that they do. The fallacy consists not in using an analogy, but either in (1) using a false analogy, one that is not a real resemblance, or in (2) using an analogy falsely, by assuming that when two things are similar in one way they will also be similar in another way.

Examples of false analogy:

(1) "The Stoical scheme of supplying our wants by lopping off our desires is like cutting off our feet when we want shoes." (Jonathan Swift)

(2) "The only proof capable of being given that an object is visible is that somebody sees it . . . similarly, the only proof capable of being given that an object is desirable is that someone desires it." (John Stuart Mill, *Utilitarianism*) (The suffix 'able' in 'desirable' means '*deserving* of being desired,' while the same suffix in 'visible' means '*capable* of being seen'. This fallacy could also be labeled as an amphiboly.)

(3) "The only freedom which deserves the name is that of pursuing our own good in our own way, so long as we do not attempt to deprive others of theirs, or impede their efforts to obtain it. Each is the proper guardian of his own health, whether bodily or mental and spiritual." (John Stuart Mill, *On Liberty*)

(4) "No body can be healthful without exercise, neither natural body nor politic; and, certainly, to a Kingdom or estate, a just and honourable war is the true exercise. A civil war, indeed, is like the heat of a fever; but a foreign war is like the heat of exercise, and serveth to keep the body in health; for in a slothful peace, both courage will effeminate and manners corrupt." (Francis Bacon)

(5) "You can't turn back the clock."

(6) Jesus once deliberately committed a fallacy of false analogy to test a

woman's faith, and he was pleased when she detected and refuted his fallacy by extending his analogy:

> "And Jesus went away from there and withdrew to the district of Tyre and Sidon. And behold, a Canaanite woman from that region came out and cried, 'Have mercy on me, O Lord, Son of David; my daughter is severely possessed by a demon.' But he did not answer her a word. And his disciples came and begged him, saying, 'Send her away, for she is crying after us.' He answered, 'I was sent only to the lost sheep of the house of Israel.' But she came and knelt before him, saying, 'Lord, help me.' And he answered, 'It is not fair to take the children's bread and throw it to the dogs.' She said, 'Yes, Lord, yet even the dogs eat the crumbs that fall from their master's table.' Then Jesus answered her, 'O woman, great is your faith! Be it done for you as you desire.' And her daughter was healed instantly."
> (Matthew 15:21–28)

5E, The Argument from Silence

When a speaker or writer is silent about x, we cannot conclude that he does not believe in x, or that there is no x. The fallacy called the "argument from silence" does just that. E.g.: "Notice that this author never once refers to her husband. And there is no evidence whatever of any reference to her husband, in any documents of her time or later, by her friends or by her enemies. Therefore she must have been unmarried."

Western legal systems recognize this fallacy in the principle that "silence betokeneth nothing" (used by Thomas More in his trial: see *A Man For All Seasons*) and in the Fifth Amendment (the accused is allowed to refuse to answer a question, and this cannot be used as positive evidence against him).

Historical textual scholars often commit this fallacy, arguing from a text's silence. From the fact that Descartes does not mention anything about the Masons or the Rosicrucians, some conclude that he could not have belonged to these societies, as some claim he did. Others argue that his silence is evidence that he *did* belong to them, since they are *secret* societies and silence is exactly what we would expect to find in their members! (This is arguing in a circle, a form of begging the question.) Both arguments, of course, are fallacious and prove nothing.

5F, Selective Evidence

This extremely common fallacy consists simply in referring only to the evidence that tends to support your hypothesis and ignoring the evidence that tends to refute it. Pessimists will point to many ways in which life is getting worse: increased rates of suicide, divorce, depression, new diseases, teenage crime, domestic violence, etc.; while optimists will point to many ways life is getting better: increased wealth, medical discoveries, treatment of the handicapped, technological efficiency, communications, etc. The fallacy is so common and so simple that it is pointless to multiply examples. It is perhaps the most basic of all mistakes for a scientist: letting his hypothesis control his data rather than vice versa.

5G, Slanting the Question

This is a fallacy that occurs especially in polls. Pollsters can obtain almost any result they want if only they slant the question in a certain way. E.g. one pollster will ask: "Do you support the right of a woman to freely choose whether or not to carry her pregnancy to term?" Another will ask: "Do you support the right to life of all human beings at all stages of development from conception to natural death?"

Individuals, of course, also frequently slant the question in conversation. E.g. "Don't you think people are entitled to basic health care?" vs. "Do you think we should be forced to pay for socialized medicine?" Or: "Does a good society give all children a free basic public education?" vs. "Should our children be propagandized in government schools?"

Section 6. Procedural fallacies

We now turn to fallacies of procedure, or logical protocol. They all violate basic logical justice. The arguments may be formally valid, but they are used, or treated, wrongly. These fallacies are just as common in argument as others, but less often recognized in logic textbooks. They do not have technical titles.

6A, "Refuting" an Argument by Refuting Its Conclusion

We do not refute an argument simply by refuting its conclusion. What refutes an *argument* is an analysis of the argument that finds in it a term used ambiguously or a false premise or a logical fallacy, thus showing how the argument went wrong and why it does not prove its conclusion. What refutes an argument's *conclusion* (which is a single proposition) is another argument proving the contradictory of that conclusion. Arguers often assume that they have completed their job when they only refute a conclusion and do not refute the argument that supposedly proves it. But they have not. For they have only put forth an apparently-equally-good argument to prove the opposite conclusion; they have only engaged in offensive logical warfare and not defensive; they have left the original argument still standing. The result of this is not to prove or convince, but to paralyze the mind of a rational and objective listener, for the listener now finds himself suspended between two arguments, and two conclusions, that seem equally convincing.

The 18th century philosopher Immanuel Kant thought this was all that could ever be done with regard to metaphysical questions. He thought that "pure reason," i.e. the use of reason beyond sense experience, always resulted in logical standoffs or "antinomies" where equally good and equally irrefutable arguments for two contradictory propositions could be found. He called these "antinomies of pure reason." For instance, that space and time are infinite *and* that they are finite; or that the human will is free rather than necessitated or determined, *and* that it is necessitated or determined rather than free. Kant thought this situation showed that we should be skeptical of the possibility of metaphysics.

But this conclusion need not follow. First, even if metaphysical arguments did lead to antinomies, that would not prove the questions are somehow wrong: that is a *non sequitur*. Second, the antinomies might be psychological rather than logical, subjective rather than objective. Third, the antinomies can be answered; mistakes can be found in at least one of the arguments on each side in any "antinomy," usually an ambiguous term. Fourth, they *must* be answerable, in principle. For two contradictory conclusions cannot both be true, therefore they cannot both be proved by perfectly good arguments.

But when you leave an argument "hanging" instead of showing its weakness, and then go off and create another one, you neglect half your work. That is like sending good batters to the plate but no fielders to the field, hoping that you score more runs than your opponent even without any defense. That might possibly win a baseball game but not a logical debate, for you do not win a logical debate by simply scoring the most runs, so to speak, i.e., inventing the largest number of arguments.

6B, Assuming that Refuting an Argument Refutes Its Conclusion

This is the opposite error from the previous one. Fallacy 6A was "all offense and no defense"; fallacy 6B is "all defense and no offence." Fallacy 6A was offering a counter-argument without showing an error (ambiguous term, false premise, or logical fallacy) in your opponent's argument; fallacy 6 is showing the error in your opponent's argument and thinking that settles the matter, thinking that refutes your opponent's conclusion. It does not. Just because someone offers a weak argument for a conclusion, that does not show that the conclusion is false. There are weak as well as strong arguments for atheism, e.g., and also for theism. The weakness of a weak argument for atheism ("if God existed, my puppy wouldn't have died") does not prove theism, and the weakness of a weak argument for theism ("God must exist because the universe is very big and powerful") does not prove atheism. There will always be some bad arguments for true conclusions.

6C, **Ignoring the Argument** (Arguing "Beside the Point")

More radical, even, than giving only half a refutation (6A and 6B) is giving none at all, ignoring your opponent's argument altogether and, after politely waiting until he is finished, starting up as if he had not said anything at all. People often do this because they are poor listeners; they just wait their turn to speak, and then speak without *responding* to what was already said.

E.g. a Protestant propagandist might "refute" the Catholic argument for papal infallibility by pointing to the corrupt Borgia popes. This not only confuses moral infallibility (which is not claimed) with doctrinal infallibility (which is) but ignores the Catholic argument whose premises are tradition and the authority of the Church, and turns to another issue instead. Or a Catholic propagandist might "refute" the Protestant argument for Justification by Faith Alone by pointing out that belief in that doctrine would encourage him, personally, to commit crimes since good or evil works do not contribute to one's justification, ignoring the Protestant argument from Biblical exegesis of Romans and Galatians.

Here is a famous philosophical example of ignoring the argument: Samuel Johnson's "refutation" of Berkeley's argument against the existence of matter: "We stood talking for some time together of Bishop Berkeley's ingenious sophistry to prove the nonexistence of matter and that everything in the universe is merely idea. I observed that though we are satisfied his doctrine is not true, it is impossible to refute it. I shall never forget the alacrity with which Johnson answered, striking his foot with mighty force against a large stone, till he rebounded from it, 'I refute him thus.'" (*Boswell's Life of Johnson*)

Ignoring the argument is obviously a weakness, but an unscrupulous sophist can sometimes turn this weakness into an apparent strength if he has enough chutzpah to do it with an arrogant, sneering rhetorical flourish. For instance, Karl Marx, in *The Communist Manifesto*, replies to the ten commonest charges against communism (such as "it abolishes families," "it abolishes nationality," "it abolishes effort") not by answering them but by simply claiming that *capitalism* is guilty of all these charges (which is the *tu quoque* fallacy), and then concludes, "As for the charges brought against communism from a religious, philosophical, and in general, an ideological viewpoint, does it take much intelligence to realize that they are not worthy of consideration?"

It is an old preacher's trick: "when your point is weak, holler like hell."

6D, **Substituting Explanations for Proofs**

When we give a proof, we claim to have slammed the door shut, so to speak; we claim to prove that our conclusion *must* be true and its contradictory *cannot* be true. When we give an *explanation*, we claim only to have opened the door, so to speak: to open the mind to the likelihood that x is the explanation for y. Since explanations claim less than proofs, they are less controversial, less threatening, less confrontational; so it is tempting to use them instead of proofs. This is not a fallacy, if we know what we are doing; but it is a fallacy when we confuse the two and think that our explanation amounts to a proof.

E.g. Darwinian Natural Selection explains the fossil record, and does so more scientifically than any other hypothesis. However, Natural Selection is an explanation, not a proof. First of all, it is not put forward as a proof of the fossil record (for no one questions that record; it is not controversial; it is not a conclusion of an argument, but it is *data*). It is put forward as a hypothesis that explains the fossil record. Second, the Darwinian argument for Natural Selection, including the evidence of the fossil record, amounts to a probable argument, but not a "door-shutting" proof – at least so far. Copernicus's heliocentric hypothesis too was only an explanation, not a proof, until subsequent observations refuted the alternative Ptolemaic geocentric hypothesis.

Similarly, the Freudian *explanation* of religion as fear-induced father-figure-fantasy does not *prove* religion is an illusion, any more than the religious *explanation* of Freud's atheism as his own Oedipus complex *proves* that Freud was wrong about God.

6E, Answering Another Argument than the One Given

Students on tests often change the question given to them from one that they cannot answer to one that they can, and then answer it. Similarly, in the middle of an argument we often hear someone come up with a brilliant refutation – of an argument that was not given. He has slain the enemy, but the wrong enemy. Perhaps he hopes that the brilliance of his refutation will distract attention away from his sidestepping the original argument.

An example: "Slavery is morally wrong. It violates a basic human right." "Oh, I know that argument. You think it's always wrong to have a slave, because it's always harmful, and makes for suffering and misery. But it doesn't. Sometimes some people are happier as slaves. Sometimes the relationship to a master is a good one. And sometimes slavery is the only alternative to death – for captured soldiers in war, for instance, in many parts of the ancient world. Your argument ignores special cases like that." (But the original argument was not that slavery was wrong because it always made slaves unhappy, but because it violated a universal human right.)

Another example: "Plato argued against democracy in this way: he said a just state is like a just soul, and a just soul is not a democracy but an aristocracy, with reason ruling desires and necessary desires counting for more than unnecessary ones." "What a silly argument! 'Old Plato said it, so it must be true,' right? Hey, haven't you ever heard of the fallacy of the appeal to authority?"

6F, Shifting the Burden of Proof

The "burden of proof" or "onus of proof" is a matter of protocol, or interpersonal rules in debate. The one who has this "burden of proof" has to prove his case; if he does not, he loses the debate.

Who has the burden of proof? This varies with the situation. Sometimes it is the one who denies, sometimes the one who affirms. Sometimes it is the first to speak, sometimes the second.

In science, an idea is "guilty until proved innocent," so to speak: a crucial principle of the scientific method is to accept no idea until you have adequate proof for it. (What counts as "adequate proof" also varies with the situation.) But in ordinary conversation, an idea is "innocent until proved guilty," so to speak: we believe what our friends say until we have good reason to disbelieve it. If a physicist says he has discovered how to make cheap cold fusion, or if a theologian says he has discovered the date of the end of the world, the burden of proof is on him, and our rightful reply is, "Prove it!" But if Aunt Harriet says the dirty little diner downtown serves the best apple pie you've ever tasted in your life, or if your brother says he saw a police car crash into the front door of the city library, you don't say "Prove it." The burden of proof is on you if you doubt it. This is not a matter of logic but of personal protocol.

It becomes a matter of logic when, in debate, the original strategy is implicitly changed. E.g. in court a prosecuting attorney may badger the defense to prove its case as if the accused were guilty until proved innocent rather than innocent until proved guilty; or a moralist crusading for prohibition may demand proof that alcohol contributes to the health of bodies or societies. In a debate about a controversial practice that used to be illegal or unavailable, such as cloning or surrogate motherhood, the one who attacks the new procedure often assumes that the burden of proof is on the "new kid on the block," on the new permissiveness, while the one who defends it often assumes that any practice, like a person, is innocent until proved guilty. Who has the burden of proof here is itself a matter of serious argument, but this should be agreed on *before* argument proceeds, and whoever assumes the burden of proof should not "cop out" on giving such a proof (i.e. proving his case) by simply accusing his opponent of not proving *his* case.

6G, Winning the Argument but Losing the Arguer – or Vice Versa

"Winning the argument but losing the arguer" means ignoring the personal, psychological factor and ending up being distrusted and treated as an enemy or a threat by the person you wanted to persuade. Good logic is an instrument of persuasion; it is only one ingredient in a larger interpersonal situation; and those who love logic and are good at it often forget this context. Intelligent people's minds are not changed by bad logic, but they are not changed by bad personal tactics either.

The more common mistake today is probably the opposite of this fallacy: using tactics of personal appeal such as friendliness to substitute for good reasons, using the subjective element as a substitute for the objective element in dialogue. There is a brilliant example in "A Man for All Seasons," where the Duke of Norfolk is trying to persuade Thomas More to approve King Henry VIII's divorce, as the Duke and all his friends have, even in violation of Thomas's own conscience: "Couldn't you see your way clear to come with me, Thomas – for friendship's sake?" And Thomas replies, "And when you go to Heaven for obeying your conscience, and I go to Hell for disobeying mine, will you come with me – for friendship's sake?"

Both the personal and the impersonal dimensions are necessary as two parts of all interpersonal argument, and neither one can make up for the lack of the other.

Section 7. Metaphysical fallacies

These are not included in most logic textbooks, but since this one is more philosophical than most, and since these fallacies are quite common and quite destructive, and since metaphysics is at the root of all the other divisions of philosophy, it is fitting to briefly expose beginners to a few of the most common of these fallacies so that they will be forewarned and forearmed if and when they meet them in more advanced studies.

7A, **Reductionism, or "Nothing Buttery"**

This is probably the most pervasive metaphysical fallacy of modern thought: love is nothing but lust, mind nothing but brain, philanthropy nothing but enlightened self-interest, man nothing but an ape, an ocean nothing but trillions of tons of hydrogen, oxygen, and sodium chloride, and thinking nothing but cerebral biochemical computing. Whenever we hear the phrase "nothing but," a bell of suspicion should ring.

Its most usual form is the reduction of form to matter. This is common in our materialistic age. The above examples are only six out of thousands. In all these cases, the predicate is only the matter or raw material that the subject is made of, not its form or essence or nature.

Some examples of reductionism:

"Words are nothing but wind, and learning is nothing but words, therefore learning is nothing but wind." (Jonathan Swift, *A Tale of a Tub*)

"What do you read, my lord?" "Words, words, words." ("Hamlet")

"Why are you so surprised?" said the retired star to the children. "Because in our world a star is only a big ball of gas." "Even in your world, that is not what a star is, only what it is made of." (C.S. Lewis, *The Voyage of the Dawn Treader*)

7B, The Fallacy of Accident:
Confusing the Accidental with the Essential

An obvious example of this fallacy is racism, which takes an accident of the person (his race) and treats it as essential, as if different races were different *species*. It is equally possible, and more fashionable today, to commit the fallacy in reverse: to take something essential and treat it as accidental. For instance, the heterosexuality of the family, the competitiveness of a game like soccer, or the objectivity and universality of moral law. Whether or not it is good for two homosexual (*or* heterosexual) adults of the same gender to raise children, a "family" without any father or without any mother does not possess the whole essence of a *family*. Whether or not it is beneficial to children's self-esteem for adults to remove the concept of "winning," "losing," and "points scored" from soccer, if you do that then what you have left is not *soccer*. Whether the idea of real universally binding and unchanging moral obligations is an enlightened or an unenlightened idea, and whether it makes us happy or miserable, a "morality" without real universals, or absolutes, is simply not *morality*; it is utility or psychological integration or something else.

The field of Biblical interpretation shows how both forms of the Fallacy of Accident are equally possible. An example of absolutizing the relative would be insisting that no woman may ever appear in church without a hat because St. Paul told the Corinthian women to wear one. (In ancient Corinth, prostitutes advertised themselves by letting their hair hang loose in public.) An example of relativizing the absolute would be insisting that the divine commandment against adultery could not apply to those who felt "truly in love."

Examples of the Fallacy of Accident: (NB: many of these are also *non sequiturs*.)

1. "A great nose indicates a great man." (Cyrano de Bergerac)

2. "How can Van Gogh be a good painter? Look how immoral a life he led."

3. "There is an incredible amount of empty space in the universe. The distance from the sun to the nearest star is about 4.2 light years, or 25 followed by 12 noughts miles. . . . And as to mass: the sun weighs about 2 followed by 27 noughts tons, the Milky Way weighs about 160,000 times as much as the sun [*sic*] and is one of a collection of galaxies of which, as I said before, about 30 million are known [*sic*]. It is not very easy to retain a belief in one's own cosmic importance in view of such overwhelming statistics." (Bertrand Russell, *Unpopular Essays*, pp. 85–86)

4. A refutation of Russell's fallacy above: "We have discovered our own insignificance in discovering how tiny the earth is and how utterly immense the universe is." "In that case, we have also discovered that an elephant is somewhat more significant than a man, and a tall man is slightly more significant than a short man." (This is an example of refutation by *reductio ad absurdum*: see p. 294.)

5. "This medicine must be good for me; it tastes awful."

7C, **Confusing Quantity with Quality**

This confusion can also work both ways. *Quality* may be *quantified* by the claim that I.Q. tests (or multiple choice exams in a philosophy course!) measure wisdom, or that statistics can measure exactly how much better Pepsi tastes to people than Coke, or that all of a painting can be expressed in a digital mathematical formula without omitting anything. (This last example comes from the parable of French philosopher Henri Bergson (1859–1940) about mathematical bees.) The *qualification* of *quantity* occurs when it is claimed that *numbers* have personalities, colors, sounds, moral values, or inherent but inexpressible mystical significance. The quantification of quality is much more fashionable today; the qualification of quantity was more fashionable in ancient times. Each era, like each person, tends to overemphasize what they are good at.

7D, **"The Fallacy of Misplaced Concreteness":**
Confusing the Abstract with the Concrete

The concepts in metaphysics are very abstract. These abstractions (such as "being," "causality," and "essence") are usually expressed by nouns. Nouns also express concrete individual things. It is easy to confuse these two kinds of nouns, and treat an abstraction as if it is a concrete reality. This is "the fallacy of misplaced concreteness." (Whitehead coined the phrase.)

Two famous examples of this fallacy[1] are Plato's Theory of Forms and Humanism's worship of "humanity." Plato believed that abstract essences or Forms like beauty, justice, horseness, redness, goodness, and the like were a whole other realm or "world" of real things (this is the "Extreme Realism" defined on page 42) rather than *aspects* of things abstracted from those things by the mind. He noted that red things change, while redness does not; that beautiful things are mixed with ugliness, while beauty is not; that just actions are relative, but justice is absolute; and he taught that true wisdom was the knowledge of this higher world of unchangeable, perfect, absolute realities.

It is reasonable to hold that these Forms exist, indeed, as ideas in the mind of God; but not in themselves, as independent entities or substances. It is also superfluous, as Aristotle pointed out, to suppose that whenever there exist two of any kind of thing (e.g. two men) there exists also a third thing, viz. the common essence. There is indeed a common essence, but that essence is not a "third man." If it were, there would have to be a fourth "man" common to the "third man" and the other two men, *et cetera et cetera ad infinitum.*

"The love of Humanity" can also be a fallacy of misplaced concreteness if the abstraction "humanity" substitutes for concrete individuals as objects of love. This is what Dickens calls "telescopic philanthropy" (in *Bleak House*),

---

1 Though both are controversial, and some would defend these two examples as not fallacious at all.

substituting concern for faraway groups like "the poor" and abstractions like "justice in the Near East" for concrete human beings and problems in our own families and lives. As Linus says in a "Peanuts" comic strip, "I have no problem with Humanity. It's people I can't stand." Or as G.K. Chesterton put it,

O how I love Humanity
With love so pure and pringlish,
And how I hate the horrid French,
Who never will be English!

When we treat abstractions like "causality" and "substance" as concrete entities, we become subject to critiques like Hume's, in which he points out that no one ever observed "causality," or "substance," only particular things and events. Even the self is not an observable object that we can catch by a kind of inner observation. Hume erroneously deduced from this premise the conclusion that there *was* no such thing as causality or substance or even any substantial self. This is itself a fallacy: a *non sequitur*. But his error was provoked by the fallacy of misplaced concreteness on the part of those who thought of causality as a kind of river of force, or substance as a kind of foundation for the building of accidents, or the self as a kind of ghost or "little man inside pulling strings." (Thus Hume's critique was also an example of the "straw man" fallacy.)

7E, Confusing Logical, Physical, and Psychological Causes

See p. 81, paragraph 1, for this fallacy.

7F, Confusing Essence and Existence (The Existential Fallacy)

One example of this fallacy is rather rare and esoteric: Sartre's claim that man's essence is simply to exist, that we arbitrarily construct our own essence. Another, broader example is the claim that a thing has no essence, that it simply exists as an unintelligible, absolutely indefinable something. A thing may be unintelligible *to us*, but nothing can be unintelligible in itself. Even God is fully intelligible – to God. There is a difference between saying that God has no essence and saying that God's essence is existence, or not distinct from existence. The latter is simply to say that God exists necessarily, without needing a cause.

An opposite form of this metaphysical fallacy is the attempt to think about existence as if it were an essence. (This is the metaphysical mistake made, e.g., in one version of St. Anselm's "Ontological Argument," treating the predicate "existence" as if it were an essence or quality or definable perfection. If you have never heard of this argument, see page 284 or ask your teacher.) Since all that is conceivable is essence, we have no concept of existence. Existence appears only in a judgment ("that *is*," "this *is* that"). It is a metaphysical fallacy to treat existence as an essence.

The confusion between essence and existence can be logical as well as metaphysical: see the discussion of existential propositions on page 150. We will see later how modern logic's unnecessary assumption that all particular propositions assert existence and all universal propositions are only about essences has provoked modern logicians to reject the traditional Square of Opposition (page 179).

7G, Confusing the Natural with the Common

The *natural* is inherent and unchangeable; the merely *common* is accidental and changeable. It is human *nature* to want property; it is *common* in our age to want a lot more than we can use. It is *natural* to wear clothes; it is *common* in our day to wear jeans. It is *natural* (in accord with human nature) to love beauty; it is *common*, in some cultures, to be fascinated with ugliness for its shock value.

Here too the confusion can work either way. Reducing the natural to the common is the more fashionable fallacy in our society, since the very concept of a nature, and of human nature, is rejected by skepticism and nominalism. Treating the common as the natural was the more common (but not more natural!) fallacy of past generations: e.g. assuming that it was simply part of human nature to have a social class system, or kings. Many of today's controversies are about whether some practice or desire is unnatural or just uncommon, or even whether there is any meaning at all to the concept 'unnatural.'

* * * * *

There are no exercises at the end of this long chapter on the 49 fallacies. Examples have been integrated into the text instead. Why? Because it is the hardest topic in logic for fair and useful quizzes and tests, since there is almost always some overlapping among the fallacies, especially if there are a large number of them to learn. (And 49 is a large number!) Very often, when one primary fallacy is committed, another, secondary fallacy is too, at least in an implicit way. Often there are three or four good answers to the question "identify the fallacy." So the correct answer is often a matter of interpretation, with some reasonable doubt as to which is the best. "Name the fallacy" exercises often resemble the game "Pin the Tail on the Donkey." This stands in striking contrast to the rest of logic, where the correct answers are almost always "black and white" and unarguable.

So, instead of the pain of exercises, we have included the pleasure of an old, charmingly out-of-date, satirical short story entitled "Love Is a Fallacy." It will stick with you, as a "big picture," longer than many little flea-like exercises.

"Love Is a Fallacy"
by Max Schulman (from *The Many Loves of Dobie Gillis*)

Cool was I and logical. Keen, calculating, perspicacious, acute and astute–
I was all of these. My brain was as powerful as a dynamo, as precise as a
chemist's scales, as penetrating as a scalpel. And – think of it! – I was only eight-
een.

It is not often that one so young has such a giant intellect. Take, for example, Petey Bellows, my roommate at the university. Same age, same background,
but dumb as an ox. A nice enough fellow, you understand, but nothing upstairs.
Emotional type. Unstable. Impressionable. Worst of all, a faddist. Fads, I submit,
are the very negation of reason. To be swept up in every new craze that comes
along, to surrender yourself to idiocy just because everybody else is doing it –
this, to me, is the acme of mindlessness. Not, however, to Petey.

One afternoon I found Petey lying on his bed with an expression of such
distress on his face that I immediately diagnosed appendicitis. "Don't move," I
said. "Don't take a laxative. I'll get a doctor."

"Raccoon," he mumbled thickly.

"Raccoon?" I said, pausing in my flight.

"I want a raccoon coat," he wailed.

I perceived that his trouble was not physical, but mental. "Why do you want
a raccoon coat?"

"I should have known it," he cried, pounding his temples. "I should have
known they'd come back when the Charleston came back. Like a fool Ispent all
my money for textbooks, and now I can't get a raccoon coat."

"Can you mean," I said incredulously, "that people are actually wearing raccoon coats again?"

"All the Big Men on Campus are wearing them. Where've you been?"

"In the library," I said, naming a place not frequented by Big Men on
Campus.

He leaped from the bed and paced the room. "I've got to have a raccoon
coat," he said passionately. "I've got to!"

"Peter, why? Look at it rationally. Raccoon coats are unsanitary. They shed.
They smell bad. They weigh too much. They're unsightly. They – "

"You don't understand," he interrupted impatiently. "It's the thing to do.
Don't you want to be in the swim?"

"No," I said truthfully.

"Well, I do," he declared. "I'd give anything for a raccoon coat. Anything!"

My brain, that precision instrument, slipped into high gear. "Anything?" I
asked, looking at him narrowly.

"Anything," he affirmed in ringing tones.

I stroked my chin thoughtfully. It so happened that I knew where to get my
hands on a raccoon coat. My father had had one in his undergraduate days; it lay

now in a trunk in the attic back home. It also happened that Petey had something I wanted. He didn't have it exactly, but at least he had first rights on it. I refer to his girl, Polly Espy.

I had long coveted Polly Espy. Let me emphasize that my desire for this young woman was not emotional in nature. She was, to be sure, a girl who excited the emotions, but I was not one to let my heart rule my head. I wanted Polly for a shrewdly calculated, entirely cerebral reason.

I was a freshman in law school. In a few years I would be out in practice. I was well aware of the importance of the right kind of wife in furthering a lawyer's career. The successful lawyers I had observed were, almost without exception, married to beautiful, gracious, intelligent women. With one omission, Polly fitted these specifications perfectly.

Beautiful she was. She was not yet of pin-up proportions, but I felt sure that time would supply the lack. She already had the makings.

Gracious she was. By gracious I mean full of graces. She had an erectness of carriage, an ease of bearing, a poise that clearly indicated the best of breeding. At table her manners were exquisite. I had seen her at the Kozy Kampus Korner eating the specialty of the house – a sandwich that contained scraps of pot roast, gravy, chopped nuts, and a dipper of sauerkraut – without even getting her fingers moist.

Intelligent she was not. In fact, she veered in the opposite direction. But I believed that under my guidance she would smarten up. At any rate, it was worth a try. It is, after all, easier to make a beautiful dumb girl smart than to make an ugly smart girl beautiful.

"Petey," I said, "are you in love with Polly Espy?"

"I think she's a keen kid," he replied, "but I don't know if you'd call it love. Why?"

"Do you," I asked, "have any kind of formal arrangement with her? I mean are you going steady or anything like that?"

"No. We see each other quite a bit, but we both have other dates. Why?"

"Is there," I asked, "any other man for whom she has a particular fondness?"

"Not that I know of. Why?"

I nodded with satisfaction. "In other words, if you were out of the picture, the field would be open. Is that right?"

"I guess so. What are you getting at?"

"Nothing, nothing," I said innocently, and took my suitcase out of the closet.

"Where you going?" asked Petey.

"Home for the weekend." I threw a few things into the bag.

"Listen," he said, clutching my arm eagerly, "while you're home, you couldn't get some money from your old man, could you, and lend it to me so I can buy a raccoon coat?"

"I may do better than that," I said with a mysterious wink and closed my bag and left.

"Look," I said to Petey when I got back Monday morning. I threw open the suitcase and revealed the huge, hairy, gamy object that my father had worn in his Stutz Bearcat in 1925.

"Holy Toledo!" said Petey reverently. He plunged his hands into the raccoon coat and then his face. "Holy Toledo!" he repeated fifteen or twenty times.

"Would you like it?" I asked.

"Oh yes!" he cried, clutching the greasy pelt to him. Then a canny look came into his eyes. "What do you want for it?"

"Your girl," I said, mincing no words.

"Polly?" he said in a horrified whisper. "You want Polly?"

"That's right."

He flung the coat from him. "Never," he said stoutly.

I shrugged. "Okay. If you don't want to be in the swim, I guess it's your business."

I sat down in a chair and pretended to read a book, but out of the corner of my eye I kept watching Petey. He was a torn man. First he looked at the coat with an expression of a waif at a bakery window. Then he turned away and set his jaw resolutely. Then he looked back at the coat, with even more longing in his face. Then he turned away, but with not so much resolution this time. Back and forth his head swiveled, desire waxing, resolution waning. Finally he didn't turn away at all; he just stood and stared with mad lust at the coat.

"It isn't as though I was in love with Polly," he said thickly. "Or going steady or anything like that."

"That's right," I murmured.

"What's Polly to me, or me to Polly?"

"Not a thing," said I.

"It's just been a casual kick – just a few laughs, that's all."

"Try on the coat," said I.

He complied. The coat bunched high over his ears and dropped all the way down to his shoe tops. He looked like a mound of dead raccoons. "Fits fine," he said happily.

I rose from my chair. "Is it a deal?" I asked, extending my hand.

He swallowed. "It's a deal," he said and shook my hand.

I had my first date with Polly the following evening. This was in the nature of a survey; I wanted to find out just how much work I had to do to get her mind up to the standard I required. I took her first to dinner. "Gee, that was a delish dinner," she said as we left the restaurant. Then I took her to a movie. "Gee, that was a marvy movie," she said as we left the theater. And then I took her home. "Gee, I had a sensaysh time," she said as she bade me good night.

I went back to my room with a heavy heart. I had gravely underestimated the size of my task. This girl's lack of information was terrifying. Nor would it be enough merely to supply her with information. First she had to be taught to *think*. This loomed as a project of no small dimensions, and at first I was tempted to give her back to Petey. But then I got to thinking about her abundant physical charms and about the way she entered a room and the way she handled a knife and fork, and I decided to make an effort.

I went about it, as in all things, systematically. I gave her a course in logic. It happened that I, as a law student, was taking a course in logic myself, so I had all the facts at my finger tips. "Polly," I said to her when I picked her up on our next date, "tonight we are going over to the Knoll and talk."

"Oo, terrif," she replied. One thing I will say for this girl: you would go far to find another so agreeable.

We went to the Knoll, the campus trysting place, and we sat down under an old oak, and she looked at me expectantly. "What are we going to talk about?" she asked.

"Logic."

She thought this over for a minute and decided she liked it. "Magnif," she said.

"Logic," I said, clearing my throat, "is the science of thinking. Before we can think correctly, we must first learn to recognize the common fallacies of logic. These we will take up tonight."

"Wow-dow!" she cried, clapping her hands delightedly.

I winced, but went bravely on. "First let us examine the fallacy called Dicto Simpliciter."

"By all means," she urged, batting her lashes eagerly.

"Dicto Simpliciter means an argument based on an unqualified generalization. For example: Exercise is good. Therefore everybody should exercise."

"I agree," said Polly earnestly. "I mean exercise is wonderful. I mean it builds the body and everything."

"Polly," I said gently, "the argument is a fallacy. *Exercise is good* is an unqualified generalization. For instance, if you have heart disease, exercise is bad, not good. Many people are ordered by their doctors *not* to exercise. You must *qualify* the generalization. You must say exercise is *usually* good, or exercise is good *for most people*. Otherwise you have committed a Dicto Simpliciter. Do you see?"

"No," she confessed. "But this is marvy. Do more! Do more!"

"It will be better if you stop tugging at my sleeve," I told her, and when she desisted, I continued. "Next we take up a fallacy called Hasty Generalization. Listen carefully: You can't speak French. I can't speak French. Petey Bellows can't speak French. I must therefore conclude that nobody at the University of Minnesota can speak French."

"Really?" said Polly, amazed. "*Nobody?*"

I hid my exasperation. "Polly, it's a fallacy. The generalization is reached too hastily. These are too few instances to support such a conclusion."

"Know any more fallacies?" she asked breathlessly. "This is more fun than dancing even."

I fought off a wave of despair. I was getting nowhere with this girl, absolutely nowhere. Still, I am nothing if not persistent. I continued, "Next comes Post Hoc. Listen to this: Let's not take Bill on our picnic. Every time we take him out with us, it rains."

"I know somebody just like that," she exclaimed." A girl back home – Eula Becker, her name is. It never fails. Every single time we take her on a picnic –"

"Polly," I said sharply, "it's a fallacy. Eula Becker doesn't cause the rain. She has no connection with the rain. You are guilty of Post Hoc if you blame Eula Becker."

"I'll never do it again," she promised contritely. Are you mad at me?"

I sighed. "No, Polly, I'm not mad."

"Then tell me some more fallacies."

"All right. Let's try Contradictory Premises."

"Yes, let's," she chirped, blinking her eyes happily.

I frowned, but plunged ahead. "Here's an example of Contradictory Premises: If God can do anything, can He make a stone so heavy that He won't be able to lift it?"

"Of course," she replied promptly.

"But if He can do anything, He can lift the stone," I pointed out.

"Yeah," she said thoughtfully. "Well, then I guess He can't make the stone."

"But He can do anything," I reminded her.

She scratched her pretty, empty head. "I'm all confused," she admitted.

"Of course you are. Because when the premises of an argument contradict each other, there can be no argument. If there is an irresistible force, there can be no immovable object. If there is an immovable object, there can be no irresistible force. Get it?"

"Tell me some more of this keen stuff," she said eagerly.

I consulted my watch. "I think we'd better call it a night. I'll take you home now, and you go over all the things you've learned. We'll have another session tomorrow night."

I deposited her at the girls' dormitory, where she assured me that she had had a perfectly terrif evening, and I went glumly home to my room. Petey lay snoring in his bed, the raccoon coat huddled like a great hairy beast at his feet. For a moment I considered waking him and telling him that he could have his girl back. It seemed clear that my project was doomed to failure. The girl simply had a logic-proof head.

But then I reconsidered. I had wasted one evening: I might as well waste another. Who knew? Maybe somewhere in the extinct crater of her mind a few embers still smoldered. Maybe somehow I could fan them into flame. Admittedly it was not a prospect fraught with hope, but I decided to give it one more try.

Seated under the oak the next evening I said, "Our first fallacy tonight is called Ad Misericordiam."

She quivered with delight.

"Listen closely," I said. "A man applies for a job. When the boss asks him what his qualifications are, he replies he has a wife and six children at home, the wife is a helpless cripple, the children have nothing to eat, no clothes to wear, no shoes on their feet, there are no beds in the house, no coal in the cellar, and winter is coming."

A tear rolled down each of Polly's pink cheeks. "Oh, this is awful, awful," she sobbed.

"Yes, it is awful," I agreed, "but it's no argument. The man never answered the boss's question about his qualifications. Instead, he appealed to the boss's sympathy. He committed the fallacy of Ad Misericordiam. Do you understand?"

"Have you got a handkerchief?" she blubbered.

I handed her a handkerchief and tried to keep from screaming while she wiped her eyes. "Next," I said in a carefully controlled tone, "we will discuss False Analogy. Here is an example: Students should be allowed to look at their textbooks during examinations. After all, surgeons have X rays to guide them during an operation, lawyers have briefs to guide them during a trial, carpenters have blueprints to guide them when they are building a house. Why, then, shouldn't students be allowed to look at their textbooks during an examination?"

"There now," she said enthusiastically, "is the most marvy idea I've heard in years."

"Polly," I said testily, "the argument is all wrong. Doctors, lawyers, and carpenters aren't taking a test to see how much they are learned, but students are. The situations are altogether different, and you can't make an analogy between them."

"I still think it's a good idea," said Polly.

"Nuts," I muttered. Doggedly I pressed on. "Next we'll try Hypothesis Contrary to Fact."

"Sounds yummy," was Polly's reaction.

"Listen: If Madame Curie had not happened to leave a photographic plate in a drawer with a chunk of pitchblende, the world today would not know about radium."

"True, true," said Polly, nodding her head. "Did you see the movie? Oh, it just knocked me out. That Walter Pidgeon is so dreamy. I mean he fractures me."

"If you can forget Mr. Pidgeon for a moment," I said coldly, "I would like to point out that the statement is a fallacy. Maybe Madame Curie would have discovered radium at some later date. Maybe somebody else would have discovered it. Maybe any number of things would have happened. You can't start with a hypothesis that is not true and then draw any supportable conclusions from it."

"They ought to put Walter Pidgeon in more pictures," said Polly. "I hardly ever see him any more."

One more chance, I decided. But just one more. There is a limit to what flesh and blood can bear. "The next fallacy is called Poisoning the Well."

"How cute!" she gurgled.

"Two men are having a debate. The first one gets up and says, 'My opponent is a notorious liar. You can't believe a word that he is going to say.' . . . Now, Polly, think. Think hard. What's wrong?"

I watched her closely as she knit her creamy brow in concentration. Suddenly a glimmer of intelligence – the first I had seen – came into her eyes. "What chance has the second man got if the first man calls him a liar before he even begins talking?"

"Right!" I cried exultantly. "One hundred per cent right. It's not fair. The first man has *poisoned the well* before anybody could drink from it. He has hamstrung his opponent before he could even start. . . . Polly, I'm proud of you."

"Pshaw," she murmured, blushing with pleasure.

"You see, my dear, these things aren't so hard. All you have to do is concentrate. Think – examine – evaluate. Come now, let's review everything we have learned."

"Fire away," she said with an airy wave of her hand.

Heartened by the knowledge that Polly was not altogether a cretin, I began a long, patient review of all I had told her. Over and over and over again I cited instances, pointed out flaws, kept hammering away without letup. It was like digging a tunnel. At first everything was work, sweat, and darkness. I had no idea when I would reach the light, or even *if* I would. But I persisted. I pounded and clawed and scraped, and finally I was rewarded. I saw a chink of light. And then the chink got bigger and the sun came pouring in and all was bright.

Five grueling nights this took, but it was worth it. I had made a logician out of Polly; I had taught her to think. My job was done. She was worthy of me at last. She was a fit wife for me, a proper hostess for my many mansions, a suitable mother for my well-heeled children.

It must not be thought that I was without love for this girl. Quite the contrary. Just as Pygmalion loved the perfect worman he had fashioned, so I loved mine. I decided to acquaint her with my feelings at our very next meeting. The time had come to change our relationship from academic to romantic.

"Polly," I said when next we sat beneath our oak, "tonight we will not discuss fallacies."

"Aw, gee," she said, disappointed.

"My dear," I said, favoring her with a smile, "we have now spent five evenings together. We have gotten along splendidly. It is clear that we are well matched."

"Hasty Generalization," said Polly brightly.

"I beg your pardon," said I.

"Hasty Generalization," she repeated. "How can you say that we are well matched on the basis of only five dates?"

I chuckled with amusement. The dear child had learned her lessons well.

"My dear," I said, patting her hand in a tolerant manner, "five dates is plenty. After all, you don't have to eat a whole cake to know that it's good."

"False Analogy," said Polly promptly. "I'm not a cake. I'm a girl."

I chuckled with somewhat less amusement. The dear child had learned her lessons perhaps too well. I decided to change tactics. Obviously the best approach was a simple, strong, direct declaration of love. I paused for a moment while my massive brain chose the proper words. Then I began:

"Polly, I love you. You are the whole world to me, and the moon and the stars and the constellations of outer space. Please, my darling, say that you will go steady with me, for if you will not, life will be meaningless. I will languish. I will refuse my meals. I will wander the face of the earth, a shambling, hollow-eyed hulk."

There, I thought, folding my arms, that ought to do it.

"Ad Misericordiam," said Polly.

I ground my teeth. I was not Pygmalion; I was Frankenstein, and my monster had me by the throat. Frantically I fought back the tide of panic surging through me. At all costs I had to keep cool.

"Well, Polly," I said, forcing a smile, "you certainly have learned your fallacies."

"You're darn right," she said with a vigorous nod.

"And who taught them to you, Polly?"

"You did."

"That's right. So you do owe me something, don't you, my dear? If I hadn't come along you never would have learned about fallacies."

"Hypothesis Contrary to Fact," she said instantly.

I dashed perspiration from my brow. "Polly," I croaked, "you mustn't take all these things so literally. I mean this is just classroom stuff. You know that the things you learn in school don't have anything to do with life."

"Dicto Simpliciter," she said, wagging her finger at me playfully.

That did it. I leaped to my feet, bellowing like a bull. "Will you or will you not go steady with me?"

"I will not," she replied.

"Why not?" I demanded.

"Because this afternoon I promised Petey Bellows that I would go steady with him."

I reeled back, overcome with the infamy of it. After he promised, after he made a deal, after he shook my hand! "The rat!" I shrieked, kicking up great chunks of turf. You can't go with him, Polly. He's a liar. He's a cheat. He's a rat."

"Poisoning the Well," said Polly, "and stop shouting. I think shouting must be a fallacy too."

With an immense effort of will, I modulated my voice. "All right," I said. "You're a logician. Let's look at thing logically. How could you choose Petey

Bellows over me? Look at me – a brilliant student, a tremendous intellectual, a man with an assured future. Look at Petey – a knothead, a jitterbug, a guy who'll never know where his next meal is coming from. Can you give me one logical reason why you should go steady with Petey Bellows?"

"I certainly can," declared Polly. "He's got a raccoon coat."

IV: Definition

Section 1. The nature of definition (B)

Definition is crucial to logic. For a definition tells us what a thing is; and if we do not know what a thing is, by the first act of the mind, we cannot know what to predicate of it in the second act of the mind, and thus we have no premises for our reasoning (the third act of the mind).

This is the most important chapter of the first third of this book, for the first third is about terms, and the main problem with terms is ambiguity, and definition is the way to clear up ambiguity in our terms.

It is also the simplest chapter of the first part of this book, for the principles of good definitions are very simple. The *practice* of these principles, however, is not simple. Most of our problems in communication come here: in trying to understand what we mean by our terms, trying to "come to terms" with each other.

Definition is crucial to the "Socratic Method." The archetypal philosopher, Socrates, usually spent more than half of each of his dialogues defining terms. The most famous and influential book in the whole history of philosophy, Plato's *Republic*, spends most of its time in defining just one term, "justice." Book I of the *Republic* is an excellent reading exercise for the student of definitions; it consists in Socrates evaluating three definitions of justice and finding them wanting. He does this by increasingly complex arguments. (Arguments can be means to the end of constructing a good definition, just as good definitions can be means to the end of constructing good arguments.)

Definition is to comprehension what division is to extension. A definition analyzes, or takes apart, the comprehension of a term, by subdividing the aspects of its essential meaning ("species") into genus (the common aspect) and specific difference (the specific, proper aspect); while a division analyzes the extension of a term, in subdividing its population into sub-groups.

A definition tells us *what a thing is*. The ideal definition, an "**essential definition**," tells us the thing's essence, by giving its *genus* and *specific difference*. That is the maximum for a definition. The minimum for an acceptable definition is that it at least distinguishes the thing defined from all other things, so that we will not confuse it with other things. The maximum, or perfect, idea of a thing is both *clear* and *distinct*; but if we cannot have perfect clarity, we should at least have perfect distinctness. If we cannot know exactly what a thing is, we should at least know what it isn't, that is, know its limits. "Definition" comes from *de-finio*, which means *to set limits around* a thing.

The importance of definition can hardly be overestimated. It perfects the first act of the mind in telling us what a thing is. If we do not know what a thing is, we simply do not know *what* we are talking about.

This is the most basic reason why symbolic logic alone is radically inadequate for philosophy: it cannot deal with what a thing is. It is at least implicitly Nominalist (see Chapter I, Section 3, pages 41–43): it excludes the very notion of essences.

Section 2. The rules of definition (B)

There are six rules for a logically acceptable definition:

1. **A definition should be coextensive with the thing defined: neither too broad nor too narrow.** (This is the most important rule, and the hardest to obey. It concerns the extension of the term rather than the comprehension)
2. **A definition should be clear, not obscure.**
3. **A definition should be literal, not metaphorical.**
4. **A definition should be brief, not long.**
5. **A definition should be positive, not negative, if possible.** (Only negative realities call for negative definitions.)
6. **A definition should not be circular.** (The term defined cannot appear in the definition.)

These six rules can be condensed to three:

A definition must be:
1. **coextensive**
2. **clear, literal, and brief**
3. **not negative or circular**

Section 3. The kinds of definition

Here is a division of (good) definitions:

   I. Nominal
   II. Real
      A. Essential
      B. Non-essential
         1. by properties
         2. by accidents
         3. by causes
            a. by efficient cause

b. by final cause
c. by material cause
4. by effects

Thus, the kinds of definitions are:
1. **nominal** (a definition of the *word* rather than the thing designated by the word)
2. **essential** (genus plus specific difference)
3. **by properties** (in the technical sense of the *predicable* 'property' [see page 57])
4. **by accidents** (the difficulty here is piling up enough accidents to limit the extension so that the definition is not too broad).
5. **by efficient cause** or agent (often called a "genetic" definition): e.g. "A solar eclipse is an astronomical event caused by the moon blocking the sun's light from some part of the earth by coming between the sun and the earth." "An acorn is a seed produced by an oak tree." "Anthrax is the disease caused by the bacteria *anthracis*."
6. **by final cause** or purpose: e.g. "A house is a machine for living." (Le Corbusier) "An eye is an organ for seeing." "A pen is an instrument for writing with ink."
7. **by the material cause** or contents: "Water is two parts hydrogen and one part oxygen." "Fish are animals with gills." "The helium atom has two protons and one neutron in its nucleus."
8. **by effects**: e.g. "A carcinogen is any thing or event that tends to cause cancer."

The "four causes" are explained more extensively on pages 202–5. One of the four causes, the formal cause, is omitted in this list because a definition by formal cause would be the same thing as an essential definition.

Nominal definitions are definitions of a *name*, or a *word*, not necessariy of a reality. They answer the question "How is this word used?" rather than "what is this thing?" Dictionary definitions are usually intended only to be nominal definitions.

Nominal definitions can be subdivided into (a) definitions that give the usual or *conventional* meaning of the word and (b) those that give a *specialized* meaning, often a meaning suggested or stipulated by the writer, such as: "Let us define a 'socially acceptable practice' as any practice that over 50% of the society approves." (These are called "**stipulative definitions**.") Nominal definitions can also define a word by giving (c) a synonym, (d) the etymology of the word, or (e) examples of its use – though giving examples is not, strictly speaking, *definition* at all. In Plato's *Meno*, Socrates shows how inadequate it is to try to give a definition by examples only, in criticizing Meno's attempts to define "virtue" in general by giving examples of particular virtues.

Since nominal definitions are not, strictly speaking, definitions of things at all, but only of words, we cannot strictly apply to them the rules for definitions. Even so, they should at least avoid the two most important errors in definitions, "too broad" and "too narrow."

It is sometimes difficult to decide whether a given definition is nominal or real. If you are intending to give a nominal definition, it is good to clarify this intention by italicizing or putting quotation marks around the word you are defining.

Essential definitions. The ideal definition gives the essence or whatness or nature of the thing defined by analyzing the meaning (or comprehension) of this essence into two parts: (1) the generic or general or common part and (2) the specific or differentiating or proper part. These two parts are both "comprehended by" (included in) the "comprehension" (inner meaning) of the term.

The generic part tells us what general class the thing essentially belongs to: Man is an animal, triangles are plane figures, hammers are tools, monarchy is a form of government, Christianity is a religion.

The *genus* given should be the "*proximate genus*," the narrowest genus: not "substance" or "organism" but "animal" for "man"; not "figure" but "plane figure" for "triangle"; not "society" but "government" for "democracy."

The *specific difference* tells us how the thing defined differs from all other members of its genus: man is rational, triangles are three-sided, hammers strike nails, monarchy is rule by one, Christianity believes that "Jesus is Lord" (divine). An essential definition, thus, gives the *species* (= genus + specific difference) of the thing defined.

Properties can substitute for specific differences, but then we have a definition by property instead of by essence: e.g. "Man is the animal that writes"; "triangles are plane figures whose interior angles add up to 180 degrees."

A review of the predicables (page 56) may be necessary here. It is essential to remember that "species" does not mean "any man-made classification at all in which a more general class is subdivided into more specific classes." A thing's "species" is its *essence*. or, in Aristotle's words, "what is predicated essentially of many different individuals": e.g. Socrates, Plato, and Aristotle are all *men*. (They are all Greeks too, but that is not *essential*.)

And a "genus" is *not* just "any man-made general class," but *the common part of the essence*, or in Aristotle's words, "what is predicated essentially of several things that differ in species": men, monkeys, dogs, sharks, guppies, clams, robins, hawks, snails, possums, alligators, and snakes are all *animals*.

Finally, a "specific difference" is *the differentiating part of the essence*, or, in Aristotle's words, "what makes one species different from another within a genus." Man is the only *rational* animal; triangles the only *three-sided* enclosed plane figures, etc.

The species is the complete essence, including both the genus and the specific difference. In terms of a term's comprehension, the genus is one part of the species. (Animality is part of humanity.) In terms of extension, a species is part of a genus. (Humanity is part of the animal kingdom.)

* * * * *

Most arguments about definitions are about whether or not the definition is too broad or too narrow. This is one of the most important first steps in any philosophical argument, as can be seen by reading the dialogues of Plato. Such arguments are not only about words but about reality, since definitions, like any propositions, are either true or false. However, *one cannot argue about nominal definitions* except in terms of usage: is this how the term is in fact usually used? Nominal definitions, like languages, are man-made, socially constructed conventions rather than universal objective truths; they are *invented* rather than *discovered*. Especially, *one cannot argue about stipulative definitions*, for they are neither true nor false, not acts of intellect that claim to discover objective truths, but proposals of will ("Let us use the term X to designate Y and Z"). Stipulative definitions simply create new nominal definitions. And one can argue about nominal definitions only in terms of practicality of usage.

Socrates always preferred ordinary language definitions to technical or stipulative ones. Most subsequent philosophers (and "experts" in every field) have tended to prefer what a populist might call "witch doctor languages," technical terminologies understood only by the elite, the inner circle in power. It is a very good exercise to translate "witch doctor languages" into ordinary language. This is both useful for others, who do not understand the terminology, and useful for ourselves, since translating is a test as to whether we understand the *concept* or only the *words*. Great philosophers like Aristotle can define difficult terms by one-syllable words. (See Aristotle's definition of truth on page 144.)

The following chart provides examples of each kind of definition for three simple concepts.

KIND OF DEFINTION	OF 'MAN'	OF 'TRIANGLE'	OF 'DEMOCRACY'
too broad	two-legged animal	plane figure	form of government
too narrow	male rational animal	enclosed plane figure with three equal sides	government by direct popular rule
obscure	an ontological synthesis of molecular and self-referential intentionality	the two-dimensional figural gestalt for geodesic domes	participatory or semi-participatory plebiscitarianism

KIND OF DEFINTION	OF 'MAN'	OF 'TRIANGLE'	OF 'DEMOCRACY'
metaphorical	a ghost in a machine	the geometrical image of the Holy Trinity	a bunch of blind bats discussing the definition of daylight
too long	the most para-doxical and multi-dimensional creature in nature, exhibiting both visually detectable physical attributes and that form of consciousness which can become progressively more aware of a plurality of propositional truths by reasoning	a two-dimensional geometrical figure composed of no more and no less than three finite straight lines all of whose end points touch those of another, thereby enclosing a finite space	that form of government whose essential features include popular recall of elected officials, referenda on selected issues, majority rule, and legal equality of essential rights for all citizens
negative	neither ape nor angel	neither a one-dimensional line nor a three-dimensional solid, and neither a square nor a circle	"the most imperfect form of government ever invented except all the other ones" (Winston Churchill)
circular	the creature with human attributes	the shape of any triangular object	government by democratic process
nominal	the species called *"homo sapiens"*	English word for the following figure: Δ	English word for *arche* by *demos*
essential	rational animal	three-sided enclosed plane figure	government by popular sovereignty
by property	the animal that speaks	enclosed plane figure with 180° in its three interior angles	form of government in which laws are determined by popular consent
by accidents	the animal with two legs and no feathers	favorite geometrical figure of the late medieval mystics	form of govern-ment most preva-lent in 20th-century Europe

KIND OF DEFINTION	OF 'MAN'	OF 'TRIANGLE'	OF 'DEMOCRACY'
by efficient cause	creature whose soul is directly created by God	enclosed plane figure generated by the meeting of three straight lines	form of government created by the American "Founding Fathers" and ancient Greeks
by final cause	the creature who seeks Truth, Goodness, and Beauty as ends	geometrical figure providentially designed to image the Trinity in two dimensions	government designed for the most participation by the most people
by material cause	the creature composed of an animal body and a rational soul	two-dimensional figure that contains a finite space, three straight lines, and three angles	government composed of enfranchised populace and their elected representatives
from effects	creature who produces culture	the geometrical figure that caused Hegel to invent his dialectic	government that makes all its citizens responsible for governing

Section 4. The limits of definition

At least five things cannot be properly defined (although we can still say true and useful things about them, and distinguish them from things with which they might otherwise be confused):

(1) What is *infinite* cannot be defined, for a "definition" (*de-finio*) of a thing means telling the limits or boundaries of that thing, and what is infinite has no limits or boundaries. The only definition possible for something infinite is a negative one. Thus "eternity" means "not-time," and "infinity" itself means "not-finitude." It is, of course, impossible to define God, if God is infinite being or an infinite being or the infinite being. (However, it is possible to define finite gods, like the Greek Olympians. But see point 2 below.)

As far as God is concerned, we can only say (a) what God is not or (b) what God is like. But this is not to *define* God, for each of these two choices violates a rule of definition. (a) If we use literal, univocal language, we can only say what God is *not*, not what God *is*. (E.g. God is not a man, God is not a body, God is not in time.) But God is not a negative thing, like nonbeing or death or evil. So a negative definition of God would violate one of the rules of definition (rule #5). (b) If we use analogical or metaphorical language, we can speak positively, but only to say what God is *like*, not what God *is*, literally. (E.g. we can say that God is a Father, God is Love, God is a King. But God is not a human biological father or the changeable human passion of love, or an earthly political ruler.) And of course non-literal language violates another rule of definition (rule #3).

(2) *Individuals* cannot be defined by essential definitions, only species can. For there is no specific difference to distinguish one individual from another; the specific difference differentiates one *species* from another. Thus, a description that puts together enough accidents to distinguish the individual from all others is used as a substitute for a definition: e.g. "the tall, thin, brown-haired Dutchman who taught in the philosophy department at Boston College in 1978."

(3) The *summa genera* or highest genera – i.e. the categories (see page 54) – cannot be properly defined because there is no genus for them, no higher class above them.

(4) *Being* itself, which is not contained in any of the categories and is universal in them all (for they all *are*), cannot be defined, for the same reason.

(5) And the "*transcendentals*," the absolutely universal properties of all being, cannot be properly defined any more than being can. These are traditionally listed as (a) *something*, (b) *one*, (c) *true*, (d) *good*, and (e) *beautiful*. (Others should probably be added, e.g. "able to act" and "related.") Everything that is, is (a) something (that's obvious!); (b) one (even if it is one group, one class, or one pair); (c) ontologically true, i.e. intelligible or knowable; (d) ontologically good (for it is desirable, valuable, willable, for something); and (e) beautiful (for it pleases, by its goodness, the consciousness of one who knows it in its truth).

We can describe the transcendentals but not define them. E.g. the transcendental "one" means "not divided in itself and divided from others," and "beauty" means "that which, being seen, pleases" (*id quod videtur placet*).

Exercises: We include a plethora of exercises on definitions because they are fundamental to philosophy, because they involve not only issues of logical form but also substantive issues of content, and because they are fun and profitable to argue over.

I.   Give a good definition for each of the following. Label what kind of definition you are giving. Try to give an essential definition if possible. If possible, have others evaluate and argue about your definitions.
     1. logic
     2. science
     3. induction
     4. deduction
     5. reasoning
     6. proposition
     7. term
     8. (H) abstraction (noun)
     9. (H) concrete (adjective)
     10. accident
     11. property
     12. definition

13. (H) religion
14. (E) truth
15. fate
16. essence
17. (E) courage
18. angel
19. plant
20. planet
21. (E) square
22. noun
23. abortion
24. death
25. charity
26. money
27. (H) eggbeater

II. First classify, then evaluate, each of the following definitions. If it is too broad or too narrow, say why: what is there in the subject that is not in the predicate if the predicate is too narrow, and what is there in the predicate that is not in the subject if the predicate is too broad? The definitions quoted from literary sources (section B) especially are designed to stimulate fruitful philosophical arguments.

A. Shorter, easier exercises:
1. Life is the most vivid of all dreams.
2. Marriage is a voluntary, lifelong, monogamous covenant relationship between a man and a woman.
3. "A man's religion is what he does with his solitude."
4. A bishop is a clergyman who exercises episcopal functions.
5 Trade is the interchange of goods.
6. (E) Love is "a something we know not what."
7. Life is the sum of vital forces.
8. Life is the opposite of death.
9. (E) Life is a bowl of cherries.
10. (E) Life is when you're breathing.
11. Life is what happens between birth and death.
12. Memory is the storehouse of the mind.
13. A university is a place for acquiring a great deal of knowledge on a great deal of subjects.
14. Security means contentment.
15. (E) A separation is not a divorce.
16. "Personality is the ability to say Yes; character is the ability to say No." (Ann Landers)
17. (E) Personality is the quality of being a person.

18. Personality is what makes friends.
19. "A person is the non-objectifiable subject of all objectification, such as knowing, doubting, believing, wondering, loving, hating, choosing, desiring, feeling, or sensing an object; and since a subject is not an object, it cannot be an object of definition."
20. A circle is something round.
21. A school is a means of transferring words from a teacher to a student in lectures and from the student back to the teacher in tests without either of the two necessarily knowing what they are saying.
22. A "MaeWest" is an inflatable life preserver for pilots who fall into the sea.
23. A tiger is a large feline mammal with transverse, tawny stripes.
24. A plant is a non-sentient organism.
25. A clock is an artificial device for telling time.
26. "Effervescent" means "bubbling."
27. A honeycomb is a structure of adjoining hexagonal cells made of wax by bees for storing honey.
28. A saddle is a seat for a rider on an animal.
29. (E) Man is an animal endowed with the faculty for articulate speech.
30. (E) Arteriosclerosis means hardening of the arteries.
31. (E) A wound is a physical injury caused by breaking the skin.
32. A policeman is a watchdog for criminal activities.
33. A vice is a bad habit.
34. Economic solvency is not having any debts.
35. A student is one who studies.
36. (E) Man is a mortal being.
37. Man is the animal which can go to Heaven.
38. Man is the only animal which can be insane.
39. Man is the animal that produces 3.141 pounds of dung per pound of body weight annually.
40. Virtue is the ability to control passions.
41. A body is a material substance.
42. A body is a substance made of extended parts.
43. (E) Goodness is whatever makes you happy.
44. (E) Goodness is what the lawmaker defines as acceptable.
45. (E) Goodness means kindness.
46. (E) Reality is whatever I know.
47. (E) A logroller is a roller of logs.
48. (E) Being is what bees do.
49. (E) "Architecture is frozen music."
50. (E) "Philosophy" means "the love of wisdom."

B. Quotations
1. "Philosophy is unintelligible answers to insoluble problems." (Henry Adams)

2. (E) "A philosopher is a blind man in a dark room looking for a black cat that isn't there." (Lord Bowen)
3. (E) "A philosopher is one who contradicts other philosophers." (William James)
4. (E) "Philosophy is common sense in a dress suit." (Oliver S. Braston)
5. (E) "Religion is the opiate of the people." (Marx)
6. "Love is nothing else but an insatiate thirst of enjoying a greedily desired object." (Montaigne)
7. (E) "Law is whatever is boldly asserted and plausibly maintained." (Aaron Burr)
8. "Law is , , . an ordinance of reason for the common good, promulgated by him who has care of the community." (Thomas Aquinas)
9. "A figure is that which is enclosed by one or more boundaries." (Euclid)
10. "Faith is the substance of things hoped for, the evidence of things not seen." (Hebrews 11:1)
11. "Faith is when you believe something that you know ain't true." (attributed to a schoolboy by William James in "The Will to Believe")
12. (E) "Economics is the science which treats of the phenomena arising out of the economic activities of men in society." (John Maynard Keynes, *Scope and Methods of Political Economy*)
13. "Justice is health of soul." (Plato)
14. "Justice, for each part of the soul or the state, is doing one's own proper work." (Plato)
15. (E) "We see that all men mean by justice that kind of state of character which makes people disposed to do what is just and makes them act justly and wish for what is just." (Aristotle, *Nicomachean Ethics*)
16. "'The true,' to put it very briefly, is only the expedient in the way of our thinking, just as 'the right' is only the expedient in the way of our behaving." (William James, "Pragmatism's Conception of Truth")
17. (E) "By good, I understand that which we certainly know is useful to us." (Spinoza, *Ethics*)
18. "Happiness is the satisfaction of all our desires." (Kant, *Critique of Pure Reason*)
19. (E) "The word happiness indicates the extent to which the innate and acquired components of sensory-motor function approach an optimum relationship between the antagonistic processes of individualization and socialization so that the movements of the individual are contributing directly or indirectly to larger and more complex electron-proton aggregates or larger and more complex social organizations." (A.P. Weiss, *A Theoretical Basis of Behavior*)
20. (E) "Inquiry is the controlled or directed transformation of an indeterminate situation into one that is so determinate in its constituent distinctions and relations as to convert the elements of the original situation into a unified whole." (John Dewey, *Logic: The Theory of Inquiry*)

21. "Grief for the calamity of another is *pity*, and ariseth from the imagination that the like calamity may befall himself." (Hobbes, *Leviathan*)
22. "Conscience is an inner voice that warns us somebody is looking." (H.L. Mencken)
23. (E) "Religion is a complete system of human communication (or a 'form of life') showing in primarily 'commissive,' 'behabitive,' and 'exercitive' modes how a community comports itself when it encounters an 'untranscendable negation of possibilities.'" (Gerald James Larson, "Prolegomena to a Theory of Religion," *Journal of the American Academy of Religion*)
24. "When we talk of any particular sum of money, we sometimes mean nothing but the metal pieces of which it is composed; and sometimes we include in our meaning some obscure reference to the goods which can be had in exchange for it, or to the power of purchasing which the possession of it conveys." (Adam Smith)
25. "But in practice a citizen is defined to be one of whom both the parents are citizens; others insist on going further back, say to two or three more ancestors. This is a short and practical definition; but there are some who raise the further question how this third or fourth ancestor came to be a citizen. Gorgias of Leontini, partly because he was in a difficulty, partly in irony, said: 'Mortars are what is made by mortar-makers, and the citizens of Larissa are those who are made by magistrates; for it is their trade to make Larissaeans.' Yet the question is really simple, for, if according to the definition just given they shared in the government, they were citizens. This is a better definition than the other. For the words "born of a father and a mother who is a citizen" cannot possibly apply to the first inhabitants or founders of a state." (Aristotle)
26. "By liberty is understood, according to the proper signification of the word, the absence of external impediments." (Thomas Hobbes)
27. (E) "We are willing to treat the term 'religious sentiment' as a collective name for the many sentiments which religious objects may arouse." (William James)
28. (E) "It is almost a definition of a gentleman to say that he is one who never inflicts pain." (Newman)
29. "Man is a thinking reed." (Pascal)
30. "Knowledge is true opinion." (Plato, *Theaetetus*)
31. "The Master said, 'Yu, shall I teach you what knowledge is? When you know a thing, to recognize that you know it, and when you do not know a thing, to recognize that you do not know it: that is knowledge.'" (Confucius, *Analects*)
32. "The word *body*, in the most general acceptation, signifieth that which filleth, or occupieth some certain room, or imagined place, and dependeth

not on the imagination, but is a real part of that we call the universe." (Hobbes, *Leviathan*)

33. "War . . . is an act of violence intended to compel our opponent to fulfill our will." (Von Clausewitz, *On War*)

34. (E) "Political power, properly so called, is merely the organized power of one class for oppressing another." (Karl Marx & Friedrich Engels, *The Communist Manifesto*)

35. "To sneeze is to emit wind audibly by the nose." (Samuel Johnson, *Dictionary*)

36. "I would define 'political correctness' as a form of dogmatic relativism, intolerant of those, such as believers in 'traditional values,' whose positions are thought to depend on belief in objective truth." (Philip Devine, *Proceedings of the American Philosophical Association* June, 1992)

37. (E) "The word 'reality' has whatever significance we choose to give it." (Reuben L. Goodstein, "Language and Experience")

38. (E) "Truth is whatever my colleagues in my department let me get away with saying." (Stanley Fish)

39. "The meaning of a statement is the method of its verification." (Friedrich Waismann, *Erkenntnis* I)

40. "Evolution is an integration of matter and concomitant dissipation of motion, during which the matter passes from an indefinite, incoherent homogeneity to a definite, coherent heterogeneity, and during which the retained motion undergoes a parallel transformation." (Herbert Spencer, *Principles of Biology*)

41. "A friend is a person with whom I may be sincere." (Emerson)

C. Chestertonianisms. Some of these are definitions, others are critiques of definitions, perhaps some are neither, but all are provocative. Chestertonisms have been described as verbal potato chips: you can't eat just one.

1. "There is above all this supreme stamp of the barbarian: the sacrifice of the permanent to the temporary."

2. "It is not bigotry to be certain we are right; but it is bigotry to be unable to imagine how we might possibly have gone wrong."

3. "Bigotry may roughly be defined as the anger of men who have no opinions."

4. "Bigotry is an incapacity to conceive seriously the alternative to a proposition."

5. "Shakespeare has been optimistic when he felt pessimistic. This is the definition of a faith. A faith is that which is able to survive a mood."

6. "What we suffer from today is humility in the wrong place. . . . A man was

meant to be doubtful about himself, but undoubting about the truth; this has been exactly reversed."

7. "The false theory of progress . . . maintains that we alter the test instead of trying to pass the test. . . . If the standard changes, how can there be improvement, which implies a standard? . . . Progress itself cannot progress. . . . Progress should mean that we are always changing the world to suit the vision. Progress does mean (just now) that we are always changing the vision."

8. "Art is limitation. . . . If, in your bold creative way, you hold yourself free to draw a giraffe with a short neck, you will really find that you are not free to draw a giraffe. . . . You can free things from alien or accidental laws but not from the laws of their own nature. You may, if you like, free a tiger from his bars, but do not free him from his stripes. . . . Do not go about as a demagogue encouraging triangles to break out of the prison of their three sides."

9. "Tradition is only democracy extended through time. It is trusting to a consensus of common human voices. . . . Tradition may be defined as an extension of the franchise. Tradition means giving votes to the most obscure of all classes, our ancestors. It is the democracy of the dead. Tradition refuses to submit to the small and arrogant oligarchy of those who merely happen to be walking about."

10. "Obviously a suicide is the opposite of a martyr. A martyr is a man who cares so much for something outside him that he forgets his own personal life. A suicide is a man who cares so little for anything outside him that he wants to see the last of everything."

11. "They have invented a phrase that is a black-and-white contradiction in two words – 'free-love,' as if a lover ever had been, or ever could be, free. It is the nature of love to bind itself, and the institution of marriage merely paid the average man the compliment of taking him at his word."

12. "Strictly speaking, there is no such thing as a. . . . Peasant. Indeed, the type can only exist in community. . . . One must not think primarily of a French Peasant, any more than of a German Measle. The plural of the word is the proper form; you cannot have a Peasant till you have a peasantry The essence of the Peasant ideal is equality; and you cannot be equal all by yourself."

D. Evaluate the following evaluation of a definition:

"What is a fairy-story? In this case you will turn to the *Oxford English Dictionary* in vain . . . its leading sense is said to be (a) a tale about fairies . . . (b) an unreal or incredible story, and (c) a falsehood. The last two senses . . . [are] hopelessly vast. But the first sense is too narrow. . . . Especially so if we accept the lexicographer's definition of *fairies*: 'supernatural beings of diminutive size'. . . . *Supernatural* is a dangerous and difficult word in any of its senses, looser or stricter. But to fairies it can hardly be applied. . . . For it is man who is, in contrast to fairies, supernatural (and often of diminutive stature); whereas they are natural, far more natural than he. Such is their doom." (J.R.R. Tolkien, "On Fairy Stories")

E. Explain the following argument about a definition of justice by Plato: "But take this matter of doing justice. Can we say that it really consists in nothing more nor less than telling the truth and paying your debts? Are not these acts sometimes just and sometimes unjust? Suppose, for example, a friend who has lent us a weapon were to go mad and then ask for it back. Surely everyone would say that we ought not to do that; it would not be just to do it, or to tell the whole truth to the madman. Acting justly, then, cannot be defined as telling the truth and paying your debts."

F. What is the implied definition of "miracle" in the following? "The story of the whale swallowing Jonah, though a whale is large enough to do it, borders greatly on the marvelous; but it would have approached nearer to the idea of miracle if Jonah had swallowed the whale." (Thomas Paine, *The Age of Reason*)

G. Plato having defined man as a featherless biped, Diogenes ran to the marketplace, bought a chicken, plucked out all its feathers, ran back into Plato's classroom, threw the plucked chicken at Plato's feet, and said to the class, "Behold Plato's man!" On which account Plato added to the definition: "with broad, flat nails." (Diogenes Laertius)

V. The Second Act of the Mind: Judgment

Section 1. Judgments, propositions, and sentences

It is very useful at various points in this book, especially at the beginning of a new section such as this one, to go back and review the Introduction, Section 4 (all of logic in two pages, pp. 26–27) or Section 5 (the Three Acts of the Mind, pp. 28–34). For that is like a road map that tells you where you are, how everything in the landscape is related to everything else, where it all fits. Without this sense of place, without this outline, you may feel lost and confused, and this feeling will permeate every new detail you learn.

We now begin exploring the second act of the mind, **judgment**, and its logical product, the **proposition**, which is expressed linguistically in a **declarative sentence**. The distinction, *within* the second act of the mind, between judgments, propositions, and sentences is not absolutely crucial, but what is absolutely crucial for all subsequent progress in logic is the distinction between judgment and the other two acts of the mind: the distinction between judgments and concepts and the distinction between judgments and arguments – or, in terms of the *products* of these three acts of the mind, the distinction between propositions and terms and the distinction between propositions and syllogisms. These two distinctions are expressed in language, respectively, in the distinction between sentences and words and in the distinction between sentences and paragraphs. If this paragraph was at all confusing to you, please reread pp. 28–34.

Propositions are most clearly and sharply distinguished from both terms and arguments by the fact that *only propositions can be either true or false*. Terms are only clear or unclear, whether these terms stand by themselves or form parts of propositions. Propositions are either true or false, whether they stand by themselves or form parts of arguments. Arguments as a whole are neither true nor false; each proposition *within* an argument is either true or false. Arguments as a whole are either logically valid or logically invalid, depending on whether or not the conclusion necessarily follows from the premises.

The individual mind's inner, private *judgments* are expressed in *propositions*, which are universal and public statements that might be thought of as photographs of judgments or footprints of judgments or fossils of judgments. A single proposition is the meaning common to all the different languages' declarative sentences that express that proposition. "Being is good," "*Ens est bonum*," "*Das Sein ist gut*," "*L'Etre est bon*," and "*Ousia ariston estin*," are all the same proposition in five different sentences, in five different languages.

There are four other kinds of sentences, which are not declarative sentences and do not claim to be true. These are not propositions. They are: (1) interrogative sentences, which ask questions (e.g. "What time is it?"), (2) imperative sentences, which issue commands or requests (e.g. "Please pass the mustard"), (3) exclamatory sentences, which directly express emotion (e.g. "Ouch! Good grief!"), and (4) performatory sentences, which act to effect changes ("I baptize you . . .").

The Importance of Propositions

This second third of this logic text is shorter than the first or third thirds, but it is just as important. For propositions, and only propositions, contain truth; and truth is the aim and end and goal of reason. The first and third acts of the mind are means to the end of truth; only the second act of the mind contains or attains that end. One means to this end is clarifying and defining terms, understanding the terms which make up the content of a proposition. Another means to truth is arguing, trying to prove new propositions (conclusions) from other propositions (premises). Since the end is more important than the means, truth is more important than definitions and arguments. And it is here, in the second act of the mind, that we find truth.

When we hear others speaking, or when we read what others have written, we notice two things present in our consciousness: the objective and the subjective, the things said and our emotional reactions to these things. We are bored, interested, moved, scared, irritated, depressed, cheered, disgusted, threatened, or attracted by what we hear or read. It is absolutely essential – not only for logic but for all education and in fact for civilization, honesty, and sanity – that we distinguish these two things, the objective and the subjective; that we understand, and concentrate on, not only our own feelings and reactions to what is said but also *what is said*, what is given to us, our verbal *data*. We cannot justly and intelligently react to what is said if we do not understand what is said, what is objective to us; or if we cannot distinguish the objective from the subjective, distinguish what is said from our personal reaction to it. So the first thing we must do is to find out *what is said*, what truth-claims are contained in this discourse that is spoken or written – that is, what propositions are being uttered.

This is the simple and obvious core of the art of reading, and this is one of the most useful parts of logic. For the complaints that students can no longer read seem to be increasing every generation. After a century of universal public education, Americans do not know how to read or write as well today as they did a hundred years ago. If you doubt this, compare newspapers or elementary reading textbooks for any grade a century ago with those today.

One of the best remedies for bad reading and writing is good logic, especially the analysis of propositions. For *thinking* clearly, *expressing* your thoughts clearly (in writing or speaking), and *interpreting* another's expressions (written or spoken) clearly are three arts that are very closely allied; no one of them can be done well without doing the other two. And the part of logic that is most directly related to this is the part that studies propositions.

Subject and Predicate

After the mind has understood the nature or essence or "whatness" of something by forming a concept, it then goes on to relate two of these concepts to each other by making a "judgment." We *judge* that "all men are mortal" or that "apples are fruits" or that "apples are vegetables." (False judgments are judgments too.)

The mind's act of judgment, expressed in the logical structure called a "proposition" and in the linguistic structure called a "declarative sentence," always has two parts, for it relates to each other two concepts which are expressed in two terms and two words or phrases. One is the "subject" and the other is the "predicate.".

The **subject** is what we are talking about. The **predicate** is what we say about it.

It is easy to identify the subject and predicate of a proposition if you know grammar. For the logical subject and predicate are always the same as the grammatical subject and predicate.

The subject and predicate of a proposition are not interchangeable, like the two parts of an equation on the two sides of the equal sign. "2+2=4" means the same thing as "4=2+2"; but "God is love" does not mean the same thing as "Love is God." There is no subject or predicate in an equation, but there is always a subject and a predicate in a proposition, and they perform different functions.

To see this, remember that a declarative sentence is an act of communication between two people, the speaker (or writer) and the listener (or reader). What the speaker says to the listener in a proposition is this: I am going to say something about subject S. I assume you already know something about S; that you know what S means. S is old, S is behind us. And now I am going on to something new, I will say something new about S, I will predicate (affirm or deny) P of S. Perhaps you did not know before that S is P. In other words, S is my "sermon topic" and P is my "sermon." S is my title and P is my essay.

Thus "God is love" means: "I will tell you something new or remarkable or worth saying about God – the God I assume you know something about already. And what I will tell you is that God is love." This is news. This is controversial, and arguable. This may be true or it may be false. But whether it is true or false, its meaning is not the same as the meaning of "Love is God." "Love is God" means: "I will tell you something about love, the love you already know (presumably the human love we all experience): this is God, this is ultimate reality, seek no further. That is my news, that is my controversial and arguable sermon." You can see that these two propositions, "God is love" and "Love is God," say something very different, in fact two different religions. The first is a form of Theism, the second is a form of Humanism. No matter which of these two may be true or false, they mean very different things. Perhaps both are true (though they seem to contradict each other), perhaps both are false (some atheists would say so), perhaps the first is true and the second is false (most theists would say so), and perhaps the first is false and the second is true (most humanists would say so); but they are different propositions.

The Kinds of Propositions

We have been speaking only of **simple propositions**, with one subject and one predicate. These are called **categorical propositions** in logic. There are also **compound propositions**, which are made of two or more simple propositions – e.g. "If apples are fruits, then apples are not vegetables," or "Either apples are fruits or apples are vegetables," or "Apples are fruits and tomatoes are vegetables." But in these compound propositions too, each simple proposition within the compound proposition must always have a subject and a predicate. We will study compound propositions a few chapters later. There are three kinds: **hypothetical** ("if . . . then . . ."), **disjunctive** ("either . . . or . . ."), and **conjunctive** ("both . . . and . . ." or "not both . . . and . . .").

Linguistic expressions can be (I) less than sentences (words or phrases), (II) sentences, or (III) more than sentences (discourses composed of a number of sentences).

Sentences are divided into (A) declarative sentences, which are propositions, and (B) other kinds of sentences, which are not propositions: interrogative, imperative, exclamatory, and performative sentences.

Propositions are divided into (1) simple (also called "categorical") propositions and

(2) compound propositions.

Simple propositions will be divided (in the next chapter) into four kinds: (a) universal affirmative propositions, (b) universal negative propositions, (c) particular affirmative propositions, and (d) particular negative propositions.

Compound propositions will be divided into (a) hypothetical ("if . . . then . . .") propositions, (b) disjunctive ("either . . . or . . .") propositions, and (c) conjunctive ("both . . . and . . ." or "not both . . . and . . .") propositions.

The following outline should help to orient us, like a wide-ranging road map:

Linguistic expressions:
I. Less than sentences (terms)
II. Sentences
    A. Declarative sentences (propositions)
      1. Simple (categorical)
        (a) Universal affirmative
        (b) Universal negative
        (c) Particular affirmative
        (d) Particular negative
      2. Compound
        (a) Hypothetical
        (b) Disjunctive
        (c) Conjunctive
    B. Non-declarative sentences
      1. imperative
      2. interrogative
      3. exclamatory
      4. performative
III. More than sentences (arguments)

There are other possible divisions of propositions. The most important division of all is the division into true and false. Each kind of proposition above can be either true or false. We may not *know* whether a given proposition is true or false, but *every proposition must be either true or false.* Either there are exactly 91,199 craters on the moon larger than Meteor Crater in Arizona, or not. Either the Chicago Cubs are under a curse, and will never win a World Series until the end of the world, or not.

Because we sometimes do and sometimes do not know whether a proposition is true or false, we can also divide propositions into *three* kinds, (a) true (i.e. known to be true), (b) false (i.e. known to be false), and (c) unknown. This division violates one of the rules of logical division, since it simultaneously uses two standards: true vs. false and known vs. unknown. (See p. 64, rule 3.) However, in dealing with the Square of Opposition (Chapter VII, Section 2) the classification of propositions into true, false, and unknown, which results from doing two different divisions at once, is very useful and time-saving.

Aristotelian vs. Modern Logic on What Propositions Do

What, exactly, does a proposition do? It affirms or denies one term (the predicate) of another (the subject). It asserts that all or some of the subject is or is not the predicate.

There are two ways to look at this. Modern logic texts look at it in terms of extension, and of class inclusion. This is why they call simple propositions "categorical" propositions: because they relate two "categories" to each other. In modern logic, "categories" is meant in the broad sense of *any* classes or sets of things. But in traditional, Aristotelian logic, "categories" is meant in the more restricted sense explained above in Chapter II, Section 2 (page 54). In Aristotelian logic, categories are objectively real kinds, not man-made sets; natural rather than artificial.

They are not just any classes but only the ten highest genera (substance, quality, quantity, relation, time, place, action, passion, posture, possession). But in modern logic, any things in the world can simply be classified at will into mental boxes, and then those boxes are compared as to population (extension, not comprehension). Thus in modern logic "all men are mortal" means "the set of beings that we classify as men is included in the larger set of beings that we classify as mortals." This is a perfectly legitimate thing to do, but in Aristotelian logic a proposition does more than that. It deals also with the real natures of things, our knowledge of these natures, and the expression of that knowledge and those natures in the meanings (comprehension) of terms. Thus "all men are mortal" means that all beings that have the essence of humanity have the property of mortality as part of that essence, or a consequence of that essence.

The two significant differences here are (1) that modern logic deals with extension, not comprehension; class inclusion, not essences or natures of things; because it tends to be nominalistic and skeptical of "essences" or "natures" (see pages 19–23 and 43–46); and (2) that in modern logic these "classes" of things that are related in a proposition as subject and predicate are thought to be constructed rather than discovered. They are created by our act of classifying, for whatever purposes we may have. Modern logic manipulates class concepts; traditional logic explores the natures of things.

Section 2. What is truth? (P)

Truth is the point and purpose and goal of propositions. But what is truth?

This question "What is truth?" is really one of the easiest of all philosophical questions to answer. We all know what truth is, and where it is. The difficult thing is not to define or locate truth, but to pursue it and find it. Truth is like a Siberian tiger: we all know what Siberian tigers are and where they live, but actually hunting and capturing one is disconcertingly difficult.

Let us begin with the question of *where* truth is. Where does truth live? What is the house of truth? What sort of things can have "truth"?

We say certain "ideas" are true or false or that certain "thoughts" are true or false. The words "ideas" and "thoughts" are rather vague and generic, and from a logical point of view we must distinguish three different kinds of "ideas" or "thoughts," namely the three acts of the mind (conceiving, judging, and reasoning), their three mental products (concepts, judgments, and arguments), their three logical expressions (terms, propositions, and syllogisms), and their three linguistic expressions (words or phrases, declarative sentences, and paragraphs). Truth and falsity reside only in the second of each of these sets of three things.

As we have already seen, truth does not reside in concepts or in arguments but only in judgments. The terms that express concepts are either unambiguous or ambiguous, but never true or false. Only when two terms are combined in a proposition can there be truth or falsity. The syllogisms that express arguments are either logically valid or invalid, but never true or false. Each proposition in a syllogism is either true or false, but the syllogism as a whole is not.

Modern logic obscures this distinction because it reduces *validity* to *truth*. It interprets a syllogism like "all A is B and all B is C, therefore all A is C" as simply the claim that the following proposition is true: "All cases of proposition p (that all A is B) being true together with proposition q (that all B is C) being true are also cases of proposition c (that all A is C) being true."

Truth does not reside in any other *logical* entities than propositions, but it does reside elsewhere than in propositions. For example, we use the word "true" to refer to a quality that resides in some *things*, insofar as they conform to a standard by which the mind judges them. We say "This is true money, but that is counterfeit." "This is a true (original) Van Gogh, but that a copy." "The publican had true piety, but the Pharisee had false piety." "He is true to his promises." "What the prophet says will come true." This kind of truth – the truth in things, ontological truth – is *the conformity of the thing to the mind*, to an idea or design or standard in a mind, human or divine; whereas logical truth, i.e. propositional truth, as we shall see, is *the conformity of the mind to the thing*.

According to religious Judaism, Christianity, and Islam, the ultimate "house of truth" is the mind of God. God *invents* the truth of the universe, as His art; man *discovers* it, as his science. Human science is the indirect reading of the divine mind.

We also use the word "true" to refer to a quality that resides in *persons*, insofar as they are authentic, reliable, and honest. "He's a true man; she's a true woman." "True" here means "true to his word, trustable, faithful." (There is a distinctive Hebrew word for this: *emeth*.) *God* is called "faithful and true" (*emeth*) in the Hebrew scriptures.

Once we have our answer to *where* truth is, it becomes easier to answer our second question, *what* truth is, especially if we confine our answer to *logical* truth. Aristotle defined truth, and what everyone does in fact mean by truth, in the most simple and commonsensical possible way when he said, "If a man says of what is that it is, or of what is not that it is not, he speaks the truth, but if he says of what is not that it is, or of what is that it is not, he does not speak the truth." There you have it: the answer to "What is truth?" in one 48-word sentence, and not one word of more than one syllable! The ability to speak advanced wisdom in words of one syllable is a true test of a philosopher, or at least a good philosophy teacher. As G.K. Chesterton says, "Most of the machinery of modern language is labour-saving machinery; and it saves mental labour very much more than it ought. . . . Long words go rattling by us like long railway trains. . . . It is a good exercise to try for once to express any opinion one holds in words of one syllable. If you say, 'The social utility of the indeterminate sentence is recognized by all criminologists as a part of our sociological evolution towards a more humane and scientific view of punishment,' you can go on talking like that for hours with hardly a movement of the gray matter inside your skull. But if you begin 'I wish Jones to go to gaol [jail] and Brown to say when Jones shall come out,' you will discover, with a thrill of horror, that you are obliged to think." (*Orthodoxy*)

Telling the truth means "telling it like it is," and knowing the truth means "knowing what is." Truth is the conformity of thought to thing, mind to reality, thought's subject to thought's object. And we express what-is in true *propositions* (and what-is-not in false propositions).

Even if you say (as some philosophers do) that truth is what works (Pragmatism), or that truth is the ontological size of an idea (Monism), or that truth is the coherence of an idea with other ideas (Idealism), you are still always presupposing Aristotle's commonsensical definition (often called "the correspondence theory of truth") by saying that this (your definition) is *in fact* what truth really is; you are trying to "tell it like it is": that truth *really is* what works, or ontological size, or coherence.

A technical point, but an important one: to speak accurately, Aristotle's theory is more sophisticated than the one modern philosophers often call the "correspondence theory" [usually associated with Locke]. Locke's is a "picture theory" while Aristotle's is a "formal identity theory." Locke believed that our ideas are *copies* of reality and that what we know immediately and first of all is our own ideas. This logically leads to skepticism [though Locke did not draw this consequence], for if we never know reality directly and immediately, we can never be sure which pictures of it truly correspond to it and which do not. In contrast, Aristotle taught that the very same identical "form" or essence [e.g. appleness] that exists in reality [in the apple] materially and individually and concretely, is abstracted by the mind and exists in the mind immaterially and universally and abstractly.)

Section 3. The four kinds of categorical propositions (B)

Every proposition has a **matter**, or content, and a **form**. The matter of a proposition is its two terms, its subject term and its predicate term. The content of these two terms is almost infinitely variable. Propositions can say anything about anything. But the *form* of a simple (categorical) proposition consists in only two variables: the "**quantity**" and the "**quality**."

The "quantity" of a proposition means how much of the subject we are talking about, *all* or *some*. The quantity is either **universal** (all) or **particular** (some).

The "quality" of the proposition means whether it is **affirmative** or **negative**, whether the predicate is affirmed of the subject or denied of the subject.

The "matter," then, is the two terms, and the "form" tells how these two terms (the subject and the predicate) are related to each other.

Since a proposition can be either universal or particular in quantity and either affirmative or negative in quality, there are four possibilities:

A: universal affirmative propositions (e.g. "All men are mortal.")
E: universal negative propositions (e.g. "No men are mortal.")
I: particular affirmative propositions (e.g. "Some men are mortal.")
O: particular negative propositions (e.g. "Some men are not mortal.")

The four logical forms of categorical propositions are called A, E, I, and O for short. This tradition comes from medieval Latin: A and I are the first two vowels in the Latin word *affirmo*, which means "I affirm." An A proposition is universal and affirmative (all S is P) and an I proposition is particular and affirmative (some S is P). E and O are the first two vowels in the Latin word *nego*, which means "I deny." An E proposition is universal and negative (no S is P), and an O proposition is particular and negative (some S is not P).

Singular Propositions

There are really six kinds of propositions rather than four because there are really three kinds of quantity: universal, particular, and singular. **Singular propositions** do not talk about either all of a class *or* some of a class because they do not talk about a class at all, but about an individual. E.g. "Socrates was bald," or "The next sound you hear will be the hyena." Since we cannot divide the extension of a concrete individual thing or person, as we can divide the extension of a class, there can never be a singular proposition that begins with "some." That is, *singular* propositions are not *particular* propositions. The terminology of logic at this point can be misleading, since in ordinary language "particular" has two meanings: "some members of this class" and "this one concrete individual." In logic we use "particular" only in the first sense.

Instead of treating singular propositions as a third kind of quantity, neither universal nor particular, we can treat them all as universal propositions, since they always refer to all of the individual they refer to. An individual cannot be divided. "Socrates is mortal" means "Socrates as a whole is mortal, all Socrates is mortal." (You might think that only part of Socrates is mortal since his body can die but his soul cannot. But even so, the concrete individual person Socrates, who has both a body and a soul, is mortal, i.e. can die, because his body and soul can be divided from each other.) So we will not need six forms of propositions (universal affirmative, universal negative, particular affirmative, particular negative, singular affirmative, and singular negative) but only four, since we can treat singular propositions as universal propositions.

Only Four Forms of Propositions

We also need not subdivide particular propositions, though we could. More precise specifications of "some," such as "most" and "many," can all be included under "particular," rather than multiplying the forms of propositions to more than four.

There is an immense advantage in reducing all simple propositions to only these four forms. For if we have only four forms, we have a very limited number of possibilities for combinations and relations among them, and thus we have only a small number of simple rules about them. Fitting the infinitely varied content of ordinary-language propositions into one of four and only four logical forms is like fitting millions of soldiers into only four ranks, or millions of people into only four sizes of T-shirts. It is a "Procrustean bed."

The price we have to pay for this simplification is that just as some people just don't fit into Small, Medium, Large, or Extra Large T-shirts, some parts of the meaning of some ordinary-language propositions occasionally cannot be put into the simplified scheme of four forms. Sometimes this missing meaning can be put into the matter, or content, and sometimes it has to be ignored and omitted for the time being. The two most usual losses are "certainly" vs. "probably" and "many" vs. "few." For instance, in the proposition "Man is certainly mortal," "certainly" is not part of the subject or the predicate, but expresses the necessity of the relationship between man and mortality. This is dealt with in an advanced form of logic called "modal logic," but not here in this elementary treatment. "Only a few men are heroes" loses part of its meaning (the specification of quantity) when translated into "some men are heroes" or into "some men are not heroes," or even into both.

Section 4. Logical form (B)

We need to translate or re-express ordinary language propositions into a stricter logical form for two reasons: (1) to more clearly understand what they say and (2) to calculate whether arguments that contain these propositions are valid or invalid.

All propositions must fit into one of the four following molds:

(1) Universal affirmative (A) proposition: All [S] is [P]
(2) Universal negative (E) proposition: No [S] is [P]
(3) Particular affirmative (I) proposition: Some [S] is [P]
(4) Particular negative (O) proposition: Some [S] is not [P]

Here are a few examples of the difference between ordinary language and logical form.

Ordinary language: "Birds fly."
Logical form: All [birds] are [things that fly]

Ordinary language: "Absolute perfection no mortal will ever attain."
Logical form: No [mortals] are [ones who will ever attain absolute perfection]

Ordinary language: "Not all is gold that glitters."
Logical form: Some [that which glitters] is not [gold]

Before you have taken a logic course it is almost impossible to understand why it is so important to put propositions into such strict logical form. It seems clumsy, artificial, and "picky." Why then must we use logical form? The usefulness of logical form is similar to the usefulness of numbers. Once things are reduced to quantity, many calculations can be made about them with great efficiency, clarity, and certainty. It is similar to the binary, zero-sum language of computers: translating everything into this digital format gives us great power and efficiency in calculating. (Symbolic logic is *all* calculating; Aristotelian logic, however, is not *no* calculating.) In a much more modest way, once we (1) separate the form from the matter by putting the matter inside the square brackets, and (2) reduce the forms of propositions into four and only four, we can then calculate many things on the basis of the form alone.

For instance, once we reduce "all men are mortal," and "all pigs are green" to the same form, the "universal affirmative" proposition **All [S] is [P]**, we can then tell that the argument "All pigs are green and all philosophers are pigs, therefore all philosophers are green" is logically valid, formally valid, even though all of its propositions are false. It has the exact same logical form as the argument "All men are mortal, and all Greek philosophers are men, therefore all Greek philosophers are mortal," all of whose propositions are true.

When we determine whether an argument is logically valid or invalid (in Part III), we do so on the basis of the form alone, abstracted from the truth of the content or matter. In order to do that, we need to distinguish the form and the matter, by translating the ordinary language propositions into logical form, so that we can see these two things, the form and the matter, distinctly. Once a proposition is in logical form, we can see at a glance what is its matter and what is its form. For logical form puts all its matter, its content, i.e. the subject and predicate terms, inside square brackets and puts all its form outside the brackets.

In order to put all the complex variety of ordinary language propositions into only four rigid logical forms, leaving no room for variation, all the variation has to go into the matter, the S and P terms inside the brackets. It is an enormously efficient simplification.

Though it seems "picky," it is important to use brackets when writing propositions in logical form – much more important than you probably think. *If you "cheat" and drop them, you will almost inevitably make many sloppy mistakes later.* Insistence on being careful about this tiny and nitpicking detail will probably make a surprising difference in clarity later in dealing with complex arguments. They are like curbs at the sides of streets or frames around pictures.

We have *four* forms because we have two variables with two possibilities for each: two possible quantities (universal or particular) and two possible qualities (affirmative or negative).

The **quantity** is indicated by the **quantifier**, which is the word before the subject in logical form. "All" and "No" are universal quantifiers; "Some" is the particular quantifier.

The other variable in a proposition's form is the **quality**: a simple proposition is either *affirmative* or *negative*, depending on whether it *affirms* its predicate of its subject (S *is* P) or *denies* its predicate of its subject (S is *not* P).

The quality is indicated by the **copula**, which is the "is" or "is not" (for singular subjects), "are" or "are not" (for plural subjects). The copula comes between the subject and the predicate in logical form.

No other verb can be a copula, only "is" or "is not" (or "are" or "are not.") The copula is almost more like an equal sign than like a word; it expresses the relation between the subject and the predicate, as an equal sign expresses the relationship between the two sides of an equation. However, remember that in ordinary language "is" does *not* mean the same thing as an equal sign: see above, page 140, "Subject and Predicate."

When the main verb of an ordinary-language proposition is "is," that verb can be used as the copula in our logical-form translation of the proposition. But when the main verb is not "is" (or "is not"), we need to insert an "is" into the logical form to make the copula. Every logical-form proposition needs a copula, and no other word is allowed as the copula, for that would give us more than two copulas and thus more than four forms, and that would make subsequent calculations based on the form alone much more complex.

So "Some men are mortal" translates word for word into logical form, but "A few bad apples corrupt the whole barrel" does not. "A few" becomes "some," and "corrupts the whole barrel" becomes the predicate. ("Corrupts" is not a copula; it is part of the predicate term.) But if we were then simply to insert the affirmative copula, we would get the grammatically unintelligible "Some bad apples are corrupts the whole barrel." What can we do to amend that?

Here is what we must do. In strict logical form, each term, predicate as well as subject, needs to be a noun, a noun phrase, or a pronoun. The reason for this is so that each term can be independent, and shift positions if necessary, from subject to predicate or from predicate to subject. (And this will be necessary later, when dealing with arguments.) But a verb or an adjective cannot be a subject. Only a noun (or a noun phrase or a pronoun) can be a subject. Since every predicate must be able to be used also as a subject, it must be changed into a noun. So "corrupts the whole barrel" is changed into *"that which* corrupts the whole barrel."

We will be using "that which" so often in this way that it is convenient to use the abbreviation "tw" for it. We need to add "that which" before a verb, when the predicate is a verb, and "that which is," or "twi," before an adjective, when the predicate is an adjective. But we do not need to use "twi" before a term that is *already* a noun.

IF PREDICATE IS . . .	USE . . .
a verb e.g. "X grows y"	tw (that which) All [X] is [tw grows y]
an adjective e.g. "X is large"	twi (that which is) All [X] is [twi large]

When translating from ordinary language to logical form, the basic and universal rule is that *we may change the wording if necessary but never the meaning.* When we change "A few apples corrupt the whole barrel" to "Some [apples] are [that which corrupt the whole barrel]," we have changed the wording (in two places) to get the proposition into logical form, but we have not changed the meaning.

Existential propositions. Some propositions do not relate two terms, subject and predicate, but simply assert the existence of the subject: e.g. "God is," or "Santa Claus doesn't exist," or "There are four kinds of propositions." When we say "God is," we are not using "is" as a copula, for there is no predicate after it, but we are using it to assert existence and deny nonexistence. The simplest way to treat existential propositions at this point is to reduce them to standard-form propositions with "that which exists" as their predicate. However, if we get into more advanced logic we will see that these existential propositions have importantly different meanings and obey different rules than others.

So the four (and only four) strict logical forms for all simple propositions are:

A: All [S] is [P]
E: No [S] is [P]
I: Some [S] is [P]
O: Some [S] is not [P]

The Ambiguity of "All S is not P"

The form for the E, "No S is P," does not begin with either "all" or "some" but with "no." The word "no" does double duty: it indicates both universality of quantity and negativity of quality. Thus in the logical form for the E, the apparently-affirmative copula "is" is really negative.

Why don't we use "all S is not P" for our logical form for the E proposition? That would conform to the form of the other three kinds of propositions, where the only quantifiers are "all" or "some" and where "is" is always the affirmative copula while "is not" is always the negative copula.

The answer is that in the English language, "all S is not P" is ambiguous. It has two very different meanings. Only one of these two meanings is that of an E proposition, that every S fails to be a P. The other meaning of "All S is not P" is, very strangely, that *some* S is not P. In the ordinary English that we all speak every day without thinking about it, "*all* S is not P" often means "*some* S is not P."

This sounds confusing or even ridiculous only in a logic course; outside the classroom we all understand it intuitively without hesitation. When I say, "*All* lawyers are not crooks," I am not saying that no lawyers are crooks. I am responding to a prior assertion or belief, implied or expressed, that all lawyers are crooks, and I am denying that. How do I deny the idea that all lawyers are crooks? There are three ways to express this denial:

(1) I can say "Some lawyers are not crooks."
(2) I can say "Not all lawyers are crooks."
(3) I can say "*All* lawyers are not crooks."

In the first case, my proposition is a straightforward O proposition.

In the second case, I insert a "not" before "all lawyers are crooks." "Not all lawyers are crooks" means "It's not true that all lawyers are crooks." If I can find some lawyers who are not crooks, I have disproved the idea that all lawyers are crooks. But instead of saying "some lawyers are not crooks," I express the very same meaning in these different words: I say, "Not all lawyers are crooks." This is really an O proposition, and we can call it the "tricky O" proposition. It is an O that looks a bit like an E.

The third case is even trickier, because it looks even more like an E, and can be called the "very tricky O." When I accent the "all" in "*all* lawyers are not crooks," I mean the same thing as in the two cases above. The meaning is an O.

So we need one totally unambiguous logical form for the E proposition, and "all S is not P" is not unambiguous (since it may mean either the E or the "very tricky O"), so we use the unambiguous "no S is P" instead.

The logical form for an O proposition is "some S is not P," and this can also be ambiguous if we *accent* the word "some," thereby implying that "some *and only some* S is not P." We do not use accents, or anything ambiguous, in logical form. *In logical form, "some" does not mean "only some," or "some but not all"* (we could call this *the strong meaning of "some"*) but *"at least some"* (we could call this *the weak meaning of "some"*).

Section 5. Euler's Circles (B)

Euler's Circles are a useful visual image for the four kinds of categorical propositions. They were invented by the 18th-century Swiss mathematician Leonhard Euler, who drew four different circle diagrams for the four different kinds of propositions to show the different relations between S and P that each of these four assert. These circles are useful both for understanding just what is asserted by each of the four kinds of propositions and also for a very quick and easy way of checking syllogisms for validity (page 237).

Interpreting the Four Forms

Just what does each of these four propositions mean?

The A proposition affirms that every S is a P, that all S's are P's, that if it's S it must be P. In terms of comprehension, the A proposition means that P is part of the meaning of S. In terms of extension, the A proposition asserts that the whole class of S's, or the whole population of S's, is included in the class of P's. To understand "all stallions are horses," imagine the population of each term inside a fenced-in corral. "All stallions are horses" asserts that the corral containing stallions is contained by the corral containing horses. The circumference of the circles are like the fences around the corrals.

A:

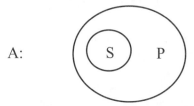

The particular affirmative proposition (I) asserts that some S is P. In terms of comprehension, this means that P is part of the meaning of some S's. In terms of extension, it means that some S's are included in the class of P's.

Remember that "some" here does *not* mean "some *and only some, but not all.*" It means simply "some," that is, "*at least* some," or "some and *perhaps* all, but perhaps not." When you say "some" in logic, you do not commit yourself to either "all" or "not all." You do not "read between the lines." "Some" means simply "some" and nothing more, in logical form.

But if someone else has *accented* the word "some" in ordinary language, this implies "*only* some," or "some *and not all.*" When someone says, "Well, *some* lawyers are honest," he implies that only some but not all lawyers are honest. In ordinary language the main thrust of "*Some* lawyers are honest" (with an accented "some") is really negative, though it looks like an I. This ambiguity could be classified under the "fallacy of accent." (See above, page 75.) The only way to reveal the negative aspect is to add a second proposition, an O, So the sentence "*Some* lawyers are honest" with accent is really equivalent to "Some lawyers are honest (I) *and* Some lawyers are not honest (O)."

The Euler diagram for an I proposition puts part of the S circle, or S class, into P, and leaves the rest of it in dotted lines outside P. The dotted lines signify the unknown. When we know only that "some S is P," we know only that some S is within P, we do not know whether or not some S is also outside P. But we make room for that possibility by the dotted lines.

I:

The universal negative proposition (E) asserts that no S is P. In terms of comprehension, P does not belong to S; in terms of extension, the populations of P and S exclude each other, so that there is nothing that is a member of both classes, S and P. Thus the circles are exclusive, neither inclusive, as with an A proposition, nor partly overlapping, as with an I proposition.

E:

The Euler diagram for an O puts *part* of the class (or circle) of S outside P (i.e. in "*not*-P"), but leaves the other part dotted, or unknown. If we know only that "some S is *not* P" (i.e. that some S is outside P), we do not know whether or not it is also true that some S *is* P (i.e. that some S is also inside P).

O: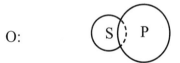

Section 6. Tricky propositions

Besides the "tricky O," there are other forms of propositions that are tricky:

Exclusive propositions begin with the word "only." The main thrust of such propositions is negative, even though there is no "no" in the ordinary language. The "only" functions negatively. E.g. "Only men are allowed into the men's room" means not merely that all men are allowed into the men's room, or that some men are allowed into the men's room, but that no one but men is allowed into the men's room, that no non-men are allowed into the men's room.

There are two equally good ways to translate an exclusive proposition: (1) we could translate "Only men are allowed into the men's room" into "No non-men are allowed into the men's room," in the form of an E proposition; (2) or we can translate it into an A proposition as follows: "Only men are allowed into the men's room" becomes "All who are allowed into the men's room are men." "Only S is P" can be reworded as "All P is S." The rule is always that we may change the wording but never the meaning.

Another, different kind of exclusive proposition begins not with "only" but with "*the* only." These are easy to reword. "The only S is P" means simply "All S is P." ("The only" = "all.") E.g. "The only good Yankee is a dead Yankee" means that "All good Yankees are dead Yankees." "The only ones allowed into the men's room are men" means "All who are allowed into the men's room are men."

Exceptive propositions begin with "all except. . . ." These propositions really say *two* things and should be translated into two propositions. "All humans except the first humans had human parents" means both that "All humans who were not the first humans had human parents" and that "The first humans did not have human parents." "Every animal except man lacks reason" means both that "All non-human animals lack reason" and that "Man does not lack reason."

Indesignate propositions. Some propositions have no words to indicate quantity, and we have to intuit whether they are meant as universal or particular. E.g. "people are fickle," or "cliffs are dangerous," or "fans swarmed the field." Clearly, "cliffs are dangerous" is an A and "fans swarmed the field" is an I, but "people are fickle" might be meant either universally ("All people are fickle") or particularly ("Some people are fickle"); it is hard to tell which. One helpful rule here is that if the predicate belongs to the subject by nature (or essentially), the proposition is universal; if only by accident, the proposition is particular. Thus cliffs are by nature dangerous, and since all cliffs have the nature of cliffs, all cliffs are dangerous. But fans do not swarm the field by nature, just because they are fans, so that proposition is particular. As to "People are fickle," if "fickle" means "somewhat fickle" or "capable of being fickle," this belongs to man by nature and thus to all men, so the proposition is universal; but if "fickle" means "very fickle" or "surprisingly fickle" or "unusually fickle," this is accidental and the proposition is particular.

So to decide whether indesignate propositions are universal or particular, we must look at the comprehension. If the predicate belongs to the subject necessarily, because of the nature of the subject as such, it is universal; if not, it is particular. Thus the meaning of maxims like "Great books deserve to be taught" is universal, while the meaning of rough generalizations like "White men can't dance" is not.

Note that we are only speaking of *meaning* here, not *truth*. Do not try to determine the meaning of someone else's proposition by imposing what you believe is true onto it. That would be confusing *interpretation* (of what the proposition means) with *belief* (what you think is true). (See page 355, point A.)

More specific quantifiers: Sometimes, we cannot fit all the quantitative meaning into our strict logical form. "A few," "many," "most," "a small quantity of" and "a fairly large percentage of" all have to become "some." What do we do with exact numbers, e.g. "Three ships took Columbus to America"? "Three" cannot become "all"; and we cannot have more than two quantities, "all" and "some," or else we would multiply our logical forms so much that we could not make simple rules about them, as we will be doing for the rest of the book. We could just say "Some" instead of "three," but that would lose an important part of the meaning. So it is best to put exact numbers into the matter or content of the term, with an "all" added: e.g. "Three ships took Columbus to America" becomes: "All [three ships] are [tw took Columbus to America]."

"Few" vs. "A few": Propositions beginning with "a few" are straightforward I propositions, but propositions beginning with "few" are usually O propositions, because their main intent is negative. "Few Hittites could read" means to say something about Hittite illiteracy more than Hittite literacy, so it is best to translate it as "some Hittites are those who could not read." Yet it seems to imply that *some* Hittites *could* read, so it also implies an I. It is really *two* propositions.

Other quantifiers: sentences beginning with "every," "each," "everyone," "anyone," "whoever," "any," "everything," "one who," "that which," "anything," and the like are obviously universal. Sentences beginning with "a few," "few," "many," "most," "a group of," and the like are particular.

Temporal quantifiers. Sometimes time words do the job of quantifiers, "never" indicating an E, "always" an A, and "sometimes" or "occasionally" an I or an O. E.g. "Hyenas never really laugh" becomes "No [hyena] is [tw really laughs]" and "Water is always H_2O" becomes "All [water] is [H_2O]." But sometimes the temporal word is part of the meaning of a term, e.g. "Socrates is the philosopher I always teach first to beginners."

Compound propositions. We do not have strict logical forms for compound propositions yet, and the forms we will use for them are more symbolic and quasi-mathematical than those for simple propositions. (In fact, symbolic logic is much more useful there than Aristotelian logic.) But even at this point we should be able to recognize them, their distinction from simple propositions, and the three kinds of them: hypothetical ("if . . . then . . .") propositions, disjunctive ("either . . . or . . .") propositions, and conjunctive ("both . . . and . . ." or "not both . . . and . . .") propositions.

When a single compound sentence contains more than one simple proposition without being either hypothetical or disjunctive, it is usually conjunctive: e.g. "To be a philosopher is not merely to have subtle thoughts, nor even to found a school, but so to love wisdom as to live according to its dictates." (Thoreau, *Walden*)

Exercises: Identify each of the following as (a) not a proposition at all, (b) a simple (categorical) proposition, or (c) a compound proposition. If it is a simple proposition, put it into strict logical form.

The clearest way to do this is in three steps:

First, decide whether it is a proposition.

Second, if it is, decide whether it is an A, E, I, or O.

Third, write down the logical form for whichever type of proposition you have decided it is, A, E, I, or O, with the brackets empty.

Fourth, put the words for the subject and the predicate into the brackets.

There is a veritable plethora of exercises here, as there were for definitions and as there will also be for enthymemes (abbreviated syllogisms: page 264), since these are the three most useful and basic exercises in logic, one for each of the three acts of the mind. To do the basics well is more useful than to do everything else but to do it poorly; and you learn to do the basics well only by habit, which comes from much practice. Most of the 174 propositions that follow are a treasure trove of wisdom as well as good exercise.

A. Some relatively easy propositions:
  1. Some sentences can't be classified as any kind of proposition at all.
  2. Every single person in this room and in the room next door too – you know, that big ugly room with the air conditioner in it.
  3. Come here, you ungrateful cur!
  4. Socrates was a philosopher.
  5. *All* philosophy professors aren't absent-minded.
  6. I itch.
  7. Nothing matters.
  8. Everything except the observer of every thing in the universe is a thing in the universe.
  9. Mad Cow Disease is no myth.
  10. Some gamblers are just lucky and some aren't.
  11. The fish does not exist that I can't catch.
  12. Alexander the Great was Aristotle's student.
  13. Not one of the Greeks at Thermopylae escaped.
  14. Everyone who knows that everyone is a fraud, is a fraud.
  15. Not everyone worth meeting is worth befriending.

B. Some famous quotations:
  1. "Many a wit is not a whit wittier than Whittier."
  2. "Charity begins at home."
  3. "A thousand Swedes ran through the reeds chasing one Norwegian."
  4. "I hereby dub thee Knight of the Round Table."
  5. "Every little breeze seems to whisper 'Louise'."
  6. "Halt! Who goes there?"
  7. "I love you."
  8. "If you continue to turn the crank of that torture rack, you will in all probability detach all four of my limbs from their sockets."

9. "Black, black, black is the color of my true love's hair."
10. "He jests at scars who never felt a wound."
11. "No one is free who does not command himself."
12. "Every man is a good judge of his own interests."
13. "Familiarity breeds contempt."
14. "Loose lips sink ships."
15. "Damn the torpedoes; full speed ahead!"
16. "What this country needs is a good five cent cigar."
17. "A chicken in every pot."
18. "History never repeats itself."
19. "Happy the country that has no history."
20. (Chinese curse:) "May you live in interesting times."
21. "Now fades the world with all its glamour."
22. "What man has done, man can do."
23. "He who is not with me is against me."
24. "He who laughs last, laughs best."
25. "Uneasy lies the head that wears the crown."
26. "Nothing that is morally wrong can be politically right."

C. Quotations from the classics:
1. "They also serve who only stand and wait." (John Milton, "On His Blindness")
2. "A good talker, even more than a good orator, implies a good audience." (Leslie Stephens)
3. "None think the great unhappy but the great." (Edward Young)
4. "We make a ladder of our vices if we trample those same vices underfoot." (St. Augustine)
5. "No person except a natural born citizen shall be eligible to the office of President." (U.S. Constitution)
6. "Those who do not complain are never pitied." (Jane Austen)
7. "If an angel were to tell us anything of his philosophy, I believe many propositions would sound like 2 x 2 = 13." (George Lichetenberg)
8. "The world is a looking glass and gives back to every man the reflection of his own face." (William Makepeace Thackeray)
9. "No man can live without joy." (St. Thomas Aquinas)
10. "Only the adventurous can understand the greatness of the past." (Alfred North Whitehead)
11. "I know no thought that more wonderfully concentrates a man's mind than the thought that he must hang tomorrow morning." (Samuel Johnson)
12. "Born of the sun, they traveled a brief while toward the sun, and left the vivid air singed with their honour." (Stephen Spender)
13. "It is useless to attempt to reason a man out of a thing he was never reasoned into." (Jonathan Swift)

14. "Work is the curse of the drinking class." (George Bernard Shaw)
15. "Man is neither angel nor brute, and the unfortunate thing is that he who would act the angel acts the brute." (Pascal)
16. "Some books are to be tasted, others to be swallowed, and some few to be chewed and digested." (Francis Bacon)
17. "Abandon all hope, ye who enter here." (Dante)
18. "Cleopatra's nose: if it had been shorter, the whole history of the world would have been changed." (Pascal)
19. "The mass of men lead lives of quiet desperation." (Thoreau)
20. "All happy families resemble one another; every unhappy family is unhappy in its own fashion." (Tolstoy)
21. "For all have not the gift of martyrdom." (John Dryden)
22. "What is the use of running when you are on the wrong road?" (John Ray)
23. "Nothing is demonstrable unless the contrary implies a contradiction." (Hume)
24. "Either death is a state of nothingness and utter unconsciousness, or . . . there is a change and migration of the soul from this world to another." (Plato)
25. "The moving finger writes; and, having writ, moves on; not all your piety nor wit shall lure it back to cancel half a line, nor all your tears wash out a word of it." (Edward Fitzgerald) (There are 4 propositions here!)
26. "Twas brillig, and the slithy toves did gyre and gimble in the wabe; All mimsy were the borogoves, and the mome raths outgrabe." (Lewis Carroll)
27. "If thy Superior drawl or hesitate in his words, pretend not to help him out or prompt him." (*The School of Manners, or Rules for Children's Behaviour*, 1701)
28. "The only thing necessary for the triumph of evil is for good men to do nothing." (Edmund Burke)
29. "Industrious and intelligent boys who live in the country are mostly well up in the cunning art of catching small birds at odd times during the winter months." (*A Plain Cookery Book for the Working Classes* by Charles Elme Francatelli, 1861)
30. "Fear God. Honour the King. Reverence thy Parents. Submit to thy Superiors. Despise not thy inferiors. Be courteous with thy Equals. Pray daily and devoutly. Converse with the Good. Imitate not the wicked. Hearken to Instruction. Be desirous of Learning. Love the School. Be always cleanly. Study Vertue. Provoke no Body. Love thy Schoolfellows. Please thy Master. Let not play entice thee. Restrain thy Tongue. Covet future Honour, which only Vertue and Wisdom can procure. (*The School of Manners*, 1701)
31. "'Bah!' said Scrooge, 'Humbug!'" (Dickens)
32. "The silken, sad, uncertain rustling of each purple curtain thrilled me." (Edgar Allen Poe)

33. "In the beginning there was no baseball." (J.B. Phillips)
34. "I ain't ever had a job; I just always played baseball." (Leroy Robert "Satchel" Paige)
35. "God created man in his own image and man has been returning the compliment ever since." (George Bernard Shaw)
36. "Man was created a little lower than the angels, and has been getting a little lower ever since." (Josh Billings)
37. "Through love all things become lighter which understanding thought too heavy." (Hatif)
38. (An extremely difficult proposition to put into logical form is Churchill's famous praise of the pilots of the Royal Air Force): "Never has so much been owed by so many to so few."

D. From the *Dhammapada* (the sayings of Gautama Siddhartha, the Buddha)
   1. "Whatever we are is caused by what we think."
   2. "Speak or act with an impure mind, and trouble will follow you as the wheel follows the ox that draws the cart; speak or act with a pure mind, and happiness will follow you as your shadow."
   3. "In this world, hate never yet dispelled hate."
   4. "The fool who knows he is a fool is that much wiser; the fool who thinks he is wise is a fool indeed."
   5. "It is better to conquer yourself than to win a thousand battles."
   6. "Be quick to do good; if you are slow, the mind, delighting in mischief, will catch you."
   7. "He who seeks happiness by hurting those who seek happiness will never find happiness."
   8. "Hurt rebounds."
   9. "The world is on fire, and are you laughing? You are deep in the dark, and will you not seek light?"
   10. "An ignorant man is an ox; he grows in size, not wisdom."
   11. "Consider the world: a bubble, a mirage."
   12. "If you let go of winning and losing, you will find joy."
   13. "How easy it is to see your brother's faults, how hard to face your own."
   14. "The way is not in the sky, the way is in the heart."
   15. "The mind speaks but the body knows."

E. From Shakespeare
   1. "What's done cannot be undone." (*Macbeth* V ,1)
   2. "Sweet are the uses of adversity." (*As You Like It* II ,1)
   3. "All's Well That Ends Well" (title)
   4. "Cowards die many times before their deaths; the valiant never taste of death but once." (*Julius Caesar* II, 2)
   5. "Crabbed age and youth cannot live together." ("The Passionate Pilgrim")

6. "Fair is foul, and foul is fair." (*Macbeth* I, 1)

7. "Halt! Who goes there?" "Nay, answer me." (*Hamlet* I, 1)

8. "To thine own self be true, and it must follow, as the night the day, thou canst not then be false to any man." (*Hamlet* I, 3)

9. "Some rise by sin, and some by virtue fall." (*Measure for Measure* II, 1)

10. "Golden lads and girls all must, as chimney-sweepers, come to dust." ("Cymbeline" IV, 2)

11. "Ah, what a sign it is of evil life, where death's approach is seen so terrible!" (*Henry VI Part II*, III, 3)

12. "Our remedies oft in ourselves do lie, which we ascribe to heaven." (*All's Well That Ends Well* I, 1)

13. "How weary, stale, flat, and unprofitable seem to me all the uses of this world!" (*Hamlet* I, 2)

14. "Lord, what fools these mortals be!" (*A Midsummer Night's Dream* III, 2)

15. "The fool doth think he is wise, but the wise man knows himself to be a fool." (*As You Like It* V, 1)

16. "The course of true love never did run smooth." (*A Midsummer Night's Dream* I, 1)

17. (H) "In the most high and palmy state of Rome, a little ere the mightiest Julius fell, the graves stood tenantless, and the sheeted dead did squeak and gibber in the Roman streets." (*Hamlet* I, 1)

18. (H) "There are more things in heaven and earth than are dreamed of in your philosophy, Horatio." (*Hamlet* I, 1)

19. "If love be blind, love cannot hit the mark." (*Romeo and Juliet* II, 1)

20. "The man that hath no music in himself, nor is not moved with concord of sweet sounds, is fit for treasons, stratagems and spoils." (*The Merchant of Venice* V, 1)

21. "O that this too, too solid flesh would melt, thaw, and resolve itself into a dew! Or that the Everlasting had not fix'd His canon 'gainst self-slaughter!" (*Hamlet* I, 2)

22. "Angels and ministers of grace defend us!" (*Hamlet* I, 4)

23. "Something is rotten in the state of Denmark." (*Hamlet* I, 4)

24. "Who steals my purse steals trash." (*Othello* III, 3)

25. "Love's not Time's fool." (Sonnet 116)

26. "Once more unto the breach, dear friends, once more, or close the wall up with our English dead!" (*Henry V* III, 1)

27. "By the pricking of my thumbs, something wicked this way comes." (*Macbeth* IV, 1)

28. "A horse! A horse! My kingdom for a horse!" (*Richard III* V, 4)

29. "A rose by any other name would smell as sweet." (*Romeo and Juliet* II, 2)

30. "The serpent that did sting thy father's life now wears his crown." (*Hamlet* I, 5)
31. "If this be error and upon me proved, I never writ, nor no man ever loved." (Sonnet 116)
32. "For sweetest things turn sourest by their deeds; lilies that fester smell far worse than weeds." (Sonnet 94)
33. "Had I but served my God with half the zeal I served my King, He would not in mine age have left me naked to mine enemies." (*King Henry VIII* III, 2)
34. "For God's sake, let us sit upon the ground and tell sad stories of the death of kings." (*King Richard II* III, 2)
35. "Poor and content is rich, and rich enough." (*Othello* III, 3)
36. "If it be now, 'tis not to come; if it be not to come, it will be now; if it be not now, yet it will come." (*Hamlet* V, 2)
37. "A great while ago the world begun, with hey, ho! the wind and the rain." (*Twelfth Night* V, 1)
38. "To gild refined gold, to paint the lily . . . is wasteful and ridiculous excess." (*King John* IV ,2)
39. "All that glisters is not gold." (*The Merchant of Venice* II, 7)
40. "Not all the water in the rough, rude sea can wash the balm off from an anointed king." (*King Richard II* III, 2)
41. "That man that hath a tongue, I say, is no man if with his tongue he cannot win a woman." (*Two Gentlemen of Verona* III, 1)
42. "Now the hungry lion roars, and the wolf behowls the moon." (*A Midsummer Night's Dream* V, 1)
43. "O all you host of heaven! O earth! What else? And shall I couple hell? O, fie! Hold, hold, my heart; and you, my sinews, grow not instant old, but bear me stiffly up." (*Hamlet* I, 5)
44. "To be or not to be: that is the question." (*Hamlet* III, 1)
45. "My words fly up, my thoughts remain below; words without thoughts never to heaven go." (*Hamlet* III, 3)
46. "Alas, poor Yorick!" (*Hamlet* V, 1)
47. "To err is human; to forgive, divine." (though sometimes attributed to Shakespeare, this is really from Alexander Pope, *Essay on Criticism*)
48. "Horatio, I am dead." (*Hamlet* V, 2)
49. "Good night, sweet prince, and flights of angels sing thee to thy rest." (*Hamlet* V, 2)

F. From G.K. Chesterton:
   1. "As long as you have mystery, you have health; when you destroy mystery you create morbidity." (*Orthodoxy*)
   2. "Thoroughly worldly people never understand the world." (*Orthodoxy*)
   3. "If a thing is worth doing, it's worth doing badly."

4. "Men did not love Rome because she was great. She was great because they had loved her." (*Orthodoxy*)
5. "The man who makes a vow makes an appointment with himself at some distant time and place." ("A Defense of Rash Vows")
6. "A great classic means a book which one can praise without having read." ("Tom Jones and Morality")
7. "The only two things that can satisfy the soul are a person and a story; and even a story must be about a person." ("The Priest of Spring")
8. "Logic is a machine of the mind, and if it is used honestly it ought to bring out an honest conclusion." (*Varied Types*)
9. "There is a very real thing which may be called the love of humanity; in our time it exists almost entirely among what are called uneducated people, and it does not exist at all among the people who talk about it." (*Tremendous Trifles*)

G. From the Bible:
1. "No one can serve two masters. For either he will hate the one and love the other, or he will be devoted to the one and despise the other. You cannot serve God and mammon." (Matthew 6:24)
2. "Blessed are the poor in spirit." (Matthew 5:3)
3. "Great is Diana of the Ephesians!" (Acts 19:28)
4. (H) "If God so clothes the grass of the field, which today is alive and tomorrow is thrown into the oven, will he not much more clothe you, O men of little faith?" (Matthew 6:30)
5. "Those who take the sword shall perish by the sword." (Matthew 26:52)
6. "Whatever a man soweth, that shall he also reap." (Galatians 6:7)
7. "A soft answer turneth away wrath." (Proverbs 15:1)
8. "He who is not with me is against me." (Matthew 12:30)
9. "And at noon Elijah mocked them, saying, 'Cry aloud, for he is a god; either he is musing, or he has gone aside, or he is on a journey, or perhaps he is asleep and must be awakened.'" (I Kings 18:27)
10. "A good tree cannot bring forth evil fruit." (Matthew 7:18)
11. "Whoever brings back a sinner from the error of his way will save his soul from death and will cover a multitude of sins." (James 5:19)
12. "If I speak with the tongues of men and of angels but have not love, I am a noisy gong or a clanging cymbal." (I Corinthians 13:1)
13. "My beloved is mine, and I am his." (Song of Songs 2:16)
14. "Who is she that looketh forth as the morning, fair as the moon, clear as the sun, terrible as an army with banners?" (Song of Songs 6:10)
15. "Love is strong as death." (Song of Songs 8:6)

16. "O that his left hand were under my head and his right hand embracing me!" (Song of Songs 8:3)
17. "Some boast of chariots, some of horses, but we boast of the name of the Lord our God." (Psalm 20:7)
18. "All things work together for good for those who love God." (Romans 8:28)
19. "Even though I walk through the valley of the shadow of death, I fear no evil." (Psalm 23:4)

Section 7. The distribution of terms

Each term in a categorical proposition – the subject and the predicate – is either **distributed** or **undistributed**. A term is distributed if it is universal; that is, if the proposition claims to know something about *all* of the class of things referred to by the term. A term is "undistributed" if it is particular, i.e. if the proposition claims to know only about *some* of the class.

We need to know whether each term is distributed or undistributed in order to test arguments for validity (which we will learn in Chapter XI), since some of the rules for validity depend on the distribution of the terms. This knowledge is also illuminating for other reasons; e.g. it shows us that an E proposition claims the most knowledge because it distributes both its terms, and an I proposition claims the least because both its terms are undistributed.

It is very easy to see whether the subject term is distributed or undistributed, because once the proposition is in logical form the quantifier tells us this explicitly. The subject of a universal proposition (A or E) is always distributed (universal), and the subject of a particular proposition (I or O) is always undistributed (particular). When we say "all men are mortal," we are obviously claiming to know something about all men; when we say "some men are heroes," we are claiming to know something about only some men, not necessarily all.

The predicate term is also either distributed or undistributed, for we are claiming to know something about either all or some of the class of things referred to in that term. But there is no quantifier word ("all," "no," or "some") before the predicate to tell us, as there is before the subject. It is the copula, i.e. the quality of the proposition (affirmative or negative), that tells us the distribution of the predicate. (Remember, the copula in an E, "no S is P," is really negative even though it seems to be affirmative. It is written as "is" instead of "is not" because the initial "no" makes the copula to mean "is not." We would have used the form "all S is not P" for the E proposition if it were not for the confusion with the "very tricky O." See page 151 above.)

The predicate of an affirmative proposition is always undistributed; the predicate of a negative proposition is always distributed. That is the simple, universal rule.

			SUBJECT	PREDICATE
UNIVERSAL	affirmative	A:	Distributed	Undistributed
	negative	E:	Distributed	Distributed
PARTICULAR	affirmative	I:	Undistributed	Undistributed
	negative	O:	Undistributed	Distributed

Here is the explanation. An affirmative proposition *in*cludes its subject in its predicate, as can be seen from its diagram in Euler's circles. But when we include S in P, we include S in part of P, as we include a necklace in part of a jewelry box. This is true whether we are talking about all S (an A) or some S (an I). Whether it is a whole necklace or part of a necklace, we include it in part of the box. So we are referring to only part of the box, part of the predicate. An A or an I proposition claims to know only some of its predicate.

But a negative proposition *ex*cludes its subject from *all* of its predicate. "No S is P" means "No S is any kind of P at all." When we exclude a necklace from a jewelry box, we exclude it not only from one corner of the box, but from the whole box.

This is true even if the subject is only particular. In an O proposition ("some S is not P") the subject ("some S") is particular, but that particular part of S is excluded from *all* of P, like part of a necklace being excluded from all of the box.

It will be useful to symbolize the distribution of terms by writing little d's and u's above them and to the right like exponents in math (d for distributed and u for undistributed) when we use logical form. That way, we can see the distribution of terms at a glance, and this will save us time later when we examine arguments for validity. For three of the six formal fallacies in syllogisms depend on the distribution of terms.

> A: All S^d is P^u
> E: No S^d is P^d
> I: Some S^u is P^u
> O: Some S^u is not P^d

Exercises on distribution of terms:
1. Which one of the following propositions has a distributed predicate? (a) Some planets aren't life-supporting. (b) Every nation is mortal. (c) Some life-supporting bodies are parents. (d) All these yaks are diseased. (e) Socrates was mad.

2. Which one of the following propositions has an undistributed predicate? (a) No A proposition has a distributed predicate. (b) Some I propositions do not have distributed predicates. (c) Every E proposition must have an undistributed predicate. (d) E propositions don't have undistributed predicates. (e) Some O propositions don't have distributed predicates.

3. Which of the following five sentences above, in question 2, is false?

4. Which of the following propositions has an undistributed subject? (a) Man as such is not mortal. (b) None of the suspects told the truth. (c) All men are mortals. (d) Some good things are bad for you. (e) Socrates was not mad.

5. The predicate of an O proposition is (a) always distributed (b) always undistributed (c) sometimes distributed and sometimes undistributed (d) there is no way to tell

6. The distribution of the subject of an A proposition is (a) always less than that of the predicate (b) always more than that of the predicate (c) always the same as that of the predicate (d) sometimes more and sometimes less than that of the predicate

7. The distribution of the subject of an I proposition is . . . (same four options as question 6)

8. The distribution of the subject of an O proposition is . . . (same four options as question 6)

VI. Changing Propositions

Section 1. Immediate inference

Inference is the third act of the mind: moving from premise or premises to conclusion, drawing a conclusion from one or more premises. It is a synonym for reasoning or arguing. What an inference or argument claims is that *if the premise(s) is (are) true, then the conclusion must be true*; that its conclusion must logically follow from its premises.

When there is only one premise, we have **immediate inference**. When there are two or more premises, we have **mediate inference**, since the conclusion is drawn not from the first premise alone, immediately, but only through the mediation of at least one other premise.

But why are we studying a kind of *inference* ("immediate inference") here in the unit on the second act of the mind?

Because "immediate inference" is not really inference at all! Inference means moving from one piece of knowledge (the premises) to another (the conclusion). But in immediate inference, the single premise and the conclusion are not really different. The conclusion is not new knowledge. It only rearranging what we already knew in the premise, stating the same content in a different form.

To see the difference, compare the following two arguments. The first is an immediate inference, and the second is a mediate inference.

(1) No apes are angels.
Therefore no angels are apes.

(2) Angels are pure spirits.
Pure spirits are not confined by space.
Therefore angels are not confined by space.

When we know that no apes are angels, we already know that no angels are apes. An E proposition mutually excludes its subject and predicate. We see *immediately* that if the subject is excluded from the predicate, that means that the predicate is excluded from the subject. We do not really infer a new conclusion; we only express the knowledge we already had – that S and P are excluded from each other – in different words.

But in the second example we might know both of the premises without ever bringing them together in our mind and drawing the conclusion. We might have thought that angels *are* confined by space, that only a certain finite number of angels could dance on the head of a pin, because we never noticed that the two premises necessarily prove the conclusion that angels are *not* confined by space. We may have known that angels are pure spirits rather than things with material bodies, and also that pure spirits without bodies are not confined by space, since space is an aspect of bodies only – we may have known both of these premises to be true without knowing the conclusion to be true until this argument was presented to us. Quite often we do not realize the logical implications of what we already know or believe. In fact, argumentation usually consists in trying to convince someone of a conclusion he does not yet accept on the basis of premises that he already does accept. If he already accepted the conclusion, you would not *need* to prove it to him; and if he did not accept the premises, you *could* not prove it to him.

But what "immediate inference" really is, is merely changing a single proposition in form. There are two ways of doing this: **conversion** and **obversion.**

It may be useful at this point to remind and reorient ourselves by an outline:
I.   Terms
II. Propositions
III. Arguments (inferences)
    A. Immediate inference (only one premise, and only two terms)
       1. Obversion
       2. Conversion
       3. Combined forms
    B. Mediate inference (more than one premise, and more than two terms)
       1.Deductive (usually syllogism)
         a. Simple
         b. Compound
           (1) hypothetical
           (2) disjunctive
           (3) conjunctive
       2. Inductive

Section 2. Conversion (B)

When we "convert" a proposition, we interchange the subject and the predicate. For instance, "No man is an island" becomes "No island is a man," and "Some marriages are mistakes" becomes "Some mistakes are marriages." If we look at the Euler circles for either of these two propositions, the E or the I, we will see at a glance that the conversions are valid: that if it is true that no man is an island, it must be true that no island is a man; and that if it is true that some marriages are mistakes, it must be true that some mistakes are marriages. (We can speak of "valid" and "invalid" inferences even in immediate inferences, for the truth of the conclusion either necessarily follows from the truth of the premise, or not; if so, the inference is valid, and if not, it is invalid.)

E and I propositions both convert validly, simply by interchanging the subject and predicate. However, A propositions do not. From "all men are mortal" it does not validly follow that "all mortals are men." (Apes and roses are mortal too, but they are not men.) The rule for converting an A proposition is that it converts only to an I: if all men are mortal, it follows that *some* mortals are men.

The reason for this has to do with the distribution of terms. In the E and I propositions, the distribution of the subject and of the predicate is the same. Both are distributed in the E, and both are undistributed in the I. But in the A, the two terms are different in distribution: the subject is distributed and the predicate is undistributed. So to convert an A simply to another A would violate a basic rule of inference, which is that **no term that is undistributed in the premise may be distributed in the conclusion**. For if it is undistributed in the premise, that means that we know only some of it, only part of the class. That is not sufficient reason for drawing a conclusion about all of it, about all of the class. Our knowledge of only some of this term in the premise does not warrant our claiming to know all of it in the conclusion. But that is what would happen if we converted an A simply, moving from "All (S) (distributed) is *P* (*undistributed*)" to "All *P* (*distributed*) is S (undistributed)."

In fact, this is a very common formal fallacy, **the fallacy of an illicit conversion of an A proposition**. It is usually clothed with other words and is not naked and obvious. For instance, an advertisement like "All great models use Rich-Bitch Kitsch-Stitch Lipstick. What about you?" implicitly argues that "All great models use Rich Kitsch Lipstick, therefore All who use Rich Kitsch Lipstick are great models."

Here is a famous argument from a major philosopher, John Stuart Mill, that may be interpreted as an example of the fallacy of an illicit conversion of an A proposition:

"The only proof capable of being given that an object is visible, is that people actually see it. The only proof that a sound is audible, is that people actually hear it; and so of the other sources of our experience. In like manner, I apprehend, the sole evidence it is possible to produce that anything is desirable, is that people do actually desire it."

Perhaps Mill is offering only an analogy rather than an argument. But if it is an argument, it seems to be that "Everything desirable is desired, therefore everything desired is desirable." And that is an invalid conversion of an A proposition.

(Perhaps a better way of exposing Mill's fallacy here is to say that he is equivocating on the term "desirable." "Desirable" can mean either "*capable* of being desired" or "*worthy* of being desired." In the premise, Mill uses the first sense of "desirable," and in the conclusion he uses the second. See page 102.)

It is sometimes difficult to distinguish between an illicit conversion of a simple A proposition and a compound conjunctive ("and") proposition in which subject and predicate exchange places. Here are four famous cases, in which the connective "and" might or might not be interpreted as an inference (implying "and therefore"), thus giving us the fallacy of an illicit conversion of an A:

(1) "What is rational is actual, and what is actual is rational." (Hegel)
(2) "What is fitting is honorable, and what is honorable is fitting." (Cicero)
(3) "What's thine is mine, and all mine is thine" (Plautus)
(4) "Beauty is truth, truth beauty." (Keats)

An O proposition cannot be validly converted either, for the same reason an A cannot. It *sounds* right to say "Some S is not P, therefore Some P is not S," in a dreamy sort of way, as if it were a kind of justice or equal treatment. But a glance at the Euler circle diagram for the O shows us why this is a fallacy:

"Some birds are not robins" does not mean that "Some robins are not birds." When we argue "Some S is not P, therefore Some P is not S," we violate the rule of distribution, for S was undistributed in the premise ("*Some* S") but distributed in the conclusion. For in the conclusion "Some P is not S," S is the *predicate* of a negative proposition. This gives us a second fairly common fallacy, **the illicit conversion of an O proposition**.

In the premise "Some S is not P" (above) the lines around S are partly dotted lines, symbolizing what is unknown. There are three possibilities about S: we don't know whether it (1) stops outside the border of P, (2) extends into part of P, or (3) extends into all of P. If the third possibility is true, then it is *not* true that some P is not S.

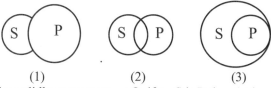

(1)   (2)   (3)

An E also validly converts to an O: if no S is P, then (at least) some P is not S. So the valid conversions are: E to E, I to I, A to I, and E to O. We can diagram them with arrows. Let an arrow represent an inference, with the premise at the beginning (the bowstring end of the arrow) and the conclusion at the end (the point of the arrow):

Table of Valid Conversions:

$$E \rightarrow E$$
$$I \rightarrow I$$
$$A \rightarrow I$$
$$E \rightarrow O$$

It is especially necessary in conversion to be sure all our terms, even the predicates, are nouns when we have translated into logical form, because in conversion the original predicate moves to the subject position, and only nouns can be subjects. "Sheep can't swim" can't convert into "Swim can't sheep," but converts into "No [things that can swim] are [sheep]." But this is clear only after putting "Sheep can't swim" into logical form first: "No [sheep] are [things that can swim]."

Section 3. Obversion (B)

Obversion is based on the principle that two negatives make a positive and cancel each other out. In obversion, we take the original proposition (the premise) and change it by doing two things: we **(1) negate the copula and (2) negate the predicate**. That is, we (1) change the quality of the *proposition*, from affirmative to negative or from negative to affirmative; and we also (2) change the quality of the *predicate* from P to non-P or from non-P to P.

Thus, when we obvert "All men are mortal" we get "No men are immortal." When we obvert "Every genius is a nonconformist" we get "No genius is a conformist." A's become E's in obversion.

And E's become A's: "No lakes are oceans" obverts to "All lakes are non-oceans"; and "No man is an island" obverts to "All men are non-islands."

I's become O's: "Some old ladies are gracious" obverts to "Some old ladies are not ungracious"; and "Some gases are noninflammable" obverts to "Some gases are not inflammable."

And O's become I's: "Some puddings are not chocolate" obverts to "Some puddings are non-chocolate"; and "Some teams are not unbeatable" becomes "Some teams are beatable."

When we negate the predicate, we must be sure to negate the whole predicate and not just part of it.

Table of Valid Obversions:

$$A \rightarrow E$$
$$E \rightarrow A$$
$$I \rightarrow O$$
$$O \rightarrow I$$

Section 4. Combined Forms: Contraposition and Inversion

We do not need to learn any new rules for contraposition, since it is nothing but a three-step process combining obversion and conversion: *first obvert, then convert (this is a "partial contraposition"), then obvert again (this is a "full contraposition").*

(A) Beginning with "All S is P," we obvert to "No S is non-P," then convert that to "No non-P is S," then obvert that to "All non-P is non-S."

(E) Beginning with "No S is P," we obvert to "All S is non-P, then convert to "Some non-P is S," then obvert to "Some non-P is not non-S."

(I) Beginning with "Some S is P," we obvert to "Some S is not non-P," but this is an O and we cannot convert an O. So there is no contrapositive to an I.

(O) Beginning with "Some S is not P," we obvert to "Some S is non-P," then convert to "Some non-P is S," then obvert to "Some non-P is not non-S."

Thus the end results of contraposition are:

(A) "All S is P" is "All non-P is non-S."

(E) "No S is P" becomes "Some non-P is not non-S."

(O) "Some S is not P" also becomes "Some non-P is not non-S."

We also need no new rules for inversion, which is either partial (first convert, then obvert) or full (first convert, then obvert, then convert):

(A) Beginning with "All S is P," we convert to "Some P is S," then obvert to "Some P is not non-S" (partial inversion). But we cannot convert this because it is an O.

(E) Beginning with "No S is P," we convert to "No P is S," then obvert to "All P is non-S" (partial inversion), then convert to "Some non-S is P" (full inversion)..

(I) Beginning with "Some S is P," we convert to "Some P is S," then obvert to "Some P is not non-S" (partial inversion). But we cannot convert this because it is an O.

(O) Beginning with "Some S is not P," we cannot convert this because it is an O.

It is not necessary to learn separate rules or tables for contraposition or inversion, for two reasons. First, contraposition and inversion is too complex to be practically useful in most ordinary-language situations. Second, there is nothing more in them than successive obversions and conversions, so the rules for conversion and obversion suffice.

Similarly, it is not necessary to learn rules or tables for inversion, which is only: first convert, then obvert (= "*partial inversion*"), then convert again (= "*full inversion*").

Exercises:

A. Convert each of the following if possible. First, translate into logical form.
   1. "God helps those who help themselves."

2. "Bigger fish eat little fish."
3. "All who are not for us are against us."
4. "No man is a hero to his valet."
5. "Some books are to be chewed and digested."
6. (H) "Not all is gold that glitters."
7. "Beauty is truth."
8. "Love never ends."

For additional practice, add the propositions in Exercises A–G on pages 156–63.

B. Obvert each of the above propositions.

C. Give the partial contrapositive, full contrapositive, partial inverse, and full inverse for each of the above propositions.

D. Explain the following, from Samuel Taylor Coleridge. (Watch out for the"very tricky O.")

"Sir, I admit your general rule
That every poet is a fool,
But you yourself may serve to show it,
That every fool is not a poet."

E. Evaluate the following inferences: First, find out what kind of inference it is. (If you do not translate the propositions into logical form, you probably will not be able to do this clearly.) Then determine whether the inference is valid or invalid by applying the appropriate rules.

1. "If God is male, then male is God." (Mary Daly)
2. No unintended inference is pernicious. Therefore all unintended inferences are non-pernicious, and so, some non-pernicious things must be unintended inferences.
3. No snarks are boojums. Therefore no boojums are snarks. Therefore all boojums are non-snarks. Therefore some non-snarks are boojums. Therefore some non-snarks are not non-boojums.
4. Not all lawyers are Republicans, therefore not all Republicans are lawyers.
5. At least one being is not temporal, therefore some being is atemporal.
6. At least one red thing is rotten, therefore at least one rotten thing is red.

VII. Contradiction

Section 1. What is contradiction? (B)

In logic, "contradiction" does not mean the subjective, psychological relation between two human beings who disagree with each other, but the objective, logical relation between two propositions that cannot both be true at the same time and also cannot both be false at the same time.

For instance, suppose you and your spouse are discussing the fact that your son's career makes it necessary for him and his wife to live in separate cities for a few weeks. You evaluate the situation pessimistically by repeating the proverb "Out of sight, out of mind," while your spouse evaluates the same situation optimistically by repeating the proverb "Absence makes the heart grow fonder." Are the two of you contradicting each other or not? If one is right, must the other be wrong?

Or, as you pitch in to help cook a Thanksgiving turkey, someone in the kitchen tells you, "No, no; for 'too many cooks spoil the broth.'" But someone else says, "Yes, yes, for 'many hands make light work.'"

Or, as you wonder whether or not to rush into something new, one person advises you, "Look before you leap," while another says, "Strike while the iron is hot," and "He who hesitates is lost."

Proverbs often seem to contradict each other when they do not if they refer to different situations. They are not as universal as they seem, and two non-universal propositions do not contradict each other. "Out of sight, out of mind" is true of weak relationships, "absence makes the heart grow fonder" is true of strong ones. "Too many cooks spoil the broth" is true in skilled work, but "many hands make light work" is true in unskilled work.

The reason these proverbs do not contradict each other is that they do not cover the same territory, so to speak; each one is speaking about a different thing or a different set of things or a different situation. If one person says "many lawyers are crooks" and the other says "many lawyers are not crooks," they do not contradict each other, because both subclasses of lawyers exist. But if one says "all lawyers are crooks" and the other says, "no, at least some lawyers are not crooks," those two propositions contradict each other.

It is crucially important in logic to know when two propositions contradict each other and when they do not. One of the most common reasons why debates and arguments fail to resolve a controversial issue and reveal the truth is a lack of clarity about what really contradicts what.

The conditions for contradiction are very simple, very stringent, and very limited. **Two propositions contradict each other only when the truth of either one necessarily means the falsity of the other,** *and* **the falsity of either one necessarily means the truth of the other. And this happens only between propositions that (a) have the same subject and predicate, and (b) differ in both quantity and quality.**

There are only two sets of contradictory propositions: (1) propositions with the form "All S is P" and "Some S is not P," and (2) propositions with the form "No S is P" and "Some S is P." *The only sets of propositions that contradict each other are an A and an O, or an E and an I, with the same subject and predicate.*

Exercises: Put each proposition into logical form and write its *contradictory* also in logical form.

1. "No man is a hero to his valet."
2. "Full many a flower is born to bloom unseen."
3. "Nobody doesn't like Sara Lee."
4. "A thing of beauty is a joy forever."
5. "It's a dirty bird that fouls its own nest."
6. "A fair face may be a foul bargain."
7. "Red sky in the morning, sailors take warning; red sky at night, sailor's delight."
8. "There's many a slip 'twixt the cup and the lip."
9. "A good conscience is your best pillow."
10. "None but the brave deserve the fair."
11. "Sometimes a man's gotta do what a man's gotta do."
12. "Not all mistakes are stupid ones."

Section 2. The Square of Opposition

Which propositions contradict each other is made clear by the "Square of Opposition":

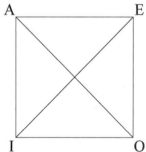

"Opposition" is a special, technical term in logic. It means **the relation between any two propositions that have the same subject and the same predicate but differ in quality or quantity or both.** Two propositions that do not have the same subject, or do not have the same predicate, are not in any kind of "opposition." Opposition exists only between two propositions with the same subject and the same predicate.

There are four different kinds of opposition: contradiction, contrariety, subcontrariety, and subalternation/superalternation:

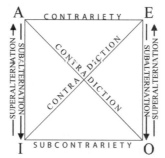

The most important kind of opposition is **contradiction**, the relation between opposed *A and O* propositions, or between opposed *E and I* propositions. (The *relation* is called "contradiction" and the two *propositions* are called "contradictories.") This is the relation diagrammed by the two diagonal lines across the center of the Square. **Of two contradictories, if one is true the other is false and if one is false the other is true.** If "all lawyers are crooks" is true, "some lawyers are not crooks" is false, and if "all lawyers are crooks" is false, "some lawyers are non-crooks" is true. (Apologies to lawyers, but stock examples stick in memory.)

There are also three other kinds of opposition besides contradiction. The most important of these is **contrariety**. The only two propositions that are **contraries** are an A and an E in opposition (i.e. with the same subject and predicate). "All S is P" and "No S is P" are contraries.

Contraries cannot both be true, but they can both be false. If "All lawyers are crooks" is true, then "No lawyers are crooks" must be false, and if "No lawyers are crooks" is true, then "All lawyers are crooks" must be false. However, both propositions can be false, if some lawyers are crooks and some are not.

The practical application of the distinction between contraries and contradictories is this: **To refute an A or E proposition, you do not need to prove its contrary, only its contradictory.** You need to show only *some* counter examples, in fact only *one*, to refute a universal. An A proposition is an affirmative universal, and an O is sufficient to refute it. If someone says "All lawyers are crooks," you have refuted him if you show that "some lawyers are not crooks." You do not need to show that "No lawyers are crooks." Similarly, an I proposition is sufficient to refute an E. If someone says "No lawyers are crooks," you have refuted him if you show that "some lawyers are crooks." You do not need to show that "All lawyers are crooks."

The relation between two opposed particular propositions, I and O, is called **subcontrariety**, and the propositions are called **subcontraries**. **Subcontraries can both be true.** This is why proverbs that seem to contradict each other often do not: because their meaning is often particular rather than universal. Two particulars do not contradict each other.

Subcontraries can both be true, but **subcontraries cannot both be false**. If "Some lawyers are crooks" is true, it may be that "some lawyers are not crooks" is also true, and vice versa. But if "some lawyers are crooks" is false, then "some lawyers are not crooks" cannot also be false. For if "some lawyers are crooks" is false, this can be only because no lawyers are crooks. If an I is false (e.g. "Some lawyers are crooks"), then its contradictory E must be true: "No lawyers are crooks." The only thing that would make it false that even some lawyers are crooks is that no lawyers at all are crooks. So if an I is false, its opposed E (its contradictory) must be true. (Remember, with contradictories, if one is false, the other must be true, and if one is true, the other must be false.) But if the E is true – if it is true that "*No* lawyers are crooks" – then it is certainly true that at least some lawyers are not crooks, and that is the O.

The relation between opposed A and I propositions, and between opposed E and O propositions, is called **subalternation**, and the propositions are called **subalternates**.

Among subalternates, if the universal proposition is true, then the particular that comes under it (i.e., its subalternate) must also be true. And if the particular is not true, then the universal cannot be true.

If "All lawyers are crooks" is true, then "Some lawyers are crooks" must be true. (Remember, in logic "some" does not mean anything more than it says; it does not mean "only some" but "at least some.") And if "No lawyers are crooks" is true, then certainly "Some lawyers are not crooks" must be true.

Also, among subalternates, if the particular proposition is false, the universal must be false. If it is false that even some lawyers are crooks, it must be false that all lawyers are crooks. And if it is false that even some lawyers are not crooks, it must be false that no lawyers are crooks.

All of this works only for propositions in opposition, not for any other propositions. The Square of Opposition is a very productive "machine," but its products are limited.

Instead of memorizing all four of these technical terms (contradiction, contrariety, subcontrariety, and subalternation) and their definitions, and then applying them, it is quicker and easier to memorize the following version of the Square of Opposition, which includes everything you will need to know for practical purposes:

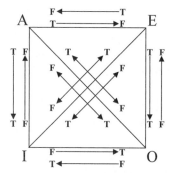

On this Square, arrows represent valid inferences. E.g., if an A proposition is true, then its opposed I must be true too. Thus, there is an arrow going down from A to I as T to T, from a true A to a true I. (Again, remember that this all works *only* for propositions that are in opposition, i.e. that have the same subject and predicate. You must first find out whether you have opposition before you can use the Square of Opposition.) But there is no arrow going up from a true I to a true A; so that is not a valid inference. There is an arrow going up from a false I to a false A, so that is a valid inference. If you know an I is false, you know its opposed A is also false.

Notice that the relationship of contradiction is the most important and the most fruitful, i.e. the one that tells you the most.

Here is another way of summarizing the Square: when you have two opposed propositions,

	A is	E is	I is	O is
If A is true	true	false	true	false
If E is true	false	true	false	true
If I is true	unknown	false	true	unknown
If O is true	false	unknown	unknown	true
If A is false	false	unknown	unknown	true
If E is false	unknown	false	true	unknown
If I is false	false	true	false	true
If O is false	true	false	true	false

The Square is a very effective machine, but it runs only on the proper fuel: two propositions in opposition and in logical form. There are three ways the Square of Opposition is useful:

(1) The cross lines tell you *what proposition contradicts any given proposition.* So if you need to refute any proposition (i.e. prove it to be false), you can look at the square to see what proposition you need to prove to be true. E.g. to refute "all lawyers are crooks" you need to prove that "some lawyers are not crooks."

(2) The arrows tell you *which inferences are valid* (but only between two opposed propositions). All inferences (between two opposed propositions) that are on this square are valid; all inferences (between two opposed propositions) that are *not* on this square are invalid. If someone has made an inference from one opposed proposition to another, you can instantly see whether it is a valid inference or not.

(3) The arrows also tell you *how to complete a valid inference* yourself from one opposed proposition to another. Just follow any of the arrows on the square.

Thus there are three kinds of questions, or exercises, for the Square:

(1) "Tell what proposition needs to be proved in order to disprove the following proposition." That is, "give the contradictory of the following proposition." The answer to this question is a *proposition*.

(2) "Tell whether the following completed inference is valid or invalid." The answer to this question is "valid" or "invalid."

(3) "If you know that the following proposition is true, or false, as given, what do you know about the following second proposition: is it true, false, or unknown?" The answer to this question is "true," "false," or "unknown" because you are here completing the inference and declaring the proposition which is the conclusion of your inference to be true, false, or unknown. (If unknown, this means you do not claim you can make an inference at all.)

Exercises:

A. To disprove each of the following propositions, what proposition must be proved? In other words, give the contradictory of each of the following propositions.
   1. "Man was born free and is everywhere in chains." (Rousseau)
   2. "There is nothing new under the sun." (Ecclesiastes)
   3. "I alone have escaped to tell you." (*Job*, quoted in *Moby Dick*)
   4. "Some hate by morning what they love by night."
   5. "*All* evil is not rooted in the love of money."
B. Evaluate the following inferences:
   1. Since it's true that some banks are not safe, it must be true that some banks are.
   2. It's false to say that no man ever lost money underestimating the intelligence of consumers. Therefore it must be true that some men did lose money underestimating consumer intelligence.
   3. It must be true that not all truths are true, because it's false that every truth is true.
   4. If love never fails, then it can't be true that some love fails.
   5. If it's false that some philosophers are insane, it must be false that all philosophers are insane.
   6. Since some students are good debaters, some students are not good debaters.

C. If you know that the proposition in column I is true or false as indicated, what do you know about the corresponding proposition in column II? Is it true, false, or unknown?

Column I	Column II
1. All snarks are boojums: false.	1. Some snarks are boojums.
2. Some snarks are boojums: false.	2. All snarks are boojums.
3. No snarks are boojums: false.	3. All snarks are boojums.
4. Some snarks are not boojums: false.	4. Some snarks are boojums.
5. Some snarks are not boojums: true.	5. No snarks are boojums.
6. Some snarks are boojums: true.	6. No snarks are boojums.
7. No snarks are boojums: true.	7. Some snarks are not boojums.
8. All snarks are boojums: true.	8. All boojums are snarks.

Section 3. Existential import (P)

A proposition has "existential import" if it means to claim the existence (or non-existence) of something. For instance, "There is no Santa Claus," "God exists," "Unicorns are not real," and "Some of the events in the popularly believed story of George Washington's life never really happened, such as his cutting down the cherry tree."

An explicitly existential proposition has no predicate distinct from its copula. It simply says that its subject exists, or does not exist.

But what of ordinary subject-predicate propositions? Do they have existential import or not?

Consider the following propositions:

1. All witches are dangerous.
2. Some witches are dangerous.
3. All leprechauns are tricky.
4. Some leprechauns are not tricky.
5. All fish have gills.
6. Some fish have gills.

Everyone knows fish exist, and everyone knows leprechauns don't, but some people think witches exist and some think they don't. But we cannot decide whether or not a proposition in itself has existential *import* (meaning) by taking polls to see how many people *believe* that the subject of that proposition exists. The objective *meaning* of a proposition is one thing; whether someone subjectively *believes* it to be true or false is another thing.

So how do we decide whether propositions that are not explicitly existential propositions have existential import or not? All modern logic texts solve this problem by claiming that all universal propositions lack existential import and all particular propositions have it. This is *not* what traditional Aristotelian logic assumes, and it seems (to this writer, anyway) a wholly unnecessary, arbitrary, and confusing assumption. For how could the proposition "all witches are dangerous" lack existential import and "some witches are dangerous" have it? Either witches exist, or not. In either case, it might be that none are dangerous, or that all are, or that some are and some are not – whether we are talking about real beings or only fictional beings. Exactly the same thing is true of leprechauns, which all of us believe are fictional, and of fish, which all of us believe are real. This is the simplest way of dealing with existential import for ordinary propositions: that *none* of them have it, that only explicitly existential propositions have it, that only explicitly existential propositions mean to assert the existence of the subject.

Modern logic texts always assume that particular propositions have existential import. But if I say "Some unicorns are fierce and some are gentle," I do not mean to assert the existence of unicorns. I only mean to distinguish, among these unicorns (all of whom have the essence of unicorns but no existence), between those that have the accident "fierce" and those that have the accident "gentle." Modern logicians could not have missed such a simple point unless they had abandoned or forgotten the elementary metaphysical distinctions between essence and existence, and between essence and accident.

Every modern logic text I can find simply asserts, without proof, that particular propositions have existential import and universal propositions do not. For instance, the latest edition (the tenth) of the world's best-selling logic text, by Copi, brings up a "difficulty" with the standard Square of Opposition: "The difficulty can be appreciated by reflecting upon I and O propositions, which surely (*sic!*) do have existential import. Thus the I proposition 'Some soldiers are heroes' says that there exists at least one soldier who is a hero. . . . But if this is so . . . we are forced to confront some very awkward consequences. [So why not question your assumption then?]

"(1) Earlier we said that an I proposition follows validly from its corresponding (opposed) A proposition by subalternation. . . . But if I and O propositions have existential import, and they follow validly from their corresponding A and E propositions, then A and E propositions must also have existential import." And the idea that universal propositions have existential import has already been denied.

"(2) Furthermore, if both universal and particular propositions have existential import, then we could never formulate a negative existential proposition.

"(3) Finally, the inference from a true A to a true I would be invalid if particulars have existential import and universals do not, for it is fallacious to derive more from less, to deduce an existential conclusion from a non-existential premise." The modern interpretation makes the Square of Opposition invalid. And yet we know commonsensically that the Square is correct, and the greatest minds since Aristotle have never thought otherwise until the advent of symbolic logic.

But no modern logic text considers denying its presupposition that I and O propositions always have existential import and A and E propositions never do, since all symbolic logic texts follow the interpretation of George Boole, the English mathematician who is one of the founders of modern symbolic logic: "In the Boolean interpretation, universal propositions are interpreted as having no existential import, while particular propositions are not interpreted in this way." (Copi, *op. cit.*, p. 201)

Yet clearly, in ordinary language, particular propositions sometimes do and sometimes do not have existential import. Just as "some" sometimes, in some contexts and tones of voice, implies "some but not all," while at other times it does not, so the initial word "some" in an I or O proposition sometimes, in some contexts, implies "some of these really existing things" while at other times it does not. "Some of our ballplayers are sick" does imply that our ballplayers exist, but "Some elves are heroic" does not imply that elves exist.

The same is true for universal propositions: sometimes there is an implication of existential import, sometimes not, and sometimes there is neither implication. Whoever says "All of our ballplayers are sick" implies real ballplayers, but whoever says "All fictions are subjective" implies that fictions are fictional! And there is a third case, which makes neither of the above implications: "All nuclear terrorists who hold the whole world hostage will be instantly executed" does not imply that there are or ever will be any such beings – nor does it imply that there are not.

By the simple and commonsensical device of not making the gratuitous assumption that all A and E propositions must lack existential import and all I and O propositions must have it, we preserve the traditional commonsensical Square. Common sense comes to the aid of common sense.

Section 4. Tricky propositions on the Square

The easiest way to deal with tricky propositions is simply to translate them into standard logical form and then to put them onto the Square. However, they can also sometimes be put directly onto the Square, as follows:

Propositions that use temporal designations like "always," "never," and "sometimes": "S is always P" is treated as an A; "S is never P" as an E; and "S is sometimes P" as an I.

Propositions that use modal designations like "necessary," "impossible," and "possible":

"It is necessary that S is P" is treated as an A; "It is impossible that S is P" is treated as an E; and "It is possible that S is P" is treated as an I.

There are also synonyms for these three modal designations, such as "it must be" for "necessary," "it can't be" for "impossible," and "it might be" for "possible."

Exceptive, exclusive, and other tricky propositions need no new Square to accommodate them; all that needs to be done is to translate them into standard form (A, E, I, or O) and proceed as usual.

Compound propositions (hypothetical, disjunctive, and conjunctive) simply cannot be dealt with by the Square, and there is no need to try to invent complex new Squares for them. It would be like trying to fit a large truck into a garage designed for a small car.

Singular propositions (like "Socrates is fat") can go on the Square by being translated into universals ("All Socrates is fat"), as we have already done. But there are no particular singular propositions; we cannot talk about "Some Socrates." In this case, and in this case only, the A and the E are contradictory: If it is true that Socrates is fat, then it is false that he is not; If it is false that he is fat, then it is true that he is not; If it is true that he is not, then it is false that he is; and If it is false that he is not, then it is true that he is.

The same is true of explicitly *existential propositions with singular subjects*: there are only two possibilities, that it is, or that it is not; and these two are contradictory.

But explicitly existential propositions whose subject is *not* singular but either particular or universal can go on the square just as other propositions do, for they too are either A, E, I, or O, even though they have no predicate distinct from the copula (except "real" or "unreal").

Tricky Exercise: Where is the fallacy in the following nine-step inference? Each step is either an obversion, a conversion, or an opposition, and each single step seems valid. Yet the first premise is obviously true and the final conclusion is obviously false. We cannot validly prove a false conclusion from premises that are not false, so where is the erroneous step? (Hint: page 170, last paragraph.)

1. Let us assume that all men are mortal.
2. Since wise men are part of the class "men," it follows that wise men are mortal. You may consider this an immediate inference from an A to an I, from "all men" to "some men," or else as an implied syllogism. You have not yet learned the rules of the syllogism, but obviously it is valid to argue that "all men are mortal, and wise men are men, therefore wise men are mortal."
3. And if all wise men are mortal, then no wise men are immortal, by obversion.
4. And if no wise men are immortal beings, then no immortal beings are wise men, by conversion.
5. And if it is true that no immortal beings are wise men, it is false that some immortal beings are wise men, by contradiction on the Square of Opposition.
6. And this conclusion, that "some immortal beings are wise men," says the

same thing as "some immortal beings are not unwise men," by obversion. So if 5 is false, 6 is false also.

7. But if it is false that some immortal beings are not unwise men, then it must be true that all immortal beings are unwise men, by contradiction on the Square of Opposition.
8. And if it is true that all immortal beings are unwise men, then it is true that some unwise men are immortal beings, by conversion.
9. Thus we have proved that some unwise men are immortal beings, i.e. that some students who flunk logic will never die.

Section 5. Some practical uses of the Square of Opposition

Squares structurally similar to the Square of Opposition can be made for a variety of things other than A, E, I, and O propositions in opposition, to classify and summarize possibilities at a glance. Of course, the rules of the Square of Opposition do not apply in the same way to these "squares," since they have at their four corners not opposed A, E, I, and O propositions but instead variables such as "yes" and "no" to two different questions or "more" and "less," or "time" and "space," or "past" and "future," or "east" and "west."

Take the "square" in which the four corners represent opposite answers to two different questions. These answers can be either an absolute, simple Yes and No, or a more relative and gradual More and Less. The famous argument called "Pascal's Wager" is an example of a "square" with simple Yes or No answers to two questions. Pascal argued as follows: In objective fact, either God exists, or not. And in any individual's subjective choice, either he chooses to believe in God, or not. So there are four possibilities: (1) God exists and I believe in Him; (2) God exists and I don't believe in Him; (3) God doesn't exist and I believe in Him; and (4) God doesn't exist and I don't believe in Him.

S U B J E C T I V E L Y		OBJECTIVELY	
		God exists	*God does not exist*
	I believe	(1) Gain: Everything Loss: Little or Nothing	(3) Gain: Nothing Loss: Nothing
	I do not believe	(2) Gain: Nothing Loss: Everything	(4) Gain: Nothing Loss: Nothing

Once these four possibilities are set up, Pascal calculates the possible gain and loss in each case. We want to gain two things, he argues: truth and happiness, the two absolute desires of everyone. But we cannot be sure which of these two propositions is true: that God exists or that He does not. We gain the truth in two of the four cases: (1) and (4), for our belief matches reality in both cases. We lose the truth in the other two cases, (2) and (3), since our belief fails to match reality in those cases. But if we believe that we cannot know which is more likely, we cannot decide whether or not to believe on this basis. We have a 50-50 chance of winning the truth no matter whether we choose Yes or No. So far we have no clear reason for "betting" for God or against Him. But if we turn to our other goal, happiness, we have good reason for "wagering" that God exists rather than not. For if God does not exist, there is no meeting Him after death, no Heaven or Hell, no infinite and eternal gain or loss; thus there is little difference between believing and not believing, since there is in the end nothing to gain or to lose. But if God does exist and I must believe in Him and accept His gift of Heaven in order to attain Heaven, then believing in Him (possibility #1) gives me infinite gain but little or no loss; while not believing in Him (possibility #2) gives me little or no gain but infinite loss. Thus my only chance of winning is the combination (1) and my only chance of losing is the combination (2). So belief is a very reasonable "wager."

Here is an example of the other kind of "square," with gradual or relative answers, "more affirmative" vs. "more negative." Avery Dulles has proposed a classification of four ideological attitudes toward Church and State in contemporary America. "Traditionalism" is more positive toward the Church and more negative toward the current State; "Neo-conservatism" is more positive toward both; "Liberalism" is more positive toward the State and negative toward the Church and "Radicalism" is more negative toward both.

Toward the Church

		Positive	Negative
	Positive	Neo-conservatism	Liberalism
Toward the State			
	Negative	Traditionalism	Radicalism

Sometimes the traditional Square is useful, without modification, in distinguishing four possible positions. For instance, in the debate about abortion, one may believe that (A) all fetuses are persons, (I) at least some fetuses are persons, (E) no fetuses are persons, or (O) at least some fetuses are not persons; and this would give us four different positions on abortion if we assumed that persons may not be killed but non-persons may: (A) that all abortions are wrong, (I) that at least some are wrong, (E) that none are wrong, and (O) that at least some are not wrong.

Alternatively, if we assumed that fetuses *are* persons, we could then go on to distinguish four beliefs about a right to life: (A) that *all* persons have the right to life (and therefore all abortions are wrong), (I) that at least *some* persons have the right to life (and therefore that at least some abortions are wrong), (E) that *no* persons have the right to life (and therefore that no abortions are wrong), and (O) that at least *some* persons do *not* have the right to life (and therefore that at least some abortions are not wrong).

Those who debate important and divisive moral issues like abortion often do not clearly distinguish what propositions they claim are true, or claim to know are true. It is often assumed that there are only two possible positions when there are in fact four because there are two variables, not one. A "square" can reveal this. Sometimes the variables are the same as they are on the real Square, viz. universal vs. particular and affirmative vs. negative. At other times, the two variables are different (as in the Avery Dulles example).

Contradictions with Sets of Propositions

Do sets of propositions, like political party platforms, contradict opposite sets of propositions, like opposing party platforms? Is it logically possible to agree with both Democrats and Republicans platforms?

Obviously, the answer is: in part but not wholly if some of the planks in one platform (i.e., some propositions) contradict some in the opposing platform and others do not. E.g., it is logically possible to agree with the Democratic platform about stricter laws to protect the environment and with the Republican platform about lowering taxes. But because we vote for one party or the other, we sometimes assume it's a "package deal" with no "line-item veto."

When asked for our opinion on some controversial issue, we often fail to make distinctions but instead just "feel" that one side is right *in toto* and the other side wrong. But there may be multiple propositions, or a set of propositions, held by each side. E.g., when we are asked "how we feel" about homosexuality, we should first demand of ourselves that feelings be based on thinking. And since thinking makes distinctions, while feelings do not, we *might* insist on distinguishing between attitudes toward people and attitudes toward actions, and between legality and morality, and thus favor laws to protect homosexuals from discrimination while also believing that homosexual acts are immoral, without any logical contradiction.

Sometimes people do not notice that a set of propositions, all of which they believe, contains a contradiction between two of these propositions, or, more hiddenly, between one proposition and *two* others taken together. E.g., according to polls, about two-thirds of Americans believe that abortion is the killing of an innocent human life, and about two-thirds of Americans believe that abortion should be legal, yet well over two-thirds believe that all human lives should be protected by law. But any two of those three propositions, taken together, contradict the third one. The logic is like that of the stock insult: "You can be honest, or intelligent, or (fill in your favorite villain: Fundamentalist, Liberal, Capitalist, Socialist, etc.), or any two of them, but not all three." (Work it out.)

VIII. The Third Act of the Mind: Reasoning

Section 1. What does "reason" mean? (P)

"Man is a rational animal." That was the classical definition of man. The modern mind tends to object to two things in this definition: (1) Its larger meaning of "man" and (2) its larger meaning of "rational."

(1) In *all* books written in English until fairly recently we find the larger, or inclusive, use of "man" to mean both men and women equally. But current feminist fashion insists on an exclusively masculine meaning to "man" (which this author would call not "inclusive" but "exclusive," in fact "male chauvinism"). They would use not "man" but "humanity" to designate both males and females equally. But this is a confusion, because "humanity" is an abstract term, designating a quality, as in "humanity vs. divinity," while "man" is a concrete term, as in "God and man" or "a man or an animal"). The new usage, which is exclusive and "sexist," calls itself "inclusive" and it accuses the traditional inclusive usage of exclusivism and sexism!? (See also page 36, footnote 1.)

(2) The larger, older meaning of "rational" includes wisdom, intuition, understanding of the nature or essence of a thing (the "first act of the mind"), self-knowledge, moral conscience (awareness of good and evil), and the appreciation of beauty, as well as reasoning and rational calculation (the "third act of the mind").

Even in this larger, ancient sense of "reason," human reason has weakness as well as power. Compared with angels (pure spirits), we are like slowly crawling insects: we must gather all our data from our five senses, and we must usually proceed slowly, step by step, deducing or inducing one thing from another. In these two ways our rational knowledge is indirect: it depends on prior sense experience and it depends on prior knowledge. Angels, in contrast, have something like direct mental telepathy with the mind of God, or at least with the essences of things as God knows them, immediately and intuitively.[1]

---

1 This is simply the definition of an angel, whether or not angels are real, whether or not there is good reason for believing they are real, and whether or not those reasons amount

On the other hand, the human mind has a remarkable power compared with even the highest animal intelligence. Human reason surpasses animal intelligence in at least three ways:

First, though all human knowledge begins in experience, we can acquire knowledge beyond experience, and even with certainty, through deductive reasoning. For instance,

☆ If we know that *everything that has atoms must be able to reflect light,*
☆ And if we know that *all little green men on Mars have atoms* (i.e. if there are little green men on Mars, they must have atoms),
☆ Then we know with certainty that *all little green men on Mars (if there are any) must be able to reflect light,* even though we have never seen little green men on Mars, and even though we do not know whether or not there are little green men on Mars. This is quite remarkable.

Second, we can know not only particular truths beyond our immediate experience, but also *universal truths,* such as "2+2=4" or "all men are mortal." This power presupposes the first power, the power to know beyond experience, for experience never presents universals, only particulars. We can know universals by abstracting them from the particulars that we experience, e.g. "human nature" from human beings or "life" from living things.

Third, we can know *necessary and unchangeable truths*; we can know not only that such and such happens to be the case, but also that it must necessarily and always be the case. If A is B and B is C, then A must *necessarily* be C. This is even more than the power to know universal truths. Not all universal truths are necessary. "All human babies come from human mothers" is a universal truth (so far) but not a necessary truth, and it will cease to be true when someone clones a human being. "All my ties are four-in-hand" is true but not necessarily true, since I could have had some bow ties too, and probably will have some in the future. But "all men are mortal" or "all triangles have 180 degrees in the sum of their three interior angles" are not only *universal* truths (true of *all* men or *all* triangles) but also *necessary* truths, truths that *must* be so and cannot ever cease to be so.

Section 2. The ultimate foundations of the syllogism (P)

The power of deduction to give us certain knowledge, as expressed in a syllogism such as the classic "All men are mortal and[2] Socrates is a man, therefore Socrates is mortal," comes from the inherent, self-evident, and necessary truth of the following principles:

to proofs. We are not assuming the existence of angels, or of God, but using the concept of an angel to understand the nature of human reason by contrast.

[2] 'And' often indicates a relation between two premises.

(1) *"Whatever is universally true of a subject must be true of everything contained in that subject"* – that is, if x must be true of all S, then x must be true of every single S. This is known technically as the *dictum de omni*, or "the law about all." Because of this principle, we can be certain that if *all* men are mortal, and Socrates is *a* man, Socrates must be mortal. Whatever is true of a universal is true of all its instances, for a universal is "uni-versa," "one-in-many," one and the same in all its instances. It is the universal that is the foundation of the syllogism.[3]

(2) *"Whatever is universally false of a subject must be false of everything contained in that subject"* – that is, if x is not-true of all S, of S as such, then x must not be true of any single S. This is called the *dictum de nullo*, or "the law about none." It is the negative version of principle (1). Because of this principle, we can be certain that if *no* men are angels, and Socrates is *a* man, Socrates must not be an angel.

(3) Now combine these two principles with the third principle that *"two things identical with one and the same third thing are identical with each other,"* and you get the syllogism. For the "third thing" is the "middle term," the common term with which the other two terms are compared. In the classic example above, "Socrates" and "mortal" are both compared with a common third term, or "middle term," "men." (See below, pages 215–19 on the importance of the middle term.) If all *men* are mortal and Socrates is *a man*, then Socrates must be mortal.

(4) The negative corollary of principle (3) is that if there are two things, one of which is identical with a third thing and the other of which is not, then those two things are not identical with each other. In the syllogism "No men are angels, and Socrates is a man, therefore Socrates is not an angel," "Socrates" and "angel" are both compared with the common third term, or "middle term," "men."

(5) Principles (3) and (4), in turn, assume the *Law of Identity* (*"a thing is what it is"*).

(6) And the negative corollary of the Principle of Identity is the *Law of Non-Contradiction* (*" a thing is not what it isn't; x is not non-x"*).

(7) Finally, it also assumes that *a thing is either x or not x*. A predicate must be either affirmed or denied of a subject; there is no third possibility. A proposition is either true or false, there is no third possibility. This is the *Law of Excluded Middle*. (All these principles, especially this last one, assumes no ambiguity of terms.)

On these principles, all of which are logically self-evident "tautologies," the syllogism rests.

---

3   This is why modern logicians, who are usually nominalists, do not think much of syllogism. Nominalism is the denial of any real universals. See also the next chapter for more historical and logical detail on this controversy (pages 219–30).

Tautologies

A "tautology" is a proposition that does not need to be proved because it is logically self-evident. It "proves itself," so to speak, because if you deny it, you must contradict yourself. Examples are: "Frogs are frogs," "Whatever animal has teeth and claws, has claws," "If I exist, I exist," and "Nothing that is divisible is indivisible at the same time." A tautology can be defined in three ways: (a) a proposition that is true because of its logical form, whatever its content, (b) a proposition whose contradictory is self-contradictory, or (c) a proposition whose predicate is necessarily contained in its subject.

Though a proposition may be self-evident objectively, in itself, it may not be self-evident subjectively, to a given human mind. For instance, "angels are not confined to space" and "whatever has color must have size" are both self-evident in themselves, but not to a person who does not understand the nature of angels and space, color and size well enough to know that these connections are necessary.

Sometimes the term "tautology" is used for *any* objectively self-evident proposition, but more usually it is used in a narrower sense, only for propositions that are *explicitly* self-evident, verbally self-evident, independent of the meaning of the terms. If we use this narrower sense, "All red ties are red," "All red X's are X's," and "All red gloms are gloms" are tautologies, but "no angels have bodies" and "All men have bodies" are not.

What about a proposition like "You will pass this course if you work hard enough"? This is a tautology if "hard enough" means "hard enough to pass"; for then the proposition means "If you work hard enough to pass, you will pass," or "If you pass because you work hard enough, then you will pass." And that is clearly a tautology. However, if "hard enough" means "hard enough to satisfy the teacher," then it is not a tautology.

A tautology tells us no new information. "This candidate will be elected if there is sufficient support" is a tautology, like "you will pass if you work hard enough," though it sounds as if it is saying something informative. It says only that if there is sufficient support for him to be elected, then there will be sufficient support for him to be elected. If you contradict the proposition, you contradict yourself: it cannot be true that the candidate will be elected even if there is not sufficient support for him to be elected.

Tautologies are necessarily true. Their contradictories are *necessarily* false, logically impossible. Other propositions are true (or false) only because of some other things being true; that is, they are *contingently* true (or false). "Water runs downhill" is contingently true, true only because of gravity. In a universe where matter repels instead of attracts, it would *not* be true. Necessary truths are truths that are true *in all possible worlds*.

We cannot imagine or conceive the opposite of a necessary truth. For instance, we cannot imagine, or conceive, or tell a story about, a world in which 2+2=5. We can, however, imagine the opposite of any contingent truth if we have a lively enough imagination – like a world without gravity. "Dead bodies decay (when there is normal heat and air) and do not come back to life" is a truth about all dead bodies; but it is a contingent truth, and we can imagine (and even believe) a miracle happening, in which a dead body does not decay but comes back to life. That would be a violation of physical law, but physical laws are only contingent truths, true only because something else is true in this particular world, which might not be true in some other possible world. But we cannot even conceive, and therefore we literally cannot believe, any violation of a logical law, since logical laws are necessary truths, true of all possible worlds, so that a proposition that violates a logical law is strictly meaningless.

For instance, "A man walked on water" may be a miracle, but it is not a self-contradiction. "A man walked on water and didn't walk on water at the same time" is a self-contradiction, if there is no ambiguity in the terms. (Of course, surfers walk on water in a sense. But though that may be *almost* as wonderful as what Jesus did, it's not quite the same.) "God can give man free choice, so that man is free to choose between good and evil, and at the same time withhold free will from man, so that man never chooses evil" is a self-contradictory and thus strictly meaningless proposition. It does not become meaningful because it is predicated of God. God, if He exists and created the physical universe, can over-ride its physical laws; but even God cannot violate logical laws, because these laws are not dependent on the temporal nature of the creation but on the eternal nature of the Creator.

– If, of course, God exists. It is not clear what reality these laws are dependent on if there is no God; but in any case they are eternal, unchangeable, necessary truths. If God exists, these laws are descriptions of the nature of God. This is a useful explanation of the distinction between necessary and contingent truths even for atheists, for it is the *meaning* of "God," or the *concept* of God, that is relevant here. The distinction holds conceptually whether there is a real God or not.

Section 3. How to detect arguments

We can evaluate arguments as valid or invalid only after we find them. Not all written or spoken discourse contains arguments, and discourse that *does* contain arguments is usually like a tide pool containing crabs: you have to hunt for them to find them.

Detecting arguments is like crabbing. Suppose we are fishing for crabs with a net. We must (1) first detect the presence of a crab before we can hope to (2) get it into our net; and we usually must get it into our net before we can (3) tell whether it is one of the edible kind of crabs or not. These three steps apply to arguments as well as crabs. The critical question about any argument is (3) whether it is logically valid or not, whether the mind can accept it, whether it is mentally edible, so to speak. But before we can determine that (3), we must first

(2) be clear about what the argument is saying, and we do this by putting it into logical form, especially the form of a syllogism. That corresponds to the net. (Advanced fishermen might do without a net, and advanced logicians can bypass the step of putting ordinary-language arguments into logical form, but beginners in logic definitely need to put an argument into logical form before they can see whether it is valid or not, just as beginning crabbers need to get the crab in the net before they can see whether it is edible or not.) But even before we can do this (2), we must first (1) detect the presence of an argument, as we detect the presence of a crab. If we wave our net of syllogism randomly, we will probably not find an argument in it. For there is much more in human linguistic communication than arguments, just as there is much more in the sea than crabs.

Detecting the presence of an argument is not something that can be taught mechanically. It is intuitive "seeing." There are mechanical principles for testing the *validity* of an argument, and we will learn these shortly; but there are no mechanical principles for testing for the *presence* of an argument.

However, there are indicators. One is the presence of the essential *structure* of an argument, and another is certain *key words*.

(1) The essential structure of every argument consists of a relationship between its two parts: premises and conclusion. The conclusion is what you are trying to prove; the premises are your reasons, your evidence, your proof. The relationship between them can be put in different ways: we can say that the conclusion "follows from" the premises, or that the premises "entail" the conclusion, or "prove" the conclusion, or that the premises are the "reasons" for the conclusion, or that the conclusion is true *because* the premises are true, or that (in a deductive argument but not an inductive one) *if* the premises are true, *then* the conclusion *must* be true.

In "All men are mortal and Socrates is a man, therefore Socrates is mortal," the conclusion is "Socrates is mortal" because that is what you are trying to prove; and the premises are "All men are mortal" and "Socrates is a man" because that is your reason for believing that Socrates is mortal, that is your proof that Socrates is mortal, that is your evidence that Socrates is mortal. The word "therefore" asserts your claim that the premises have this logical relation to the conclusion, that they prove the conclusion to be true.

(2) There is usually a key word indicating this premise-to-conclusion relation. "Therefore" is the formal, proper word, but there are many others. The following is a list of "conclusion indicators." The proposition that *follows* these words is usually the conclusion of an argument; and the proposition that *precedes* these words is usually a premise (thus argument-indicator words usually indicate *both* the conclusion *and* a premise):

"therefore"
"hence"
"it follows that"

"consequently"
"in consequence"
"which shows that"
"so"
"then" (after "if")
"indicates that"
"implies that"
"entails that"
"so you can see that"
"we can conclude that"
"we can infer that"
"we may deduce that"
"points to the conclusion that"
"which means that"
"which shows that"
"leads one to believe that"
"bears out the point that"
"proves that"
"thus"
"as a result"
"accordingly"
"for this reason" (followed by a comma)

The following words are premise-indicators. The proposition which *follows* any one of them is usually a premise of an argument; and the proposition which *precedes* them is usually the conclusion:

"because"
"since"
"for"
"as"
"on the assumption that"
"if"
"if we assume that"
"if we suppose that"
"in view of the fact that"
"let us assume that"
"may be inferred from"
"may be deduced from"
"follows from"
"as shown by"
"inasmuch as"
"as indicated by"

"the reason is that"
"for the reason that"
"for this reason" (followed by a colon)

There could be a very short third list of double-premise-indicators. There would be only two words on this list: 'but' and 'and,' both of which are often used to connect two premises (e.g. "No angel is mortal, *but* he is mortal, therefore he is not an angel," or "All men are mortal *and* Socrates is man, therefore Socrates is mortal") But 'but' and 'and' have so many other functions that they do not *usually* function as double-premise-indicators, while the words on the other two lists *do* usually function as conclusion-indicators or premise-indicators.

Section 4. Arguments vs. explanations

Most of the words in the two lists above could also indicate the presence of explanations rather than arguments, so we must distinguish these two things.
Compare the two following:

(1) "He must be guilty because he has shifty eyes."
(2) "He is absent because he is ill."

(1) is an argument (a weak one), but (2) is an explanation, not an argument. In (1), we try to *prove* that he must be guilty, and the evidence we use to prove it is that he has shifty eyes. In (2), we do not try to *prove* that he is absent; we already know that to be true. That is not controversial, or in question; there is no need to prove it. Instead, we try to *explain, or give the cause* of his absence. We say that cause is his illness. But in (1), we do try to prove that he is guilty, for that is in question, that is controversial, not agreed, or not known. And his shifty eyes are brought up as evidence that supposedly proves that he is guilty. The implied syllogism is:

All who have shifty eyes are guilty.
And he has shifty eyes.
Therefore he is guilty.

It is a weak argument because the first premise, which was implied rather than stated, is pretty obviously not true. But if instead we use the true premise that "*Some* who have shifty eyes are guilty," the resulting syllogism is formally invalid or fallacious:

> Some who have shifty eyes are guilty.
> And he has shifty eyes.
> Therefore he is guilty.

It is a mistake to do that kind of thing with "He is absent because he is ill," to express it as a syllogism, for it is not trying to prove that he is absent, as a controversial, arguable proposition, at all. Instead of *proving* that he is absent, it *assumes* it, and then *explains* it by giving its cause.

How do we recognize this difference between arguments and explanations? We just "see" it, intuitively or instinctively, by understanding the meaning of the words and the context. There is no better explanation. Outside of logic classes, few people ever have any trouble making that distinction; only in logic classes do students get confused about it. The best way to distinguish them is simply to drop the context of "a logic textbook" and imagine you are talking to a friend.

Section 5. Truth and validity (B)

Arguments are either logically **valid** or logically **invalid**. If they are logically invalid, they contain a logical **fallacy**. The word "fallacy" has a specific and narrow meaning in logic. Not every *mistake* is a *fallacy*. An error of fact, like the belief that the earth is flat, is not called a fallacy in logic, though sometimes it is called that in ordinary language. Only an argument can be fallacious, not a proposition. A fallacy is a mistake in *reasoning*. A fallacy makes an argument logically "invalid." An argument without any fallacies is logically valid: its conclusion follows necessarily from its premises.

To review the threefold structure of logic once again:

Terms are never true or false, and never logically valid or invalid (fallacious), but only clear or unclear (ambiguous).

Propositions are never valid or invalid (fallacious), but only true or false. And each term within a proposition is either clear or unclear.

Arguments are either valid or invalid (fallacious). Each proposition in an argument is either true or false, and each term is either clear or unclear.

So a good argument is one whose terms are all clear, whose propositions are all true, and whose logic is valid. A bad argument is one with an unclear term or a false proposition or a logical fallacy.

Truth is a relationship between a single proposition and the real world, or the nature of things, or "objective reality," or what is "outside of" (independent of) the proposition and the mind that expresses it. *Validity* is a relationship *between propositions*: between the premises of an argument and the conclusion of the argument.

We have already studied "material fallacies," fallacies of content, wrong uses of the *content* in arguments. We are now about to study "formal fallacies," fallacies of logical form. Logical form is the relationship between, or arrangement of, terms and propositions (that is, the content, or matter) in an argument.

To understand what makes an argument invalid, we need to understand what makes one valid. An argument (we speak only of a *deductive* argument here) is valid if the premises necessitate the conclusion, if they prove the conclusion, if their being true makes it necessary that the conclusion be true. So in a valid argument, the premises cannot be true without the conclusion being true. If we know that the premises are true, we can be sure that the conclusion is true. This is the point of "validity": it assures us that it is safe to move to the conclusion if we have already moved to, or occupied, the premises – like a step across a river in a battle.

A valid argument gives us *certainty* about its conclusion. It is not absolute certainty but relative certainty, that is, certainty relative to the premises. It is conditional certainty or hypothetical certainty: certainty that *if* the premises are true, then the conclusion must be true. But it *is* certainty, which is a currently unfashionable thing; it is "rigid" and iron and awful and unchangeable. If all A is B and all B is C then all A *must* be C, necessarily and everywhere, for everyone and forever. At no time or place or culture or world can it change. Changes might take place in the laws of physics: water might run uphill tomorrow, or a galaxy of antimatter and antigravity might be discovered; but in all possible worlds the fundamental laws of logic must hold. Miracles might happen; the fundamental laws of the universe might be set aside by the Creator of the universe; but even the Creator cannot violate logical laws. If God exists, logical laws are the laws of the divine nature. Even God cannot both exist and not exist at the same time. A meaningless self-contradiction does not suddenly become meaningful because you add the words "God can do this" to it. And this is so not because we say so, because the human mind has legislated these laws. The laws of logic are not invented, they are discovered; they are objective truths. (Of course, the language systems we use to formulate them are invented, and our process of coming to learn them is subjective.)

In a previous chapter, we made the point (which some will find startling and even offensive) that it is very easy to define "truth." However, it is far from easy to find it, and to be sure when you have found it. We now make another point some will find surprising: it is easy to know with certainty whether an argument is valid. However, this is not enough: an argument is totally satisfactory only if it meets *three* criteria, and it is far from easy to know whether an argument is good by the other two criteria: whether all the terms are unambiguous and whether all the premises are true.

In any deductive argument, assuming the terms are clear, there are four possibilities:

(1) The premises are true and the logic is valid.

(2) The premises are true and the logic is invalid.

(3) At least one of the premises is false and the logic is valid.

(4) At least one of the premises is false and the logic is invalid.

Only in the first case can we know that the conclusion is true. In the other three cases, we do not know whether the conclusion is true or false.

LOGIC

		VALID	INVALID
PREMISES	*TRUE*	Conclusion true	Conclusion unknown
	FALSE	Conclusion unknown	Conclusion unknown

We can also know that an argument whose conclusion is false and whose logic is valid must have at least one false premise.

LOGIC

		VALID	INVALID
CONCLUSION	*TRUE*	Premises unknown	Premises unknown
	FALSE	At least one premise must be false	Premises unknown

This is equally important for practical purposes, since we often argue "backwards," so to speak, proving that a premise must be false from the fact that the conclusion is false (if the logic is valid), instead of "forwards," proving that a conclusion must be true from the fact that the premises are all true (if the logic is valid). These are the two most usual strategies in arguing: reasoning backwards, or "upstream" from pollution downstream (a false conclusion) to pollution upstream (a false premise); or reasoning forwards, or "downstream" from unpolluted (true) premises to an unpolluted (true) conclusion. And both strategies depend on this principle about the relationship between truth and validity in an argument.

We cannot validly argue in any other way. E.g., we cannot validly argue that if the premises of a valid argument are false, then the conclusion must be false too; that pollution upstream proves pollution downstream, so to speak; that if the argument is consistent, false premises must lead to a false conclusion just as surely as true premises lead to a true conclusion. That mistake comes from thinking of an argument as a sort of mathematical equation, with the premises on one side and the conclusion on the other. But a mathematical equation is reversible, while an argument is not. (Neither is a proposition simply reversible, as we have seen previously (page 140): the subject and the predicate are not interchangeable, but perform different functions.) In a valid argument, true premises entail a true conclusion (arguing "downstream"), but a true conclusion does not necessarily entail true premises. And a false conclusion entails false premises (arguing "upstream") but a false premise does not necessarily entail a false conclusion. The conclusion might be true by accident.

So only the two following inferences are correct:

1. **If the argument is valid and the premises are true, then the conclusion must be true.** (This is one mode of correct argument; we could call it *"arguing forward."*)
2. **If the argument is valid and the conclusion is false, then at least one premise must be false.** (This is the other mode of correct argument; we could call it *"arguing backward."*)

Here are two examples of valid arguments with false premises but a true conclusion:

All evil spirits are birds.   The earth is a star.
And all sparrows are evil spirits.   And no stars are fish.
Therefore all sparrows are birds.   Therefore the earth is not a fish.

In both cases above, the premises are false, and the argument is valid, yet the conclusion happens to be true (by accident).

The practical point of this is that *you do not refute a conclusion by showing that it follows from false premises.*

Suppose someone has just given a logically valid argument for a conclusion you disagree with, but this argument has one or more false premises in it. You point out these false premises. What have you accomplished? Something, but not everything. You have refuted his *argument* but not his *conclusion*. You have only shown that your opponent's argument has not proved his conclusion, as he claimed. His argument is inconclusive because it has a false premise. The conclusion is still in doubt. It is neither proved to be true, as your opponent has claimed, nor is it proved to be false.

And just because a valid argument has a true conclusion, that does not mean it has true premises. We must be careful not to think of an argument as a reversible equation. Like a river, an argument carries us in one direction, downstream: we can move from true premises to a true conclusion – we can know that if the premises are true, then the conclusion be true – but we cannot reverse this and know that if the conclusion is true the premises must be true. (We can, however, deduce that if the conclusion is false, at least one of the premises must have been false, just as we can deduce that if garbage is flowing down the river, someone must have unloaded it upstream.)

The practical point in strategy of arguing here can be summed up as the following:

(1)   You do *not* prove that a premise is true by showing that from it a true conclusion logically follows.
(2)   You do *not* prove that a conclusion is false by showing that it logically follows from a false premise.
(3)   You *do* prove that a premise is false by showing that from it a false conclusion logically follows.
(4)   You *do* prove that a conclusion is true by showing that it logically follows from true premises.

These situations all concern *valid* arguments. Here are some other situations with invalid arguments. When you have an invalid argument, you know nothing about truth and falsity:

(5)   You do *not* prove that a conclusion is false by showing that the argument is invalid. An invalid argument can have a true conclusion:

> The sky is blue
> And grass is green
> Therefore man is mortal

(6)   You do *not* prove that an argument is invalid by showing that its conclusion is false. A false conclusion can emerge from a valid argument if it has false premises:

> All pigs are purple
> And all purple things are immortal
> Therefore all pigs are immortal

(7)   You do *not* prove a conclusion is true by showing that the argument is valid. The premises must also be true. The example above (6) is a valid argument but has a false conclusion.

(8)   You do *not* prove an argument valid by showing that its conclusion is true. Example (5) above has a true conclusion but it is an invalid argument.

Arguing "Forward"

If Premises Are . . .	And Argument Is . . .	Then Conclusion Is . . .
TRUE	**VALID**	**TRUE**
TRUE	INVALID	UNKNOWN
FALSE	VALID	UNKNOWN
FALSE	INVALID	UNKNOWN

Arguing "Backward"

If Conclusion Is . . .	And Argument Is . . .	Then Premises Are . . .
TRUE	VALID	UNKNOWN
FALSE	**VALID**	**ONE FALSE**[4]
TRUE	INVALID	UNKNOWN
FALSE	INVALID	UNKNOWN

Imagine a spy trying to get out of East Berlin into West Berlin. In order to succeed in getting to West Berlin, he has to pass three checkpoints: Able, Baker, and Charlie. If he fails at any of one or more of the checkpoints, he fails to get out. The spy symbolizes an argument, and escape to West Berlin symbolizes proving its conclusion to be true. The three checkpoints are the three questions of logic, one for each of the "three acts of the mind" (see the charts on pages 32–33). Checkpoint Able checks for ambiguous terms. Checkpoint Baker checks for false premises. Checkpoint Charlie checks for logical fallacies.

---

4   At least one, possibly more.

We can know (1) that if the spy passes all three checkpoints, he succeeds (this is arguing "forward"); and that (2) if he does not succeed, he has failed at least one checkpoint (this is arguing "backward"). (3) We also know that if he has passed two of the three checkpoints and yet has not succeeded in getting to West Berlin, he must have failed the remaining checkpoint.

Thus we know (1) that if an argument has no ambiguous terms, false premises, or logical fallacies, its conclusion must be true; and that (2) if the conclusion is *not* true, it must have failed at least one of the three checkpoints. (3) We also know that if the argument with the false conclusion has passed any two of the three checkpoints, it must have failed the remaining one.

Exercises on the relationship between truth and validity·
Which of the following statements can we know to be true, assuming unambiguous terms? (This is probably the dullest, most abstract, and least interesting exercise in this book.)

1. If a premise is false and the argument is invalid, the conclusion must be false.
2. If a premise is false and the argument is invalid, the conclusion must be true.
3. If a premise is false and the argument is valid, the conclusion must be true.
4. If a premise is false and the argument is valid, the conclusion must be false.
5. If a premise is false and the conclusion is false, the argument must be invalid.
6. If a premise is false and the conclusion is false, the argument must be valid.
7. If a premise is false and the conclusion is true, the argument must be invalid.
8. If a premise is false and the conclusion is true, the argument must be valid.
9. If the premises are true and the argument is valid, the conclusion must be true.
10. If the premises are true and the argument is valid, the conclusion must be false.
11. If the premises are true and the argument is invalid, the conclusion must be false.
12. If the premises are true and the argument is invalid, the conclusion must be true.
13. If the premises are true and the conclusion is true, the argument must be valid.
14. If the premises are true and the conclusion is true, the argument must be invalid.
15. If the premises are true and the conclusion is false, the argument must be valid.
16. If the premises are true and the conclusion is false, the argument must be invalid.
17. If the argument is valid and the conclusion is false, at least one premise must be false.
18. If the argument is valid, the conclusion is false, and one premise is true, the other premise must be false.
19. If the conclusion is false, then either the argument is invalid or a premise is false.
20. If one premise is false, the conclusion true, and the argument valid, the other premise must be true.

IX: Different Kinds of Arguments

Section 1. Three meanings of "because"

In distinguishing arguments from explanations, it is necessary to distinguish three different meanings of the word "because" (and sometimes also the word "cause") which are often confused:

(1) the physical relation between cause and effect
(2) the logical relation between premise and conclusion
(3) the psychological relation between motive and act

(1) The relation between cause and effect is easily understood. When we say "I will die because of cancer," we point to death as the effect and cancer as the cause. When we say "The Red Sox did not win a World Series for 86 years because of the Curse of the Bambino," we point to their 86-year drought as the effect and the Curse as the cause. (More prosaic minds can substitute weak pitching as the cause.)

(2) The relation between premise and conclusion is different. It is a *logical* relation, not a *physical* (#1) or *psychological* (#3) relation. When we say "I will die because all men die and I am a man," I point to the truth of "I will die" as the conclusion that is proved, and I point to "all men die and I am a man" as the two premises which together prove that conclusion. When we say "Since the Red Sox finally defeated the Yankees in the playoffs, God must have converted and is not a Yankee fan any more," we point to God's conversion as our conclusion and the Red Sox victory as our reason for believing that conclusion. When we say "He believes in Heaven because there has to be perfect justice in the end," we point to his conclusion that Heaven exists and to the fact (or claim) that there must be perfect justice in the end as his premise or logical reason for believing it.

(3) "Because" can also indicate a psychological motive for a mental or physical act. When I say "I think I will die today because I am feeling despair,"

I point to my belief that I will die today as my mental act and to my feeling of despair as my motive, or moving force leading me to this belief. It is not a physical cause, nor is it a logical reason. I am giving the subjective cause for my believing it rather than the objective cause of its really happening. I am giving a motive for the subjective, psychological act rather than either a logical reason proving the conclusion or a physical cause causing the event. When I say "I always expect the Red Sox to blow a lead because I'm a New England pessimist," I'm pointing to my pessimism as the psychological motive or moving cause for my belief. When I say "He believes in Heaven because he's afraid to die," I'm pointing to his fear of death as the subjective, psychological moving cause of his belief in Heaven. I'm not saying his fear of death is a logical proof of Heaven, nor that it is the physical cause or creator of Heaven.

The psychological "because" is the reason children first give, since we know our own subjective feelings most easily. The causal "because" is the next reason we give, for physical sensations of physical things come easy and early to us. The logical "because" is the last and most advanced reason we give, for it is the most abstract and difficult. The first "because" is subjective and immaterial, the second is objective and material, the third is objective and immaterial.

A very common fallacy today is to confuse two of these "becauses," to substitute the psychological "because" for the logical "because." (This is essentially the "genetic fallacy": see page 81.) We live in the psychological era. We think we refute an idea when we uncover its psychological origins. For example, if belief in God can be shown to be motivated by fear (as Freud says), we think that proves the belief is false. But this is a confusion. The objective logical proof, reason, or evidence for a belief is independent of the believer's subjective psychological motives. You do not logically refute an idea by pointing to suspicious motives, but by pointing to inadequate evidence. Freud's critique of religion is a long, complex, clever, and detailed version of exactly this fallacy. It amounts to: "God does not exist because people are terrified of a universe without a father-figure." *After* we know an idea is false, we naturally wonder what psychological motives could have led people to believe it, and then we rightly point to the psychological motive. Pointing to the motive *instead* of to the reasons, "refuting" the motive instead of the idea, is a form of "the genetic fallacy."

Note that both "because" #2, the logical reason, and "because" #3, the psychological motive, are causes of *thinking*, while "because #1" is a cause of *being*. When someone says "It's going to rain because the sky is full of dark clouds," he is giving a cause of the *being* of the rain; when he says "It must be raining because the streets are wet," he is only giving a cause of his *thinking* that it is raining; for the wetness of the streets does not *cause* the rain to be. And when someone says "I think it must be raining, because everything else has gone wrong in my day so far," he is giving a merely psychological and subjective "because," an irrational cause of his believing that it is raining rather than a rational one.

The difference between motives ("because" #3) and reasons ("because" #2) is that motives are psychological "efficient causes" of beliefs while reasons are "formal causes." To see what this means, we need to look at one of the most useful ideas ever discovered, Aristotle's notion of the "four causes." It is an idea that is so basic that it is a criterion of being educated, a condition for being civilized.

Section 2. The four causes (P)

Be sure you understand the above explanation of the distinction between arguments and explanations before reading this section.

Causes can be used either (1) as *arguments*, to prove some controversial idea which some people think to be true and others false, or to predict some as-yet-unseen and unknown future event, or (2) as *explanations* for an idea that is not controversial because it is already known or admitted to be true, or for an event that is past or present and already seen or known.

There are four kinds of causes, therefore four kinds of causal explanations, as well as four kinds of causal arguments.

Two of the four causes, the "efficient cause" and the "final cause," are *extrinsic* to the effect. The other two causes, the "formal cause" and the "material cause," are *intrinsic* to the effect. What we mean by "cause and effect" in ordinary language today is usually restricted to the efficient cause, or at most to the efficient cause and the final cause. However, we still use the word "because" for all four causes, whether in causal explanations or causal arguments.

We take the two intrinsic causes (or "becauses") first. The *formal cause* is the essence, or essential nature, of a thing, *what* it is. This is expressed in a definition, most perfectly in an essential definition (see page 123). The formal cause of an acorn is to be the seed of an oak tree. The formal cause of an operation is to be a surgical intervention into a human body. The formal cause of this book is to be an elementary Aristotelian logic text. The formal cause of a river is to be a large body of water flowing between two banks. The formal cause of "butterflies in the stomach" is to be a feeling of agitation in the lower abdomen.

The *material cause* is the contents or raw material of a thing: what it is made of. The material cause of an acorn is pulp and shell. The material cause of an operation is an incision and the repair of some body part. The material cause of this book is all its words, topics, and chapters. The material cause of a river is water. The material cause of "butterflies in the stomach" is palpitation of the nerves.

Now the two extrinsic causes. The *efficient cause* is the agent that makes, moves, or changes the effect. The efficient cause of an acorn is an oak tree. The efficient cause of an operation is a surgeon. The efficient cause of this book is its author. The efficient cause of a river is centuries of erosion. The efficient cause of the feeling of "butterflies in the stomach" can be fear, or falling in love, or hearing transcendently beautiful music, or indigestion.

The *final cause* is the end, goal, or purpose of something, whether this purpose is conscious or not, and whether the thing is artificial or natural. The final cause of an acorn is to grow into an oak tree. The final cause of an operation is to heal a disease. The final cause of this book is to teach logic. The final cause of a river is to flow to the lowest possible point. The final cause of "butterflies in the stomach" is to warn the body to act differently somehow, e.g. to avoid foods that cause indigestion.

A historical sidebar on final causes: Modern philosophy tends to be very suspicious of final causes or "teleology" (from *telos*, the Greek word for purpose) anywhere except in consciously purposive human activity. (Some philosophers even deny it there and say man is just a complex machine.) But it is reasonable and commonsensical to believe that "there is a purpose for everything," even though that purpose is not always known or present to human minds (as distinct from the mind of God). The reason for thinking that everything must have a final cause is that just as the efficient cause of any thing is the reason why its matter is now determined to have this form rather than another, so the final cause is the reason why the efficient cause acts as it does, toward this determinate end and not randomly. E.g. the words in this book (its content, raw material, or "matter") are formed into a logic text (its "form" or essence) *because of the purpose* of this text: to teach logic. It has seemed reasonable and "commonsensical" to almost all people in all times, places, and cultures to believe in real teleology even for mindless things in nature; for these things, after all, move in regular and predictable ways, like arrows directed to targets: dogs have puppies and puppies become dogs. The fact that we do not *know* the purposes of natural things nearly as well as we know the purposes of the artificial things we designed does not mean that there *are* no such natural purposes. (Unless everything we don't know can't be!)

There were two main reasons why belief in final causes declined in the modern West. The first was the confusion of science with scien*tism*. Early modern physical scientists discovered that when we use the scientific method, final causality was useless for its explanatory purposes (naturally, since these final causes or natural purposes are not clearly known by the human mind, since we did not design nature). But scien*tism* was the philosophical (not scientific) belief that *only* science provided objectively reliable knowledge.

The second reason for the decline of belief in final causes was a decline of belief in religion. Obviously, natural design and a cosmic Designer of nature naturally (but not *necessarily*) go together.

So the four causes, (1) formal, (2) material, (3) efficient, and (4) final, tell us a thing's (1) identity, (2) contents, (3) origin, and (4) destiny; or (1) what it is, (2) what it's made of, (3) where it came from, and (4) where it's going. Obviously, the most important application of these four questions is to ourselves. If we were to fulfill Socrates' (and Apollo's) first law, "know thyself," we would have to know the answers to these four questions about ourselves and our life. And of the four questions, the fourth is the most important, for the question of the final cause of human life is the question of the "meaning of life" or the "purpose of life" or the *summum bonum* (greatest good, ultimate end).

The four questions are obviously connected: if our origin is merely dust and chance, our essence is also merely dust and chance, and so is our destiny. If our origin is more heavenly, so is our essence and our destiny.

All four causes are always connected, since they are not merely artifices, humanly-invented methods for explaining things, but real aspects of real things. The final cause is the reason why the efficient cause imposes the formal cause on the material cause. To shelter a family is the reason why a carpenter shapes wood into a house. To teach logic is the reason why an author forms words into a logic textbook.

$$* \quad * \quad * \quad * \quad *$$

The four causes may be used as arguments or as explanations. We consider arguments first. Arguments, in moving from premises to conclusion, may move either from *cause to effect* or from *effect to cause*. When an argument moves "forward," from cause to effect, it deduces the effect from the cause, in any one of the four senses of "cause":

"The castle is made by a great artist, therefore it will be great art." This is deducing the effect from the efficient cause.

"The castle is square, therefore it will have four 90-degree interior angles." This is deducing the effect from the formal cause.

"The castle is made of strong stone, therefore it will last for centuries." This is deducing the effect from the material cause.

"The castle is designed to hold many people, therefore it will be large." This is deducing the effect from the final cause.

When an argument moves "backward," from effect to cause, it deduces the cause from the effect, in any one of the four senses of "cause":

"The castle is great art, therefore it must have been made by a great artist." This is deducing the efficient cause from the effect.

"The castle has four 90 degree interior angles, therefore it is square." This is deducing the formal cause from the effect.

"The castle has lasted for centuries, therefore it must be made of strong stone." This is deducing the material cause from the effect.

"The castle is large, therefore it must be designed to hold many people." This is deducing the final cause from the effect.

Explanations, as distinct from arguments, always explain the effect by the cause and not vice versa.

Explanations can use any one of the four causes:

"Man is morally responsible because he is rational." (explanation by formal cause) (Reason is not the *efficient* cause of moral responsibility, for reason does not act on man as a carpenter acts on wood. Rather, moral responsibility is due to man being the kind of being he is, namely rational.)

"I am reading this logic book to become a more critical thinker." (explanation by final cause)

"This book is abstract because it is written by a philosophy professor." (explanation by efficient cause)

"This book is long because it includes all of traditional logic." (explanation by material cause)

Exercises: Identify which of the four causes is used in each of the following explanations or arguments; and tell whether it is an explanation or an argument:

1. I'm getting a college degree to get a better job.
2. It's loud because it's a rock concert.
3. I study logic because I think it will raise my grade point average in other courses.
4. He's throwing the textbook at the wall in frustration because he's studying logic.
5. Toilet paper is absorbent because of its capillary structure.
6. This footprint must be that of a six-toed sloth, because that's the only animal with six toes.
7. I play tennis just to relax.
8. Stadiums are strong because they're made with steel-reinforced concrete.
9. Men pitch baseballs faster than women because they have more upper body muscle strength.
10. Women's voices are higher than men's because their vocal cords are different.
11. The ball will land in the seats because the home run hitter is up.
12. Children ask questions because the reason we're here is to know truth.
13. The tide is high because the moon is full.
14. The iron filings are moving because there's a magnet here.
15. It's water because it's two parts hydrogen and one part oxygen.
16. E.T. is a person because he can communicate.

Section 3. A classification of arguments

We can classify arguments by different standards:

(1) By form: Arguments may be either **immediate inference** (Chapter VII) or **mediate inference**. Immediate inference contains only one premise and only

two terms; mediate inference contains at least two premises and at least three terms.

Immediate inference includes **opposition, obversion, conversion**, and **contraposition.**

Within mediate inference, arguments may be either **deductive** or **inductive**. Deductive arguments begin with a general, or universal, premise and usually apply it to a particular case in the conclusion. Inductive arguments begin with particular, individual, specific cases and usually generalize to a more universal conclusion. Deductive arguments claim certainty; inductive arguments claim only probability. We will deal with induction in Chapter XIV.

Deductive arguments are usually syllogisms, either **simple syllogisms**, composed only of simple (categorical) propositions, or **compound syllogisms**, which contain at least one compound proposition. There are different rules for each kind of syllogism. We will deal with syllogisms in Chapters X, XI, and XII.

Within compound syllogisms, there are three basic types: **hypothetical, disjunctive**, and **conjunctive**. We will deal with them in Chapter XIII.

(2) By causality: Any kind of deductive argument may also be divided into **arguments from cause to effect**, or **arguments from effect to cause**. Both of these in turn can be divided into four kinds depending on which of the four causes is used: formal, material, efficient, or final.

(3) By direction of movement: We may move from an argument's premise to its conclusion, or we may move from a conclusion back to its premise. The objective logical structure of the argument is the same in each case, but our subjective psychological process is different. Sometimes we deduce a new conclusion from a given premise, and sometimes we trace a given conclusion back to its not-given but implicit premise, arguing that in order to reach a given conclusion you need to assume such and such a premise.

(4) By length: Any of the above kinds of arguments may also be divided into one-step arguments and multiple arguments. Multiple arguments are simply chains of simple arguments, where the conclusion of the first step becomes a premise for the second step.

(5) By strategy: Multi-step arguments can be put together either linearly or cumulatively. A **linear argument** is like a river that begins at one place, with one premise, and takes a number of turns, adding other premises, like tributaries, usually using multiple arguments in a chain, and finally reaching one destination, the conclusion. Socrates' arguments are usually of this nature and usually contain many steps. A **cumulative argument** is like a number of rivers all running into the same lake. It uses different premises, and different, independent arguments, often of different types, all to establish the same conclusion. This is the kind of argument most often used in debate or in informal conversation.

Section 4. Simple argument maps (B)

The patterns of arguments can be made clear by a very simple form of argument map, in which the movement from premises to conclusion is symbolized by an arrow, with the conclusion at the point of the arrow and a premise at the feathered end of the arrow. Two premises joined together in a syllogism look like a marriage in a genealogical table. For instance, take the classic

> All men are mortal.
> Socrates is a man.
> Therefore Socrates is mortal.

The argument map for this argument would be the following:

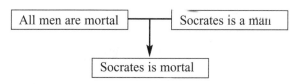

The horizontal line between the two premises is like a marriage: only when conjoined together do these two premises produce the legitimate child, their conclusion.

At some point in the future it may be useful to save time by the abbreviation of using symbols for whole propositions instead of writing them out; but at this point, to avoid any possibility of confusion, you should take the time to patiently write out the whole proposition in each box when using argument maps.

Take the following linear argument:

> All that is material is extended in space.
> And all that is extended in space can be divided.
> Therefore all that is material can be divided.
> And all that can be divided can be destroyed.
> Therefore all that is material can be destroyed.

The argument map here is simply:

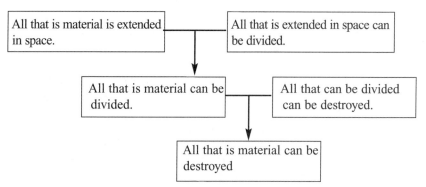

Now take the following cumulative argument: "There must be a life after death, because life would be unendurable otherwise, and because nearly every culture in history teaches it, and because there has to be a final judgment, and also because we're not just bodies but spirits too."

Here, four different premises all are brought up to prove the same conclusion. The argument map for this argument would be:

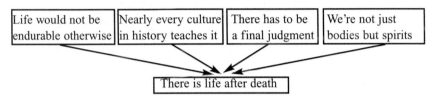

There is no horizontal line between the premises because each one is "unmarried," so to speak: independent.

In the next few chapters we will learn how to judge how strong each of these arguments is. An argument map does not evaluate the *strength* of an argument, but only diagrams its *strategy*. The strength of an argument depends on three things: whether the terms are clear, whether the premises are true, and whether the logical progressions are logically valid. We have already studied terms and the technique for making them clear: definition. We will soon study the rules for judging whether any given argument is logically valid or invalid. But there is no one technique or set of rules for judging whether any given proposition is true or false.

The following argument is more complex:

> "If there were a God, the world would be perfect, and this world is far from perfect. Besides, science can explain everything real without God. And psychology can explain all our subjective fantasies and fallacies and faiths without God, because it can trace them all back to fear or ignorance – for instance, ignorance of the forces of nature led the Greeks to believe that a god made thunder. So it seems more rational to me to be an atheist."

The first thing to do in approaching any argument is to find its conclusion. This is usually intuitively obvious, but even if it is not, there is usually a "conclusion indicator" (see the list above, on pages 191–92). Here, it is the word "so." The conclusion also usually comes either last or first. Here the conclusion is that "it is more rational to be an atheist." Each of the three separate arguments that come before this conclusion is a different reason for believing it. Thus, the overall argument is cumulative. However, the last of the three separate arguments is itself linear, For it supports its point with a "because" and a "for instance," a premise and an example. (Examples often function as premises for inductive arguments.) So our argument diagram here would be more complex:

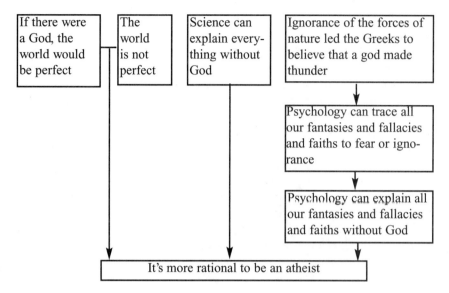

This argument is more complex for a number of reasons.

For one thing, it is a combination of a cumulative argument (overall structure) and a linear argument (third reason, on the right).

For another thing, the first argument (on the left) has two premises, the second argument (in the middle) has only one, and the third argument (on the right) has three.

The two premises of the first argument fit together to prove the conclusion that "it is more rational to be an atheist."

The second argument has a hidden premise that is not expressed, "If science can explain everything without God, then it's more rational to be an atheist." We will learn how to "smoke out" these hidden premises later.

The third argument offers the proposition "psychology can explain all our fantasies and fallacies and faiths without God" as a reason for the conclusion "it is more rational to be an atheist," identifying this proposition about psychology as a premise by putting the word "because" before it; then it offers a reason for believing *this* premise, namely that "it (psychology) can trace them (all our fantasies, fallacies, and faiths) back to fear and ignorance." (This becomes clearer when we translate pronouns into the nouns they stand for – one of the techniques we will utilize when we learn to put arguments into logical form.) Then it gives a reason for believing that "it can trace them back to fear and ignorance" by the example of the Greeks believing that a god made thunder.

When we are confronted with a complex argument, consisting of a series of separate arguments, it is always best to use an argument map first. It is like consulting a road map before going on a trip to a place you have never visited before. Each arrow on the argument map will be a separate logical argument which you will have to (1) identify (locate), then (2) classify (as inductive or deductive, simple syllogism or something else), and then (3) evaluate (as logically valid or invalid). Argument maps help you to do the first of these three steps. You identify each separate argument, and its relation to the other separate arguments, as well as its place in the overall argument, by such argument maps. Only then are you ready to classify and evaluate each of these separate arguments without confusing one with another. You will learn the rules to use in evaluating each kind of argument (the third step) in the following chapters. You will also learn the forms and structures of each kind of argument (the second step), so that you can identify which kind of argument you have. You cannot apply the rules for inductive arguments to arguments that are deductive, for instance, or vice versa. You cannot apply the rules that distinguish valid from invalid *simple* syllogisms if you have a *compound* syllogism. Each kind of argument has a different set of rules, so you must (1) first identify each distinct argument, then (2) classify it (determine what kind of argument it is), and then (3) evaluate it by its appropriate set of rules. More complex arguments maps are presented on page 282. You might be able to do a few of the exercises on these more complex arguments, on page 285. Try them.

Section 5. Deductive and inductive reasoning (B)

There are two fundamentally different kinds of reasoning, deductive and inductive. One of the differences between them is their premises: inductive reasoning uses particular or specific or individual premises and usually moves to a more general conclusion, while deductive reasoning begins with a general, or universal, premise and usually moves to a less general conclusion.

This general rule needs to be qualified, however. It does not mean that in a deductive argument the conclusion must be an I or an O proposition; it is often an A or an E proposition. But it is always an application of one of the premises, which acts as a principle, to a case in point of it; and this *usually* makes the conclusion less universal, but not always. In the classic syllogism "All men are mortal, and Socrates is a man, therefore Socrates is mortal," the conclusion is less universal than one of the premises (the first one). In the following syllogism, the conclusion, though an A, is also less universal than the first premise:

> All men are mortal.
> And all Irishmen are men.
> Therefore all Irishmen are mortal.

(For "all men" is more universal than "all Irishmen.") But in the following syllogism, the conclusion is just as universal as the premise:

> All bachelors are unmarried men.
> No unmarried men are men who have wives.
> Therefore no bachelors are men who have wives.

The clearest difference between deduction and induction is that the premises of induction come from sense observation, which is always of individual cases; while at least one of the premises of deduction comes from intellectual understanding, which always includes something universal.

Just as deduction does not *always* move from the universal to the more particular, induction does not always move from the more particular to the more universal. Some kinds of inductive argument do not end in a general conclusion: e.g. many arguments from analogy and causal arguments.

Here is another kind of inductive argument with a singular conclusion:

> I am a professor and I am absent-minded.
> And she is a professor and she is absent-minded.
> And they are professors and they are absent-minded.
> And he is a professor.
> Therefore he is probably absent-minded.

A second difference between induction and deduction is that deduction always claims certainty for its conclusion, while inductive reasoning claims only probability. Obviously, if all A is B, then this A is B too (deductive); while if this A is B, it does not follow with certainty that all A is B (inductive). An inductive argument claims to give good reasons for its conclusion, but they are not good enough for certainty, only some degree of probability. Thus deductive arguments are either simply valid or simply invalid, while inductive arguments are better or worse, more or less probable.

An inductive argument can claim certainty only if it is a "complete induction," that is, covers all cases. If I know there are only ten people in my class, and if I have examined each one and determined that he is over 18, I can conclude with certainty that all the people in my class are over 18.

Deductive and inductive arguments have totally different sets of rules. The rules for deductive arguments are "tight," certain, and infallible. (Obviously, the people who use the rules are not!) A computer can determine whether any deductive argument is formally valid or invalid. But the rules for inductive arguments are not "tight" but "loose." An inductive argument is like a plane that is flown "by the seat of your pants" while a deductive argument is like a plane flown by instruments.

Section 6. Combining induction and deduction: Socratic method (P)

Socrates was the first person who seemed to know exactly what he was doing in using both inductive and deductive reasoning together. His typical method of arguing combined the two as follows:

(1) First, a **question** arises: e.g. Is it true that political justice is simply whatever is in the interest of the stronger, as Thrasymachus the Sophist maintains in Book I of the *Republic*?

(2) We begin by making relevant sense observations of **examples** of justice. A just doctor heals and improves the weaker man, the patient who is sick; a just teacher of horse handling teaches and improves the weaker man, the man who does not know how to handle horses; and so with other cases.

(3) We then make an **inductive generalization** on the basis of these examples (and this is inductive reasoning): it seems that justice is in the interest of the weaker rather than the stronger.

(4) The fourth step is **understanding the necessity of this universal** which we have arrived at, by understanding the reason for it: justice is always in the interest of the weaker because of what justice essentially is, by its own nature. In step three we know the *fact*; in step four we understand the *reason* for it.

(5) We can then proceed to the **application of the universal to the particular by deduction**. We apply our general principle to the specific example under discussion, political justice, by deductive reasoning: Since justice is in the interest of the weaker, not the stronger; and since political justice is a form of justice; therefore political justice too must be in the interest of the weaker, not the stronger.

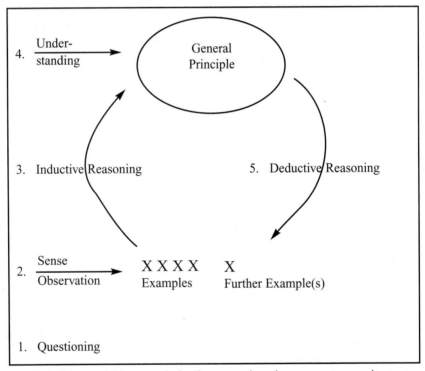

Step 4 is crucial because inductive reasoning alone cannot prove its general conclusion with certainty. So if the general principle that has been arrived at by induction is not known with any more certainty than the inductive argument gives it (in step 3), then when we use it as the premise of a deductive argument (in step 5), that premise will still only be *probably* true, and the conclusion of the deductive argument will also be only probably true, even though its connection with its premises is certain. It is certain that *if* all swans are white and this is a swan, this is white; but if it is not certain that all swans are white, then it is not certain that this swan is white.

The step in Socratic method *between* the inductive reasoning and the deductive reasoning is not a step of reasoning but understanding; a first-act-of-the-mind insight into the universal that has been discovered by inductive reasoning. And only when this insight understands the *necessity* of this universal principle can that principle be known with certainty and not only with probability, which is all that induction gives. Only then can that principle yield certainty in the conclusion that follows from it by deductive reasoning. For instance.

(1) We wonder whether we are going to die.

(2) We look around for relevant evidence and we observe in experience that each individual human being that we know of who has lived in the past has died. We know a few of these deaths from direct experience, and we know most of them through authorities like obituary columns and history books. We also know that each individual living in the present believes himself to be mortal.

(3) From this data base, we arrive by induction at the principle that "all men are mortal." So far this is only probable, its probability increasing as the data base increases.

(4) Then we come to understand that mortality is a property, and not just an accident, of man; that man is mortal by nature, since man by his nature has an animal body, which is an organic, interdependent system of material organs all of which are needed in order for it to live, and any one of which can be destroyed simply by separating some of its material parts from others by a rock or a knife or a fire.

(5) Having understood that "all men are mortal" by necessity, our deduction that "all men are mortal, and I am a man, therefore I am mortal," can give us a conclusion we can be certain is true, for it not only validly follows from its true premises but validly follows from its *certainly* true premises.

This is the overall epistemological pattern of the logic of the Socratic Method. What is more famous, and more typically associated with Socrates, is the methodological format *within* step five, the famous art of cross-examination (probably imitated from Athenian court cases) in which Socrates (a) does not lecture but asks his opponent questions, eliciting "yes" or "no" answers, (b) does so in a "dialectical" way, that is, in the form of "either-or" dilemmas, and (c) uses long, multi-step *reductio ad absurdum* arguments to refute one horn of the dilemma, thus proving the other. These are the "signature" details of Socratic method, and the larger context of the five steps is usually forgotten; but that larger context is Socrates' even more fundamental contribution to the art of philosophical argument. Aristotle, who disagrees with much of Socrates' (or Plato's) philosophy (e.g. the metaphysical Theory of Forms, the anthropological dualism of body and soul, and the epistemological rationalism and theory of knowledge as "recollection" of innate ideas), agrees with and uses these five steps himself. In fact, these five steps are not some specialized, esoteric method proper to Socrates alone, or the Greeks alone, but they constitute the most natural and complete movement of human knowledge.

From the Aristotelian point of view, six alternative theories of knowledge can be seen to exaggerate one of the steps, or to omit one of the steps, or to wrongly order the steps, of this Socratic scheme. (1) Dogmatism (in the popular sense) omits step one, the question, or the questionableness of the question. (2) Skepticism denies that we can go beyond Step 1 and have any reliable knowledge even in Step 2, sense perception. (3) Radical empiricism denies that we can go beyond Step 2. (3) Moderate Empiricism denies that we can go beyond Step 3, reliable but only probable generalizations from sense experience. (4) Extreme Rationalism claims that Step 4, understanding essences, is innate rather than dependent on experience. (5) Rationalism claims that Step 5, deductive reasoning, can be certain without depending on Step 2, sense perception. And (6) Kantian Idealism gets all the parts together but orders them wrongly, working the circle backwards, imposing categories (essences) on experience rather than deriving them from it.

The reason why Socrates' argument in Book I of the *Republic* is not satisfying to him (see the last paragraph of Book I), and why it should not be satisfying to us, is that Step 4 is missing (an understanding of the essential nature of justice); and this is supplied by the rest of the *Republic*. The argument in Book I is formally valid (and, by the way, very complex; an argument map of all its steps would look like an archery contest), and its observational data base and its inductive reasoning (Steps 2 and 3) are sound. But that is all. This example (the difference between Book I and Books II–X of the *Republic*) illustrates the inferiority of modern symbolic logic to classical Socratic-Aristotelian logic. Correct manipulation of symbols according to computer-like rules of consistency, plus empirical evidence, is not enough to convince human beings of a truth, even if expressed in all the complex and sophisticated techniques of symbolic logic, because human beings are "rational," and "rational" means not merely *calculating* but *understanding*; not merely the third act of the mind but the first; not merely the fifth step of the Socratic Method but the fourth. That is why Plato put this step at the *top* of his "divided line" in Book 6 of the *Republic*, which summarizes the steps of the education of the philosopher.

X. Syllogisms

Section 1. The structure and strategy of the syllogism (B)

The syllogism is the heart of logic. It is the easiest, most natural, and most convincing form of argument. Its structure is so simple and perfect that to everyone it is convincing and to some it is even beautiful. Consider the classic example:

> All men are mortal.
> And Socrates is a man.
> Therefore Socrates is mortal.

(We keep using the same simple, well-known examples not out of a lack of imagination but out of compassion for beginners, because they are simple, clear, and easily remembered.) We can see from this example the essential ingredients in the structure of a syllogism:

There are **three propositions: two premises and one conclusion.**
There are **three terms. Each term is used twice.**
The subject of the conclusion is called **the minor term.**
The predicate of the conclusion is called **the major term.**
The term which appears in each premise but not in the conclusion is called the **middle term.**
The premise containing the major term is called **the major premise.**
The premise containing the minor term is called **the minor premise.**

You cannot tell which premise is the major premise and which is the minor premise until you have first identified which term is the major term and which is the minor term. And you do this only by looking at the conclusion. So to analyze a syllogism,

(1) First identify the conclusion.
(2) Then identify the minor and major terms. (They are, respectively, the subject and the predicate of the conclusion.)
(3) Then identify the major and minor premises. (They contain, respectively, the major and minor terms.)

(4) Finally, identify the middle term as the term that is left, the term that is not in the conclusion but is in each premise.

From now on we will use the following standard abbreviations:

S = the minor term
P = the major term
M = the middle term

We use S for the minor term because it is always the subject (S) of the conclusion. It is *not* always the subject of the minor premise, however. Sometimes it is and sometimes it is not. But even when it is the predicate of the minor premise, we will use the symbol S for it, since it is always the subject of the conclusion.

We use P for the major term because it is always the predicate (P) of the conclusion. It is not always the predicate of the major premise, however. Sometimes it is and sometimes it is not.

We use M for the middle term no matter where it appears in the premises. It may be the subject of both premises, or the predicate of both, or the subject of one and the predicate of the other.

(All this technical terminology is necessary if we want to analyze arguments clearly and judge them as valid or invalid.)

It is conventional to place the major premise first, then the minor premise, and last the conclusion, when putting a syllogism into logical form. But in ordinary language, the three propositions in a syllogism can occur in any order whatsoever. In fact, one of them is often omitted, and implied or "kept in mind." (This kind of syllogism is called an "enthymeme," from the Greek word for "kept in mind." It is the commonest form of all in ordinary language.) The order of the premises is not important. When you put in a syllogism in logical form, the only rule about the order of the three propositions is that the conclusion is always put last. The major premise does not *have* to be put first, unless your instructor is very picky. (But there are often good reasons for being picky.)

Using this terminology, we can now understand the *strategy* of the syllogism. It can be summarized in the following diagram:

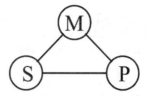

The conclusion is what we are trying to prove. It is a single proposition, with a subject and a predicate, S and P. We want to prove that P can be affirmed of S, that S and P belong together (if the proposition is affirmative); or that P must be denied of S, that S and P do not belong together (if the proposition is negative). To do this, we relate both S and P to the same common third term, M. The middle term is the *touchstone*; we test whether or not S and P belong together by *touching both to M*, as we would test whether two magnets have the same polarity by touching them both to the same third magnet to see whether they react to it in the same way or in opposite ways.

Imagine a bridge over a river. The middle term is the middle of the bridge. S and P are the two ends of the bridge, where it touches the land. The major and minor premises are the two halves of the bridge: the major premise connects M (the middle of the bridge) with P (one end of the bridge) and the minor premise connects M with S (the other end of the bridge). It is M that either holds the bridge together or makes it fall apart. The middle term is the center and key of the syllogism, the hinge on which it turns.

Let us look at two different cases: a syllogism with an affirmative conclusion and a syllogism with a negative conclusion.

Case #1: an affirmative conclusion. If both S and P are related affirmatively to M in the premises, then S and P must be related affirmatively to each other in the conclusion. It is an axiom in algebra that two quantities equal to a common third quantity are equal to each other. Although S and P are not quantities, and the copula ("is") is not the same as the equal sign in mathematics, yet the axiom is applicable here too: if S and M agree, and if M and P agree, then S and P agree.

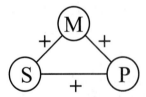

(2) Case #2: a negative conclusion. If S and P are related to M in opposite ways in the premises – if one of them is related to M affirmatively and the other negatively – then S and P must be related to each other negatively in the conclusion. The axiom here is that "Two quantities, one of which is, and the other of which is not, equal to a common third quantity, are not equal to each other."

There are two forms of the negative syllogism, since it may be either S or P that agrees with M.

(2A) If S and M agree, but M and P do not, then S and P do not:

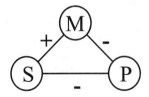

For example: No mortals are gods.
                    And all men are mortals.
                    Therefore no men are gods.

(2B) And if S and M do not agree, but M and P do, then S and P do not:

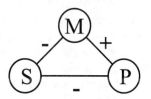

For example: Computers are machines.
                    And humans are not machines.
                    Therefore humans are not computers.

(3) What if S and P are both related to M negatively? Then we know nothing about how they are related to each other. We cannot prove a negative conclusion from two negative premises. For instance,

                    No men are insects.
                    And no insects write logic books.
                    Therefore no men write logic books.

is obviously an invalid argument. Its premises are both true, but its conclusion is false.

Imagine S, M, and P as warring nations, which can be either allies or enemies. (In affirmative propositions the two terms are like allies; in negative propositions they are like enemies.) Let us look at three possible cases: (1) no negative premises, (2) one negative premise, and (3) two negative premises.

(1) If S and M are allies, and M and P are allies, then S and P must be allies. (E.g. if France and England are allies, and England and America are allies, then France and America must be allies.)

(2A) If S and M are enemies, and M and P are allies, then S and P must be enemies. (E.g. if America and Germany are enemies, and Germany and Italy are allies, then America and Italy must be enemies.)

(2B) If S and M are allies, and M and P are enemies, then S and P must be enemies. (E.g. if England and America are allies, and America and Japan are enemies, then England and Japan must be enemies.)

(3) If S and M are enemies, and M and P are enemies, then S and P may be allies or enemies. (E.g. if America and Germany are enemies, and Germany and Russia are enemies, then America and Russia may be either allies or enemies.) The saying is not always true that "the enemy of my enemy is my friend." But the ally of my enemy must be my enemy.

Exercises: True or false?
1. The middle term always appears once in the major premise.
2. The middle term always appears once in the minor premise.
3. The minor term is always the predicate of the minor premise.
4. The middle term is never the predicate of two premises.
5. No syllogism can have only two terms.
6. No one syllogism can have four terms.
7. The major term can never be the subject of the conclusion.
8. In the syllogism "no A is B and some C is B, therefore some C is not A," the major premise comes first.
9. (H) In the syllogism "You smell and I don't, therefore I'm not you," the middle term is "one who smells."
10. "All cardinals are red, therefore some red things are cardinals" is a syllogism.

Section 2. The skeptic's objection to the syllogism (P)

A classic objection to the syllogism comes from ancient skeptics, who argued that every syllogism rests on its unproved premises; these need to be proved by other syllogisms, which in turn rest on unproved premises, *et cetera et cetera ad infinitum.*

Take our old friend "All men are mortal, Socrates is a man, therefore Socrates is mortal." It claims that we can know that Socrates is mortal because this conclusion necessarily follows from the two premises. But, the skeptic points out, these premises may be false. Just because the syllogism is logically valid does not mean that its conclusion must be true. "All trees are cats, Socrates is a tree, therefore Socrates is a cat" is logically valid, but its conclusion is false because its premises are false. So, the skeptic argues, we need to prove that the premises are true before we can know that any conclusion is true. How shall we prove the two premises? We need two more syllogisms. But the syllogism that proves each premise is subject to the same problem as the initial syllogism: its premises are either unproved (in which case we do not know that its conclusion is true), or have to be proved by other syllogisms with other premises, which in turn are either unproved or need to be proved by assuming other premises, *et cetera, et cetera ad infinitum.* We have an infinite regress of premises.

Aristotle answered this argument very simply: there is no infinite regress of premises. The regress stops because all proof depends on self-evident, "self-proving" premises. These are of two kinds: direct sense experiences and tautologies (see page 189). We know that some fire is hot (by sense experience) and that 2+2=4 (by reason) *not* because we *prove* either of these two things but because we directly experience them. We experience the heat of fire with our senses and we experience the self-evident truth of 2+2=4 with our intelligence.

We do not deduce the rest of our knowledge from tautologies; they are not the starting points of our learning. Sense experience is. Tautologies are the final court of appeal, so to speak: if any argument violates a tautology, a self-evident logical law, that fact alone shows that the argument is invalid. This is how we ultimately prove that a given argument is valid or invalid, if challenged.

For instance, suppose someone challenges the syllogism "All men are mortal, and Socrates is a man, therefore Socrates is mortal." Suppose someone says, "Why can't the premises be true and the conclusion false?" Our reply is that if you say this is so, you are contradicting yourself, for you are saying both that Socrates is mortal and that he is not. If Socrates is not mortal – if the conclusion is false – then at least this one man is not mortal. (For you have already admitted that Socrates is a man.) But the admission that at least one man is not mortal contradicts the other premise you admitted, namely that *all* men are mortal. So you are contradicting yourself. The law of non-contradiction is the ultimate tautology in logic, the ultimate court of appeal.

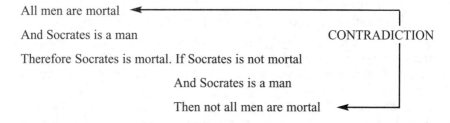

All men are mortal

And Socrates is a man   CONTRADICTION

Therefore Socrates is mortal. If Socrates is not mortal

    And Socrates is a man

    Then not all men are mortal

(1) **The Law of Non-contradiction** can be formulated in various ways. Aristotle's formulation is that "The same property cannot both belong and not belong to the same subject at the same time in the same respect." A tree cannot be at the same time taller than a cat and not taller than a cat. Aristotle's formulation is in terms of the relation between the two terms (subject and predicate) of a simple proposition. Modern symbolic logic usually formulates it in terms of the relation between two whole propositions in a compound, hypothetical proposition: "If p is true, then p is not false." Or "No proposition can be true and false at the same time."

In terms of real beings, the law states that **nothing can both be and not be** (at the same time). In terms of terms, it states that **S cannot both be P and not be P.** In terms of propositions, it states that **a proposition p cannot be both true and false.** The general formulation which covers all three is that *x is not non-x,* whether x is a term, a proposition, or a real thing.

(2) The **Law of Identity** says that *x is x.* In terms of real beings, **whatever is, is.** In terms of terms, **whatever is x, is x.** In terms of propositions, **if p is true, p is true.**

(3) The **Law of Excluded Middle** says that *either x or non-x.* In terms of real beings, **everything must either be or not be.** In terms of terms, **S must be**

either P or non-P. In terms of propositions, **either p or non-p; every proposi-tion must be either true or false.** There is no third, middle possibility between true and false.

These are the three tautologies which, together with direct sense experience, constitute Aristotle's answer to the skeptical objection to syllogism.

These "Laws of Thought" are not merely *imperatives* or ideals or principles which we *ought* to follow in our thinking; they are also *facts*, statements about the real world, in fact about everything that exists. The Greeks would call them *logoi* rather than *nomoi*: unchangeable and necessary laws of the very nature of things, objective truths that we discover, rather than normative laws that we make and can disobey. "Thou shalt not kill" is a normative law, an imperative, an ideal; and it can be and is disobeyed. But the Law of Non-contradiction is a necessary law, a fact rather than an ideal, and it can never be disobeyed. Insofar as the law of non-contradiction is a normative law for thought ("Thou shalt not contradict thyself"), it is not always obeyed by us, by our minds, by "subjective reality;" for we often commit fallacies of contradiction. But the Law of Non-Contradiction (x is not non-x) is always and necessarily obeyed by objective reality, by things – all things. It *is in fact true of* all things. Nothing ever is what it is not. The same is true of the Law of Identity: it is always in fact true of all things. Nothing ever fails to be what it is. And it is also true of the Law of Excluded Middle: everything either is, or is not. These are not just laws of thought, they are laws of things. They are metaphysical laws, ontological laws.

We sometimes say things that seem to contradict these laws, but they never do. For instance, we say, "He's not himself today," which seems to contradict the law of identity. But we are equivocating: we mean that "his felt self is not his ideal self today," or that "his *de facto* self is not his *de jure* self today."

We might want to follow Leibniz's suggestion and add a fourth law, the **"Principle of Sufficient Reason": everything that is has a sufficient reason why it is–both why it *exists* and why it is *what* it is,** why it is that something rather than something else.

. Also, **everything that acts or changes has a reason or cause why it acts or changes.** This **"Principle of Causality"** is a corollary of the "Principle of Sufficient Reason." In other words, everything that has existence, essence, and activity or change has a reason for its existence, its essence, and its activities or changes. Nothing is arbitrary, meaningless, and irrational in itself. Though we obviously do not *know* the reason for everything, there *is* a reason for every-thing.

One simply cannot think coherently without believing this principle. If things could exist or change without any reason, something could simply pop into existence in front of you right now – a tiny green tiger, for instance – for ab-solutely no reason at all. It could come to be without anything at all causing it to come to be. No sane human being in the history of the world ever believed in this "pop theory." Only a madman or a philosopher could dream of defending it.

The puzzling question then arises: How do we know these four principles, the heart of reason itself? By reason? Or by "faith"? Or by something else?

From the time of Descartes, philosophers for two centuries have tried to prove them, to rationally validate reason itself. Most philosophers today believe the attempt is intrinsically impossible, and begs the question, for it would have to use reason to prove reason, thus assuming the validity of the reason it uses.

Is the alternative faith? Aldous Huxley wrote: "All science is based on an act of faith – faith in the validity of the mind's logical processes, faith in the explicability of the world, faith that the laws of thought are laws of things."

Pascal put the puzzle in a theological context: our minds are like computers, and their innate hardware, including these Laws of Thought, have been programmed into us either by a wise and trustable intellect (God), or by an unwise and/or untrustworthy intellect (anything from a brilliant but fallible extraterrestrial to the Devil), or by no intellect at all but by blind chance. If either of the two latter possibilities is the true one, then our intellect is not to be totally trusted. Therefore the rationalist, who wants to trust reason above all else, must begin not with reason and proof but with an act of faith.

Perhaps what Huxley and Pascal call "faith" is not the opposite of reason but the heart of reason: a direct insight into the necessary truth of the self-evident. If "reason" means only calculation and proof, as it does for Descartes and his successors, including symbolic logicians, this insight is not "reason." But if "reason" means what it did to Socrates, Plato, and Aristotle, then this is the most rational knowledge possible.

Philosophers of a Kantian type maintain that this not an insight into truth at all but simply a psychological fact about how our minds have to work. But is it then a *limitation* that we cannot believe in meaninglessness, irrationality, and self-contradiction? "Romanticists" like Walt Whitman and Nietzsche seem to have believed just that. Whitman wrote, in "Song of Myself," "Do I contradict myself? Very well, then, I contradict myself. I am large. I contain multitudes." And Nietzsche encouraged potential "overmen" to "have chaos in yourselves." But surely this is self-defeating, for if the laws of non-contradiction and identity are not true, then "I contradict myself" means "I do *not* contradict myself," and "Have chaos" means "Do *not* have chaos."

Section 3. The empiricist's objection to the syllogism (P)

A second objection to syllogism has become so common that it is often taken for granted in modern philosophy. It comes from two main modern sources: David Hume, the 18th century Scottish philosopher, and John Stuart Mill, the 19th century English philosopher, both of whom were nominalists in metaphysics, (probably) atheists in theology, determinists in cosmology, materialists in anthropology, empiricists in epistemology, and utilitarians in ethics. (These six positions tend to go together as part of a single "package deal.")

The objection is that the syllogism is a fake, to put it bluntly; that it claims to yield new knowledge but does not and cannot; that deduction never proves anything at all. For either the conclusion merely repeats in different words what has already been stated in the premises, or not. If it does merely repeat the premises, then it is like immediate inference, in which the original proposition or premise is merely reworded or changed around; no new knowledge is gained. There is no more in the conclusion than in the premises. If it does *not* merely repeat the premises, it commits the fallacy of *non sequitur*, "it does not follow," for there is more in the conclusion than in the premises.

So if there is *not* more in the conclusion than in the premises, the syllogism is a tautology; and if there is, then it is a *non sequitur*. Thus the syllogism is either a trivial tautology or an invalid *non sequitur*.

Take the classic case, "all men are mortal, and Socrates is a man, therefore Socrates is mortal." Mill argues that we could never know the premise that all men are mortal *unless we already knew* that *Socrates* was mortal. For (assuming that Socrates is a man) if Socrates is *not* mortal, then not all men are mortal. So instead of the universal premise being evidence or *reason* for the particular conclusion, it is the other way round: the universal premise actually *presupposes* the truth of the particular conclusion. The conclusion is the premise, and the premise is the conclusion. Syllogisms really work backwards. That is Mill's objection.

Here is our answer to Mill's objection. It comes from experience, from data, from the way we all actually do in fact reason. Let's look at a very ordinary, typical case of reasoning by syllogism. Suppose you the student now say, "I hate logic." I ask you why. You say, "Because it's confusing, and I hate confusing subjects." You are giving me a syllogism to justify not thinking about the problem of the syllogism. Your syllogism is:

> All confusing subjects are subjects I hate.
> And logic is a confusing subject.
> Therefore logic is a subject I hate.

John Stuart Mill would not accept your argument. He would say, How can you know that every confusing subject is one you hate (your major premise) unless you had first experienced every single confusing subject in the world, including logic?

The answer, of course, is that *we learn not only by experiencing particulars but also by understanding universals.* Once we have experienced *some* confusing subjects, we can abstract the universal principle from the particular case. We understand that every confusing subject will be unattractive precisely *because* it is confusing. This is not an accident, it is a property.

The same is true regarding the "all men are mortal" syllogism. We *understand* that all men *must* be mortal because they must have organic bodies, although not all men must be white or between three and seven feet tall. We understand the difference between a property and an accident; we understand what necessarily follows from the essence *because we understand the essence.*

A similar dilemma may be raised against any single proposition: that either the predicate merely repeats the subject, or not. If it does, if S and P are the same, then the proposition is a mere tautology; if it does not, if S and P are not the same, then the proposition is false when it says that S "is" P. In fact it violates the law of identity, for it says that "S is not S." (If S is P and P is not S, then S is not S!) At this point perhaps we need a devious but clever President to remind us that "it all depends on what the meaning of 'is' is."

The answer to this dilemma is that P is neither identical with S nor contrary to S but one of the aspects of the meaning of S: either its genus (that aspect of its essence which it has in common with other things) or its specific difference (that aspect of its essence which distinguishes it from the rest of its genus) or its species (the whole essence, genus plus specific difference) or a property (an aspect of its nature which necessarily and always follows from its essence, but which is not the very essence) or an accident (which is neither an aspect of its essence nor necessarily and always follows from its essence, thus is sometimes present and sometimes not). In other words, the doctrine of the predicables is our answer to this dilemma, and it will be our answer to the Hume-Mill objection too.

"S is P" is not like "2+2=4", since P can reveal five different aspects of the comprehension of S. But modern symbolic logic has no doctrine of the predicables. It ignores the comprehension of a term, for this means its nature or essence, and this notion conflicts with nominalism. It also ignores the distinctively human power to comprehend a term's comprehension, and uses only those data-processing and calculating powers of the mind that we share with a computer, thus in practice reducing the human mind to a computer, "natural intelligence" to "artificial intelligence." There is, thus, an important human and philosophical issue at the heart of the divide between classical and modern logic. Whether this last sentence is true or not is precisely one of the issues that divide the two logics. But modern logic cannot help us argue about that issue! A merely formal, algebraic, computer-language logic cannot deal with the issues about the nature of man and knowledge that are part and parcel of the very essence of philosophy, because it cannot deal with essences, natures, universals.

Mill intended his dilemma against syllogism to show the superiority of induction to deduction; but in fact it is equally fatal against induction. For an inductive argument which draws a universal conclusion from particular instances is also subject to the same dilemma of "tautology or *non sequitur.*" If it is a complete induction, i.e. if the premises cover all instances of the universal conclusion, then it is a tautology; if not, it is a *non sequitur.* "John, Jim, Joe, and Jeb are each members of the Issaquah Barbershop Quartet, and each one is male, therefore all members of the I.B.Q. are male" is a tautology (since a quartet by definition has only four members). But "John and Jim are members of the I.B.Q, and each is male, therefore all members of the I.B.Q. are male" is a *non sequitur*. How could science generalize from a few observations of a few falling bodies to the universal rule that "*all* freely falling bodies accelerate at the rate of 32.2 feet per second per second" without committing a *non sequitur*? And it is impossible to observe *all* freely falling bodies in the world. The larger the number of instances observed, the more *probable* is the universal conclusion, of course; but it is *merely probable*. What makes it more than probable? It is only probable that a coin will come up heads half the time; but it is more than probable that falling bodies will accelerate at 32.2 feet per second per second. What is only probably true is also possibly false. The truth of an A proposition is rendered probable if its opposed I proposition is true (and this is induction); but the truth of an O is also compatible with the I being true; and if the O is true then the A is *not* true, since the A and the O are contradictory.

It is a common misunderstanding that modern science relies on induction rather than deduction and therefore is impervious to Mill's critique of deduction. It is true that modern science is vastly superior to pre-modern science partly because it relies on experience and observation rather than authority, tradition, and speculation. But science is not identical with induction. It depends on deduction as well as induction. For science is predictive, and all prediction is deductive and syllogistic.

Prediction is syllogistic because it is like mathematics. When the scientist predicts, he is using his equations and formulas as a major premise, and the specific material and natural forces that he observes as a minor premise, i.e. an instance or example of the formulas. To take a very simple example, "2+2=4" could be a major premise, and then it could be applied to apples as follows:

Any two things, if added to two things of the same kind, will be four things of that kind.

Two apples added to two apples are two things added to two things of the same kind.

Therefore two apples added to two apples will be four apples.

Mill's critique of the syllogism applies just as much to this syllogism as to any other. Modern science, with its emphasis on mathematics, induction and concrete experience, is no more exempt from Mill's critique than ancient philosophy, with its emphasis on syllogism, deduction, and abstraction.

To understand this, we must understand the analogy between inductive reasoning and abstraction. Induction, like deduction, is *reasoning*, and therefore comes under the third act of the mind, not the first; while abstraction comes under the first act of the mind, not the third; yet there is an analogy between the two.

Abstraction is the process by which we form a universal concept on the basis of experiencing a number of particular instances of it – for instance, understanding "man" or "human nature" from having experienced some individuals of this species. Aristotle gives this famous image for it: "It is like a rout in battle stopped by first one man making a stand and then another, until the original formation has been restored. When one of a number of logically indiscriminable [identical in essence] particulars has made a stand [in the mind], the earliest universal is present in the soul" (*Posterior Analytics* 100a). Abstraction mentally separates this universal, common essence from the individuating accidents such as gender, race, height, age, clothing, etc. Intelligent minds do it quickly, after only a few examples; slower minds take longer and need more examples, more experience.

Induction: Just as abstraction is the power of the mind to move from sensed particulars to an understood universal (e.g. from men to Man) in the first act of the mind (understanding), so induction is the power in the third act of the mind (reasoning) to move from a number of singular propositions, which are the reports of sense observations, to a universal proposition – e.g. from "these men are mortal" to "all men are mortal."

How is this done? Let us look at a specific instance. There are two peasants on a medieval feudal manor. Neither has ever been away from his little bit of land; neither has ever seen more than 500 different human beings; but one (let's call him Odo) has a bright and quick mind while the other (Bozo) has a dim and slow one. One day both see something they never saw before: slave traders with black men on chains, coming to the manor to sell the black men as slaves. Odo says: "What a terrible thing to do: treating those humans like animals!" Bozo replies, "What do you mean, human beings? They have black skin. They can't be human beings. They must be animals. And it's perfectly all right to chain animals and sell them, so it's not a terrible thing at all."

Note that both Odo and Bozo use the same logical principles of the syllogism. Odo is implicitly arguing:

Treating humans like animals is wrong.
Chaining and selling humans is treating humans like animals.
Therefore chaining and selling humans is wrong.

Chaining and selling humans is wrong.
What those traders are doing is chaining and selling humans.
Therefore what those traders are doing is wrong.

Bozo agrees with Odo's first syllogism, but not with the second premise of his second syllogism, because he does not recognize that these black men are human beings. Why not? Because he did not abstract as well as Odo. All Bozo did was to abstract the sensed constants from the sensed variables. All humans he ever saw had two legs, two eyes, hair, white skin, the power of speech, and a Frankish accent. Some were male, some female; some old, some young, some tall, some short. So he knew that not all humans were male, or old, or tall. But he did not know that not all humans were white, or Frankish. Odo, however, not only abstracted the sensed constants from the sensed variables, like Bozo, but also abstracted the *essence* from the *accidents* among the sensed constants. He understood that the power of speech was part of the human essence but the color of skin was not.

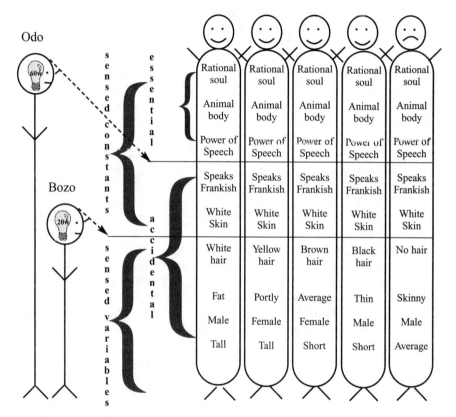

The materialist and empiricist and nominalist ignores this distinctively human power, the power not shared by animals, cameras, or computers: the power to abstract and understand essences. In other words, the modern nominalist logician has no doctrine of the predicables; he cannot distinguish an accident from an essential property.

Finally, let us answer Mill logically, in his own terms, about the syllogism. He claims that all syllogisms really beg the question, and work backward, from conclusion to premise. Let us look at two kinds of syllogisms. In the first kind, all the predicates are accidents. In the second, some are properties.

First kind of syllogism:
All the books in my bookcase are paperbacks.
That book is a book in my bookcase.
Therefore that book is a paperback.

Second kind of syllogism:
All men are mortal.
Socrates is a man.
Therefore Socrates is mortal.

Mill is right about the first kind of syllogism but wrong about the second. There is no way to know that all the books on your bookcase are paperbacks without first looking at each one, including this one. So the conclusion ("this book is a paperback") must be known to be true *before* the premise ("all the books in my bookcase are paperbacks") can be known to be true. For all of the predicates in this syllogism are accidents of their subjects. It is accidental to a book to be a paperback or a hardcover. It is accidental to a book to be on my bookcase or not. If a proposition has an accident as its predicate, the only way to be sure it is true is by experience, by observation. The mind cannot tell, just by understanding the essence of a book, whether it is a paperback or not and whether it is on my bookcase or not. We know this not *a priori*, prior to sense experience, but only *a posteriori*, posterior to experience.

But the opposite is true of the second syllogism. We have *a priori* knowledge that all men are mortal; we can know that all men are mortal before we experience all men, i.e. every single man. (We can never experience every single man, of course; there are over 6 billion of them alive, and many dead, and many not yet born.) We can know that all men are mortal by understanding the essence of the subject "man." Man is a rational animal, with a rational soul and an animal body. This is his essence. We can understand the animal part of his essence well enough to understand why everything with an animal body must be mortal. We know that all men are mortal not by examining every individual man with our senses but by examining the universal essence of man with our mind. Until modern times, the word "reason" meant that power of understanding (the first act of the mind) as well as the power of computer-like deduction (the third act of the mind).

The source of Mill's error is his Nominalism. It is only through the universal – specifically, through the middle term – that syllogism works. And in every syllogism the middle term must be universal ("distributed") at least once; otherwise we have the fallacy of Undistributed Middle. (See pages 246–48.) Nominalism denies universals; no wonder it denies syllogism.

Nominalism also undermines induction, for nominalism reduces universals to man-made groupings of individuals into artificial classes set up for accidental purposes. According to Nominalism there is no objectively right or wrong way of grouping many individuals into a class, since there is no common nature or essence in the individuals that really and objectively constitutes that class. All we can do is whatever we desire to do: e.g. we can classify men and trees together as "tall" or "handsome" or "things that make me smile"; or we can classify men and mud and marshmallows together as "soft" or "things that begin with the letter 'm.'" Reason is a servant of desire – and this is another, connected, doctrine of this philosophical school that includes Hobbes, Hume, Mill, Freud, Darwin, and Marx. Aristotle offers us the alternative in the famous formula that "one can know a universal without knowing all its particulars" (*Posterior Analytics* 71a, 26ff.).

Nominalism amounts to denying that we can know what an apple is. All human thought and speech use universal concepts. The only exceptions are proper names; all other names are "common," and Aristotelian realism (the alternative to Nominalism) is "common sense." The denial of this common sense has permeated modern philosophy. Especially in the 20th century, the dominant philosophy in all English speaking countries has been some form of Positivism. This is a word with many meanings, but essentially it designates the constellation of six "isms" already enumerated: nominalism in metaphysics, atheism in theology, determinism in cosmology, materialism in anthropology, empiricism in epistemology, and utilitarianism in ethics.

Its logical form was first called "Logical Positivism" in its landmark manifesto *Language, Truth and Logic* by A.J Ayer (1926); then "analytic philosophy," when it was softened and modified a bit, since the fundamental claim of this manifesto was not only mistaken but self-refuting, self-contradictory. The basic claim was that the only two kinds of meaningful propositions were tautologies and empirically verifiable or falsifiable propositions (essentially, what Kant called "analytic *a priori* judgments" and "synthetic *a posteriori* judgments"). This claim is immediately self-contradictory, for it itself is neither a tautology nor empirically verifiable, therefore meaningless by its own criteria.

What is relevant here is to see that nominalism naturally results in such a narrow either/or. If there are no real universals, then all knowledge of objective reality is of concrete individuals, and this comes only by sense observation. Man is essentially reduced to an animal plus a computer in his powers of knowing. The distinctively human dimensions of reason have been abolished – by human reason! This is not intellectual humility; it is intellectual suicide.

A popular argument of the modern Nominalist against the old notion of reason is that it was arrogant and aprioristic, that it ignored experience and held back the progress of science, and that the modern concept of reason is more humble and scientific. The history of science, the Nominalist argues, is a garbage can full of abstract "essences" which have been discarded. For instance, Aristotle thought that fire rose because it was the essence of fire to move toward the heavens.

It is true that the knowledge of universal essences by abstraction is by its very nature (i.e. its essence!) subject to error, and history is full of errors that came from its misuse. But "the misuse of a thing does not take away its proper use." (*Abusus non tollit usum.*) All human knowledge is subject to error, and its history is full of examples of them. But at least metaphysical realism explains why abstraction can be valid; Nominalism cannot explain even that. Realism is embarrassed by reason's errors, but Nominalism is embarrassed by reason's success!

Much of the progress of science consists in a better understanding of the *nature* of things. For instance, modern physicists no longer claim that it is fire's essence to move toward the heavens, because they claim to know more about the *nature* of fire, and other bodies, than Aristotle did – and this claim itself cannot be made by a Nominalist.

Section 4. Demonstrative syllogisms

Some syllogisms leave us uncertain about the truth of their conclusions even when there is no ambiguous term, no false premise, and no fallacy, because we are uncertain about the truth of one of the premises.

Sometimes this is simply because one of the premises, though necessarily true in itself, is not known with certainty but only with "right opinion," as Plato put it. Sometimes it is because the premise is in itself only probable, not certain – in which case the conclusion too can be only probable, not certain. For instance,

Traveling faster than light is impossible.
And getting to another galaxy in a single lifetime is traveling faster than light.
Therefore getting to another galaxy in a single lifetime is impossible.

Is this conclusion absolutely certain? Many things deemed "impossible" by science in one age have been proven possible in a later age. Do we know with certainty that both the premises are true? The first premise rests on the nearly unanimous authority of current scientists, but that is only human authority, and not absolutely certain. The second premise rests on the assumption that the human life-span can never be radically expanded – and that is even less certain. So the conclusion, while very probable, is not certain.

But even when both premises are known to be certainly true, our mind (and not just our feelings) is more totally satisfied by one kind of syllogism than by another. For one syllogism may give the real reason why the conclusion is true (this reason resides in the middle term), while another may not. Both kinds of syllogism can be logically valid, but only the first kind is called a "perfect demonstration," or an argument *propter quid* ("because of this"), since it gives the real cause of the conclusion being true.

To see this distinction, contrast the following two syllogisms:

(1) Whatever is composed of parts is destructible.
    Whatever is material is composed of parts.
    Therefore whatever is material is destructible.

(2) Whatever is material is able to reflect light waves.
    Consciousness is not able to reflect light waves.
    Therefore consciousness is not material.

Both syllogisms are logically valid, and both have true premises, but (1) is more convincing than (2). Why?

Because in (1), the middle term is the real reason or cause for the conclusion being true, while in (2) it is not. Matter is in reality destructible because it is composed of parts; its parts actually make it destructible, decomposable, splittable. But consciousness is not immaterial because it cannot reflect light waves. The inability to reflect light waves does not actually cause the immateriality of consciousness. Rather, it is an effect of it.

Take another example:

Whatever is material is able to be moved from one place to another
Numbers are not able to be moved from one place to another
Therefore numbers are not material.

It is not the absence of being able to be moved from one place to another that makes numbers immaterial. The middle term does not give the real reason for the conclusion.

When the middle term does give the real reason or cause for the conclusion being true, we have what is classically called a "demonstrative syllogism." It is also sometimes called a "perfect demonstration" – perfect because our mind is satisfied, since we know not only the fact (the conclusion) but also the reason for it (the middle term). In a non-demonstrative syllogism, we have indeed proved the fact (the conclusion), and we can be certain that it is true if we are certain *that* the premises are true; but not *why*: we do not yet know the real reason or cause why it is true. So our mind is not totally satisfied.

A classic example of the difference between a valid non-demonstrative argument and a valid demonstrative argument is the difference we have already referred to (page 214) between Book 1 of Plato's *Republic* and Books 2 through 10. Socrates is dissatisfied at the end of Book 1 because although he has proved that justice is more profitable than injustice, he does not yet know why, since he does not yet know the essence of justice, what justice is. He has not yet deduced justice's "profitability" from its essence. Only after finding the essence of justice (a long process in the *Republic*) can he know that this essence of justice is the real reason why justice must always be more profitable than injustice. This essence, expressed in his definition of justice, is the middle term of his basic syllogism. (It is basically that justice is that virtue in a soul or in a state by which each part performs its natural function with its proper particular virtue, in harmony with the other parts. Justice is to the soul or the state what health is to the body.)

The most practical application of this distinction between demonstrative and nondemonstrative syllogisms comes when we are trying to *construct* syllogisms. To make a syllogism, you must find an appropriate middle term. To make a *demonstrative* syllogism, you must find a middle term that tells us the real reason for the conclusion. For instance, suppose you wanted to prove to someone who admired Hitler that Hitler was not a great man. You *could* argue this way:

Hitler was hated by nearly all the world.
Whoever is hated by nearly all the world was not a great man.
Therefore Hitler was not a great man.

But the middle term here is not the cause of Hitler's lack of greatness, so you have not constructed a demonstrative syllogism, though it is a valid one. It would be better to use instead a syllogism whose middle term gives the actual cause, e.g.:

Hitler was a tyrant.
A tyrant is not a great man.
Therefore Hitler was not a great man.

Still another reason why some syllogisms are more convincing than others – this time a purely psychological reason – is because their arrangement of terms is clearer and stronger. Affirmative propositions are clearer and stronger than negative ones, and universal propositions are clearer and stronger than particular ones, so the most convincing and simple form of syllogism is one with three A propositions, arranged in perfect order like the circles on a dart board. It could be called a "bull's eye syllogism." E.g.:

All men are mortal.
All sages are men.
Therefore all sages are mortal.

This is more convincing than

All sages are men.
No men are immortal.
Therefore no immortals are sages.

Yet the second syllogism is just as valid as the first, and comes to the same conclusion. (The two conclusions are partial contrapositives.) It does give the real reason for the conclusion, so it is a demonstrative syllogism. But it is not a perfect one because it does not give this reason as clearly as the "bull's eye syllogism" does.

Classic logic texts usually included a chapter on "reducing to the first figure" (see pages 257–58), i.e. changing a syllogism around so that the order of terms was that of a "bull's eye syllogism," because we are more easily persuaded by a perfectly-formed argument.

Section 5. How to construct convincing syllogisms (B)

Constructive logic is as important as critical logic; making your own good syllogisms is as important as evaluating others' syllogisms. Fortunately, this is quite easy to do – so much so that it is often omitted entirely in logic texts. The basic steps are:

1. Know what conclusion you want to prove.
2. Put your conclusion into logical form. This will give you your two terms, S and P.
3. The key step in constructing a convincing syllogism is to find a good middle term, one that naturally joins the other two terms. This is best done by instinct and intuition, by imitation and practice and habituation. Since the middle term is really the reason for the conclusion, all you have to do is ask yourself what *is* the reason for your conclusion, and you will have your middle term. Ask yourself what is the *real* reason for your conclusion, and you will make a *demonstrative* syllogism.
4. Finally, check your syllogism for validity. (The fastest way is by Euler's circles, page 237.)

Suppose you want to prove that "you should never trust a pit bull." First, put it into logical form. You're really trying to prove something about pit bulls, not about "you," so you need to reword your proposition. You could put it into a negative logical form ("No pit bulls are to be trusted") or an affirmative form ("All pit bulls are untrustworthy"). All other things being equal, the affirmative form is easier and clearer.

Now you ask yourself "Why?" Why do you believe all pit bulls are untrustworthy? You will probably immediately come up with a reason, e.g. "They're all aggressive by nature, even when tamed." So there is your middle term:

All pit bulls are aggressive by nature even when tamed.
Whatever is aggressive by nature even when tamed is untrustworthy.
Therefore all pit bulls are untrustworthy.

Pit bull owners will still disagree with you, but at least you have something to argue about. Your conclusion is now based on two premises, not just feeling or prejudice. And the premises are a bit harder to refute than the conclusion. At least, more people agree with the premises than with the conclusion. That's the whole strategy of the syllogism: to lead people from premises they already believe to a conclusion they do not.

Or suppose you want to prove that Utopianism is an illusion, that a perfect society can never exist on earth. First, formulate your conclusion: "No perfect society is something that can exist on earth." Then ask yourself "Why?" What is there about a perfect society that makes it impossible, or what is there about things on earth that make them all imperfect? Formulating the question in the first way might give you a syllogism like

No perfect society is something that can be made by imperfect people.
Everything that can exist on earth is something made by imperfect people.
Therefore no perfect society is something that can exist on earth.

Or if you formulate the question in the second way, you might come up with a syllogism like

> All things on earth are infected with weakness, ignorance, and death.
> Nothing infected with weakness, ignorance, and death is a perfect society.
> Therefore nothing on earth is a perfect society.

The more you do it, the more easy and natural it becomes. Appropriate middle terms begin to leap out at you; and this clarifies your own reasons as well as furnishing you with arguments to persuade others.

Exercises
A. Test your intuitive sense of valid and invalid arguments by telling whether you think each of the following syllogisms is valid or invalid.

1. All dead men are men.
   Some men bleed.
   Therefore some dead men do not bleed.

2. No dead men are live men.
   All live men bleed.
   Therefore no dead men bleed.

3. Only live men bleed.
   Dead men are not live men.
   Therefore dead men don't bleed.

4. All who bleed are alive.
   Dead men aren't alive.
   Therefore dead men don't bleed.

5. Dead men don't hiccup.
   Whoever doesn't hiccup, doesn't bleed.
   Therefore dead men don't bleed.

6. John is a dead man.
   John does not bleed.
   Therefore some dead men do not bleed.

7. All who bleed have bodies that are doing something.
   Most dead men do not have bodies that are doing something.
   Therefore dead men do not bleed.

8. Dead men don't stop their own bleeding.
   Those who stop their own bleeding do not bleed.
   Therefore dead men do not bleed.

9. All men who don't bleed are impervious to hemophilia.
   Dead men are impervious to hemophilia.
   Therefore dead men are men who don't bleed.

10. Some dead men are not yet in *rigor mortis*.
    Some who are not yet in *rigor mortis* bleed.
    Therefore some dead men bleed.

B. For each of the following conclusions, construct a valid syllogism without any *obviously* false premises, by finding an appropriate (realistic, convincing) middle term. Make it a demonstrative syllogism if possible. Though you have not yet learned the rules for discriminating valid from invalid syllogisms, you have an innate, intuitive sense of that, which you used in evaluating the syllogisms in exercise A; use it again here in constructing syllogisms.

1. Courage is a virtue.
2. Not all great men are patriotic.
3. Giving makes you happy.
4. Somebody farted.
5. Slavery is morally wrong.
6. Whatever has color, has size.
7. Power is not happiness.
8. All men by nature desire to know.
9. Some valid syllogisms do not convince anyone to believe their conclusion.

C. The following exercises are more difficult because they require you to see both sides of a controversial issue. Construct convincing syllogisms to prove *both* of each pair of contradictory conclusions. This is a good exercise not only in logic but also in practical psychology, "getting into" other minds.

1A. Some things that cause contentment are harmful.
1B. No things that cause contentment are harmful.

2A. Beauty is in the eye of the beholder. (Beauty is subjective.)
2B. Beauty is not in the eye of the beholder. (Beauty is not subjective.)

3A. The human soul is immortal.
3B. The human soul is not immortal.

4A. Moral rightness changes with time and place.
4B. Moral rightness does not change with time and place.

5A. God exists.
5B. God does not exist.

6A. Man is essentially good.
6B. Man is not essentially good.

7A. Democracy is the best form of government.
7B. Democracy is not the best form of government.

8A. Capital punishment is morally right.
8B. Capital punishment is not morally right.

9A. All abortions are morally wrong.
9B. Not all abortions are morally wrong.

D. Whenever we have two apparently good syllogisms which prove conclusions that contradict each other, which you constructed in exercise C, we must have in *at least one* of each pair of syllogisms either a term used ambiguously, or a false premise, or a logical fallacy. In this exercise you are to find one of these three possible weaknesses in *both* arguments of each pair. You probably consider the syllogism that proves the conclusion you agree with to be the stronger one, so it is a challenging and useful exercise to try to find the weakness that your opponent will find in that one, i.e. in your own argument, as well as the weakness in his.

XI. Checking Syllogisms for Validity

There are four ways to check syllogisms for validity: Euler's Circles, Aristotle's six rules of the syllogism, Venn diagrams, and "Barbara Celarent." We will explore them in order of difficulty, starting with the easiest.

Euler's Circles are (1) not *always* reliable, for there is no clear way to use them on some syllogisms that contain I or O propositions. However, they are (2) the easiest of all four methods, and (3) they do give a graphic explanation of why any syllogism is valid or invalid.

Aristotle's six rules are not only the oldest but also the best way of judging syllogisms, for (1) they are always reliable, (2) they are easy to understand and remember, and (3) they explain why each invalid syllogism is invalid, which fallacy is committed.

Venn diagrams are (1) always reliable, and (2) fairly easy to learn; however, they (3) do *not* show *why* any syllogism is valid or invalid. It is not absolutely necessary to learn Venn diagrams, since Aristotle's six rules do all that Venn diagrams do and more; but they are a useful second way of checking.

"Barbara Celarent" is the first line of a medieval list of artificial names which is a clever and charming but complicated and cumbersome way of judging the validity of a syllogism by its structure of mood and figure. (This will be explained shortly.) It is (1) universally reliable, but (2) the most difficult of all to use, and (3) it does not show why any syllogism is valid or invalid. This historical curiosity will be explained briefly, but it is an unnecessary extra, useful mainly for mental exercise.

Section 1. Euler's Circles (B)

Not only can most syllogisms be checked for validity by Euler's Circles, but the strategy of the syllogism can be seen most clearly by this method. However, it will not give a clear result for some syllogisms with I or O premises (perhaps 5–10% of the syllogisms you will meet).

If your memory is a little dim, you should first review the four Euler diagrams for the A, E, I and O propositions. (See page 152.)

The technique for evaluating syllogisms by Euler's Circles is very simple:

just diagram *both* premises by Euler diagrams, superimposing one on the other. This is possible because there is always a common term to any two propositions in a syllogism. A syllogism has only three terms, remember; if there are more than three, we have either no syllogism at all, or a syllogism with "the Fallacy of Four Terms," or perhaps two syllogisms in a chain. (We will soon learn how to detect these patterns.)

Take the easiest case first, our old friend "All men are mortal, and Socrates is a man, therefore Socrates is mortal." We first diagram "all men are mortal" in Euler circles:

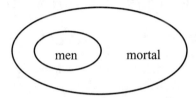

Then we superimpose the diagram for the second premise, "Socrates is a man," on our diagram for the first premise, like a double exposure in photography, thus showing how the two premises look together. The circle for "man" is already there, so all we have to do is to include the term "Socrates" in it. For in an A proposition (such as "Socrates is mortal"), the subject is included in the extension of the predicate, as a sub-population is included in a population. (In terms of *comprehension*, on the other hand, the predicate is part of the (meaning of the) subject).

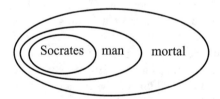

Now we simply look to see whether we necessarily have the conclusion in the diagram of the premises. For the conclusion does not add any new data to the premises. The premises by themselves supply all the data, or information; and the conclusion only reveals the truth that is already implicit in the premises. So if a syllogism is logically valid, we can see the conclusion in the premises simply by looking at the Euler diagram of the two premises superimposed on each other. In this case, we see that "Socrates is mortal" necessarily follows.

Now let's take an example of a syllogism with a negative premise and a negative conclusion:

> No creatures are perfect.
> And all angels are creatures.
> Therefore no angels are perfect.

We first diagram the first premise, "no creatures are perfect":

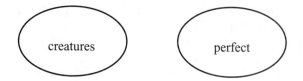

Then we add to this "all angels are creatures":

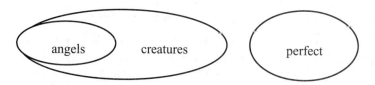

Then we simply look to see whether the conclusion necessarily follows, that "no angels are perfect." It does.

When we have a syllogism with a particular proposition in it, Euler's Circles become a bit harder to use; for the diagram for a particular proposition has a dotted line in it, signifying that we do not know how far this class extends. For instance, suppose we have the syllogism

Some fish have teeth.
Whatever has teeth can bite you.
Therefore some fish can bite you.

We first diagram "whatever has teeth can bite you." (Always diagram the universal premise first.)

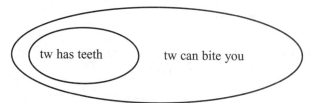

Then we add the I proposition "some fish have teeth":

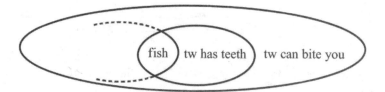

The dotted line signifies that we do not know whether or not some fish do *not* have teeth. (Remember, "some" must be interpreted to mean "at least some," that is, "some and perhaps all" rather than "only some, some and not all" – unless there is some clear indication, in the words that we are given, that it is meant in the second, stronger sense. We must not "read between the lines" or "read into" the data we are given.)

Euler's Circles show that this conclusion necessarily follows.

However, suppose we have the syllogism:

Some fish have teeth
And all fish have gills
Therefore some things that have teeth have gills

These two premises are more difficult to diagram together, because the relation between the terms "things that have teeth" and "things that have gills" is not clear. (Try it.) You probably cannot tell just from your attempt to diagram these two premises together that the conclusion does indeed necessarily follow.

Sometimes we can handle syllogisms with I or O propositions in Euler's circles if we draw not just one but a number of dotted lines to show that there are a number of possibilities. For instance, take the syllogism

Some good generals are not good politicians.
This man is a good politician.
Therefore this man is not a good general.

First, diagram the universal premise, the second one:

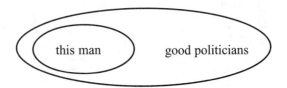

Then, superimpose the other premise, the first one It is an O, and can be drawn with just one dotted line, as follows:

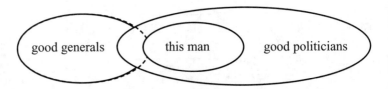

But it can also be drawn with as many as three other dotted lines, because we do not know what part of P ("good politicians") the *rest* of S ("good generals") takes up:

It may be (1) that there are no good generals that are good politicians; or it may be (2) that the line goes somewhere partially through "good politicians," so that there are some good generals outside good politicians, some good generals inside good politicians, and some good politicians outside good generals; or it may be (3) that S ("good generals") totally surrounds P ("good politicians"), so that all of "good politicians" is inside "good generals." We do not know which of these three possibilities is the case just from knowing that "Some S is not P." So we do not know the relation between "this man" and "good generals." The syllogism is invalid.

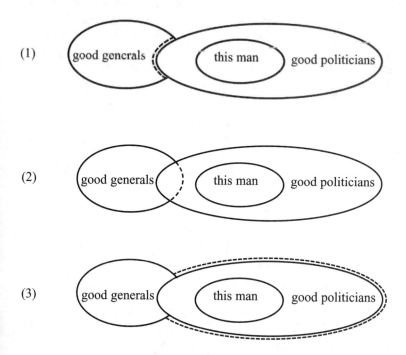

(1)

(2)

(3)

When using Euler's Circles to check a syllogism, if one of the premises is an I or an O proposition, we should include all the possible dotted lines for all the possibilities when we diagram the I or O. For if there is *any* possibility that the premises can be true without the conclusion being true, the argument is invalid.

Take, for instance, the following syllogism:

> Some persons are handicapped.
> And no Greek gods are handicapped.
> Therefore some Greek gods are not persons.

Let us begin by diagramming the E premise (the second one):

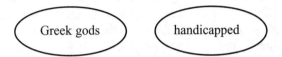

Now we superimpose the I premise. But where does the dotted line go, the line that contains the persons that are *not* handicapped? It might go (1) nowhere at all outside the class of the handicapped, and thus overlap no part of the class "Greek gods." In other words, it might be true that there are no non-handicapped persons. (In fact this *is* true if we do not limit "handicapped" to overt physical disabilities; and we can all learn this important lesson about ourselves from more obviously handicapped people!) Or (2) the dotted line might overlap part of the class "Greek gods"; it might be that there are some non-handicapped persons who are Greek gods and some who are not. Finally, (3) it might be that "non-handicapped persons" totally encompass the class "Greek gods."

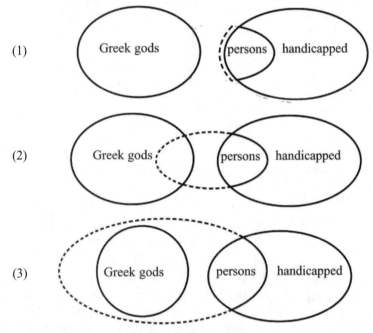

Since we do not know, just from the I proposition, which of these three possibilities is the case, we should diagram all three of them and then see whether the conclusion necessarily follows in all three cases – which it does *not* here, and so the syllogism is invalid.

Section 2. Aristotle's six rules (B)

These are the oldest and also the most helpful of all the ways of checking syllogisms. They were discovered by the same genius who first clearly discovered the theory of the syllogism itself.

To be valid, any syllogism must obey all six of these rules. If it disobeys any one, it is invalid.

You need not memorize the *numbers* of the rules, or even the exact words of the rules themselves; for you will quite quickly remember them just by using them over and over again in doing many exercises. By the way, one of the ways logic (and philosophy) is unlike languages is that deliberate memorization is almost never useful. For you either understand what you are memorizing, or not. If you do, then you need not try to memorize it because you will remember it naturally and spontaneously by the mere fact of understanding it. If you do *not* understand it, then it will be very difficult for you to remember it. So it is almost always more time efficient, as well as more pleasant, to spend your time trying to understand rather than trying to memorize.

The Rules

Rule 1: A syllogism must have three and only three terms. The usual violation of this rule is called **The Fallacy of Four Terms.**

Rule 2: A syllogism must have three and only three propositions. There is no named fallacy for the violation of this rule.

Rule 3: The middle term must be distributed at least once. The violation of this rule is called **The Fallacy of Undistributed Middle.**

Rule 4: No term that is undistributed in the premise may be distributed in the conclusion. The violation of this rule is called **The Fallacy of Illicit Minor** or **The Fallacy of Illicit Major**, depending on whether it is the minor term or the major term that contains the fallacy.

Rule 5: No syllogism can have two negative premises. The fallacy here is called simply the fallacy of **Two Negative Premises.**

Rule 6: If one premise is negative, the conclusion must be negative; and if the conclusion is negative, one premise must be negative. (No name for this fallacy; just the rule.)

In addition to these six rules, there are two corollaries, which are not *necessary* to know but are very helpful. They are not necessary to know because every syllogism which violates one of the two corollaries also violates one of the six rules. They are very helpful because sometimes the violation of one of the two corollaries is more obvious and quickly detectable than the violation of one of the six rules.

Corollary One: No syllogism may have two particular premises.

Corollary Two: If a syllogism has a particular premise, it must have a particular conclusion.

The first two rules concern the essential structure of the syllogism.
The next two rules concern the distribution of terms.
The last two rules concern negative propositions.
And the two corollaries concern particular propositions.

Explanations of the Rules

Rule 1 can be readily understood by remembering our triangle diagrams of the syllogism above, which show the importance of the middle term (pages 216–18). If we have fewer than three terms, we do not have a middle term at all. If we have more than three terms, we have more than one middle term, and then we do not have a single standard of comparison for the other two terms, the major and minor terms.

The Fallacy of Four Terms can be either explicit or implicit. It is explicit when there are four explicitly different terms. For instance,

> Whatever is in sense experience is material.
> And all knowledge comes from sense experience.
> Therefore all knowledge is material.

Both premises are true, and the syllogism *seems* formally valid – in fact it seems to be a "bull's eye syllogism" – yet the conclusion is false. The fallacy here consists in the fact that there are two middle terms: "what *is in* sense experience" and "what *comes from* sense experience." The two are not the same. *Wisdom*, e.g., comes partly *from* wide experience, but does not reside *in* experience; while *time*, e.g., is *in* experience but does not *come from* it.

The other form of the Fallacy of Four Terms is more common because it is more hidden. Here, the middle term is explicitly one but implicitly two because it is ambiguous. In fact, there is a special name for the fallacy, **The Fallacy of Ambiguous Middle.** For instance,

> "All power tends to corrupt." (Lord Acton)
> "Knowledge is power." (Francis Bacon)
> Therefore knowledge tends to corrupt.

It takes some understanding, or intuition, or "reading between the lines" to see this point, but once it is made it seems fairly obvious: that when Lord Acton said that "all power tends to corrupt," he meant *political* power, whereas when Francis Bacon said that "knowledge is power," he meant not political power but intellectual power, especially scientific knowledge that led to technological power over the forces of nature.

Rule 2, that there must be three and only three propositions in each syllogism, needs no explanation. This rule flows from the essential structure of the syllogism. Any argument that violates this rule is not a syllogism at all. Therefore you will never find a syllogism that violates this rule, so there is no named fallacy for it.

An argument with four or more propositions is usually a chain of syllogisms called an 'epicheirema." (You will learn about these later.)

Arguments with only two propositions (one premise and one conclusion) and only two terms are immediate inferences: conversion, obversion, or contraposition.

Arguments with only two propositions stated *but with three terms* are usually "enthymemes," abbreviated syllogisms. One of the three propositions of the syllogism is "kept in mind" (the meaning of "enthymeme"), or implied rather than expressed. These are genuine syllogisms, and they are in fact the commonest of all forms of argument in ordinary language. The next chapter will explore them in depth.

Enthymemes do not violate rule 2 even though they contain only two *expressed* propositions, for the third proposition is *implied*. It is really there and operating on an unconscious level, just as many things do in your life. For instance, "Man is mortal because he is material" is an enthymeme, an abbreviated form of

> All that is material is mortal. (implied premise)
> Man is material. (expressed premise)
> Therefore man is mortal. (expressed conclusion)

And "No mere man can know everything, so you can't either" is an enthymeme, an abbreviated form of

> No mere man can know everything. (expressed premise)
> You are a mere man. (implied premise)
> Therefore you can't know everything. (expressed conclusion)

When we study how to find the implied, missing premise in any given enthymeme, you will come to recognize the structure of an enthymeme very clearly, so that you will not confuse it with a violation of Rule 2. When you see two propositions with a premise indicator or a conclusion indicator, and a total of three terms in the two propositions, you probably have an enthymeme.

Rules 3 and 4 concern the distribution of terms. Since we need to know whether each term is distributed (universal) or undistributed (particular), it is a useful and time-saving device to write a little "u" for "undistributed" or a little "d" for "distributed" after each term, where we write an exponent in math, a little above and to the right, so that we can check at a glance for violations of rules 3 and 4.

It may be useful at this point to review the distribution of terms:

> Universal propositions have distributed subjects
> Particular propositions have undistributed subjects
> Negative propositions have distributed predicates
> Affirmative propositions have undistributed predicates

Proposition	Subject	Predicate
A	d	u
E	d	d
I	u	u
O	u	d

(At this point, if you are not sure you understand what it means for a term to be "distributed" or undistributed," or how to recognize in any given case whether any particular term is distributed or undistributed, review pages 163–65 before going on with this chapter.)

Rule 3 concerns the hinge and center of the syllogism, the middle term.

The reason the middle term must be distributed at least once is this: if it is not, then the minor term and the major term may be related to two totally different parts of the extension of the middle term, thus giving us the equivalent of the fallacy of four terms. It is the relationship which the major and minor terms bear to the middle term (in the major and minor premises) that justifies the relationship they bear to each other in the conclusion. If they are related to different middle terms (the Fallacy of Four Terms explicitly), or if they are related to a middle term with two different meanings (the Fallacy of Four Terms implicitly), or if they are related to different parts of (the extension of) the middle term (the Fallacy of Undistributed Middle), we have essentially the same fallacy: the middle term is not functioning as it must.

Let us begin with an example of a syllogism whose middle term functions correctly:

> Babies are not sages.
> And saints are sages.
> Therefore babies are not saints.

The first premise excludes babies from the whole extension of sages. Then the second premise includes all saints in some part of the class of sages. It does not matter how large or small that part is; all saints are in it. And no babies are. Therefore no babies can be saints. The Euler diagram shows this:

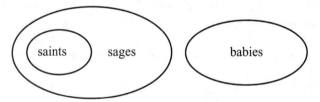

There are no dotted lines, no particular propositions, no uncertainties. We are sure about the relationship of the other two terms to the middle term, and thus to each other.

Contrast now an invalid syllogism, which uses its middle term wrongly, committing the fallacy of Undistributed Middle:

> All dogs are animals.
> And all cats are animals.
> Therefore all dogs are cats.

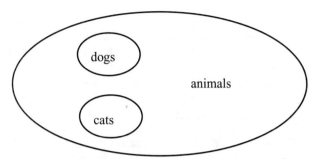

No one would be fooled by this argument, because everyone knows the conclusion is false, though both premises are true. But people might be fooled by an argument with the same logical form but a different content, such as:

> All Communists insist on the abolition of private property.
> This candidate insists on the abolition of private property.
> Therefore this candidate must be a Communist.

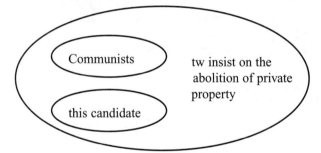

No, he might be against private property for other reasons. He might be an anarchist, or a spiritualist who wants to deny all material property because he believes matter is an illusion; or a monk who wants the whole world to live in a global monastery, or a tyrant who wants to possess all property himself.

But the form of this deceptive argument is exactly the same as the form of the first one (about cats and dogs), which is not deceptive because of its clearer content. The common form is:

> All P is M
> And all S is M
> Therefore all S is P

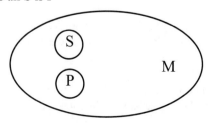

P and S are not necessarily compared with, or related to, the same part of the extension of M here. Perhaps S is one kind of M and P is another. Or perhaps they are the same. We do not know from this syllogism, because neither premise has a distributed (universal) middle term.

This pattern will be found very frequently. Undistributed Middle is probably the most common violation of the rules of the syllogism, and this pattern (two A premises with the same predicate) is the most common pattern for it.

Rule 4 could be called the No Trespassing rule. Think of the line between the premises and the conclusion as a property line. Only those who belong on the property may enter it; only those terms which have produced their credentials can cross over into the conclusion. If a term is so weak, so to speak, that it is undistributed in the premise, it cannot suddenly become strong and distributed in the conclusion. If all we know about a term in the premise is a partial knowledge, a knowledge of *some* of its extension (and that is what "undistributed" means), then that is all we are justified in claiming to know in the conclusion when that term reappears. To go from undistributed to distributed would be like a magician pulling a live rabbit out of a dead hat. It would be a trick. And there are no tricks in logic.

For instance, take the following syllogism:

> Compassion is a virtue.
> Justice is not compassion.
> Therefore justice is not a virtue.

Let's first test this syllogism by Euler circles, and then by the six rules. The Euler diagram shows how both premises can be true without the conclusion being true, for there are two possibilities:

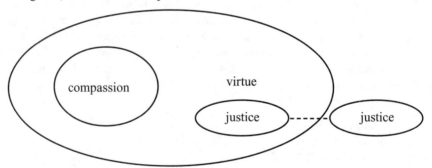

And Euler circles must be drawn for all possibilities to see whether there is any possibility that the premises can be true without the conclusion being true. (For this reason, it is sometimes easier to use the six rules than to use Euler circles.)

The six rules reveal the fallacy here as "illicit major": the major term, "virtue," moves from being undistributed in the major premise to being distributed in the conclusion. The predicate of the conclusion is the major term. This is "a virtue." This same term occurs also in one of the premises, which makes that premise the major premise. The premise is: "Compassion is a virtue." This is an A proposition. The predicate of an A proposition is undistributed. But this same term ("a virtue") is distributed in the conclusion. The syllogism thus violates Rule 4: no term undistributed in the premises may be distributed in the conclusion. The syllogism is fallacious: Illicit Major.

Another example of the same fallacy (Illicit Major) shows how Euler's Circles can be more difficult to use than the six rules:

> A healthy life is worth living.
> Some lives are not healthy.
> Therefore some lives are not worth living.

Here is one possible diagram for the premises, which seems to show that the syllogism is valid:

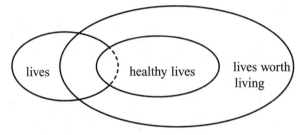

But here is another possible diagram of the premises, which shows that it is invalid:

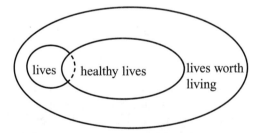

For if there is any possibility of the premises being true without the conclusion being true, the argument is invalid.

Consider the following syllogism:

> No violence is just.
> All violence is aggression.
> Therefore no aggression is just.

Perhaps all three propositions are true, but the syllogism is invalid because the minor term, "aggression," moves from being undistributed in the minor premise to being distributed in the conclusion. The Euler diagram here again also shows the fallacy, but only if we draw both possible diagrams for the premises:

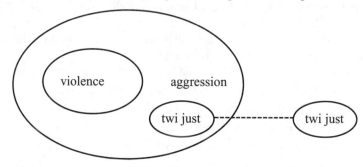

When it crosses the line from premises to conclusion, a term may move from distributed to undistributed, or it may remain undistributed, or it may remain distributed, but it may not move from undistributed to distributed. From distributed to distributed, from undistributed to undistributed, and from distributed to undistributed are all OK, but not from undistributed to distributed. From distributed to undistributed is OK – a term may move from being distributed in the premise to being undistributed in the conclusion – because if we know about all of the term in the premise (which is what "distributed" means), we are justified in claiming to know about *some* of that term (undistributed) in the conclusion; from "all" we can infer "some." But from "some" we cannot infer "all."

	OK	OK	OK	invalid
Term in the premise	d	u	d	u
	↓	↓	↓	↓
Same term in the conclusion	d	u	u	d

Rule 5 forbids two negative premises, and the reason is again the middle term. When both the major and minor terms are related negatively to the middle term, we do not know how they are related to each other. Remember, it is not necessarily true that "the enemy of my enemy is my friend," or (analogously) it is not necessarily true that two things that do not "match" a common third thing do not "match" each other. They may, or they may not.

For instance, take the following two syllogisms, both having the same logical form:

Odd numbers are not even numbers.   Birds are not fish.
Three is not an even number.   Humans are not fish.
Therefore three is not an odd number. Therefore humans are not birds.

The conclusion of the second happens to be true, but its premises do not prove it. The conclusion of the first is obviously false, and it is easier to see why its premises do not prove it. But the first syllogism is in exactly the same logical situation. They have the same logical form:

> No P is M
> No S is M
> Therefore no S is P

Rule 6 is similar to Rule 4 in that it is a kind of "No Trespassing" rule. Rule 4 state that if a *term* is undistributed in the premise, it must also be undistributed in the conclusion. Rule 6 states that if the premises contain a negative *proposition*, the conclusion must also be negative, and vice versa. (There is no "vice versa" clause in Rule 4.) There will also be a third "No Trespassing" rule, Corollary 2, which states that if one premise is particular, the conclusion must also be particular.

Consider these two syllogisms, which violate Rule 6 as well as Rule 5:

No dogs are angels.   No philosophers are angels.
And no mammals are angels.   And no lawyers are angels.
Therefore all dogs are mammals.   Therefore all philosophers are lawyers.

The first conclusion happens to be true, and the second false, but exactly the same logical form is used:

> No S is M
> And no P is M
> Therefore All S is P

That this syllogistic form is invalid, can be seen by the Euler Circle diagram:

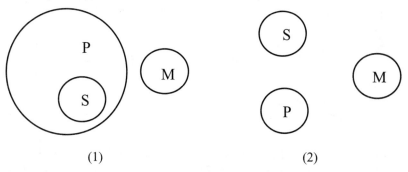

(1)   (2)

Remember, if there is any way we can diagram the premises without having the conclusion, the argument is invalid. Both of the two diagrams above have faithfully diagrammed the two premises, but the second one does not yield the conclusion.

Corollary 1 forbids any syllogism to have two particular premises. Any syllogism that violates this rule will also violate Rule 3 or 4. For example:

Some swans are white.	Some jewels are green.
And some white things are beautiful.	And some green things are alive.
Therefore some swans are beautiful.	Therefore some jewels are alive.

Here again we have the same logical form, and both syllogisms contain two true premises, but only the first has a true conclusion. The conclusion is true "by accident," so to speak; it does not necessarily follow from the premises. The fallacy is Undistributed Middle. Or consider the following:

Some onions are not smelly.	Some sheep are not black.
And some smelly things taste good.	And some black things are animals.
Therefore some onions do not taste good.	Therefore some sheep are not animals.

Here again in both cases we have true premises but only in the first case do we have a true conclusion, by accident. It does not follow from the premises. The two syllogisms have the same logical form and both commit the fallacy of Illicit Major:

Some S is not M
And some M is P
Therefore some S is not P

The corollary is a useful time-saver because the fallacy of two particular premises can be detected at a glance, while you have to mark each term with a "d" or a "u" before you can tell whether a syllogism commits the fallacies of Undistributed Middle, Illicit Major, or Illicit Minor.

Corollary 2 ("If one premise is particular, the conclusion must be particular") is another "No Trespassing" rule. The "weakness" of particularity in the premise must be reflected in the conclusion. *The conclusion always follows the weaker premise*: particular or negative.

Any syllogism that violates Corollary 2 will also violate either Rule 3 or Rule 4, and commit Undistributed Middle, Illicit Major, or Illicit Minor. E.g.:

All dogs are animals.
Some dogs are poodles.
Therefore all poodles are animals.

All three propositions are true, but the conclusion does not follow from the premises: there is Illicit Minor. If the terms in the conclusion were reversed, it is still Illicit Minor:

All dogs are animals.
Some dogs are poodles.
Therefore all animals are poodles.

It is a little easier to spot the fallacy of a particular premise without a particular conclusion than to spot Illicit Major or Illicit Minor, so this corollary too is a time-saving device.

Exercise A: Test each of the following syllogisms and the ones on page 234 by the six rules:

1. Some children smoke.
    Some who smoke get cancer.
    Therefore some children get cancer.

2. Saints are never joyless.
    Some joyless people are popes.
    Therefore some popes are not saints.

3. Peace is good.
    War is not peace.
    Therefore war is not good.

4. Some people are magnets for trouble.
    No ombudsmen are magnets for trouble.
    Therefore some ombudsmen are not people.

5. Everything in Massachusetts is in America.
    Everything in Boston is in America.
    Therefore everything in Boston is in Massachusetts.

6. No one who does not wonder philosophizes.
    Conformists do not wonder.
    Therefore conformists do not philosophize.

7. Whatever is divine is supernatural.
    Whatever is supernatural can perform miracles.
    Therefore whatever is divine can perform miracles.
    Man cannot perform miracles.
    Therefore man is not divine.

8. All mortal things are made of parts.
    The soul is not made of parts.
    Therefore the soul is not mortal.

9. Nothing immortal is made of parts.
    Man is made of parts.
    Therefore man is not immortal.

10. Whatever does not listen to reason, cannot be governed by reason.
    Falling in love does not listen to reason.
    Therefore falling in love cannot be governed by reason.

11. A john is a toilet.
    No toilet is an apostle.
    Therefore John is not an apostle.

12. Fools are never blessed.
    But some fools are lucky.
    Therefore not all lucky people are blessed.

13. All bachelors are unmarried men.
    No married woman is a bachelor.
    Therefore no married woman is an unmarried man.

14. Constancy is confidence.
    Constancy is a virtue.
    Therefore confidence is a virtue.

15. Foolhardiness is virtuous.
    Foolhardiness is confidence.
    Therefore some confidence is not virtuous.

16. Some books are sources of amusement.
    All logic books are books.
    Therefore some logic books are sources of amusement.

17. Whoever intentionally kills another should die.
    Soldiers intentionally kill another.
    Therefore soldiers should die.

18. John loves Jesus.
    Jill loves John.
    Therefore Jill loves Jesus.

19. Gorillas are nonhumans.
    Humans can speak.
    Therefore gorillas can't speak.

Exercise B: The following syllogisms need to be translated into strict logical form first. All three propositions are stated, but in ordinary language, as in "real life." Remember to identify the conclusion first, and put all three propositions in the syllogism into logical form. Then check for validity.

1. No one philosophizes who can not wonder, and computers cannot wonder, therefore no computer philosophizes.
2. "Objection 1:•*It seems that* mercy cannot be attributed to God, for mercy is a kind of sorrow, as Damascene says, but there is no sorrow in God; and therefore there is no mercy in Him." (St. Thomas Aquinas, ST I,21,3)
3. Not all syllogisms are silly, for only persons are silly, and nothing but non-persons are syllogisms. (Hint: reword the more complex proposition, which is more flexible and changeable, to conform to the terms of the more simple propositions, which are less flexible and changeable. Remember that you may never change the meaning of a proposition, only the wording.)
4. Most subjects that tend to withdraw the mind from pursuits of a low nature are useful. But classical learning does not do this, and therefore it is not useful.
5. Bacon was a great statesman. He was also a philosopher. We may infer from this that any philosopher can be a great statesman.
6. Happiness is always desired for its own sake and never as a means to anything else. Pleasure is always desired for its own sake and never as a means to anything else. Therefore happiness is identical with pleasure.
7. All immoral companions should be avoided, and some immoral companions are intelligent persons, therefore some intelligent persons should be avoided.
8. Apes are never angels, and philosophers are never apes, therefore philosophers are never angels.
9. Mathematics improves the reasoning powers. But logic is not mathematics. Therefore logic does not improve the reasoning powers.
10. "Is a stone a body? Yes. Then is not an animal a body? Yes. Are you an animal? I think so. Therefore you are a stone, being a body." (Lucian) (There are *two* syllogisms here.)
11. "His imbecility of character might have been inferred from his proneness to favorites, for all weak princes have this failing." (De Morgan)
12. Rational beings are responsible for their actions. Brute animals are not responsible. Therefore they are not rational.
13. Any honest man admits his rival's virtues. Not every scholar does this. Therefore some scholars are not honest.
14. "Since all knowledge comes from sensory impressions, and since there's no sensory impression of substance itself, it follows logically that there is no knowledge of substance." (Robert Pirsig, *Zen and the Art of Motorcycle Maintenance*, paraphrasing Hume.)
15. "Because intense heat is nothing else but a particular kind of painful sensation; and pain cannot exist but in a perceiving being; it follows that no intense heat can really exist in an unperceiving corporeal substance." (George Berkeley, *Three Dialogues between Hylas and Philonous*)
16. "Since fighting against neighbors is an evil, and fighting against the

Thebans is fighting against neighbors, it is clear that fighting against the Thebans is an evil." (Aristotle, *Posterior Analytics*)

17. "Whenever I'm in trouble, I pray. And since I'm always in trouble, there is not a day when I don't pray." (Isaac Bashevis Singer) (Hint: you will need to change the wording of these three propositions, without changing their meaning, to put the argument into the form of a three-term syllogism.)

18. "The after-image (idea) is not in physical space. The brain process is. So the after-image is not a brain-process." (J.J.C. Smart, "Sensations and Brain Processes," *Philosophical Review* 4/59)

19. "According to Aristotle, none of the products of Nature are due to chance. His proof is this: That which is due to chance does not reappear constantly nor frequently, but all products of Nature reappear either constantly or at least frequently." (Moses Maimonides, *Guide of the Perplexed*)

20. "No man can be a rhapsode who does not understand the meaning of the poet. For the rhapsode ought to interpret the mind of the poet to his hearers, but how can he interpret him well unless he knows what he means?" (Plato, *Ion*) (This syllogism too needs rewording first.)

21. "What is simple cannot be separated from itself. The soul is simple; therefore, it cannot be separated from itself." (Duns Scotus, *Oxford Commentary*)

22. "Since morals have an influence on the actions and affections, it follows that they cannot be derived from reason, because reason alone, as we have already proved, can never have any such influence." (David Hume, *A Treatise of Human Nature*)

23. "No man should fear death, for death is according to nature, and nothing is evil which is according to nature." (Marcus Aurelius) (Hint: can you get these four terms reworded into three without changing the meaning? Is this the fallacy of four terms? Is it two syllogisms?)

24. "We define a metaphysical sentence as a sentence which purports to express a genuine proposition but does, in fact, express neither a tautology nor an empirical hypothesis. And as tautologies and empirical hypotheses form the entire class of significant [meaningful] propositions, we are justified in concluding that all metaphysical assertions are nonsensical [not meaningful]." (A.J. Ayer, *Language, Truth and Logic*)

25. "You cannot recognize non-being, nor speak of it, for that which can be thought and that which can be are the same." (Parmenides) (Is there an implied premise at work here?)

26. "Since the act of friendship is love, there are thus three kinds of friendship, according to the three objects of love: (1) friendship because of virtue, which is true and essential good, (2) friendship because of something pleasing to the senses, (3) friendship because of utility." (Aquinas)

27. "Then what are we to say about that which is holy, Euthyphro? According to you, is it not that which is loved by all the gods?" "Yes." "Just because it is holy, or for some other reason?" "No, it is just for that reason." "And so it is

because it is holy that it is loved; it is not holy because it is loved." "So it seems." "On the other hand, a thing is beloved and pleasing to the gods just because they love it." "No doubt of that." "So what is pleasing to the gods is not the same as what is holy, Euthyphro, nor, according to what you say, is the holy the same as what is pleasing to the gods. They are two different things." "How is that so, Socrates?" "Because we are agreed that the holy is loved just because it is holy, and is not holy just because it is loved. Isn't that so?" "Yes." "Whereas what is pleasing to the gods is pleasing to them just because they love it." (Plato, *Euthyphro*) (Hint: this is just one single syllogism, with just three terms.)

28. God must exist because God, by definition, lacks no perfection, and existence is a perfection.

29. "And how do you know that you're mad?" "To begin with," said the Cat, "a dog's not mad. You grant that?" "I suppose so," said Alice. "Well, then," the Cat went on, "you see a dog growls when it's angry and wags its tail when it's pleased. Now I growl when I'm pleased and wag my tail when I'm angry. Therefore, I'm mad." (Lewis Carroll)

30. You hear 'south-west' or 'south-east' but never 'south-north', because that would be a contradiction. So south cannot be north. But if what is south can at the same time be west, and west can be north, it logically follows that south *can* be north.

Section 3. "Barbara Celarent"; mood and figure

There is no need to learn this method of checking syllogisms. It is mentioned here only as a historical curiosity, like the Stanley Steamer or the catapult. It is the clumsiest and slowest way to check syllogisms for validity. But it does work.

The one thing that *should* be mastered in this section is the concept of the **mood** and **figure** of a syllogism, and the simple three-letter abbreviation for the "mood" of each syllogism. For we need to know this in order to find the missing premise of an abbreviated syllogism, or "enthymeme" (next chapter), which is one of the most practically useful techniques in all of logic.

"Barbara Celarent" is *a list of valid moods for each of the four possible figures* of a syllogism, in the form of a medieval list of Latin names, so that if you know the mood and the figure of any syllogism you simply consult the list to see whether the syllogism is valid.

The **mood** of a syllogism is the quality and quantity of its three propositions. AAA is the mood of a "bull's eye syllogism" such as the classic "all men are mortal," etc. EIO is the mood of "No dinosaurs are alive, and some dinosaurs are bigger than elephants, therefore some things bigger than elephants are not alive."

We said earlier that it was not necessary, when using Aristotle's six rules of the syllogism to check for validity, to obey the convention of always placing the major premise first. But when using "Barbara Celarent" it is, for the mood of a syllogism is always expressed in a three-letter summary that is in this order: first the major premise, then the minor premise, then the conclusion.

The **figure** of a syllogism is the placement of the middle term. There are four possibilities: the middle term can be

(1) the subject of the major premise and the predicate of the minor premise (= the "first figure")
(2) the predicate of both premises (= the "second figure")
(3) the subject of both premises (= the "third figure")
(4) the predicate of the major premise and the subject of the minor premise (= the "fourth figure")

M — P	P — M	M — P	P — M
S — M	S — M	M — S	M — S
First	Second	Third	Fourth
Figure	Figure	Figure	Figure

"Barbara Celarent" is a mnemonic device to remember the valid moods for each figure. The vowels of the names make up the mood (e.g., "**Barbara**" = AAA) and there are four lines of names for the four figures:

Barbara, Celarent, Darii, Ferio (AAA, EAE, AII, EIO)
Camestres, Cesare, Baroko, Festino (AEE, EAE, AOO, EIO)
Darapti, Disamis, Datisi, Felapton, Bokardo, Ferison (AAI, IAI, AII, EAO, OAO, EIO)
Bramantip, Camenes, Dimaris, Fesapo, Fresison (AAI, AEE, IAI, EAO, EIO)

The medievals loved these lines, for they were a key (though a slow one) that opened up all valid syllogisms and locked away all invalid ones. They also knew and used Aristotle's six rules, but the Latin verses seemed more elegant, almost a magical formula or incantation. Tastes change; the laws of logic do not.

The list of names includes other devices as well. E.g. the letter "s" after the vowels "E" or "I" indicates that when the E proposition can be converted simply ("s"), the syllogism is transformed, or "reduced" into one of the first figure, the figure which Aristotle and the medievals regarded as the most clear, simple, natural, and direct. There are also other details in the scheme, e.g. using the same initial consonant for syllogisms that can be "reduced" to each other. All this elaborate logical dancing was done naturally, easily, and without reference to a text by medieval debaters.

Section 4. Venn Diagrams

Venn Diagrams are quite efficient in distinguishing valid and invalid syllogisms; however, they do not reveal the fallacy, the reason for the invalidity. Like

"Barbara Celarent," they are not necessary to learn, for they are superfluous; they do not do anything that Aristotle's six rules do not do.

Furthermore, they presuppose and use Boole's rather than Aristotle's interpretation of all universal propositions: as lacking existential import and all particular propositions as having it. This Boolean interpretation, used in all symbolic logic, invalidated the Square of Opposition (see pages 179–81), and we gave reasons there why it is quite natural and proper to reject it.

However, since Venn diagrams have become as fashionable today as "Barbara Celarent" was in the middle ages, we should briefly summarize them, as a *present* historical curiosity.

First, we must learn how to symbolize A, E, I and O propositions in a totally new way. As with Euler's circles, each term is diagrammed by a circle. However, instead of relating the terms by *including or excluding* the S and P circles, these circles *always overlap*, giving us 4 possible classes: S, P, both S and P, and neither S nor P.

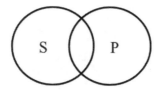

Shaded lines are used to designate which of the areas is not "occupied." Thus an A proposition, "All S is P," is interpreted to mean that there are no real beings that are S and not P – i.e. "No S is not P":

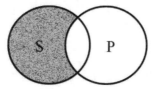

An asterisk designates which of the areas *is* "occupied." Thus an I proposition has an asterisk in that part of S that is P:

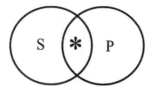

Note that the universal proposition is interpreted as not implying that any

S's exist (all it does is to deny that there are any S's that are not P), while the particular proposition is interpreted as implying that some S's exist (thus the asterisk). This is the assumption we have questioned above.

The E proposition, "No S is P," shades out the overlapping part, to show that there are no S's that are also P's:

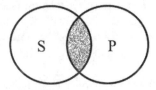

And the O proposition has an asterisk in the part of S that is *not* P (also implying that such S's exist):

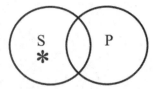

Now when we test a syllogism by Venn diagrams, we use one of the same principles as we used in Euler's circles: superimpose diagrams of the two premises on each other, and then look to see whether the conclusion necessarily follows. We do this by constructing a *three* circle diagram for each syllogism (one circle for each term), as follows:

Let us now diagram an AAA syllogism such as "All men are mortal, and Socrates is a man, therefore Socrates is mortal" – or any syllogism of the form "All M is P, all S is M, therefore all S is P."

We first shade out M's that are not P, to diagram the major premise "all M is P":

Then we add the minor premise "all S is M" by shading out all S's that are not M:

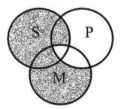

Then we look to see whether the conclusion follows, that "all S is P." All S's that are not P have been shaded out, so this does follow. It is valid.

Take an EIO syllogism (a common form, the only mood which is valid in all four figures).

No M is P
Some S is M
Therefore some S is not P

First we write down the three rings, empty:

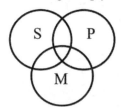

Then, diagram the major premise "No M is P" by shading out all M's that are P:

Then add the minor premise "Some S is M" by inserting the asterisk in S's M-overlapping area:

And now we see that "some S is not P" necessarily follows.

It does not matter whether we diagram the major or minor premise first, but we must always diagram the universal premise before the particular premise; otherwise, the diagram will leave some uncertainty.

Sometimes we need to diagram uncertainties as *two* possibilities in Venn diagrams, just as in Euler's circles. Take, for instance, this syllogism:

> All P is M
> Some S is M
> Therefore some S is P

First, write the three rings

Then diagram the major premise, "All P is M" by shading out all P that is not M:

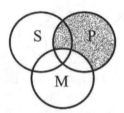

But when we come to diagram "Some S is M," we are still uncertain where to put the asterisk for S. So we have to insert two of them, since there are two possibilities. We connect them with a dotted line to show this (just as we use a dotted line for what is uncertain in Euler's circles):

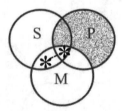

We can see that this syllogism is *not* valid because we can see a *possibility* for both premises being true yet the conclusion false.

Sometimes there is a discrepancy between Aristotle's six rules and Venn diagrams about whether the same syllogism is valid or invalid, because Venn diagrams use the Boolean interpretation of all particular propositions as existential and all universal propositions as non-existential, so that under this assumption a particular proposition can claim *more* than a universal. So because of the basic rule (common to both Aristotelian and Boolean logic) that there may not be more in the conclusion than in the premises, the Venn-Boolean system has the opposite rule from Aristotle's system: in Aristotelian logic it is fallacious to derive a universal conclusion from a particular premise; in the Venn (Boolean) system it is fallacious to derive a particular conclusion from universal premises.

A particular conclusion from two universal premises is not necessarily a fallacy by Aristotle's rules. Take the following syllogism:

All leprechauns are green.
All leprechauns are clever.
Therefore some green things are clever.

This violates none of Aristotle's six rules because if we interpret all propositions as existentially neutral, the validity of this syllogism does not depend on whether leprechauns exist or not. The term "green things" in the first premise ("all leprechauns are green") is no more nor less existential than the same term "green things" in the conclusion ("some green things are clever").

There are three reasons we do not insist on Venn diagrams for beginners: our preference for the Aristotelian over the Boolean interpretation of propositions; the fact that both Aristotle's six rules and Euler's circles reveal more simply and clearly *why* a syllogism is fallacious; and the fact that Aristotle's rules (and certainly Euler's circles) are simpler and easier to use. Aristotle's six rules may not be easier to *learn* than Venn diagrams, but once learned they are easier and quicker to *use* than Venn diagrams. You will eventually be able to recognize violations of the six rules at a glance, even in ordinary language, without translating into strict logical form, while this is not true of Venn diagrams.

XII. More Difficult Syllogisms

Section 1. Enthymemes: abbreviated syllogisms (B)

An enthymeme is a syllogism with one of its three propositions implied but not stated. The word "enthymeme" comes from the Greek "en-thymos" which means "in mind," since one of the three propositions is "kept in mind" rather than being explicitly stated in writing or speech.

This is a time-saving device, an abbreviation; and we all do it all the time. The fact that we all use enthymemes in ordinary speech shows that we all have a working knowledge of the principles of syllogistic logic in our unconscious minds. A book like this one merely brings our unconscious knowledge to consciousness, like psychoanalysis.

"The search for the tacit premise is excellent intellectual training . . . [for] most arguments are enthymemes, because almost all arguments entail unexpressed premises or assumptions. And in this broader sense the habit of searching for the tacit assumptions which are the silent determinants of one's thoughts takes on an extremely important aspect; it should be consciously cultivated." (Parker & Veatch, *Logic as a Human Instrument*)

First, Second, and Third Order Enthymemes

Enthymemes are of three types, depending on which of the three propositions is implied, or kept in mind. In "**first order enthymemes**" it is the major premise; in "**second order enthymemes**" it is the minor premise; and in "**third order enthymemes**" it is the conclusion. Third order enthymemes are relatively rare, and usually rhetorical devices, implying "draw your own conclusion." For instance, "Any candidate who can't manage his own finances, can't manage the nation's either. And this candidate can't manage his own finances." Or, "No mere mortal is infallible, and I'm only a mere mortal. (So what did you expect?)" (It is not necessary, for practical purposes, to distinguish between first and second order enthymemes, just as it is not practically necessary to distinguish between the major and minor premise.)

We deal with enthymemes in three steps:

(1) recognition that we have an enthymeme,

(2) finding the missing premise, and

(3) testing for validity.

To do the third step is simply to repeat what we have learned in the previous chapter; for once an enthymeme has its missing premise supplied, it is simply an ordinary syllogism.

The first step is identical with recognizing a syllogism, even though one of the three propositions is missing. How do we recognize a syllogism? (1) First of all, we recognize the presence of *an argument of some kind* by the presence of an argument indicator (a "therefore" word or a "because" word). (2) Then, we recognize the presence of a *syllogism* by the syllogistic pattern of (a) three propositions and (b) *three connected terms,* each of which is used twice. With an enthymeme, we will find only (a) two propositions, not three; so (b) only one of the three terms will be found twice (once in each of the two propositions).

It is much easier to learn this pattern by examples than by abstract general principles. So let us begin with this example: "Teenagers can't legally buy beer in this state because they are minors" .

The overt text contains two propositions: "Teenagers can't legally buy beer in this state" and "They are minors." These two propositions are joined by the premise indicator: "because." The two propositions have one common term: "teenagers" – but this becomes clear only if we translate the pronoun "they" into its noun, "teenagers." The pattern of an enthymeme becomes even more recognizable once you translate the two propositions into logical form:

> All [teenagers] are [minors]
>
> No [teenagers] are [those who can legally buy beer in this state]

The proposition that comes after the premise indicator "because" is the premise, and the proposition that comes before "because" is the conclusion. We all understand this instinctively outside of a logic course, i.e. we understand that the reason why teenagers can't buy beer is because they're minors, not vice versa. Only in a logic course do we ever confuse premise with conclusion, and this happens only when we forget our instinctive common sense.

Finding the Missing Premise

Now we must do the remaining step, finding and supplying the missing premise. This is extremely important for two reasons. First, we cannot test the argument for validity unless all its parts are in place. Second, there is no more practical skill you can learn from a logic course than this: how to smoke out an arguer's hidden assumptions. For that is how one arguer most often succeeds in persuading another: by exposing the other's hidden assumption, the assumption that is logically necessary for the argument to be valid. Even if A's logical analysis does not persuade B to change his opinion, at least it will cause B to understand his own argument better, by exposing its necessary assumption. Then, though A and B may still disagree, their disagreement has moved to a more basic level, the level of the assumption. The dialogue can then focus on arguments for and against that assumption. In other words, deductive arguments in lived conversation often move "backward" from conclusion to premise rather than "forward."

Here is a seven step method for finding the missing premise. After a little practice, you will recognize familiar patterns and instinctively go through all seven steps quickly, almost simultaneously.

(1) Be sure you have an enthymeme. *Look for (a) an argument indicator word* (premise indicator or conclusion indicator) *and (b) two propositions, with one common term between them.* In our example the argument indicator is "because," and the common term is "teenagers."

(2) *Identify the conclusion first.* (It is usually stated. Third order enthymemes are fairly rare, and usually obvious.) In our example, the conclusion is: "Teenagers can't buy beer in this state."

(3) *Put it into logical form*: "No [teenagers] are [those who can buy beer in this state]."

(4) *Identify the expressed premise*: "They are minors."

(5) *Put it into logical form*: "All [teenagers] are [minors]." (Translating the pronoun "they" into its noun, "teenagers.")

(6) If you already have a *common term*, proceed to step (7). If you do not have an explicit common term (i.e., a word or phrase used once in each of the two propositions without any word change), and yet you sense that there is an argument here (i.e., a connection between the premise and the conclusion such that the premise is some sort of reason for the conclusion), then try rewording one of the propositions to conform to the other one, thus getting an *explicit* common term. The basic rule is that *you may change the wording but not the meaning*. Here are some of the most common wording changes:

(6a) All *pronouns should be changed* to the nouns they refer to.

(6b) If you have two words or phrases that mean exactly the same thing, they are synonyms. *Synonyms should be changed* into each other. E.g. in "Holy people aren't gloomy; that's why Stoics aren't saints," "saints" and "holy people" are synonyms.

(6c) *Word order can be changed*, e.g. passive voice and active voice can be interchanged. E.g. "I love you, therefore you cannot die" can be changed to "You are loved by me, therefore you cannot die," thus giving us the common term "you."

(6d) *Possessives can be reworded* as independent nouns. E.g. "Since he's a doctor, his bag probably contains drugs" can be changed to "He is a doctor, therefore he is one whose bag probably contains drugs."

(6e) If a short term appears alone as a complete term in one proposition and reappears as part of a longer term in another proposition, change the wording of that other proposition as follows: extract the short term from the longer term, make it the subject, and without changing its meaning, reword the rest of the proposition to fit into the predicate. (Predicates are flexible; subjects are not.) E.g. "The man who killed Kennedy must have been a sharpshooter because Kennedy was moving fast" can be changed to "Kennedy must have been killed by a sharpshooter because Kennedy was moving fast." Or "Mothers who have more than one child in China are forced to kill their second child by abortion or infanticide; therefore China is a tyrannical regime" can be changed into "China is a place where mothers who have more than one child are forced to kill their second child by abortion or infanticide, therefore China is a tyrannical regime."

(7) Once you have a common term, and the two expressed propositions are written out in logical form, it is fairly simple to *find the missing premise*:

(7a) First, write down *the mood (A, E, I, or O) of each of the two expressed propositions*, e.g. AA or IO.

(7b) From the mood of the two propositions that are already expressed, you can tell what must be *the mood of the implied but unexpressed proposition* has to be if the syllogism is not to violate rule 5 or 6 or one of the two corollaries.

For instance, if the expressed premise is an E and the conclusion is an E, the implied premise must be an A. For if it were an E or an O, the syllogism would violate rule 5 (two negative premises), and if it were an I, the syllogism would violate Corollary 2 (a particular premise with a universal conclusion).

If the expressed premise is an A and the conclusion is an A, the implied premise must be an A. This is the most common form of all, the "bull's eye syllogism."

In our example above, the premise is an A ("all teenagers are minors") and the conclusion is an E ("no teenagers can legally buy beer in this state"), so the kept-in-mind premise must be an E. An A or an I would give us a negative conclusion without a negative premise (violating rule 6); an O would give us a particular premise without a particular conclusion (violating corollary 2).

We express the mood of a syllogism by writing the mood of each proposition in order, with the conclusion last. (It is conventional to write the major premise first, but not necessary in practice; reversing the order of the two premises does not change anything.)

The following list is a streamlined version of the clumsy old "Barbara Celarent" list of valid moods. (See page 257.) Unlike the medieval list, this one does not require you to take the *figure* of the syllogism into account at all (i.e. the placement of the middle term). *Only the following moods are valid*, all others are invalid. The list need not be memorized; it is just an application of rules 5 and 6 and two corollaries.)

AAA	AEE	EIO
AAI	EAE	IEO
AII	AEO	AOO
IAI	EAO	OAO

And since we can reverse the order of the premises without changing anything, we can omit five of the twelve above, resulting in *only seven valid moods:*

    AAA   AEE   EIO
    AAI   AEO   AOO
    AII

For only the following combinations of premises, in either order, can be
valid (by rules 5 and 6):

    AA
    AE
    AI
    AO
    EI

And the conclusion that must follow each of these five, must be as follows
(by rules 5 and 6):

    AAA (or I)
    AEE (or O)
    AII
    AOO
    EIO

The reason for this limit, the reason all other moods of the syllogism are
invalid, is the "no trespassing" rule: no "weakness" in the premises can cross
over the line into the conclusion without being reflected in the conclusion. There
are two such "weaknesses": negativity and particularity. You cannot have more
in the conclusion (the effect) than you had in the premises (the cause).

(7c) Now that you have the mood of the missing premise, *write out the
"empty" logical form* for that mood, with brackets around the yet-to-be-supplied
subject and predicate terms. In our example, the missing premise is an E, so the
empty logical form is: No [ ] is [ ].

(7d) Next, *find the two terms* that are to be joined in this missing premise.
They are the two terms that have been used only once. One of them will be the
middle term, which you can identify at a glance by the fact that it is the only
term not in the conclusion. In our example, the two terms to be joined in the
missing premise are "minors" and "those who can legally buy beer in this state."

(7e) Once you have the two terms, the only decision remaining is *which of
these two terms will be the subject and which the predicate.* Try both arrange-
ments, and if one of them gives you a fallacy, drop it and use the other.

Do not think: I will use whatever order of terms gives me a *true* premise;
for there can be dispute about what is true, but there is no question about what
is fallacious. You want to *supply whatever missing premise will make the syllogism valid.* For even if you are arguing against an opponent, you want to be fair

to him and not saddle him with a fallacy he did not explicitly commit. Give him the benefit of the doubt.

If the missing premise is an E or an I, it does not matter which order the terms come in, since both the E and the I proposition can be converted.

Let's take another example:

"Blessed are the meek, for they shall inherit the earth." (Matthew 5:2)

First, we determine that we have an argument. We do this both by intuition, or common sense, and by observing the presence of an argument indicator, the word "for."

Next, we identify the conclusion.

This can be done in two ways: by common sense and by looking at the clue, the argument indicator.

Common sense tells us that the speaker is trying to get across the conclusion that the meek are blessed, and that his reason for this rather strange and controversial conclusion is that they will inherit the earth. That is what makes them blessed; that is why they are blessed. If this point does not immediately register on your logical intuition, go to the argument indicator. (Go to it anyway, to check your intuition.)

The word "for" is a premise indicator: it points to a premise, introduces a premise; a premise comes after it. So the conclusion must come before it. So the conclusion is: "blessed are the meek." The remaining proposition must be a premise: "they shall inherit the earth."

(Remember, every argument indicator indicates *two* propositions: a conclusion indicator indicates not only a conclusion after it but also a premise before it, and a premise indicator indicates not only a premise after it but also a conclusion before it.)

We have, now, an enthymeme with one premise expressed, one premise implied, and the conclusion expressed.

Now we translate the two expressed propositions into logical form.

Take the conclusion first. "Blessed are the meek." We have here a reversed word order, with the predicate first. For the subject of a proposition is what you are talking about and the predicate is what you say about it. The speaker is *not* saying: "I am going to tell you something about *blessed*. That is my sermon topic. And what I will say about it is that it is, or are, *the meek*." That simply makes no sense. Rather, he is talking about the meek and saying that they are blessed. The meek are blessed: that is the point. He uses reversed word order for poetic or rhetorical purposes.

Clearly the proposition is affirmative. But is it universal or particular? Is he saying that *some* of the meek are blessed or that *all* are? Neither "some" nor "all" is used, but "all" is implied. Why? Because it is a general and unqualified statement. Also, because the statement implies that the meek are blessed simply by being meek, simply because they are meek. So if the meek are blessed because they are meek, then all the meek are blessed, since all the meek are meek.

Thus we have our conclusion, in logical form: "All [the meek] are [those who are blessed]."

"Blessed" is an adjective, and cannot stand alone as a subject, so we add the words "those who are," changing the wording without changing the meaning. Remember, in logical form, each term must be able to stand alone as a subject or a predicate, so each term must be a noun or noun phrase, since only a noun or noun phrase can be a subject. There will be quite a few occasions where you will have to take the predicate term and put it into the subject position when you supply the missing premise; this is the main reason why logical form requires all noun terms.

Now look at the expressed premise: "They shall inherit the earth."

First, we change the pronoun to its noun, to get a common term. Who are "they"? The meek, of course, the subjects that the speaker is speaking about.

This proposition is affirmative, obviously, but is it an A or an I? Will all the meek, will the meek as such, inherit the earth? Will the meek inherit the earth because they are meek, and thus all of them will inherit the earth? That is clearly what is implied. It is an unqualified affirmation. So it is an A, just as the conclusion is.

Next, we need to change the predicate ("shall inherit the earth") to a noun phrase ("those who shall inherit the earth.")

Now we have the expressed premise in logical form: "All [the meek] are [those who shall inherit the earth]."

We have a common term between the two expressed propositions. It is "the meek." So we do not have the problem of finding or making a common term.

The next step is to write down the logical form the missing premise has to have. Is it A, E, I, or O? Since both of the two expressed premises are A, the missing premise will have to be A to avoid violating rule 5 or 6. So it will be the most typical form of syllogism, AAA, a "bull's eye syllogism." So we write out the logical form for the implied A: "all [ ] are [ ]."

Now we need to find the two terms. How? Look at the terms in the two propositions we have already written out in logical form. Remember the structure of a syllogism: Each term must be used twice. And "the meek" has already been used twice, while "those who are blessed" and "those who shall inherit the earth" have both been used only once. So each of these two terms must be used one more time, by being joined in the missing premise.

Next, we need to find what order to put them in. There are two possibilities: "All [those who shall inherit the earth] are [those who are blessed]," or "All [those who are blessed] are [those who shall inherit the earth]." Which is it?

Common sense might click in at this point and tell us the answer; but suppose it does not. In that case, let us try both possibilities, and see which one gives us a valid syllogism.

If we try as our missing premise "all [those who shall inherit the earth] are [those who are blessed]," we have the following syllogism:

All [those who shall inherit the earth] are [those who are blessed]
And all [the meek] are [those who shall inherit the earth]
Therefore all [the meek] are [those who are blessed].

This is a perfect bull's eye syllogism, and valid. But if we had used the other possibility for our missing premise, namely "All [those who are blessed] are [those who shall inherit the earth]," we would have had:

All [those who are blessed] are [those who shall inherit the earth]
All [the meek] are [those who shall inherit the earth]
Therefore all [the meek] are [those who are blessed]

And this gives us Undistributed Middle.

Now there is absolutely no reason to saddle the speaker with this missing premise ("all the blessed shall inherit the earth"), which would make his argument fallacious, since he did not commit himself to this premise. Clearly, he is implying the other premise, the one that would make his argument valid. So that is the missing premise ("all who shall inherit the earth are blessed").

Remember, if you want to criticize another person's enthymeme, it is not fair to saddle him with a premise that would make his argument invalid if there is another premise that would not. Even if you think the premise that makes his argument invalid is true, and the premise that makes his argument valid is false, not everyone will agree as to which propositions are true and which are false, but everyone *will* agree as to which arguments are valid and which are invalid. After showing that he needs such-and-such a premise to make his argument valid, then and only then is it the time to argue that this necessary missing premise is in fact false.

Exercises on enthymemes: Put each of the following enthymemes into logical form, including the missing proposition. (It will usually be a missing *premise*, but it could be the conclusion that is missing and implied.) Identify the missing proposition with an arrow, or by enclosing it in an oval, like a cartoon "balloon" surrounding a character's thoughts. Then check the syllogism for validity. (NB: There are more exercises on enthymemes than on anything else in this book because enthymemes are the most frequent form of argument found in ordinary conversation. In fact, that very sentence was an enthymeme! Can you put it into logical form?)

1. "Rational beings are accountable for their actions; irrational brutes are therefore exempt from this responsibility."
2. "Love makes the world go round, so that means it doesn't make it go flat."
3. (E) "Love is a virtue, therefore hate is not."
4. (E) "Love is an act of will, therefore it is not an emotion."

5. (E) "Everything is changeable, therefore nothing is necessary."
6. "No one can move mountains; mountains have no wheels."
7. "Only the brave deserve the fair. Therefore you are not brave."
8. "Only the brave deserve the fair, and you're not brave."
9. "Logic stinks." "Why?" "Because I hate it, that's why."
10. "Dinosaurs cannot have been warm-blooded animals because they did not have enough food to fill the needs of such an animal."
11. (E) "All treaty violations are dangerous to peace, for all things dangerous to peace are potential causes of war."
12. "Marxists have always been social radicals, since their views were always incompatible with those of the existing societies which they wanted to overthrow."
13. "You're allowed to visit the battleship on holidays, so you can see it today."
14. "Every conclusion of Bull's Equation will always be a null set, because no matter how exhaustively you search, in history or in books or in your experience or in your own imagination, you will never find a null set that is a Bull-friendly set."
15. "Not all is gold that glitters, for tin glitters sometimes."
16. "Bub must be the quarterback because the center is hiking the ball to him."
17. "Shooting a pheasant is properly pleasant, since a pheasant is pleasingly plump."
18. "God loves me, so I guess I ain't junk."
19. "Extra-mental existence is a conceivable perfection. Therefore God must have extra-mental existence."
20. "How could it be right to restrict abortion? Any restriction on a woman's right to control her own body is wrong."
21. (E) "He was not burned, therefore he did not play with fire."
22. "Not all the rich are happy. Many commit suicide."
23. (E) "Corporations cannot be outlawed, since they have no souls."
24. "How could you believe *God* gave the Jews the Ten Commandments?" "Why not?" "Because *Moses* gave them."
25. "You bug me." "Why?" "Because I hate your dog."
26. "All conifers are trees, therefore all pines are conifers."
27. "God does not exist because you can't find Him in a test tube."
28. "Not all snakes slither, since there are a lot of green things that don't slither."
29. "Heaven is not in Boston because Fenway Park is in Boston."
30. (H) "I can personally guarantee that St. Thomas loved God because for the life of me I cannot help loving St. Thomas." (Flannery O'Connor)
31. (H) "Good sense is of all things in the world the most equally distributed, for everybody thinks himself so abundantly provided with it that even those most difficult to please in all other matters do not commonly desire more of it than they already possess." (Descartes, *Discourse on Method* I,1)

32. "Forbear to judge, for we are sinners all." (Shakespeare, *Henry VI,* Part II, III,3)
33. (H) "The criminal law forbids suicide . . . the prohibition is ridiculous, for what penalty can frighten a person who is not afraid of death itself?" (Schopenhauer, "On Suicide")
34. "Wisdom is the principal thing; therefore get wisdom." (Proverbs 4:7)
35. "He who disobeys us is, as we maintain, thrice wrong: first, because in disobeying us he is disobeying his parents; secondly, because we are the authors of his education; thirdly, because he has made an agreement with us that he will duly obey our commands." (Plato, *Crito,* imagining the laws of the state arguing for themselves)
36. (II) "One may be subject to laws made by another, but it is impossible to bind oneself in any matter which is the subject of one's own free exercise of will. . . . It follows of necessity that the king cannot be subject to his own laws." (Jean Bodin, *Six Books of the Commonwealth* (1576)) (Hint: take "matters which are the subject of one's own free exercise of will" as the subject of a premise and reword the argument accordingly.)
37. (H) "Our ideas reach no farther than our experience. We have no experience of divine attributes. I need not conclude my syllogism; you can draw the inference yourself." (David Hume, *Dialogues Concerning Natural Religion*)
38. "As a matter of fact, man, like woman, is flesh, therefore passive, the plaything of his hormones and of the species, the restless prey of his desires." (Simone De Beauvoir, *The Second Sex*)
39. (H) "Although these textbooks purport to be a universal guide to learning of great worth and importance, there is a single clue that points to another direction. In the six years I taught in city and country schools, no one ever stole a textbook." (W. Ron Jones, *Changing Education*)
40. "He would not take the crown. Therefore 'tis certain he was not ambitious." (Shakespeare, *Julius Caesar,* III,2)
41. "We possess some immaterial knowledge. No sense knowledge, however, can be immaterial. Therefore, etc." (Duns Scotus, *Oxford Commentary on the Sentences*)
42. "A nation without a conscience is a nation without a soul. A nation without a soul is a nation that cannot live." (Winston Churchill)
43. (H) "The man who says that all things come to pass by necessity cannot criticize one who denies that all things come to pass by necessity, for he admits that this too happens of necessity." (Epicurus, Fragment 40)
44. (H) "We can explain nothing but what we can reduce to laws whose object can be given in some possible experience. But freedom is a mere idea, the objective reality of which can in no way be shown according to natural laws or in any possible experience." (Kant)
45. (H) "Since no man has a natural authority over his fellow . . . we must conclude that conventions form the basis of all legitimate authority among

men." (Rousseau) (Hint: this enthymeme is most easily expressed in a disjunctive syllogism, a form you have not yet learned. But it is quite simple and commonsensical. Try "all authority is either natural or conventional" as the missing premise.)

46. "Since evil occurs, God must be willing that it should occur." (William P. Montague)

47. (E) "Because you have done this, cursed are you." (Genesis 3:14)

48. "I will fear no evil, for thou art with me." (Psalm 23)

49. "An electron, when studied, had an electric charge. It has mass. It had an angular momentum. It had a magnetic moment. It had position and velocity. And these things seemed to justify the designation of it by the term 'particle.'" (W.V. Houston)

50. (H) When asked whether the Vatican should be invited to an international conference, Stalin replied, "How many legions does the Pope have?" Construe this as an argument by interpreting Stalin's question as a "rhetorical question," i.e. a declarative sentence (and therefore a proposition) masked in an interrogative form.

51. (H) "For an idea to be fashionable is ominous, since it must afterwards be always old-fashioned." (George Santayana)

52. (H) "Art indeed copies life in not copying life, for life copies nothing." (G.K. Chesterton) (Warning: this one will need some creative but faithful rewording. Give it two or three tries before looking up the answer; the effort will make you feel good afterwards, whether you get it right or not.)

53. "The most sentimental thing in the world is to hide your feelings; it is making too much of them." (G.K. Chesterton) [Hint: what is the subject, or topic, of the first proposition?]

54. "Of the two sexes the woman is in the more powerful position. For the average woman is at the head of something with which she can do as she likes; the average man has to obey orders." (G.K. Chesterton)

55. (H) "It is idle to talk of the alternative of reason and faith. Reason itself is a matter of faith. It is an act of faith to assert that our thoughts have any relation to reality at all." (G.K. Chesterton)

56. "What things may be in themselves, I know not, because a thing is never presented to me otherwise than as a phenomenon." (Kant)

57. "Love looks not with the eyes but with the mind,/ And therefore is wing'd Cupid painted blind." (Shakespeare, *A Midsummer Night's Dream*, 1, 1)

58. (E) "Metaphysical propositions are neither true nor false because they assert nothing." (Rudolf Carnap)

59. "Definitions cannot, by their very nature, be either true or false, only more useful or less so. For this reason it makes relatively little sense to argue over definitions." (Peter Berger, *The Sacred Canopy*) It is a good exercise to argue for a little while about whether Berger is right here; cf. page 127.)

60. (H) "The materials of nature (air, earth, water) that remain untouched by

human effort belong to no one and are not property. It follows that a thing can become someone's property only if he works and labors on it to change its natural state." (Locke, *Of Property*)

61. "The fact that any individual's scientific activities are socially conditioned entails that science cannot achieve objectivity." (Richard Rudner, *Philosophy of Social Science*)

62. "Be glad of life because it gives you the chance to love and to work and to play and to look up at the stars." (Henry Van Dyke)

63. "Spinoza argued that since God is the only thing that is ultimately real, the soul could be nothing else than a mode of God." (S.E. Frost, *The Basic Teachings of the Great Philosophers*)

64. (H) "Thou hast made us for Thyself, and [therefore] our hearts are restless until they rest in Thee." (St. Augustine, *Confessions* 1, 1)

65. (E) "A machine can handle information. It can calculate, conclude, and choose. It can perform reasonable operations with information. A machine, therefore, can think." (Edmund C. Berkeley)

66. "Man is the only animal that laughs and weeps, for he is the only animal that is struck by the difference between what things are and what things ought to be." (William Hazlitt) Also identify what kind of "because" this is: argument or explanation? Which of the four causes?

67. "The value of any commodity to the person who wants to exchange it for other commodities is equal to the quantity of labor which it enables him to purchase or command. Labor, therefore, is the real measure of the exchangeable value of all commodities." (Adam Smith)

68. "The good is not the same as the pleasant, my friend, nor is the evil the same as the painful. For we cease from the one pair at the same time, but not from the other." (Plato, *Gorgias*) (Hint: make "good and evil" one term and "pleasure and pain" a second.)

69. "Only man has dignity; only man, therefore, can be funny." (Ronald Knox)

70. "God must have loved the plain people; He made so many of them." (Abraham Lincoln)

71. (H) "Whatsoever we imagine is finite. Therefore there is no idea or conception of anything we call infinite." (Thomas Hobbes)

Section 2. Sorites: chain syllogisms

In ordinary conversation we often string syllogisms together to make longer arguments. The two most common forms of these strings of syllogisms are **sorites** and **epicheiremas**. The latter are both more difficult and more common, so we shall take the easier and less common form first.

A sorites (sore-*eye*-tees) is a polysyllogism, i.e. a multiple syllogism, two or more syllogisms in direct series. E.g.,

Moby Dick is a whale.
All whales are mammals.
All mammals sleep.
Therefore Moby Dick sleeps.

A sorites is a single argument in some kind of syllogistic form, yet it has more than three terms without therefore being invalid. It is really an abbreviated multiple syllogism. E.g. the above is an abbreviated form of:

Moby Dick is a whale.
And all whales are mammals.
Therefore Moby Dick is a mammal.

Moby Dick is a mammal.
And all mammals sleep.
Therefore Moby Dick sleeps.

The only difference between the first and second versions above is that the first version omits a step, viz. the conclusion of the first syllogism in the two-syllogism version: "Moby Dick is a mammal."

A sorites may be only two syllogisms together, as in the above example, or more than two, up to any number. E.g. "all A is B and all B is C and all C is D and all D is E and all E is F therefore all A is F." For instance, "suffering produces endurance, and endurance produces character, and character produces hope, and hope does not disappoint us" (Romans 5:3–5). We can translate this into:

All who suffer, endure.
All who endure, develop character.
All who develop character, have hope.
All who have hope will not be disappointed.
Therefore all who suffer, will not be disappointed.

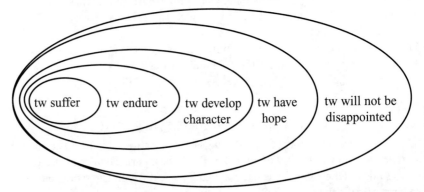

The final conclusion is implied in the quotation, as in a third order enthymeme. St. Paul seemed to be attached to this kind of sorites. There is another one in Romans 8:29–30. (Look it up. If you don't have a Bible, steal one.)

A sorites can be diagrammed most simply by Euler's circles. It is a waste of time to break a sorites down into separate syllogisms and test each one by the six rules.

There are two kinds of sorites, affirmative and negative. The affirmative form (called an "Aristotelian sorites") is simply a "bull's eye syllogism" with more than two circles around the "bull's eye," so to speak, as in the previous example. (The negative form is at the bottom of page 278.)

Most sorites are affirmative. Even when they are long, they are simple "bull's eye syllogisms." The long ones simply put more circles around the bull's eye. E.g.:

> He who drinks, gets drunk
> He who gets drunk, sleeps.
> He who sleeps, does not sin.
> He who does not sin, goes to Heaven.
> Therefore he who drinks, goes to Heaven.

Obviously there is some ambiguity operating in the terms here. (Where? Find it.) But formally the argument is valid and looks like this in Euler's circles:

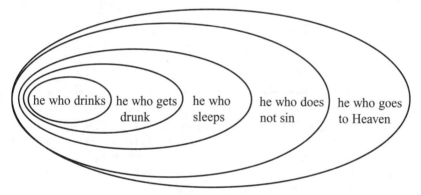

Sometimes the terms need a little rewording to go into logical form. E.g.: "Since happiness consists in peace of mind, and since durable peace of mind depends on the confidence we have in the future, and since that confidence is based on the science we should have of the nature of God and the soul, it follows that that science is necessary for true happiness" (Leibniz). Putting the propositions into more logical form, this becomes:

(1) All happiness is peace of mind
(2) All peace of mind depends on the confidence we have in the future
(3) Whatever depends on the confidence we have in the future, depends on that which is based on the science of God and the soul
(4) Therefore all happiness depends on that which is based on the science of God and the soul.

When a sorites gets this long, it is a useful and time-saving device to abbreviate the terms when drawing the Euler diagram. (However, be sure the terms are exactly worded first, before using the abbreviations, for most mistakes in sorites come from the fallacy of four terms during one of the steps, stemming from sloppy use of terminology.)

(1) All happiness (H) is peace of mind (P)
(2) All peace of mind (P) depends on the confidence we have in the future (DCF)
(3) Whatever depends on the confidence we have in the future (DCF), depends on that which is based on the science of God and the soul (DBSGS)
(4) Therefore all happiness (H) depends on that which is based on the science of God and the soul (DBSGS)

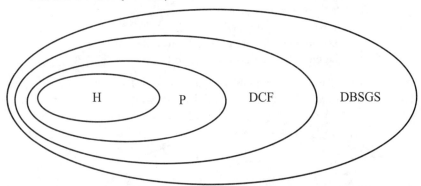

Here is another, even longer sorites from Leibniz. To save time and space, we add abbreviations for the terms as we go along. "The human soul (A) is a thing whose activity is thinking (B). A thing whose activity is thinking (B) is one whose activity is immediately apprehended and without any representation of parts therein (C). A thing whose activity is immediately apprehended without any representation of parts therein (C) is a thing whose activity does not contain parts (D). A thing whose activity does not contain parts (D) is one whose activity is not motion (E). A thing whose activity is not motion (E) is not a body (F). What is not a body (F) is not in space (G). What is not in space (G) is insusceptible of motion (H). What is insusceptible of motion (H) is indissoluble (I) (for dissolution is a movement of parts). What is indissoluble (I) is incorruptible (J). What is incorruptible (J) is immortal (K). Therefore the human soul (A) is immortal (K)" (from H.W.B. Joseph's *An Introduction to Logic*).

Though large, the Euler circle diagram for this is as simple as the last two.

The negative sorites (called the "Goclenian sorites") has only one negative premise, which is always placed last in the argument, for the sake of clarity.

     Socrates is a man.
     And all men are mortal.

And no gods are mortals.
Therefore Socrates is not a god.

It would not be *fallacious* to place the negative premise first, but it would be more *confusing* and hard to follow, therefore it is rare. One could, however, argue this way, e.g.: "No gods are mortal, and all men are mortal, and Socrates is a man, therefore Socrates is not a god" and the Euler diagram would be the same.

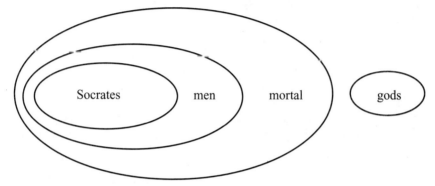

Rarely do we find a fallacious sorites, since they come in only these two clearly valid forms. This is another reason for not wasting time using the six rules or Venn diagrams on them. The main difficulty with a sorites is usually translating it from ordinary language into logical form.

Section 3. Epicheiremas: multiple syllogisms (B)

An epicheirema is a syllogism with an enthymeme attached to one or both of its premises to justify those premises. Like a sorites, it is a chain syllogism; but unlike a sorites, it is not a direct progression of circles in a Euler diagram, so it must be checked by using the six rules on each of its constituent syllogisms.

For instance, "Minds do not take up space, since they are not composed of particles of any size. Therefore they cannot be confined in prisons."

The final conclusion is that "they (minds) cannot be confined in prisons," and the (expressed) premise that justifies this conclusion is that "minds do not take up space." So the main syllogism is an enthymeme with the implied premise "whatever does not take up space cannot be confined in prisons."

All minds are things that do not take up space. (expressed premise)
All things that do not take up space are things that cannot be confined in prisons. (implied premise)
Therefore all minds are things that cannot be confined in prisons.

Or:

No minds are things that take up space. (expressed premise)
All things that can be confined in prisons are things that take up space.
(implied premise)
Therefore no minds are things that can be confined in prisons.

(When there is a choice like this, it is usually easier to reword the propositions so that you have negative terms and affirmative propositions rather than
affirmative terms and negative propositions. Most syllogisms can be reworded
into the AAA "bull's eye" format.)
However, the argument is not just a single syllogism but an epicheirema
because it adds another proposition, "they are not composed of particles of any
size," and connects that proposition to the proposition "minds do not take up
space" by a premise indicator, "since." This creates another enthymeme on top
of the first one, and this is called an epicheirema, after the Greek preposition
"epi," "on top of." (Epicheiremas can be made up of either enthymemes or full
syllogisms.)

Minds are not composed of particles of any size (expressed premise of syllogism #1)
Whatever is not composed of particles of any size does not take up space
(implied premise of #1)
Therefore minds do not take up space (conclusion of syllogism #1 and
expressed premise of #2)
What does not take up space cannot be confined in prisons (expressed premise of #2)
Therefore minds cannot be confined in prisons (conclusion of #2, final conclusion)

Sometimes both premises of the last syllogism are expressed and reasons
are added to both premises, as in the following: "Love is a virtue, because it is
a deliberate choice. But compassion is not a virtue, because it is a spontaneous
feeling. Therefore compassion is not love."

Whatever is a deliberate choice is a virtue. (implied premise of enthymeme
#1)
Love is a deliberate choice. (expressed premise of enthymeme #1)
Therefore love is a virtue. (conclusion of enthymeme # 1 and expressed
major premise of main syllogism)
Whatever is a spontaneous feeling is not a virtue. (implied premise of
enthymeme #2)
Compassion is a spontaneous feeling. (expressed premise of enthymeme #2)

Therefore compassion is not a virtue. (conclusion of enthymeme #2 and expressed minor premise of main syllogism)

Main syllogism:

Love is a virtue. (conclusion of enthymeme #1 and expressed major premise of main syllogism)
Compassion is not a virtue. (conclusion of enthymeme #2 and expressed minor premise of main syllogism)
Therefore compassion is not love. (conclusion of main syllogism)

Argument maps are often very useful for making clear the "strategy" and order of the propositions in long epicheiremas like this. (See next section.)

Take one more epicheirema, which is more complex because it requires some rewording to get it into logical form with the proper number of terms:

"Truth must necessarily be stranger than fiction, for fiction is the creature of the human mind and therefore congenial to it." (G.K. Chesterton)

It should be clear that the first proposition is the conclusion, since the premise indicator "for" comes after it.

However, there is a "therefore" near the end of the quotation, which may lead you to think (mistakenly) that what follows this "therefore" is not just a preliminary conclusion but the final conclusion. We have two conclusions: the one before "for" (remember, premise indicators always reveal conclusions, which come before them, as well as premises, which come after them) and the one after "therefore." How do we tell which is the final conclusion? By intuitively understanding the point and content of the argument, and also by the form: one formal clue is the fact that what follows "for" is another whole syllogism, in the form of an epicheirema, thus indicating that this syllogism is the reason attached on top of the premise of the main syllogism.

Thus:

Fiction is the creature of the human mind.
Whatever is the creature of the human mind is congenial to the human mind.
Therefore fiction is congenial to the human mind.
But truth is not congenial to the human mind.
Therefore truth is not fiction.
What is not fiction is stranger than fiction.
Therefore truth is stranger than fiction.

The best way to find your way through the complex jungle of propositions in longer arguments such as multiple epicheiremas is by first making argument maps, which function like road maps. To this topic we next turn.

Exercises on epicheiremas: Put each of the following epicheiremas into logical form. Supply and circle the missing, implied proposition for each enthymeme. Then check each syllogism for validity.

1. Mere matter cannot think, since it is the object of thinking. But we think, since we are thinking about thinking. Therefore we are not mere matter.
2. Not all snakes bite. For there are many reptiles that don't bite. For some lizards don't bite, and lizards are reptiles.
3. Courage is a virtue because it is a good habit. But foolhardiness is not a good habit. Therefore it is not a virtue.
4. She loves me because she laughed at my bad puns. Therefore my life is meaningful.
5. No one will ever solve the problem of evil because it's a mystery rather than just a problem. And the reason it's a mystery is that we're so involved in it that we can't be objective about it.
6. Angels do not occupy space since they are pure spirits and thus not composed of atoms. Therefore you can't confine angels in prisons.
7. No rabbit is safe, since foxes and wolves hunt them. But some Easter bunnies are safe, since they're inedible. Therefore not all Easter bunnies are rabbits.

Section 4. Complex argument maps

Arguments in practice are often long and complex, consisting of more than one or two syllogisms. Even the relatively simple, short, and straightforward patterns of enthymemes, sorites, and epicheiremas that we have just studied do not come close to exhausting the possible patterns of argument. So we need a kind of logical road map for longer and more complex arguments, to see the overall strategy of the argument, to break it down into those smaller arguments that are its parts and to see how those parts are related to each other. Only then will we be in a position to evaluate each smaller argument one by one.

Here are the three steps in mapping a long argument.

(1) First, read it through slowly and carefully. This is the step that you will be tempted to overlook or to take for granted or to do too quickly. But this is the opportunity to use your strongest logical weapon, your innate logical intuition, your ability to "see" what the point is, what the final, basic conclusion is, and what the argument is that supports it, and why it seems strong. Everyone has this innate, intuitive ability; that is the only reason logic textbooks and courses are possible – just as the fact that everyone has a moral conscience is the only reason moral systems, commandments, and ideals are possible.

When you read over the passage, do it slowly and patiently. This will actually *save* you time in the long run.

You are reading the argument for its logic, so you must ignore your feelings of agreement or disagreement, of interest or boredom, of attraction or repulsion. You need to find the formal logical structure.

Perhaps the most common cause of misunderstandings and of our inability to see eye to eye with each other is our hurry to evaluate before we receive, to talk back before listening. Premature criticism is always unfair criticism; another word for it is "prejudice," which means "premature judgment."

(2) Step two is to break the argument down into its steps. To do this, a good visual method is to mark the original text of the argument as follows:

(a) Identify each *proposition* that seems to be part of the argument by underlining it and putting a number before it.

(b) Circle each premise indicator or conclusion indicator. (Do not worry about rewording the propositions to get common terms yet. Our first task is to find the propositions and their logical relation to each other.)

(c) Now copy the propositions (or their numbers) onto a logical map, with arrows leading from premises to conclusions. We now have an overview of the strategy of the argument, so to speak.

The strategy will be cumulative, linear, or both. A cumulative argument will have many separate arguments (usually enthymemes) all leading to the same conclusion. (E.g. page 208.) A linear argument will be a multi-layered epicheirema (these will also usually be enthymemes), with premises attached to premises, and further conclusions following from conclusions. (E.g. page 284.)

(3) Only now are you in a position to *evaluate* the overall argument by evaluating each smaller argument that makes it up. Because you have the logical map, you may not need to take the time to do a three-step evaluation of every single argument step, checking for ambiguous terms, false premises, and fallacies. Rather, if you doubt the conclusion, the logical map will make it easier and clearer for you to spot where you think the overall argument's weakness is. It will usually be a premise that can be disputed; but the premise will often be the hidden and implied premise of an enthymeme, so you will have to write out each enthymeme, including the missing (implied) premises.

All arguments can be put into argument maps, no matter what rules apply in evaluating their validity. There are still three forms of deductive argument which we have not covered: hypothetical, disjunctive, and conjunctive syllogisms, i.e. syllogisms that begin with an "if . . . then . . ." premise, an "either . . . or . . ." premise, or a "both . . . and . . ." or "not both . . . and . . ." premise. The rules for these syllogisms are different from those for simple ("categorical") syllogisms; but even without having studied these rules, you can do argument maps for these syllogisms just as for categorical syllogisms.

Take the following example, from Plato's *Republic*. (We identify the propositions by number, as suggested above.)

(1) "A bad soul must rule badly, but a good soul well."
    "Yes, it must be so."
(2) "Now did we not agree that a bad soul is an unjust soul and a good soul a
    just soul?"
    "We did."
(3) "Then the just soul must rule well and the unjust soul badly."
    "So it seems by your reasoning."
(4) "But further, one who rules well is blessed or happy, and one who does not
    is miserable."
    "Of course."
(5) "Then the just soul is happy and the unjust miserable."
    "Let it be so."
(6) "But to be miserable is not profitable, and to be happy is."
    "Of course."
(7) "Then, O Thrasymachus, blessed among men, the just is always profitable
    and the unjust unprofitable."

Here we have a rather simple, though long, argument. What makes it simple is two things: it is linear, and it consists in complete syllogisms rather than enthymemes.

Let's write out the argument map for this argument in full verbal form. It is two exactly parallel arguments, one about injustice and the other about justice. We write out only the half about injustice: you can easily do the other half:

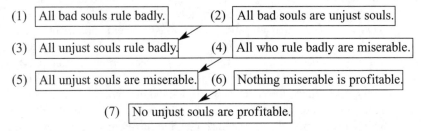

(1) All bad souls rule badly.   (2) All bad souls are unjust souls.

(3) All unjust souls rule badly.   (4) All who rule badly are miserable.

(5) All unjust souls are miserable. (6) Nothing miserable is profitable.

(7) No unjust souls are profitable.

When we put this argument into logical form, the thing that may make it confusing is that two arguments are going on at once: one about the just being profitable and the other about the unjust being unprofitable. It is difficult to put both parts of the argument (the one about justice and the other about injustice) into each proposition. But it is easy to make two overall arguments out of it, one about justice and the other about injustice.

Here is a somewhat more difficult long argument to map. It is St. Thomas Aquinas's restatement of the most argued-about argument in the entire history of philosophy, St. Anselm's famous "ontological argument," which attempts to prove that God must exist, in fact that 'God exists' is a self-evident proposition. Once again, we number the propositions. The logical connector words are our clues.

"(1) Those propositions are self-evident which are known to be true as soon as their terms are understood. (2) But as soon as the terms 'God' and 'exists' are understood, the proposition 'God exists' is known to be true. For (3) 'God' means 'that than which nothing greater can be conceived'; and (4) that which exists only mentally but not actually is not that than which nothing greater can be conceived, because (5) that which exists both mentally and actually is greater than that which exists only mentally. Therefore (6) God does not exist only mentally, but actually. Thus (7) the proposition 'God exists' is known to be true as soon as its terms are understood. (8) It is therefore a self-evident proposition."

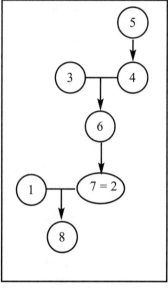

Each arrow on the map – that is, each syllogism – in this argument still must be put into logical form. But the argument map aids that process, for it tells you what propositions make up the premises and conclusions of each argument, and whether each syllogism is a simple syllogism, an epicheirema, or an enthymeme. For if two connected, "married" arrows lead to it, it is a simple syllogism rather than an enthymeme, since the two horizontal arrows symbolize its two premises, showing that it does not have any missing premise. If it has an arrow from only one premise to a conclusion, it is probably an enthymeme. If it has an arrow leading to one of its premises from one or more other premises, this shows that it is an epicheirema.

Exercises: Make argument maps for each of the following. Some of them are very difficult, especially the first two. Proposition numbers are supplied for some of them. Before you focus on the logical form, read each one slowly and thoughtfully, since understanding the logical form depends on understanding the content, the meaning and "point" of the argument.

1. (H) "In a well-ordered republic it should never be necessary to resort to extra-constitutional measures; for although they may for the time be beneficial, yet the precedent is pernicious, for if the practice is once established of disregarding the laws for good reasons, the laws will in a little while be changeable under that pretext for evil reasons. Thus no republic will ever be perfect if she has not by law provided for everything, having a remedy for every emergency, and fixed rules for applying it. And therefore I will say in conclusion that those republics which in time of danger cannot resort to a dictatorship, or some similar authority, will generally be ruined when grave occasions occur." (Machiavelli, *The Prince*)

2. "A question arises: whether it is better to be loved than feared, or feared than loved? One should wish to be both, but because (1) it is difficult to unite them in one person, (2) it is much safer to be feared than loved, when of the two one must be dispensed with. Because (3) this is to be asserted in general of men: that they are ungrateful, fickle, false, cowards, covetous . . . (4) Men have less scruple in offending one who is beloved than one who is feared, for (5) love is preserved by the link of obligation, (6) which, (7) owing to the baseness of men, (6) is broken at every opportunity for their advantage; but (8) fear preserves you by a dread of punishment which never fails." (*Ibid.*)

3. (H) "There are some philosophers who imagine we are every moment intimately conscious of what we call our *self*; that we feel its existence and its continuance in existence, and are certain, beyond the evidence of a demonstration, both of its perfect identity and simplicity. . . . Unluckily, all these positive assertions are contrary to that very experience which is pleaded for them, nor have we any idea of *self* after the manner it is here explained. For from what impression could this idea be derived? This question it is impossible to answer without a manifest contradiction and absurdity; and yet it is a question which must necessarily be answered if we would have the idea of self pass for clear and intelligible. It must be some one impression that gives rise to every real idea. But self or person is not any one impression but that to which our several impressions and ideas are supposed to have a reference. If any impression gives rise to the idea of self, that impression must continue invariably the same, through the whole course of our lives, since self is supposed to exist after that manner. But there is no impression constant and invariable. Pain and pleasure, grief and joy, passions and sensations succeed each other and never all exist at the same time. It cannot therefore be from any of these impressions, or from any other, that the idea of self is derived; consequently there is no such idea." (David Hume, *Treatise on Human Nature*)

4. "I know that nothing good dwells within me, that is, in my flesh. I can will what is right, but I cannot do it. For I do not do the good I want, but the evil I do not want is what I do. Now if I do what I do not want, it is no longer I that do it but sin which dwells in me." (St. Paul, Romans 7:18–20)

5. "We observe that rust destroys iron, mildew corn, blindness the eye, but rust and mildew do not destroy the eye, nor do blindness and rust destroy corn, nor do mildew or blindness destroy iron. Thus we see that it is the natural evil of each thing that destroys it, and only this; that is, if this natural evil does not destroy it then nothing can. For what is good cannot destroy it (since destruction is not the work of goodness), nor can what is neither good nor evil for it (for destruction is not the work of the neutral either, but only of the evil), nor can what is evil for something else, as we have seen in the examples above. If, then, there is something whose own natural evil cannot

destroy it, it is indestructible. The soul is such a thing, for its natural evils, vice and ignorance, do not ever wholly destroy it, but only weaken it. Nothing, therefore can destroy the soul. If nothing can destroy it, it is indestructible and everlasting." (summary of Plato's argument for immortality in Book X of the *Republic*)

6. "We cannot define 'religion' narrowly, as 'belief in God' because Buddhism is a religion but does not believe in God. Nor can we define religion more broadly, as 'belief in some absolute,' without God, because atheism can believe in an absolute too, but atheism is not a religion. But religion must be defined either as the belief in God or as something like an absolute without reference to God. Therefore religion cannot be defined." (from a student paper)

7. "We must explain then that Nature belongs to the class of causes which act for the sake of something. . . . A difficulty presents itself: Why should not nature work, not for the sake of something, nor because it is better so, but just as the sky rains, not in order to make the corn grow but of necessity? What is drawn up must cool, and what has been cooled must become water and descend, the result of this being that the corn grows. Similarly if a man's crop is spoiled on the threshing-floor, the rain did not fall for the sake of this – in order that the crop might be spoiled – but that result just followed. Why then should it not be the same with the parts in nature, e.g. that our teeth should come up of necessity – the front teeth sharp, fitted for tearing, the molars broad and useful for grinding down the food – since they did not arise for this end, but it was merely a coincident result; and so with all other parts in which we suppose that there is purpose? Wherever, then, all the parts came about just as they would have been if they had come to be for an end, such things survived, being organized spontaneously in a fitting way; whereas those which grew otherwise perished and continue to perish. . . . Such are the arguments (and others of the kind) which may cause difficulty on this point. Yet it is impossible that this should be the true view. For teeth and all other natural things either invariably or normally come about in a given way; but of not one of the results of chance or spontaneity is this true." (Aristotle, *Physics* II, 8)

8. (E) "All men by nature desire to know. An indication of this is the delight we take in our senses; for even apart from their usefulness they are loved for themselves; and above all others the sense of sight. For not only with a view to action, but even when we are not going to do anything, we prefer seeing, one might say, to everything else. The reason is that this, most of all the senses, makes us know and brings to light many differences between things." (Aristotle, *Metaphysics* I, 1)

9. (E) "Whoever kills a tyrant kills not a man but a beast disguised as a man. For, being deprived of all natural love for their fellow creatures, it follows that tyrants are without human sympathies, and hence are not men but wild

animals. Thus, it is clear that whoever kills a tyrant is not committing homicide, since he kills a monster and not a man." (Michelangelo, *Great Conversations*, ed. Louis Biancolli (N.Y.: Simon & Schuster, 1948), p. 281)

10. "*It seems that* God does not exist. For if one of two contraries be infinite, the other would be altogether destroyed. But the word 'God' means that he is infinite goodness. If, therefore, God existed, there would be no evil discoverable. But there is evil in the world. Therefore God does not exist. (St. Thomas Aquinas, *Summa Theologica* I, 2, 3, objection 1)

11. "We see that things which lack intelligence, such as natural bodies, act for an end, and this is evident from their acting always, or nearly always, in the same way, so as to obtain the best result. Hence it is plain that not fortuitously, but designedly, do they achieve their end. Now whatever lacks intelligence cannot move towards an end unless it be directed by some being endowed with knowledge and intelligence, as the arrow is shot to the mark by the archer. Therefore some intelligent being exists by whom all natural things are directed to their end; and this being we call God. (St. Thomas Aquinas, *Summa Theologica* I,2,3, the "fifth way")

12. "I answer that: It is impossible for any created good to constitute man's happiness. For happiness is the perfect good, which satisfies the desire altogether; else it would not be the last end, if something yet remained to be desired. Now the object of the will, i.e. of man's desire, is the universal good, just as the object of the intellect is the universal true. Hence it is evident that naught can satisfy man's will save the universal good. And this is to be found, not in any creature, but in God alone; because every creature has goodness by participation. Wherefore God alone can satisfy the will of man, as is said in the words of Psalm 102:5, "Who satisfieth thy desire with good." Therefore God alone constitutes man's happiness. (St. Thomas Aquinas, *Summa Theologica* I-II, 2, 8)

13. "Life is meaningless, since it ends in death, and death is meaningless. Death is meaningless because it is nothingness, and nothingness is the nothingness of meaning. But everything is either life or death. Therefore everything is meaningless. My proof that everything is meaningless is therefore also meaningless." (student essay)

14. "Happiness is the perfect good. But power is imperfect. For as Boethius says, 'the power of a man cannot relieve the gnawings of care, nor can it avoid the thorny path of anxiety'; and, further on, he says, 'Do you think a man is powerful who is surrounded by attendants whom he may inspire with fear but whom he fears even more than they fear him?" Therefore, happiness does not consist in power. Two reasons, in addition, show that this is true. First, because power has the character of a beginning, but happiness has the nature of an end. Secondly, because power is open to either good or evil, while happiness is man's supreme and proper good." (St. Thomas Aquinas, *Summa Theologica* I-II, 2, 4.)

XIII. Compound Syllogisms

Compound syllogisms begin with a compound proposition.

Compound propositions consist of two simple (categorical) propositions joined and related by one of three conjunctions:

(1) **"if ... then ..."** (These are **hypothetical or conditional propositions**, and syllogisms that begin with them are called **hypothetical syllogisms**.)

(2) **"either ... or ... "** (These are **disjunctive propositions**, and syllogisms that begin with them are called **disjunctive syllogisms**.)

(3) **"both ... and ..."** or **"not both ... and ..."** (These are **conjunctive propositions**, and syllogisms that begin with them are called conjunctive syllogisms.)

Compound syllogisms have a wholly different structure and wholly different rules from simple syllogisms. We cannot use Euler's circles, Aristotle's six rules, Venn diagrams, or "Barbara Celarent" in checking them. They do not have mood or figure. They do not have major, minor, and middle terms, or major and minor premises. In fact, they do not necessarily have only three terms. When they are invalid, they do not commit any of the fallacies already defined by the six rules. Virtually the only thing common to simple and compound syllogisms is the basic structure of two premises and one conclusion. To understand and evaluate them, we must begin afresh.

Section 1. Hypothetical syllogisms (B)

There are two forms of hypothetical syllogisms (i.e., syllogisms that begin with a hypothetical ("if ... then ...") proposition: **pure hypothetical syllogisms** and **mixed hypothetical syllogisms**. The first form is fairly rare, the second form is very common.

In a *pure hypothetical syllogism*, all three propositions are hypothetical propositions. E.g.,

If it rains, I will get wet.
And if I get wet, I will be cold.
Therefore if it rains, I will be cold.

This is really a simple (categorical) syllogism, in fact a "bull's eye" syllogism, in disguise, with propositions in place of terms:

> All cases of it raining are cases of my getting wet.
> All cases of my getting wet are cases of my being cold.
> Therefore all cases of it raining are cases of my being cold.

In a mixed hypothetical syllogism (which is the more common kind), only the first premise is hypothetical. The other premise and the conclusion are simple (categorical) propositions. E.g. "If you are carrying a gun, they will not let you in. And you are carrying a gun. Therefore they will not let you in."

Before we go on to distinguish the different forms of mixed hypothetical syllogisms (there are only four) and the rules for validity (they are much simpler than the rules for simple syllogisms), we should first make things shorter and easier by using a new symbol system. It is taken from modern symbolic logic, but it does not carry any philosophical baggage; it is just a much shorter and clearer way to formalize conditional syllogisms than writing out all the words. (It will not work for simple syllogisms.)

Each simple proposition will be symbolized by a single lower case letter, beginning with p, then q, then r, *etc.*

Until you have more practice with compound syllogisms, you should write out a "key" for each compound syllogism, i.e., write out the actual, fully-worded proposition next to each "p" or "q" or "r" symbol with the equal sign (=) between them. Later, you will be able to omit this on paper if it is perfectly clear in your mind, and then you can use letters alone, without the worded key.

A hypothetical proposition is two simple propositions joined by "if . . . then . . ." So it is symbolized by two letters (symbolizing the two simple propositions) joined by a sideways horseshoe (⊃), symbolizing the "if . . . then . . ."relationship. Thus "if it rains, I will get wet" is symbolized by "p ⊃ q," and the key reminds us that p = "it rains" while q = "I will get wet."

The horseshoe is also called the **"implication"** sign. "If p then q" means that "p implies q," that is, that *if p is true, then q is true.* Do not confuse "implies" with "infers." "Implies" is an objective logical relationship between propositions; "infers" is a subjective mental act made by a human mind. My mind infers a conclusion from premises, perhaps validly and perhaps invalidly. But it is *propositions* that imply other propositions. (We also use the word "imply" in ordinary language to mean something quite different: to make a veiled suggestion rather than an overt statement. Do not confuse that with logical implication.)

The proposition following the "if" is called the **antecedent**, since it antecedes, or comes before, the other proposition. The proposition following the "then" is called the **consequent**, since it is the consequent of the antecedent; it is said to be true if the antecedent is true. ("If it rains, I will get wet" means that if it is true that it rains, then it is true that I will get wet.)

We negate a proposition by putting a tilde, or curl (~) before it.

There is no Square of Opposition in compound propositions. However, there is the relationship of contradiction: p and ~p are contradictories.

Here are some hypothetical syllogisms in ordinary language to show how we symbolize them. *(The first two are valid, the last two invalid.)*

(1) "If even Socrates lacks wisdom, then no man is wise. And even Socrates lacks wisdom. Therefore no man is wise."

Key: p = "Even Socrates lacks wisdom."   Symbolization: p ⊃ q
     q = "No man is wise."   p
                                                        ∴ q

Note that even a negative proposition ("No man is wise") can be symbolized by a single letter without a tilde. The symbol p or q stands for any proposition whatever, no matter what its content.

(2) "If there is radioactivity here, it appears on this Geiger counter. And it does not appear on this Geiger counter. Therefore there is no radioactivity here."

Key: p = "There is radioactivity here."   Symbolization: p ⊃ q
     q = "It appears on this geiger counter."   ~q
                                                        ∴ ~p

(3) "If we are in a tornado, the house is falling apart. And the house is falling apart. Therefore we are in a tornado."

Key: p = "We are in a tornado."   Symbolization: p ⊃ q
     q = "The house is falling apart."   q
                                                        ∴ p

(4) "If we're lottery winners, we're rich. We're not lottery winners. Therefore we're not rich."

Key: p = "We're lottery winners."   Symbolization: p ⊃ q
     q = "We're rich."   ~p
                                                        ∴ ~q

These four forms of mixed hypothetical syllogisms are called, respectively,

(1) **Affirming the Antecedent**
(2) **Denying the Consequent**
(3) **Affirming the Consequent**
(4) **Denying the Antecedent**

They are named by what is done in the second premise. The first premise is identical in all four cases: p ⊃ q. The second premise can say one of four things: p, ~q, q, or ~p. That is, the second premise can either affirm or deny either the antecedent (p) or the consequent (q).

"Affirming the Antecedent" and "Denying the Consequent" are the two valid forms of hypothetical syllogisms. "Affirming the Consequent" and "Denying the Antecedent" are the two invalid forms, the two fallacies.

The reason for this rule is simple: more than one cause can produce the same effect. So the mere fact that the house is falling apart does not prove that a tornado is causing it (# 3 above). The house might be falling apart due to an earthquake, or termites. And the mere fact that we're not lottery winners (#4 above) does not prove that we're not rich. We might get rich through another cause, e.g. inheriting money from a dead relative, or working hard.

However, the first two forms are valid:

(1) If p is true and p's truth implies, or entails, q's truth, then q must be true. If whenever p is true, q is true too, then if p is true now, q is true now.

(2) If p implies q, and q is not true, then p is not true. If we have q *whenever* we have p, then when we do *not* have q we do not have p. For if we did have p, we would have q too.

Let us go through all four forms of a hypothetical syllogism with the same content. Let us begin with this p ⊃ q proposition: "If the wind blows, the paper falls off the desk." Now let us add the four possible second premises.

(1) Let us begin by adding p ("The wind is blowing") to p ⊃ q; i.e. let us in the second premise affirm the antecedent of the first premise. What follows? That the paper falls off the desk, q. For whenever the wind blows, the paper falls. The argument is valid.

p ⊃ q
p
∴ q

The first premise, the hypothetical proposition, may in fact be false. It claims that whenever the wind blows, the paper falls; and that is probably not true, since we could nail the paper down to the desk, so that even if the wind blows the paper would not fall. But *if* it *is* true that whenever the wind blows the paper falls, and if it is also true that the wind is blowing, then it must follow that the paper falls. "Affirming the Antecedent" is a valid form of argument.

(2) Now let us add ~q ("The paper does not fall off") instead as a second premise to the same first premise ("If the wind blows, the paper falls"). What logically follows? That the wind is not blowing, ~p. For if the wind were blowing, the paper would fall off. Another valid form: "Denying the Consequent."

p ⊃ q
~q
∴ ~p

(3) But suppose we follow "If the wind blows, the paper falls" with "The paper falls" in the second premise, and then draw the conclusion that "The wind blows." This is invalid because the conclusion does not necessarily follow. Just because the paper falls, it does not mean the wind blows; another cause could produce the same effect, such as a person blowing it off, or flipping it off – or even an earthquake. "Affirming the Consequent" is an invalid form:

p ⊃ q
q
∴ p

(4) And "Denying the Antecedent" in the second premise is also invalid. "If the wind blows, the paper falls, and the wind does not blow, therefore the paper does not fall" forgets all those other possible causes of the paper falling that were mentioned above.

p ⊃ q
~p
∴ ~q

Both fallacies make the same mistake: they begin with p ⊃ q and then proceed as if it were q ⊃ p. We can no more "convert" a hypothetical proposition than we can validly convert a simple A proposition. "Whenever the wind blows, the paper falls" does not say the same thing as "Whenever the paper falls, the wind blows." "All cases of A are cases of B" does not say the same thing as "all cases of B are cases of A."

A hypothetical syllogism can be an enthymeme, omitting any one of its three propositions, just as a simple syllogism can. And it can also be an epicheirema, adding a reason to one or both of its premises.

Thus there are three valid forms of hypothetical syllogisms and two fallacious forms. The valid forms are:

(1) the pure hypothetical syllogism:

p ⊃ q
q ⊃ r
∴ p ⊃ r

(2) Affirming the Antecedent:

p ⊃ q
p
∴ q

(3) Denying the Consequent:

p ⊃ q
~q
∴ ~p

And the two invalid forms, or fallacies, are:

(1) Denying the Antecedent:

$p \supset q$

$\sim p$

$\therefore \sim q$

(2) Affirming the Consequent:

$p \supset q$

q

$\therefore p$

If you like mnemonic devices, you could think of the abbreviations AA and DC for the two valid forms and DA and AC for the two invalid forms. Alcoholics Anonymous (AA) and Direct Current (DC) are straight (valid), while District Attorneys (DA) and Alternating Current (AC) can be crooked (invalid). If this sounds silly, forget it.

Section 2 *"Reductio ad absurdum"* arguments

In Denying the Consequent, when the consequent (q) is absurd, or obviously false, we have a *reductio ad absurdum*. This is a very common and effective strategy in argument. It is especially associated with Socrates and the "Socratic method." "Reductio ad absurdum" consists in showing that if your opponent's idea were true, absurd consequences would logically follow. Thus it is really Denying the Consequent: "if p (your idea) were true, then q (its logical consequent) would be true. But q is not true; in fact, it is obviously not true, it is absurd. Therefore p (your idea) is not true." (This argument is the more effective the more obvious it is that q is not true, i.e. the more absurd it is.)

The *reductio* is a very effective form of argument in practice because it does not begin with a premise your opponent may deny because it comes from your mind and your opinions, but it begins with your opponent's own idea or opinion, p. It says, in effect, "let us look at your idea (p); let us explore it further; let us see what consequences and conclusions it logically entails." It seems to be a "friendly" form of arguing. But if q is as "absurd" as the name claims, and if p really does imply q, the argument is really quite devastating. The only arguable question in *reductio ad absurdum* arguments usually is whether p really implies q.

There are only three ways to answer any argument – to find a formal logical fallacy, an informal fallacy or ambiguous term, or a false premise. But the logical form of the *reductio ad absurdum* (Denying the Consequent) is valid and contains no formal logical fallacy. So unless you can find an ambiguous term (i.e. an ambiguously *used* term), the only way to answer a *reductio ad absurdum* argument is to deny one of the two premises. This will probably be the first, hypothetical premise which states that p (your idea, which you think is true) entails q (the absurd consequence, which you will have to admit is false if it really is absurd). In some cases, however, you might want to deny that q is absurd and false, and this would be to deny the second premise.

The *reductio* form can be used satirically. E.g. "The government in its wisdom considers ice a 'food product.' This means that Antarctica is one of the world's foremost food producers" (George Will).

The full symbolization of this argument would be:

Key: p = Ice is a food product.   Symbolization: p ⊃ q
    q = Antarctica is one of the world's   ~q
    foremost food producers.   ∴ ~p

Another example of a satirical *reductio* is Samuel Johnson's famous refutation of moral relativism: "If he [the moral relativist] does really think that there is no distinction between virtue and vice, why, sir, when he leaves our houses let us count our spoons."

Another example is G.E. Moore's commonsensical refutation of Hume's skepticism: "I *do* know that this pencil exists; but I could not know this if Hume's principles were true; *therefore*, Hume's principles . . . are false." Here the order of the premises is reversed in the ordinary language, but we have the same logical form when we symbolize it:

Key: p = Hume's principles are true.   Symbolization: p ⊃ q
    q = I do *not* know that this pencil exists.   ~q
                                                      ∴ ~p

Another way to symbolize this argument would be as follows:

Key: p = Hume's principles are true.   Symbolization: p ⊃ ~q
    q = I *do* know that this pencil exists.   q
                                                      ∴ ~p

The example above shows that we can symbolize a negative proposition in two ways: by having the letter stand for an affirmative proposition and by putting a tilde before the letter, *or* we can keep the letter without a tilde and use our key to make clear that the letter symbolizes a negative proposition.

Here is a very abstract, high-level philosophical argument that takes the form of a *reductio ad absurdum*. It is an argument for the conclusion that numbers are objective realities rather than subjective ideas. "If number were an idea, then arithmetic would be psychology. But arithmetic is no more psychology than, say, astronomy is. Astronomy is concerned, not with ideas of the planets, but with the planets themselves, and by the same token the objects of arithmetic are not ideas either" (Gottlob Frege, *The Foundations of Arithmetic*).

This is an epicheirema because it begins with a single hypothetical syllogism but adds an additional argument (from analogy with astronomy) to support that syllogism's second premise (i.e. the categorical premise).

Not every hypothetical syllogism in the Denying the Consequent form is a *reductio ad absurdum.* But the borders between a *reductio* and any other Denying the Consequent are not sharp. It depends on how "absurd" q is, and this is often a matter of opinion. The arguments above are *reductios.* The following argument is not: "If Albert De Salvo is not the Boston Strangler, then he could not know such intimate details as these about each murder. But he does know these details. (And this is not absurd, but only surprising.) Therefore he is the Boston Strangler." But the following is a borderline case: "It is clear that we mean something, and something different in each case, by such words (as "substance," "cause," and "change"). If we did not, we could not use them consistently, and it is obvious that on the whole we do consistently apply and withhold such names" (C.D. Broad, *Scientific Thought*). Here the conclusion comes first. The argument can be symbolized as follows:

Key: p = We do not mean anything by the words   Symbolization: p ⊃ q
        'substance,' 'cause,' and 'change'   ~q
    q = We do not use these words consistently   ∴ ~p

Or:

Key: p = we do mean something by such words   Symbolization: ~p ⊃ ~q
    q = We use such words consistently   q
                                               ∴ p

Section 3. The practical syllogism:
arguing about means and ends

There are three reasons we seek knowledge by reason, Aristotle noted: (1) simply to know, for its own sake; (2) to know for the sake of doing something, for some action or practice; or (3) to know for the sake of making something, changing something, or repairing something. The first he called "theoretical" reasoning; the second, "practical" reasoning; and the third "productive" reasoning, reasoning directed toward what we now call "technology." These three motives for reasoning produce the three kinds of "sciences" that he distinguished: "theoretical sciences," "practical sciences," and "productive sciences."

Reasoning with a purely theoretical (or "speculative" or "contemplative") end comes in many different forms, and we have been exploring these different forms throughout this book. Practical reasoning, however, is much simpler: its form is usually a pure or mixed hypothetical syllogism. E.g.:

If I am to get to England by tomorrow, I must take a plane.
If I take a plane, I must buy a ticket now.
Therefore if I am to get to England by tomorrow, I must buy a ticket now.

Or simply:

If I am to get to England by tomorrow I must buy a ticket today.
I want to get to England by tomorrow.
Therefore I must buy a ticket today.

This is "practical" reasoning in the modern sense of the word "practical": pragmatic, instrumental, useful. But "practical" can also mean "moral," and this moral dimension of human practice also is often expressed in the form of hypothetical syllogisms:

If you want to be blessed or happy or perfect, you must practice all the virtues.
You do want to be blessed or happy or perfect.
Therefore you must practice all the virtues.

Some will object that this sounds too much like "the end justifies the means." But of course it does! What else could possibly justify a means? That's what "means" *means*. When we say "the end does not justify the means" we mean that a good end does not justify an *evil* means. But it surely justifies a good means. Even if you accept Kant's famous criticism of this "teleological" or "end-oriented" morality and insist that we should will our moral duty rather than our happiness, that we should try to simply "do the right thing" because it's right, it remains true that our moral reasoning usually takes the form of a hypothetical syllogism:

We must always do the right thing.
If we tell a lie, we do not do the right thing.
Therefore we must not tell a lie.

Or:

If I lie, I violate the moral imperative (the "Golden Rule" "Do as you would be done to").
I must not violate the moral imperative.
Therefore I must not lie.

Pragmatic practical reasoning differs from *moral* practical reasoning in two ways. First, in pragmatic reasoning there is no absolute good or final end (except perhaps happiness, interpreted in a purely subjective, psychological sense rather than the older, moral sense). Second, there are often many steps in pragmatic reasoning, so we often have multiple-step epicheiremas. Moral reasoning, on the other hand, usually (but not always) consists in a single syllogism.

That syllogism can be a simple syllogism:

Lying on your tax form is injustice.
Injustice should not be done.
Therefore lying on your tax form should not be done.

Or it can be a hypothetical syllogism:

If I lie on my tax form, I commit an injustice.
I should not commit an injustice.
Therefore I should not lie on my tax form.

In both forms, *there is one factual premise and one moral premise*; one "is" premise and one "ought" premise. It is their combination that makes moral reasoning.

For instance, the essential "pro-life" argument against abortion contains a moral premise and a factual premise; and there are two different "pro-choice" replies to it depending on which of the two premises is denied:

All innocent human persons have a right to life and may not be killed.
And all unborn human babies are innocent human persons.
Therefore all unborn human babies have a right to life and may not be killed.

It makes a very significant difference whether one denies the first (moral) premise or the second (factual) premise: it is the difference between a dispute about a philosophical principle and a dispute about a scientific fact.

Perhaps the most famous pragmatic practical syllogism of all time is "Pascal's Wager." Pascal argues that it is a most practical "wager" to believe in God, for: "Let us weigh gain and loss in calling heads that God is. Reckon these two chances: if you win, you win everything; if you lose, you lose nothing. Then do not hesitate: wager that He is." The argument is essentially this:

If I wager that God is (by believing in God), I can win everything and I can lose nothing.
I want to win everything and lose nothing.
Therefore I should wager that God is.

But notice that the syllogism is invalid in this form, for it is Affirming the Consequent. This reveals an important difference between a practical syllogism and a theoretical one: the "if" means something quite different. In the theoretical syllogism, "if . . . then . . ." refers to cause and effect. But in the *pragmatic* practical syllogism, "if . . . then . . ." refers to *action and consequence*, or *means and end*. In a *theoretical* hypothetical syllogism, the consequent does not justify the antecedent – you cannot affirm the consequent and thus affirm the antecedent; that is a fallacy. But in a *practical* (pragmatic) hypothetical syllogism, the consequent *does* justify the antecedent, because the consequent is the *end* and the antecedent is the *means*, and the end does justify the means in the practical order. (And if both are morally good, then the end justifies the means is the moral order too).

Exercises on hypothetical syllogisms: Put into correct symbolic form and test for validity. If there is a fallacy, name it. Remember, there may be a few enthymemes or epicheiremas too. There are no practical syllogisms here.

1. "There is no case known (neither is it, indeed, possible) in which a thing is found to be the efficient cause of itself; for in such a case it would be prior to itself, which is impossible." (St. Thomas Aquinas, *Summa Theologica* I, 2, 3)
2. "If light consisted of material particles, it would possess momentum. It cannot therefore consist of material particles."
3. "If the mountain will not come to Muhammad, Muhammad will come to the mountain. But Muhammad will come to the mountain. Therefore the mountain will not come to Muhammad."
4. "If the objective of marriage were contentment, then the discontent of either party would be a sufficient reason for annulling it."
5. "If there is such a thing as space, it must be in something. For all being is in something, and that which is in something is in space. So space will be in space, and so on *ad infinitum*. Accordingly, there is no such thing as space." (Zeno the Eleatic)
6. St. Augustine argued, against the skeptic: If you are deceived, you must exist. But you say you are deceived, therefore you can be certain you exist. But if you can be certain you exist, you can be certain of something, and if you can be certain of something, you are no longer a skeptic.
7. "But if art passes from mind to mind, it would leave one mind and abide in another; in this case, nobody would teach an art except by losing it." (St. Augustine)
8. "Total pacifism might be a good principle if everyone were to follow it. But not everyone does, so it isn't." (Gilbert Harman, *The Nature of Morality*)
9. "If a man could not have done otherwise than he in fact did, then he is not responsible for his action. But if determinism is true, it is true of every action that the agent could not have done otherwise. Therefore, if determinism is true, no one is ever responsible for what he does." (Winston Nesbit and Stewart Candlish, "Determinism and the Ability to Do Otherwise," in *Mind*, July 1978)
10. "When we regard a man as morally responsible for an act, we regard him as a legitimate object of moral praise or blame in respect of it. But it seems plain that a man cannot be a legitimate object of moral praise or blame for an act unless in willing the act he is in some important sense a 'free' agent. Evidently free will in some sense, therefore, is a precondition of moral responsibility." (C. Arthur Campbell, *In Defense of Free Will*) (Is this the same argument as #9 or not?)
11. "If there were no Un-caused Cause (First Cause), there could be no caused

causes (second causes). But there are caused causes. Therefore there must be an Un-caused Cause."

12. "As everyone knows, beauty is in the eye of the beholder. But if beauty were an objective reality, it would be in the reality of the beheld rather than in the eye of the beholder. Therefore beauty is not an objective reality." (How would someone answer this argument?)

13. "If an intelligent Creator existed, we would find design throughout the universe. We do find design throughout the universe. Therefore an intelligent Creator exists." (If this argument is invalid, how can it be changed to make it valid?)

14. "If God did not exist, we would feel so alone that we would be unable to endure a universe without Him. And this feeling can be observed to exist. Therefore God does not exist."

15. "If Papa comes home today, you will be in big trouble!" "That's true, but Papa won't come home today, so I won't be in big trouble."

16. "Whenever I eat chocolates, I get migraines. I got migraines today, so I must have eaten chocolates today."

17. "If Dr. X did not kill the officer, then he didn't kill the deputy either. And we proved that the officer was not killed by Dr. X. Therefore the deputy was not either."

18. "Confidence in promises is essential to the intercourse of human life, for without it the greatest part of our conduct would proceed upon chance. But there could be no confidence in promises if men were not obliged to perform them. The obligation, therefore, to perform promises is essential." (Stanley Jevons)

19. "'If anyone knows anything about anything,' said Bear to himself, 'it's Owl who knows something about something,' he said, 'or my name's not Winnie-the-Pooh,' he said. 'Which it is,' he added. 'So there you are.'" (*Winnie the Pooh*)

20. "Mankind, judging by their neglect of him, have never, I think, at all understood the power of Love. For if they had understood him they would surely have built noble temples and altars and offered solemn sacrifices in his honor; but this is not done." (Plato, *Symposium*)

21. "If space is finite, it must be bounded. But space cannot have a boundary, because a boundary can only separate one space from another space. What separates space from non-space is not a spatial boundary; it is a logical boundary. Therefore space is infinite." (Compare this with #5.)

22. "'To be great is to be misunderstood' I am misunderstood. Therefore I am great."

23. "Hitler knows that he will have to break us in this island or lose the war. If we can stand up to him, all Europe may be free, and the life of the world may move forward into broad, sunlit uplands; but if we fail, then the whole world, including the United States, and all that we have known and cared for, will

sink into the abyss of a new dark age made more sinister, and perhaps more prolonged, by the lights of a perverted science. Let us therefore brace ourselves to our duty and so bear ourselves that if the British Commonwealth and Europe lasts for a thousand years men will still say: This was their finest hour." (Winston Churchill, speech to the House of Commons, June 18, 1940)

24. "If men were angels, no government would be necessary." (James Madison) (Hint: this is an enthymeme with *two* propositions implied.)

25. "If Christ is not risen, then our preaching is in vain and your faith is in vain. And we are even found to be misrepresenting God, because we testified of God that he raised Christ, whom he did not raise if it is true that the dead are not raised. . . . If Christ has not been raised, your faith is futile and you are still in your sins. Then those also who have fallen asleep in Christ have perished. If for this life only we have hoped in Christ, we are of all men most to be pitied." (St. Paul, I Corinthians 15:14–19)

26. "If I had cherished iniquity in my heart, the Lord would not have listened. But truly God has listened; he has given heed to the voice of my prayer." (Psalm 66:18–19)

Section 4. Disjunctive syllogisms (B)

Disjunctive syllogisms begin with a disjunctive ("either . . . or . . .") proposition. This is symbolized by "p v q," with the "v" standing for the disjunction ("or").

Like hypothetical syllogisms, disjunctive syllogisms have four possible second premises: p, ~p, q, or ~q. Thus the four forms (which do not have names) are:

(1) p v q	(2) p v q	(3) p v q	(4) p v q
p	q	~p	~q
∴ ~q	∴ ~p	∴ q	∴ p

However, there are really only two forms, since p and q are reversible and interchangeable in a disjunctive proposition, as they are *not* in a hypothetical proposition. "Either p or q" says exactly the same thing as "either q or p." But "if p then q" does not at all say the same thing as "if q then p."

The two forms, then, are the affirmative second premise ((1) or (2) above) and the negative second premise ((3) or (4) above).

The affirmative form is invalid and the negative form is valid.

Here's why: "Either p or q" does not necessarily imply anything more than it says. It does *not* say "either p or q *but not both*." "Either p or q but not both" is called a "strong disjunction." Simply "either p or q" is called a "weak disjunction." "Either p or q" means that at least one of these two, p or q, must be true. *At least one, maybe both.* So from the affirmative second premise, which claims that one of the two alternatives is true, we cannot deduce that the other alternative could not be true as well. That is why the affirmative form is invalid (i.e. the form that has an affirmative second premise).

Some examples: Suppose someone has done something very bad. We think: this must be due to either moral wickedness (villainy) or intellectual wickedness (folly). So we say:

> Either he is a villain or a fool.
> But he's no fool.
> Therefore he must be a villain.

This is a valid argument. If at least one of the two causes, moral or intellectual badness, must have been present to account for what he did, and if one of those two was not present, then the other must have been. If the first premise is right in saying that there are only two possible causes, and if the second premise is right in saying that one of those two causes was not present, then the other cause must have been present.

But it is fallacious to argue that:

> Either he is a villain or a fool.
> and he is a villain.
> therefore he is not a fool.

For he could be both a villain and a fool; both causes might be operative; intellectual defects and moral defects might both have helped account for the effect.

Only when the first, disjunctive, proposition is a strong disjunction – only when p and q exclude each other – can we validly argue from an affirmative second premise. For instance,

> This fingerprint was made by either a man or a woman.
> It was a man.
> Therefore it was not a woman.

Since no one is both a man and a woman (though there are some confused people who sincerely believe they are), p and q here are exclusive, and the presence of one entails the absence of the other just as much as the absence of one entails the presence of the other. If and only if we know that the first premise is a strong disjunction, we can affirm in the second premise and validly argue to a negative conclusion.

Exercises: Symbolize the following disjunctive arguments and test for validity. Remember, some may be enthymemes.

1. "You must be either a liar or a fool, and you're not a fool, so you must be a liar."

2. "Either the professor's Theory of General Insanity is true, or I'm insane. But the theory is not true. Therefore I am not insane."

3. "Either the theory is insane, or I am. But I am not insane. Therefore it isn't either."

4. (H) "Since no man has a natural authority over his fellows . . . we must conclude that conventions form the basis of all legitimate authority among men." (Rousseau) (This is an enthymeme with an implied disjunctive premise about authority.)

5. "Either God or nature causes disasters. Nature causes disasters. Therefore God does not."

6. "Why, what's happened to your tail?" he said in surprise.
"What has happened to it?" said Eeyore.
"It isn't there!"
"Are you sure?"
"Well, either a tail is there or it isn't there. You can't make a mistake about it." (Winnie the Pooh)

Section 5. Conjunctive syllogisms (B)

Conjunctive syllogisms begin with a conjunctive proposition. There are two forms of conjunctive propositions, affirmative and negative. The affirmative is "both p and q" and the negative is "not both p and q." In symbolizing these we use an ampersand ("&") for "and."

The affirmative conjunctive proposition "p & q" is true only if both p is true and q is true. E.g. "both Socrates and Marx were Communists" is not true, even though Marx was a Communist, because Socrates was not. In a true/false question, if any part of the statement is false, you must mark it false as a whole.

The negative conjunctive proposition "not both p and q" is symbolized as follows: $\sim$(p & q). The tilde (negation sign) negates the whole of the parentheses that follow it, i.e. it negates the affirmative conjunctive proposition "p & q". So "$\sim$(p & q)" means "it is not the case that both p and q are true." At least one of them is false, perhaps both.

There is no common form of syllogism that begins with an affirmative conjunctive proposition; but the conjunctive syllogism beginning with a negative conjunctive proposition is quite common. Its valid form is:

$\sim$(p & q)
p
$\therefore \sim$q

And since p and q are here reversible, the following is also valid:

$\sim$(p & q)
q
$\therefore \sim$p

However, the following form is invalid:

~(p & q)

~p

∴ q

And this is really the same as:

~(p & q)

~q

∴ p

So the only conclusion we can validly prove with a conjunctive syllogism is a negative one, just as the only conclusion we can validly prove with a disjunctive syllogism is an affirmative one. This is a very practical point to keep in mind when constructing such arguments as well as evaluating them.

Some examples: "You can't both have your cake and eat it too. And you're eating it. Therefore you can't have it." This is valid. So is: "You can't both have your cake and eat it too. And you have it. Therefore you did not eat it."

"Two bodies can't both occupy the same space at once. And body #1 is in this space now. Therefore body #2 is not." This is valid.

But "You can't both have your cake and eat it too. And you do not have it. Therefore you ate it" is invalid. Perhaps you don't have your cake because you gave it away, or lost it.

"Two bodies can't both occupy the same space at once. And body #1 is not in this space now. Therefore body #2 is." This is obviously invalid.

But sometimes the fallacy is not so obvious: "No one can be stupid and be a philosopher. And he is not stupid. Therefore he is a philosopher." This is more likely to mislead because of its content. "Stupid" and "a philosopher" might be misunderstood as a strong disjunction or a complete division (see pages 62–63), i.e. both exclusive (you can't be both) and exhaustive (everyone has to be one or the other) – in which case the absence of either one would entail (imply) the presence of the other and the presence of either one would entail (imply) the absence of the other. But one can be a stupid philosopher, and one can be neither stupid nor a philosopher, so that division is neither exclusive nor exhaustive.

Transforming Syllogisms into Different Forms

The same syllogism can often be expressed in hypothetical, disjunctive, or conjunctive form. And these forms can also be interchanged with simple syllogisms. Take, e.g. the classic simple syllogism "All men are mortal, and Socrates is a man, therefore Socrates is mortal." In hypothetical form, this becomes:

If Socrates is a man, then he is mortal.

And Socrates is a man.

Therefore he is mortal.

In disjunctive form, it becomes:

Either Socrates is not a man, or he is mortal.
But he is a man (he is not not-a-man)
Therefore he is mortal.

And in conjunctive form, it becomes:

Socrates cannot both be a man and not be mortal.
But Socrates is a man.
Therefore Socrates is not not-mortal (he is mortal).

If we begin not with a simple syllogism but with a compound one, we get the same exchange possibilities:

If it rains, we will get wet.
And it will rain.
Therefore we will get wet.

All occasions of it raining are occasions of our getting wet.
This is an occasion of it raining.
Therefore this is an occasion of our getting wet.

Either it will not rain, or we will get wet.
It will not not-rain. (It will rain.)
Therefore we will get wet.

It can't be true both that it will rain and that we will not get wet.
It is true that it will rain. (It will rain.)
Therefore it is not true that we will not get wet. (We will get wet.)

Exercises on Conjunctive Syllogisms: Put into symbolic form, test for validity, *and imagine how you might reply* to each of the following. Some may be enthymemes or epicheiremas, and these may require a more complex symbolization. For an additional exercise, also transform each into disjunctive, hypothetical, and categorical forms.

1. "You can't be both you and somebody else. That's why you're not somebody else."
2. "Vampires are 'the undead.' But nothing can be both dead and undead. Therefore vampires are not dead. And nothing can be both dead and alive. Therefore vampires are alive."
3. "You can't both have your cake and eat it too. That's why you can eat your cake."
4. (A student's critique of Plato's attempt to write a philosophical dialogue on

love:) "Since the objective and the subjective attitudes are opposites, it is impossible for us to objectively reason about and subjectively experience the same thing at the same time. And you, Plato, are now objectively reasoning about love, since you are philosophizing about it. Therefore you cannot be experiencing love. But what we do not experience, we have no right to philosophize about. So you have no right to philosophize about love." (How would you answer this argument?)

5. "There is a disjunction between disjunction and conjunction; no proposition can be both. But this is a disjunction. Therefore it is not a conjunction."

6. "There is a disjunction between conjunction and disjunction. But disjunction is exclusive. Therefore conjunction is not." (Hint: this argument comes clearer when we translate it into a simple syllogism.)

Section 6. Dilemmas (B)

It is instructive to begin by quoting a typical modern logic text's attitude toward dilemmas: "The dilemma, a common form of argument in ordinary language, is a legacy from older times when logic and rhetoric were more closely connected than they are today. From a strictly logical point of view the dilemma is not of special importance. But rhetorically the dilemma is one of the most powerful instruments of persuasion and a devastating weapon in controversy" (Copi & Cohen, *Op. cit.*, p. 330).

Note first the relationship between the two reasons given for minimizing dilemmas: they are "a common form of argument in ordinary language" and they are "a legacy from older times." Note also that the author offers us a dilemma between logic and rhetoric, between "a strictly logical point of view" (i.e. a strictly formal, symbolic-logic point of view sundered from actual human use and practice), on the one hand, and "rhetoric" on the other. "Rhetoric" means "the art of persuasion," and this *can* be done by good logical reasoning without the sophistic tricks or emotional appeal which make up the negative connotation of the term "rhetoric" today. So it is a false dilemma; logical and psychological persuasiveness can and should be combined.

And a dilemma can do this.

A dilemma is a syllogism with a disjunctive ("either-or") premise and two hypothetical ("if-then") premises, one for each of the two alternatives of the disjunction. The disjunction sets up the two "horns" of the dilemma, and the hypothetical premises follow the two "horns" to their conclusion.

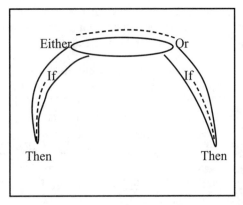

An example: Socrates, asked by a disciple whether he thought it a good idea to get married, replied Yes, because:

If you have a happy marriage, you will attain happiness.
If you have an unhappy marriage, you will attain wisdom.
You must either have a happy marriage or an unhappy one.
Therefore you will attain either happiness or wisdom.

The Four Forms of Dilemmas

A dilemma can be either simple or complex, and either constructive (affirmative) or destructive (negative). This gives us four forms: Simple Constructive, Simple Destructive, Complex Constructive, and Complex Destructive. Here are their forms:

Simple Constructive:	$(p \supset q) \& (r \supset q)$	If p, then q; and if r, then q
	p v r	Either p or r
	q	Therefore q
Complex Constructive:	$(p \supset q) \& (r \supset s)$	If p, then q; and if r, then s
	p v r	Either p or r
	q v s	Therefore either q or s
Simple Destructive:	$(p \supset q) \& (p \supset r)$	If p, then q; and if p, then r
	~q v ~r	Either not q or not r
	~p	Therefore not p
Complex Destructive:	$(p \supset q) \& (r \supset s)$	If p, then q; and if r, then s
	~q v ~s	Either not q or not s
	~p v ~r	Therefore either not p or not r

The names are taken from the conclusion: A **Simple Constructive Dilemma**'s conclusion is simple (categorical) and constructive (affirmative).

A **Complex Constructive Dilemma**'s conclusion is complex (disjunctive) and constructive (affirmative).

A **Simple Destructive Dilemma**'s conclusion is simple (categorical) and destructive (negative).

A **Complex Destructive Dilemma**'s conclusion is complex (disjunctive) and destructive (negative).

Some examples:

Simple Constructive Dilemma: "If I know any certainty, I must certainly exist; and if I am ignorant of any certainty, I must certainly exist. But I must either know some certainty or not. Thus in either case I must certainly exist."

(This is a dilemma to refute skepticism. It is essentially Descartes's "I think, therefore I exist.")

Complex Constructive Dilemma: "If God exists, then unbelievers are insane, like children who deny the existence of their own parent; and if God does not exist, then believers are insane, like adults who still believe in an invisible playmate. But either God exists, or he does not exist. Therefore either believers or unbelievers are insane."

Simple Destructive Dilemma: "If there were benevolent aliens from another planet trying to contact us, they would leave some messages; and if they were there trying to contact us, we would be intelligent enough to be worth contacting. But either they have not left any messages, or we are not intelligent enough to be worth contacting. Therefore there are no benevolent aliens from another planet trying to contact us."

Complex Destructive Dilemma: "If Jesus told the truth, then he did not deceive the world about whether he was divine. And if he was sane, then he was not deceived about whether he was divine. But either he was a deceiver or deceived about whether he was divine. (For a mere man who says he is divine is either a deceiver, if he knows this is not true, or deceived, if he thinks it is true.) Therefore Jesus either did not tell the truth or was not sane. He was either a liar or a lunatic, if he was a mere man and not the Lord."

You can see from the last two examples how much more difficult and unnatural destructive dilemmas are to construct or to follow. This is why in practice, most dilemmas are constructive, since these are much simpler and more direct.

Many dilemmas are also enthymemes, often with both the disjunctive premise *and* the conclusion omitted, since the whole argument is usually clear from the double hypothetical premise that sets up the two horns of the dilemma. And sometimes dilemmas are epicheiremas. E.g. the following dilemma is both enthymemic and epicheiremic: "If you try to steal home with the winning run, you will regret it, since you will fail. But if you do not try, you will regret it too, since you will never know whether you could have won the game if only you tried."

The power of a dilemma resides more in the matter than in the form. A dilemma is convincing as an argument to the extent that all its premises are convincingly true. A dilemma is stronger if the disjunctive premise is a tautology ("Either p or non-p" rather than "either p or q"), since "escaping between the horns" (see pages 309–10) is then impossible. And constructive dilemmas are psychologically stronger than destructive dilemmas because they are more simple, direct, and easy to follow.

The use of dilemmas is one of the fundamental features of the Socratic Method. Socrates first (1) provisionally accepts the student's opinion as an assumption, then, (2) within the horizon of this assumption, gives the student a "dialectical" choice between two horns of a dilemma, (3) then shows the student the 'if . . . then . . .' consequences of his own choice. (4) If the student then chooses the other "horn" of the dilemma, Socrates shows *its* logical consequences

(5) If the consequences of both horns of the dilemma are unacceptable, the student realizes that there is probably something wrong with his original assumption, and is led backwards, so to speak, to question this previously unquestioned assumption. It is a double *reductio ad absurdum*, which is even more effective than a single one because the student is given a choice. The dilemma leads the student to see for himself where his own premises take him. This is more effective than directly arguing against the student, which might threaten, alienate, or embitter him and put him in an adversary relationship with his teacher. (See also pages 211–14 and 350–55 on Socratic method.)

How to Construct a Dilemma

It is important in practice to know how to construct arguments as well as to deconstruct them (i.e. to analyze and criticize them).

We saw earlier that there are essentially three steps to constructing a good categorical syllogism:

(1) Formulate the conclusion you want to prove.

(2) Find an appropriate middle term to connect the subject and predicate of your conclusion.

(3) Formulate the two premises.

Constructing a good dilemma involves three steps too; the last two are similar and the first is identical to the three above.

(1) Formulate the conclusion you want to prove.

(2) Find two appropriate "horns" for your dilemma, the two alternatives which both lead to your conclusion. These should ideally be mutually exclusive and jointly exhaustive statements, x or non-x

(3) Formulate the two premises. (a) The two "horns" are your double "if . . . then . . ." premise. (b) And the disjunctive ("either . . . or . . .") premise forces your opponent to choose between these two "horns."

For instance, suppose you want to prove that "God exists." You might use these two "horns": "You must be either a theist or an atheist." Then develop the "if . . . then . . ." consequences of the two horns as follows, one quickly and the other through a long chain of consequences: "If you are a theist, you admit that God exists. If you are an atheist, you claim to know that God does not exist; and if you claim to know that God does not exist, you claim to know that God does not exist anywhere in all reality; and if you claim to know that Goes does not exist anywhere in all reality, you claim to know all reality; and if you claim to know all reality, you claim you are omniscient; and if you claim you are omniscient, you claim you are God; and if you claim you are God, you claim God exists. Therefore, if you are an atheist, you claim God exists."

The above argument is probably not going to convince many people. But it is a clever debating device. Dilemmas are usually more "fun" than serious. The above dilemma can easily be answered by escaping between the horns and embracing agnosticism.

Three Ways to Answer a Dilemma

Very rarely do dilemmas ever commit a formal fallacy. The four forms above are all valid; so if there are no ambiguous terms, the only way to respond to a dilemma is to deny one of the premises. Denying the hypothetical premise is called **"taking it by the horns."** Denying the disjunctive premise is called **"escaping between the horns."** A third way of replying to a dilemma is called **"rebuttal,"** and consists in constructing a counter dilemma which proves the opposite (i.e. contradictory) conclusion. However, this leaves the original dilemma untouched.

Even though it does not refute the original dilemma, rebuttal is the most interesting and amusing way to answer a dilemma, and history provides some famous examples. For instance, an Athenian mother tried to persuade her son not to enter politics by the following argument: "If your speech is just, men will hate you; and if is unjust, the gods will hate you. But your speech must be either the one or the other. Therefore you will be hated." The son replied, "If I say what is just, the gods will love me; and if I say what is unjust, men will love me. I must say either the one or the other. Therefore I shall be loved."

One of the most famous suits of all time was brought by the Sophist teacher Protagoras against one of his students, Euathlus. Protagoras taught the art of pleading in courts, but he charged a high fee for his instruction; and Euathlus, being clever but poor, had made a legal agreement with Protagoras that he would pay his teacher his full tuition fee only after Euathlus won his first case in court. He then delayed going to court, and Protagoras sued for his money, so Euathlus had to appear in court to defend himself against Protagoras's suit. Protagoras's argument was this: "If Euathlus loses this case, he must pay me, according to the judgment of the court. But if he wins this case, he must pay me, according to the terms of our contract. And he must either lose or win this case. Therefore he must pay me in any case." Euathlus replied: "If I win this case, I will not have to pay Protagoras, according to the judgment of the court. But if I lose this case, I will not have to pay Protagoras, according to the terms of our contract. I must either win or lose. Therefore I do not have to pay in either case." (Protagoras forgot the adage that a lawyer who tries his own case has a fool for a client.)

All three ways of answering a dilemma use the image of the "horns," as if a wild bull were charging at you. If the bull succeeds, you are pinned by his horns. (1) To "take the bull by the horns" is to remove or weaken at least one horn, which then becomes harmless – that is, to dispute the truth of one or both of the two hypothetical premises. Your opponent (the "bull") has claimed that if p, then q; you reply that this is not true: p does not necessarily imply q. (2) To "escape between the horns" is to find a safe refuge from both horns *between* them, i.e. a third possibility in addition to the two in the disjunction. It is to deny the disjunctive premise that says you must embrace one or the other of the two horns. (3) To "rebut" is to create a dilemma (a "bull") yourself, with its own horns, which pins your opponent as he pinned you.

Exercises: Put each of the following dilemmas in symbolic form, then answer each one.

1. "An unhappy alternative is before you, Elizabeth. From this day you must be a stranger to one of your parents. Your mother will never see you again if you do not marry Mr. Collins, and I will never see you again if you do." (Jane Austen, *Pride and Prejudice*)

2. "Culture is on the horns of this dilemma: if profound and noble, it must remain rare; if common, it must become mean." (George Santayana)

3. "Pain is unavoidable, for if we satisfy our desires we feel satiation and boredom; and if we do not, we feel restlessness and discomfort." (Arthur Schopenhauer)

4. (H) "A man cannot inquire either about that which he knows, or about that which he does not know. For if he knows, he has no need to inquire; and if not, he cannot inquire, for he does not know the very thing about which he is to inquire." (Plato, *Meno*)

5. King Henry VII's tax collector collected enormous amounts of taxes from the people, arguing that "If you have been spending little, you must be rich through your savings; and if you have been spending much, you must be rich in order to spend so much."

6. Caliph Omar justified burning the world's greatest library, at Alexandria, by this dilemma: "These books either agree with the Qur'an or they do not. If they agree, they are superfluous. If they disagree, they are heretical. In either case, they should be burned."

7. Socrates argued that evil is only ignorance, that no one could knowingly and deliberately choose evil. For either he knows that the act he is choosing is evil, or he does not. If he knows it is evil, he will not choose it, for no one chooses what is harmful to himself, and evil is always harmful to oneself, in body or soul. If he does *not* know the act is evil, then if he chooses it he will not be choosing it knowingly but unknowingly.

8. "Mortimer Adler wrote a great book on how to read great books, entitled *How to Read a Book*. But this book must be worthless, for either the reader already knows how to read a book before reading *How to Read a Book*, or not. If he *does* already know this, Adler's book is superfluous to him; if not – that is, if he does not know how to read a book – then he will not be able to read *How to Read a Book*, for *How to Read a Book* is a book."

9. Each religion claims to teach the most important truth in the world, the truth that is most worthy of belief. If the claim of any religion is true, then all who do not believe it are fools for not believing the thing most worthy of belief. If the claim is untrue, then all believers are fools for believing what is not believable. But each truth claim must be either true or untrue. Therefore in any case, billions of people are fools: either the believers or the unbelievers.

10. Hume argued against deduction by this dilemma: If the conclusion of a deduction does not contain anything new that is not already given in the

premises, the deduction is useless, for it yields no new knowledge; but if the conclusion does contain something new that is not in the premises, the deduction is logically invalid, for there can be no more in a conclusion than in its premises. (How would you answer this argument philosophically?)

11. "All political action aims at either preservation or change. When desiring to preserve, we wish to prevent a change to the worse; when desiring to change, we wish to bring about something better. All political action is then guided by some thought of better and worse." (Leo Strauss, *What Is Political Philosophy?*)

12. "If freedom of speech is restricted, we will cease to be a democracy. If it is not restricted, we will be at the mercy of demagogues and fanatics."

13. "Death is not to be feared, for if you are dead you cannot fear, and if you are living you are not dead."

14. "If a thing moves, it must move either in the place where it is or in the place where it is not. But it cannot move in the place where it is, for it remains therein; nor in the place where it is not, for it does not exist therein. Therefore a thing cannot move." (Sextus Empiricus, *Against the Physicists*, quoting Zeno the Eleatic)

15. "If Socrates died, he died either when he was living or when he was dead. But he did not die while living, for assuredly he was living, and as living he had not died. Nor when he died, for then he would be dead twice. Therefore Socrates did not die." (Sextus Empiricus, *Against the Physicists*)

16. If the citizens are good, laws are unnecessary to prevent evil; and if they are bad, laws are impotent to prevent evil. Therefore laws are either unnecessary or impotent.

17. [Jesus to the Pharisees:] "Whence was the baptism of John? From Heaven or from men?" [Pharisees among themselves:] "If we say, 'from Heaven,' he will say to us, 'Why then did you not believe him? [And then we fear that the people will hate us.] But if we say, 'from men,' we fear the people, for all regard John as a prophet."

XIV. Induction

Section 1. What is induction?

Induction is not a single form of argument. There are at least six different kinds of induction:

(1) generalization from experience
(2) arguments to establish a cause
(3) scientific hypotheses
(4) arguments of statistical probability
(5) arguments from analogy
(6) *a fortiori* and *a minore* arguments

What unites them all as "inductive"?

A common but inadequate definition of induction and of its distinction from deduction is that "deduction is reasoning from the universal to the particular, while induction is reasoning from the particular to the universal." This is usually but not always true. There are forms of induction which remain at the level of the particular, and there are forms of deduction which remain at the level of the universal (e.g. "All bachelors are unmarried men and no unmarried men are married men, therefore no bachelors are married men"). Valid deductive arguments can also begin with a particular premise (though they must always add at least one universal premise), e.g. "Some men are bald men, and no bald men shampoo, therefore some men do not shampoo."

There are also inductive arguments that have universal premises as well as universal conclusions, e.g. "All poodles are dogs and bark; all hounds are dogs and bark; all spaniels are dogs and bark; therefore it is probable that all dogs bark." And there are inductive arguments that have particular conclusions as well as particular premises, e.g. "Thomas was a saint and happy; Francis was a saint and happy; Theresa was a saint and happy; Catherine was a saint and happy; and John was a saint; therefore probably John was happy."

A second common definition of an inductive argument is "an argument whose premises are discovered by sense experience." The premises of deduction, since they must include at least one universal premise, are not all known by sense experience, since sense experience knows only particulars, not universals. For instance, we sense *a* man or *men*, not "man" or "all men."

However, this distinction between induction and deduction also does not always hold true. Many deductive arguments also discover their premises by sense observation: e.g. "I have observed that all the houses on Main Street are white, and #24 Main Street is a house on Main Street, therefore #24 Main Street is white." And induction also can use more than sense observation alone to find its premises. E.g. "I feel my life is meaningful, and you do too, and so do 90 out of 100 of the people I know. Therefore it is probable that most people feel their lives are meaningful."

The most unexceptionable definition of an inductive argument is one which *does not claim to prove its conclusion with certainty, even if its premises are true, but only with probability.* This is true of all six forms of induction mentioned above.

All deductive arguments are either logically valid or logically invalid by their logical form alone. Valid deductive arguments prove their conclusions with certainty (assuming the truth of the premises). But all six forms of inductive arguments fall somewhere between the two extremes of simply valid and simply invalid, and their strength derives from their matter rather than from their form. They all offer only probable reasons for their conclusions, ranging from highly probable to slightly probable.

Deduction Dependent on Induction

All of our knowledge is dependent on its beginning: our experience and observation. As Aristotle said, there is nothing in the intellect that was not first in the senses, or derived from sensation. We infer happiness from smiles, wind from leaves moving, universal human mortality from observing many individual deaths, God from observed cosmic order, or the absence of God from observed human disorder. And since experience is the basis of all our knowledge, and since induction reasons from experience, induction is the chronologically first step in reasoning. Deduction comes later and presupposes a prior induction.

Abstraction is similar to induction. Abstraction is the operation of the *first* act of the mind which leads us from a sensory awareness of particular things to an intellectual awareness of a universal nature or essence. Induction is the operation of the *third* act of the mind which *usually* leads us from a knowledge of particular truths known by experience (which make up the premises of the induction) to a knowledge of a universal truth or principle (which is the conclusion of the induction). The induction itself is an operation of the third act of the mind, reasoning, which is expressed in an argument; the knowledge of its conclusion is an operation of the second act of the mind, judgment, which is expressed in a proposition.

Both abstraction and induction are like a hunter (the mind) entering a jungle (reality) to find a tiger (a universal). As the tiger lives in the jungle, the universal exists in its particulars: justice exists in just persons and acts, redness in red things, humanity in humans. As the hunter immobilizes and cages the tiger and takes it out of the jungle into a city zoo, the mind abstracts the unchanging universal from the changing concrete things and events it is involved in (the jungle), confines it to a concept (the cage), and places it in the mental realm (the city zoo, full of caged beasts) where it can be safely and objectively studied and compared with other universals.

Zoos cannot create tigers, only receive them from jungles. Deduction receives all its data from induction. Deduction presupposes induction because no syllogism can prove its own premises. If the premises are proved by another deductive syllogism, rather than by induction, this second syllogism will also need to prove its premises, and the process will go on ad infinitum with the result that no premise will be certain, since it depends on prior premises – in which case no conclusion will be certain either. (This fact was the basis of some ancient skeptics' objection to the syllogism; see page 219.)

This process of questioning premises and tracing them back to prior premises stops in two ways. First, it stops at sense experience (and the two processes that come from it: the first-act-of-the-mind abstraction of a universal form from particular material instances of it, and the third-act-of-the-mind inductive reasoning to a universal conclusion from particular premises which are instances of it). Second, it also stops at tautologies or self-evident propositions which prove themselves, so to speak, and need no prior premises. We "just see" that $2 + 2 = 4$, or that a whole cannot be smaller than its parts, because we understand what a whole is and what a part is.

But the fact that such principles are self-evident does not mean that we did not learn them through experience, inductively. Even the law of non-contradiction itself is gradually discovered, like all universals, in and through experiencing cases of it. But we do not argue to its truth merely from our observations of some instances of it, inductively. At some point in our experience we *understand* that "x $\neq$ non-x," like "$2 + 2 = 4$" and unlike "The sky is blue," is *necessary*, not accidental; it not only *is* true but *must* be true and *cannot not* be true – really, objectively, in fact, always and everywhere.

Section 2. Generalization

Generalization is the first and simplest of the six forms of induction. Abstraction (in the first act of the mind) and inductive generalization (in the third act of the mind) both reach the universal through the particular. In abstraction, the intellect sees the universal nature (e.g. "redness") in and through a number of particular examples (e.g. "this red apple" and "that red sunset"). In generalization, the reason arrives at a conclusion (a proposition, the expression of the second act of the mind) through a process of reasoning (the third act of the mind) which begins with a number of particular truths as premises and ends with a universal truth as a probable conclusion. E.g. "This swan is white, and that swan is white, and so is that swan and that one, therefore probably all swans are white."

This form of inductive reasoning is also called "**induction by simple enumeration.**" It is the simplest form of induction. It obviously can only arrive at a probable conclusion unless we have a "**complete induction,**" in which we are sure that we have examined all the cases, i.e. each of the members of the class which is the subject of our conclusion (e.g. "Rose passed and Tim passed and Tom passed and Barbara passed and Ruth passed, and these five are the only members of the class, therefore all the members of the class passed").

The probability of the conclusion being true increases in proportion to each of the following factors: (1) How many observations, how many cases or examples are there? (2) More important, what proportion of the whole class do the cases observed constitute? If there are only 100 swans but there are 800 ducks, observing 90 swans yields more probability than observing 400 ducks. (3) How representative is the sample? Is it a fair cross-section?

There are other factors to be factored in too, such as time: Is there past precedent? Are there historical data? And will things change in the future?

The probability of a generalization increases when we add other factors to distinguish *coincidences* from *causal laws*. Superstitions often come from the confusion between coincidences and causal laws; e.g. someone probably observed 10 people walk under a ladder, observed that all 10 had bad luck shortly afterwards, and concluded that walking under a ladder causes bad luck – but it was just a coincidence. (See page 100 on the *post hoc* fallacy.)

No inductive argument can be evaluated in the same way as deductive arguments. A deductive argument is either simply valid or simply invalid; it is either-or, zero-sum, as far as logical validity is concerned. The other two factors in a deductive arguments do not usually have this zero-sum character: the truth or falsity of the premises and the meaning of the terms. Unless the premises are self-evidently true tautologies or self-evidently false self-contradictions, they are usually uncertain and disputable (though in objective fact each proposition is either true or false). And the clarity and meaning of the terms is always potentially "gray." But in an inductive argument, even the "third-act-of-the-mind" *logic* of the argument is "gray." Even if the premises are true, the conclusion follows only with probability, not certainty.

The strength of an inductive argument is not usually quantifiable (except for statistical probabilities). However, the argument becomes stronger, and the probability of its conclusion being true increases, when we apply standards such as the three factors mentioned four paragraphs above. Generalizations, like abstractions, always retain something of the character of "flying by the seat of your pants." Generalizing is much more subjective, i.e. relative to different individuals' abilities. Some people seem to have a better intuitive ability than others to generalize accurately and quickly. And one person will "just see" the truth of a generalization from a few instances, while another, slower person will require more examples. One person will leap to conclusions too quickly (the fallacy of **hasty generalization** – see page 100) while another will be more careful and discriminating. And one person will be good at inductive generalizations in one field (a field familiar to him) while another will excel in another field. The same person may be quick and accurate at one time and too slow or hasty at another. The point here is not to classify people but to avoid the expectation that induction can be as precise and impersonal as deduction.

Aristotle used the analogy of a formation in battle arising from a number of individual soldiers making a stand together, to show that the human mind is capable of this process of seeing the universal (the general principle) in the particular. "We conclude that these states of knowledge (knowing the universal from experience) are neither innate . . . nor developed from other states of knowledge, but from sense perception. It is like a rout in battle being stopped by first one man making a stand and then another, until the original formation has been restored. The soul is so constituted as to be capable of this process" (*Posterior Analytics*, 100a–b).

Exercises: Evaluate the following generalizations:
1. "The man of the machine age is a calculating animal. We live in a welter of figures, cookery recipes, railway timetables, unemployment aggregates, fines, taxes, war-debts, overtime schedules, speed limits, bowling averages, betting odds, billiard scores, calories, babies' weights, clinical temperatures, rainfall, hours of sunshine, motoring records, power indices, gas-meter readings, bank rates, freight rates, death rates, discount, interest, lotteries, wavelengths, and tire pressures." (Lancelot Hogben)
2. "After this I inquired in general into what is essential to the truth and certainty of a proposition; for since I had discovered one which I knew to be true, I thought that I must likewise be able to discover the ground of this certitude. And as I observed that in the words 'I think, hence I am,' there is nothing at all which gives me assurance of their truth beyond this, that I see very clearly that in order to think it is necessary to exist, I concluded that I might take, as a general rule, the principle that all the things which we very clearly and distinctly conceive are true." (Descartes)
3. "The demand for certainty is one which is natural to man, but is nevertheless an intellectual vice. If you take your children for a picnic on a doubtful day, they will demand a dogmatic answer whether it will be fine or wet, and be disappointed in you when you cannot be sure." (Bertrand Russell)
4. "Freeman and slave, patrician and plebeian, lord and serf, guild-master and journeyman, in a word, oppressor and oppressed, stood in constant opposition to one another." (Karl Marx and Friedrich Engels, *The Communist Manifesto*, claiming to show that all pre-communist human relationships have been oppressive)

5. Summarize and evaluate the point of the following passage: "I have never understood why there is supposed to be something crabbed or antique about a syllogism; still less can I understand what anybody means by talking as if induction had somehow taken the place of deduction. The whole point of deduction is that true premises produce a true conclusion. What is called induction seems simply to mean collecting a large number of true premises, or perhaps, in some physical matters, taking rather more trouble to see that they are true. It may be a fact that a modern man can get more out of a great many premises, concerning microbes or asteroids, than a medieval man could get out of a very few premises about salamanders and unicorns. But the process of deduction from the data is the same for the modern mind as for the medieval mind. . . . It was the misfortune of medieval culture that there were not enough true premises, owing to the rather ruder conditions of travel or experiment. But however perfect were the conditions of travel or experiment, they could only produce premises; it would still be necessary to deduce conclusions. But many modern people talk as if what they call induction were some magic way of reaching a conclusion without using any of those horrid old syllogisms. But . . . induction leads us only to a deduction. . . . Thus the great nineteenth century men of science . . . went out and closely inspected the air and the earth, the chemicals and the gases, doubtless more closely than Aristotle or Aquinas, and then came back and embodied their final conclusion in a syllogism: 'All matter is made of microscopic little knobs which are indivisible. My body is made of matter. Therefore my body is made of microscopic little knobs which are indivisible.' They were not wrong in the form of their reasoning, because it is the only way to reason. In this world there is nothing except a syllogism – and a fallacy. But of course these modern men knew, as the medieval men knew, that their conclusions would not be true unless their premises were true. And that is where the trouble began. For the men of science, or their sons and nephews, went out and took another look at the knobby nature of matter, and were surprised to find that it was not knobby at all. So they came back and completed the process with their syllogism: 'All matter is made of whirling protons and electrons. My body is made of matter. Therefore my body is made of whirling protons and electrons.' And that again is a good syllogism, though they may have to look at matter once or twice more before we know whether it is a true premise and a true conclusion. But in the final process of truth there is nothing else except a good syllogism. The only other thing is a bad syllogism, as in the familiar fashionable shape: 'All matter is made of protons and electrons. I should very much like to think that mind is much the same as matter. So I will announce . . . that my mind is made of protons and electrons.'" (G.K. Chesterton, *St. Thomas Aquinas*)

6. "Everyone has heard people quarrelling. Sometimes it sounds funny and sometimes it sounds merely unpleasant; but however it sounds, I believe we

can learn something very important from listening to the kind of things they say. They say things like this: 'How'd you like it if anyone did the same to you?' – 'That's my seat, I was there first' – 'Leave him alone, he isn't doing you any harm' – 'Why should you shove in first?' – 'Give me a bit of your orange, I gave you a bit of mine' – 'Come on, you promised.' People say things like that every day, educated people as well as uneducated, and children as well as grown-ups.

"Now what interests me about all these remarks is that the man who makes them is not merely saying that the other man's behaviour does not happen to please him. He is appealing to some kind of standard of behaviour which he expects the other man to know about. And the other man very seldom replies: 'To hell with your standard.' Nearly always he tries to make out that what he has been doing does not really go against the standard, or that if it does there is some special excuse. He pretends there is some special reason in this particular case why the person who took the seat first should not keep it, or that things were quite different when he was given the bit of orange, or that something has turned up which lets him off keeping his promise. It looks, in fact, very much as if both parties had in mind some kind of Law or Rule of fair play or decent behaviour or morality or whatever you like to call it, about which they really agreed. And they have. If they had not, they might, of course, fight like animals, but they could not *quarrel* in the human sense of the word. Quarrelling means trying to show that the other man is in the wrong. And there would be no sense in trying to do that unless you and he had some sort of agreement as to what Right and Wrong are; just as there would be no sense in saying that a footballer had committed a foul unless there was some agreement about the rules of football." (C.S. Lewis, *Mere Christianity*) (Find an inductive generalization, a hypothetical syllogism, and an argument from analogy here.)

Section 3. Causal arguments: Mill's methods

This is the most well-known kind of induction, the one whose rules are found in most logic texts and used most often in the sciences.

"Explaining things by discovering their causes" was Aristotle's definition of science; and modern science, in spite of its much "tighter" method, has not *essentially* altered that definition. Science seeks to explain things by discovering their causes (this is "pure science" or "theoretical science"), and to change things by changing their causes (this is "applied science" or "practical science": technology).

But what kinds of causes? There are at least five distinctions we need to make among causes.

(a) We have already (page 193) distinguished (1) **real causes** from **logical "becauses,"** i.e. causes of a thing's *being* from causes of our *knowledge* of it.

Science seeks *real causes*. (Even psychology seeks the real causes of knowing, feeling, *etc.*)

(b) We have also distinguished **the four causes** (page 202). Modern science seeks *efficient causes and material causes*, not formal causes or final causes. This is part of the narrowing of focus (like laser light) that distinguishes modern science from ancient science and accounts for much of its power and success.

(c) We also have distinguished **reasoning from cause to effect** from **reasoning from effect to cause** (page 204). Science usually reasons *from effect to cause*. (However, it also *predicts* effects *from* causes.) We perceive the effect, and want to find the cause: e.g. Why do I get headaches? Why are there tides? Why did this plane crash?

(d) We also need to distinguish between **necessary cause** and **sufficient cause**. A *necessary cause* is a cause *without* which the effect *cannot* happen. A *sufficient cause* is a cause *with* which the effect *must* happen. Remove the necessary cause, and you remove the effect. Produce the sufficient cause, and you produce the effect.

This distinction (d) is closely related to the one before it (c), for we can infer the cause from the effect only with necessary causes, and we can infer the effect from the cause only with sufficient causes. E.g. when we infer the presence of a foot from the presence of a footprint, we infer that a foot is a *necessary* cause for a footprint. (The inference is only probable, for footprints can also be made artificially.) And when we infer and predict future beach erosion from a hurricane, we infer that a hurricane alone is *sufficient* to cause beach erosion. Science usually seeks necessary causes, since it usually reasons from effect to cause.

(e) Finally, we must also distinguish between **ultimate and proximate causes**, or **remote and immediate causes**, or **first and second causes**. The ultimate cause of evolution may be (according to theists) divine providence, but the proximate cause may be (according to Darwin) Natural Selection. The ultimate cause of a murder may be the murderer's choice, but the proximate cause was the poison he put in the victim's food. Science seeks only proximate causes. This is one of the ways it differs from philosophy.

Mill's Five Canons of Causal Induction

In *A System of Logic* (1843) John Stuart Mill proposed five "methods of inductive inference." These are very useful practical rules for finding causes. They do not yield certainty (for we are dealing with induction here, not deduction), but they add to probability.

First Canon: Method of Agreement

"If two or more instances of the phenomenon under investigation have only one circumstance in common, the circumstance in which alone all the instances agree is the cause (or effect) of the given phenomenon."

Second Canon: Method of Difference
"If an instance in which the phenomenon under investigation occurs, and an instance in which it does not occur, have every circumstance in common save one, that one occurring only in the former; the circumstance in which alone the two instances differ is the effect, or the cause, or an indispensable part of the cause, of the phenomenon."

Third Canon: Joint Method of Agreement and Difference
"If two or more instances in which the phenomenon occurs have only one circumstance in common, while two or more instances in which it does not occur have nothing in common save the absence of that circumstance, the circumstance in which alone the two sets of instances differ is the effect, or the cause, or an indispensable part of the cause, of the phenomenon."

Fourth Canon: Method of Residues
"Subduct [subtract] from any phenomenon such part as is known by previous inductions to be the effect of certain antecedents, and the residue of the phenomenon is the effect of the remaining antecedents."

Fifth Canon: Method of Concomitant Variations
"Whatever phenomenon varies in any manner whenever another phenomenon varies in some particular manner, is either a cause or an effect of that phenomenon, or is connected with it through some fact of causation."

The essential principle behind all five of these canons is the distinction between the *necessary* and the *contingent*, or the *essential* and the *accidental*. This is translated into scientific language by being reduced to what is sensorially observable, namely the *constant* and the *variable*. Thus by observing a natural phenomenon under different circumstances, or by producing those different circumstances through a controlled experiment, the scientist tries to find the common cause of all different occurrences of the phenomenon. The philosopher would say that he is trying to distinguish the universal from the particular, the essential from the accidental, or the necessary from the contingent. But these abstract metaphysical terms are not scientifically (i.e. empirically) observable, so the scientist translates them into the observable terms, or "operational" terms, of the *constant* (or permanent or regular) and the *variable*.

The Method of Agreement

Around the middle of the 20th century the Method of Agreement was used to make an important discovery: that fluoride causes a decrease in the incidence of dental decay. The rate of decay was found to be much lower in some cities than others; the cause was not known; and investigators noticed that one circumstance common to all cities with low decay rates was an unusually high level of fluoride in their water supply. This led to the suspicion that increased fluoride caused decreased decay, and to the practice of fluoridating water supplies, with the result that dental decay was significantly decreased throughout the world.

The Method of Agreement, though its name is affirmative, is really negative: what it does is to eliminate circumstances present in some but not all cases of the phenomenon whose cause we are seeking. This can never be done completely, of course. This is one reason why neither this Method nor the other four, nor all five together, can yield certainty, as deduction can. Another reason is because the use of this method presupposes a judgment about which of many circumstances we should focus on as likely causes of the phenomenon; and this, in turn, requires an insight into the nature of things, the nature of the supposed cause and the effect. This is illustrated by a famous example of the *mis*use of the Method of Agreement: "When I drank scotch and soda, I got drunk; when I drank bourbon and soda, I got drunk; when I drank gin and soda, I got drunk. I gotta stop drinking that soda!"

The Method of Agreement can give more conclusive evidence for what is *not* a cause than for what is. For instance, it is constantly assumed that more money spent on public education causes better results, as measured by SAT scores; yet this assumption is not borne out by data. For instance, in 1992–1993 the 15 states with the top SAT scores did not include any one of the five with the highest teacher salaries, and only one of the states with the highest SAT scores was one of the ten with the highest expenditures per pupil. Four of the ten states with the highest SAT scores were among the 10 states with the *lowest* per-pupil expenditures. New Jersey had the highest per-pupil expenditures but was 39th in SAT scores. South Dakota was third in SAT scores and dead last in teacher salaries. All this data does *not* prove that being cheap causes SAT scores to increase, or that putting more money into education is a total waste; but it does help us to save time by sending us elsewhere to look for the main causes of pupil achievement.

The Method of Difference

This method doubles the data, so to speak, compared with the Method of Agreement. For instance, if half the passengers on an airplane got sick to their stomach, and all those who got sick chose the chicken for dinner while all those that did not get sick chose lasagna, we can be fairly sure the chicken, or something that came with the chicken, caused the stomach upset.

An example of the use of this method is a study of whiplash (neck pains) after rear-end auto collisions in different countries. A Norwegian researcher found that Lithuanian drivers had just as many serious accidents as drivers in other countries, but almost no whiplash. Finally, the cause of the difference emerged: Lithuanians had no personal injury insurance, very few lawyers, and free socialized medicine, so nothing could be gained by a claim of whiplash. (*The Lancet*, London, 5/4/96)

The Joint Method of Agreement and Difference

This is essentially the first two methods used together, thus increasing the probability of the conclusion. Pharmaceutical companies often use this method in testing new drugs. Two similar and typical groups of people are found. First, the first group is given the drug while the second is not. Then, after a time, the second group receives the drug while the first does not. Pasteur used this method to discover that increased temperature increased resistance to some infections, by injecting chickens with anthrax and putting some of them in a cold bath. These caught the disease and died, while the others did not. Then, when he took one chicken out of the cold bath before it died, and heated it, it completely recovered.

None of the methods can infallibly or automatically distinguish real causes from coincidences, and these must be eliminated by common sense. One study tried to find out where to put advertising inside a large one-floor discount department store by testing whether most people turned to the right or to the left first when entering the store. They arranged everything inside the store perfectly symmetrically, and they found no difference between the left-handed and the right-handed customers; but they found that while half the women turned to the left and half turned right, most of the men turned to the left. Only later did they find the cause: the prettiest female cashiers were all on the left.

The Method of Residues

This method is useful when we cannot simply and totally produce or remove the supposed cause of a phenomenon, but only produce a partial change. The simplest example I know of is the way the local dump charges me for disposing rubbish. I drive into the dump with a loaded car, get my car weighed on a scale, unload my rubbish, then drive onto the scale again where the car is re-weighed. The difference in weight is the weight of the rubbish. My vet weighs my cat the same way. The cat will not stay still on the scale, so first they weigh me holding my cat, then without her. The cause of the difference in weight is the weight of the cat.

A famous example of the use of this method was the discovery of the planet Neptune, which had never been observed visually, by the calculation that Uranus, whose orbit is next to Neptune's, moved in a slightly irregular way, with a residue of perturbation deviating from the simple elliptical orbit that all the other known planets had. This deviation could not be explained by any known visible bodies. The Method of Residues predicted that some not-yet-discovered body had to cause the residue of motion, and this body was soon discovered: the planet Neptune.

Another scientific example of the use of this method was Pascal's simple argument for the then-controversial thesis that air has weight. He wrote: "A balloon is heavier when inflated than when empty . . . if the air were [not heavy but] light, the more the balloon was inflated, the lighter the whole would be, since there would be more air in it. But since, on the contrary, when more air is put in, the whole becomes heavier, it follows that each part has a weight of its own, and consequently that the air has weight." (Pascal, *Treaties on the Weight of the Mass of the Air*)

The Method of Concomitant Variations

The first four methods all eliminate some circumstances as possible causes of a given phenomenon. When this cannot be done, the circumstance is modified instead of eliminated. For instance, increasing or decreasing certain foods or vitamins can increase or decrease certain diseases: e.g. eating one fish per week or taking one baby aspirin a day seems to decrease the risk of heart attack. A farmer finds that the more fertilizer he uses, up to a certain point, the higher or faster his crops grow. A businessman tests the efficiency of different advertising campaigns by correlating them with sales during the times he uses each one.

Coincidences can always be mistaken for causes. Yet occasionally the opposite mistake can also be made: circumstances that are apparently only coincidences can turn out to have a roundabout causal connection. For instance, a correlation was found between the years when the most spiders were found on banana boats from Latin America and the years when there were the most sunspots on the sun. Later, a causal connection was found: the sunspots, manifestations of electrical storms on the surface of the sun, produced electrical conditions in earth's atmosphere that were conducive to the fertility of banana spiders.

Another such example was a correlation between the number of storks and the number of babies in English villages. The more storks, the more babies. A *direct* causal connection was not suspected, even by the most bizarre sex education programs. When the real cause was finally uncovered, it was closer to babies causing storks than storks causing babies. Villages with high birth rates and more newlyweds had more new home construction, and storks always prefer to nest in a new chimney that has never been used by another stork. (See J.L. Casti, *Searching for Certainty* [New York: William Morrow, 1991])

The Limitations of Mill's Methods

Mill's methods are not methods of proof. They help us to discover causes and test causal hypotheses, but they do not turn induction into deduction, probability into certainty. There are two reasons for this: one quantitative, one qualitative.

First, the number of circumstances is potentially infinite, so there is no case that literally matches Mill's description of "having only one circumstance in common," and no case of "having every circumstance in common save one." We cannot examine an infinite set of circumstances.

The more important limitation of Mill's methods is qualitative: they do not tell us how to judge which of the many circumstances are relevant, i.e. likely to be causes. We must know that by intuition, understanding, experience, and common sense – something impossible to reduce to quantity and the mathematically measurable or to the empirically observable. Although the scientific method (of which Mill's five rules are an important part) appeals ultimately to mathematical and empirical standards, all great scientists must presuppose and use something more fundamental than either: human intuitive understanding.

Many times, it is this intuition more than the most explicit use of Mill's methods that finds the cause. E.g. the following example includes only a very "thin slice" of one of the five methods (which one?) but a very "thick slice" of understanding:

"Beasts do not read symbols; that is why they do not see pictures. We are sometimes told that dogs do not react even to the best portraits because they live more by smell than by sight; but the behavior of a dog who spies a motionless real cat through the window glass belies this explanation. Dogs scorn our paintings because they see colored canvases, not pictures. A representation of a cat does not make them conceive one." (Suzanne K. Langer)

Another example, typical of the "hunch" common among detectives: "'How did you know that I did manual labor? It's true as gospel, for I began as a ship's carpenter.' 'Your hands, my dear sir. Your right hand is quite a size larger than your left. You have worked with it and the muscles are more developed.'" (Arthur Conan Doyle, "The Red Headed League")

Section 4. Scientific hypotheses

The "**scientific method**" is probably the greatest single discovery in the history of science, for it is like a skeleton key that enables us to open countless other doors of scientific knowledge. It is much broader than Mill's methods of causal induction; in fact, it deserves a whole text by itself. What follows is the briefest of introductions.

Science is not esoteric. It is only an extension of principles of common sense, and the scientific method is only a refinement of the method we all use every day when we try to find a lost pet, the cause of an electrical failure, the identity of a hit-and-run driver, or the reason a friend is suddenly hostile.

The basic steps are as follows:

(1) A **problem** arises. Scientific thought, like philosophical thought, arises only when a challenge stimulates the mind to respond, like a gadfly stimulating a horse (to use Socrates' famous analogy).

(2) Before anything else, a decision is made, at least unconsciously, to address the problem critically and scientifically, i.e. to demand proof, to treat answers as false until they are proven true. This is a necessary and distinct step because we use the exact opposite of this "method of doubt" in ordinary life: we

trust books, people, sense perception, tradition, etc. until they are proved false, and we treat accused people as innocent until proved guilty. But science requires what Descartes calls "universal [or nearly universal] methodic doubt." We must **assume nothing, question everything.** This opens up the mind to possibilities we would otherwise not consider. The doubt is universal (or as nearly universal as possible) but only methodic. That is to say, it is only theoretical, not practical and lived. (In fact it is unlivable. Imagine a conversation in which everyone demanded proof for everything!) And it is a beginning, not an end; it is not a recipe for skepticism but for inquiry.

(3) A **preliminary hypothesis** is set up, a possible explanation. This precedes the collection of data (the next step), for we search for data only after we know where to search, what kind of data to search for, which data are relevant. Understanding counts more than logic here. If computers performed all the steps of the scientific method, this would be the hardest one to program them to do.

Hypotheses are only sometimes causal. That is why Mill's methods are only one part of the scientific method. Sometimes we want to know *what* rather than *why*. For instance, the hypothesis that light is composed of particles concerns the matter or content or composition of light rather than the efficient cause of it.

Which hypotheses are worth testing? What makes a hypothesis likely? We can list a number of factors, all of which are matters of practical and commonsensical judgment: (a) **relevance** to the problem, (b) **simplicity,** (c) **testability** by data (verifiability and falsifiability), (d) **compatibility** with everything else we know, both proven facts and probable theories, and (e) **power to explain or predict** future data.

From the viewpoint of the *logic* of science, testability is perhaps the most important factor. If an idea is not in principle verifiable or falsifiable by data gathered by any of the sciences, then that idea is not scientifically testable. It may still be meaningful, it may still be true, and there may still be other ways of testing it, but it cannot be called a *scientific* idea. The Freudian theory of id, ego, and super-ego, e.g., as the structure of the psyche has been criticized as an unscientific hypothesis because it excludes falsifiability in principle. If a Freudian can explain *any* possible observed psychic event as caused by id, ego, or super-ego, then the hypothesis is not testable because no observation can be specified that could refute it. It is more like a religious faith, which is not in principle falsifiable (disprovable) by *any* empirical data; e.g. no amount of injustice, or suffering would *disprove* God's goodness, for God's ways are by definition above full human understanding. The believer will not say, e.g., that a Holocaust of 6 million Jews does, but 600 does not, disprove the existence of the God of Israel. This may be reasonable, but it is not scientific. It is like trusting a friend, while science is like fingerprinting a suspect. Friendship and religion use a kind of methodic faith; science uses methodic doubt. *People* should be treated as innocent until proved guilty, but *scientific ideas* should be treated as guilty (false) until proved innocent (true).

Another philosophically-important feature of a good scientific hypothesis is *simplicity*. Simplicity in explanation is always preferable for science. If we can explain the rise of Nazism in Germany by economics, resentment at the Versailles Treaty, and the fear of Communism, it is unscientific to speak of divine providence, fate, or demons, just as it is unscientific and unnecessary to speak of the soul when doing brain surgery. But simplicity is not always desirable when our aim is not science but philosophy, or even common sense. Sometimes, more complex explanations are more adequate to the total data (e.g. the dualism of spirit and matter rather than either materialistic monism or spiritualistic monism). "Ockham's Razor," the principle that tells us to "always prefer the simpler hypothesis," has proved very fruitful and creative in science, but often fruitless and destructive in philosophy. Its natural logical consequence seems to be skepticism. (See page 112 on the fallacy of Reductionism, or "Nothing Buttery.")

(4) Relevant **data** are then collected to test the hypothesis. This is the most time-consuming and uncertain step – and usually the most important from a practical point of view. Most of the work in science today is done by millions of researchers, lab workers, and assistants rather than a few super-intelligent creative geniuses.

The data must be collected honestly and open-mindedly, not slanted to any hypothesis. The data must control the hypothesis, not the hypothesis control the data. This can be notoriously difficult when we have a personal stake in the outcome, yet it is all the more necessary then if we are to learn anything new.

For instance, a sociologist who was committed to the value of education in softening our aggressive animal instincts did research on the Germans who voluntarily performed torture and killing in the Nazi concentration camps, correlating the amount of education to the willingness to perform torture and killing, and found that there was indeed a correlation, but it was directly rather than inversely proportional.

The philosophy that labels itself "deconstructionism" challenges the fundamental principle of traditional literary criticism. Traditionally, good reading means that the text (the data) must determine and judge the reader's interpretation rather than the interpretation judge the text. Deconstructionism says it is the other way round. I will say nothing more about this philosophy because my mother would not like it; she always told me, "If you can't say anything nice about someone, don't say anything at all."

(5) The **hypothesis is refined** and made exact enough to be tested by the data. This is done in two major ways. First, the hypothesis is made testable by **deducing consequences** from it. Second, these consequences are **quantified** if possible. ("Exact sciences" are those where this is possible; "mathematically measurable" is the scientific meaning of "exact.")

For example, it was deduced that if Einstein's theory of Relativity were true, light should be curved by mass to a measurable extent such that a distant star's image would be displaced so many degrees if it passed close to the mass of the sun. Exactly this amount of displacement was observed during a solar eclipse, which made the stars along the line of sight near the sun visible during the eclipse.

(6) And this is step six: **the hypothesis is tested by observation** of the predicted consequences. This step can often be done in a much more quick and efficient way by **controlled experiment** than by simple observation.

Obviously, if the predicted consequences are *not* observed to occur, the hypothesis is shown to be inadequate. But even if the predicted consequences *are* observed, this does not *prove* the hypothesis. (To claim that would be to commit the fallacy of Affirming the Consequent.) However, it makes the hypothesis much more probable.

(7) What increasingly verifies the hypothesis is success in **predicting and controlling** what could not otherwise be predicted or controlled. At a certain point the hypothesis is verified and becomes a scientific law. There is some disagreement about where that "certain point" lies. We usually distinguish a **hypothesis**, as possible, a **theory**, as probable, and a **law**, as verified (proved).

Section 5. Statistical probability

Students will be relieved to discover that this section is very short. (Courses on statistics are usually one of the most dreaded.) But it must be mentioned, however briefly, because it constitutes one of the main kinds of inductive argument.

The two fields that spawned probability theory, and still rely on statistics the most, are gambling and insurance. Pascal – a 17th-century gambler, mathematician, and philosopher – worked out the first probability theory for gambling. (He also invented the first working computer, an adding machine.)

All forms of inductive arguments are only probable. But there are two different kinds of probability, or meanings of the word "probable," and only one of them is quantifiable statistically. (1) The probability of a penny coming down tails on any one toss is 50%. And the probability of living longer than 75 years in a time and place where the average life expectancy is 75 is slightly less than 50%. (These two examples are instances of two different kinds of quantitatively measurable probability, but we will not go into this distinction here.) (2) It is also very probable, on present evidence, that the Big Bang happened 15 billion years ago, but we cannot quantify this probability. It is probable that a certain building will not collapse, that your teacher will not pull out a gun and shoot you, and that little green men will not land a flying saucer on the White House lawn, but we cannot quantify any of these probabilities (all of which, in turn, are also different kinds of probability). If there are inductive arguments for these conclusions, the arguments can be only probable, since the conclusion of an inductive argument "follows" from its premises only with probability, not certainty. Some inductive arguments can be assigned a quantitative degree of probability; others cannot.

We must distinguish the probability of an *argument* from the probability of an *event*. We can calculate the quantitative probability of an event if we can calculate the probability of each of the simpler elements of which it is made. If these component events occur independently, we simply multiply the probability of each component event to get the probability of the composite event.

However, this is only one of two meanings of "statistical probability," namely *the number of ways an event can occur divided by the number of equipossible outcomes*. The other is *the relative frequency with which the members of a specified class exhibit a specified attribute*.

Section 6. Arguments by analogy

Many analogics are not meant as arguments at all but only as illuminating and explanatory: something within the first act of the mind, not the third. E.g. "the third base coach is called 'Windmill' because that's what he looks like when he wildly waves runners home." When analogies *are* used as arguments, they never prove their conclusion, only make it probable. They are more powerful as explanations than as arguments.

Arguments from analogy are probably the most widely used of all kinds of inductive arguments. Most of our everyday inferences are by analogy. E.g. we reason that we will enjoy a certain musician's newest song, and thus we buy her latest album, because we have enjoyed all her previous songs; or we reason that we can drive a golf ball farther if we swing the club in the same way we see the pros swing.

Arguing by analogy is really an abbreviated form of induction and deduction together. Take the classic case we have used a number of times already, Socrates' argument against Thrasymachus in Book I of Plato's *Republic*. Thrasymachus has maintained that justice is merely "the interest of the stronger"; that is, whatever the person in power judges to be in his best interest, he labels "just." Socrates argues against this by (1) first observing people who practice other arts: the horseman, the doctor, the music teacher. (2) On the basis of this observation, he makes an inductive generalization: what is just, or right, or good in all these cases is that the one in power work in the best interest of the *weaker*: the doctor heals the weakened sick patient, the teacher instructs the ignorant, the horseman trains the untrained horse or rider. The fact that the doctor, teacher, or horseman is paid for his service confirms this: justice demands he be compensated for aiding the weaker party. (3) In a perfect argument, we would then *understand why* this is not just something we happened to observe at the time but is *necessary* and unchangeable; we would have an insight into the essence involved. This step is supplied in the rest of the *Republic*, but it is not present in Book I, and that is why the argument there is only probable rather than certain, and why Socrates is not satisfied with it. (4) Having arrived at our general principle through "induction by simple enumeration" (step 2), whether we include or omit step 3, we then (4) deduce from our general principle an

application to the case we are arguing about. The general principle is that justice, or righteousness, is the advantage of the weaker, and the application is that
moral and political justice too must be not the advantage of the stronger but of
the weaker. If Socrates had shortened and simplified this already-abbreviated
argument (minus step 3) to a one-step argument by analogy, it would consist in
arguing from the cases of the doctor, teacher, and horseman to the similar case
of the politician.

Here is another example: I am lost in a jungle, very hungry, and have no
food. I wonder which of the unfamiliar fruits I see is safe to eat. I observe monkeys eating a certain fruit that looks a little like a mango, so I eat it too, since
monkeys are more similar to man than any other animal is. Instead of reasoning
in the four steps above, I have taken a short cut and reasoned directly from what
I know of mangoes (that they are safe to eat) to this mango-like fruit (that it is
too), and from monkeys to men, intuiting (or hoping) that they are similar
enough.

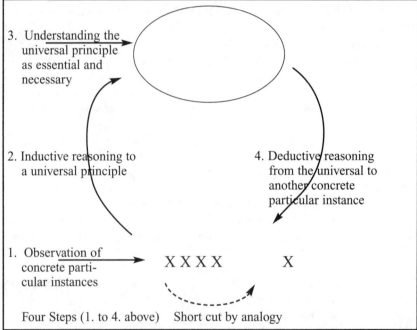

3. Understanding the
   universal principle
   as essential and
   necessary

2. Inductive reasoning to
   a universal principle

4. Deductive reasoning
   from the universal to
   another concrete
   particular instance

1. Observation of
   concrete parti-
   cular instances

X X X X   X

Four Steps (1. to 4. above)   Short cut by analogy

Obviously some arguments from analogy are better than others. Why? To
find the criteria that make arguments from analogy more or less probable, we
need to specify as exactly as possible what are the structural elements of this
argument.

The *premises* of the argument from analogy are the *observed similarities*
between two or more things in one or more ways or attributes. The *conclusion* is

that these things will also be similar in another way. Schematically, the argument from analogy looks like this:

> Entities I, II, III, and IV all have attributes A, B, and C.
> Entities I, II, and III also have attribute D.
> Therefore entity IV will probably also have attribute D.

The criteria that make an argument from analogy more probable are:
(1) The *number of entities* observed in the premises.
(2) The *variety of entities* observed in the premises.
(3) The *number of attributes* in which the entities are similar.
(4) The *relevance of these known attributes* (in which the entities are similar) to the unknown one (in which we hope they are also similar). "Relevance" here means "some kind of causal connection."
(5) The *number, variety, and importance of dissimilarities* between the entity we are reasoning about in the conclusion and the ones we see as analogical to it in the premises. Dissimilarities weaken analogies.
(6) The *boldness of the conclusion's claim*, in terms of either exactness or certainty or both. The bolder the claim, the stronger the premises must be for a good argument; the weaker the claim, the weaker the premises may be.

These criteria are not usually applicable in simple, short analogies that do not distinguish or specify a number of entities (criteria 1 and 2) or attributes (criteria 3 and 5) or the degree of exactness or certainty claimed (criterion 6). In such cases, the following two criteria suffice:
(1) How similar are the two cases? Is the similarity essential or accidental?
(2) How dissimilar are they? All analogies are similar in some ways and dissimilar in other ways. The dissimilarities will not usually be specified in the argument, since they count *against* the analogy, so you must look for them in the world. Are these dissimilarities essential or accidental?

Extending an Analogy

An argument from analogy can often be countered by *"extending the analogy,"* i.e. showing that the analogy counts *against* the conclusion it is supposed to support. Here is a famous example from the Gospels (Matthew 15:21–28):

> And Jesus went away from there and withdrew to the district of Tyre and Sidon. And behold, a Canaanite woman from that region came out and cried, 'Have mercy on me, O Lord, Son of David; my daughter is severely possessed by a demon.' But he did not answer her a word. And his disciples came and begged him, saying, 'Send her

away, for she is crying after us.' He answered, 'I was sent only to the lost sheep of the house of Israel.' But she came and knelt before him, saying, 'Lord, help me.' And he answered, 'It is not fair to take the children's bread and throw it to the dogs.' She said, 'Yes, Lord, yet even the dogs eat the crumbs that fall from their master's table.' Then Jesus answered her, 'O woman, great is your faith! Be it done for you as you desire.' And her daughter was healed instantly.

Here, Jesus praises the Gentile woman for refuting his analogy by extending it, for the analogy (the "chosen people" = the children; the Canaanite Gentiles = the dogs) was designed to test her faith and her humility, by his calculated insult, and she passed the test. It is one of the only two times Jesus ever lost an argument. See John 2:1–11 for the other. (This same example appears on page 103 as an example of the fallacy of false analogy.)

A second form of "extending the analogy" consists in extending it to absurdity. The earliest memory I have is winning an argument with my mother, who was showing me how to wipe my bum after potty training. She said, "There! See? Now it's as clean as a pillow case." I replied, "Well, why don't you sleep on it then?" Even a three-year-old knows some basic logic.

Extending an analogy to absurdity can be either a form of *reductio ad absurdum* (page 294) or a form of the *fallacy of hyperbole* (page 78), depending on whether the extension reasonably follows from the original analogy or not. And this is a matter of intuitive common sense, not logical rules.

Refutation by Logical Analogy

A common form of refutation is the *"refutation by logical analogy."* The analogy here concerns the *logical form* rather than the matter or content of the argument refuted. The strategy is to show that the argument is invalid by showing another argument of exactly the same logical form that is obviously invalid because it has obviously true premises and an *obviously* false conclusion. For instance, suppose someone has argued that

> All Fascists used torture in interrogating suspects.
> And the Israeli army used torture in interrogating suspects.
> Therefore the Israeli army were Fascists.

The refutation of this argument would begin with some phrase like "You might as well argue that" or "If you argue that way, you can also argue that," and then say

> All Fascists breathed.
> And all the Israeli army breathed.
> Therefore the Israeli army were Fascists.

For both arguments have the same fallacious form of Undistributed Middle. The underlying principle of this kind of refutation is that an argument is valid or invalid by its logical form alone, irrespective of content, and that any argument with true premises and a false conclusion is invalid.

Refutation by logical analogy may also focus on the content rather than the form of the argument refuted, by exposing the argument's implied premise (for most everyday arguments are enthymemes) and showing how false it is by deducing an obviously false consequence from it in the same field or subject matter as the original argument. E.g. "Islamic culture was imposed on Africa from abroad. Therefore it is only a veneer there, and alien." "So whatever culture is imposed from abroad is only a veneer, and alien? Then Christian culture is only a veneer and alien to Italy, because it was imposed from abroad." When the general principle that is the implied premise in the first sentence of the refutation ("So whatever culture . . .") is omitted, we have then the "short cut" of an argument by analogy.

Exercises: Evaluate the following analogies. First determine whether they are meant as *arguments* or merely as *explanations*. (Sometimes they can be interpreted either way.) If they are arguments, evaluate them by the six criteria on page 331 if possible, or at least by the two simpler criteria immediately after them, as well as by intuition and common sense.
1. "It is true that we don't have a great deal of *direct* evidence about what happens to a nation which continues to leave its budget unbalanced over a long period. But it is imperative for us to know whether we are running into national disaster by piling up our national debt, instead of cutting it down and making the budget balance. Without direct evidence, our best method is to turn to the closest thing we *do* know about, and that is the *family* budget. We know that a family cannot run up its debts forever; it will sooner or later lose the confidence of tradesmen, it will owe more than it could pay even by selling all its household goods, and it will go into bankruptcy when the creditors become insistent. This is reason enough for predicting *national* insolvency if we go on the way we have been going."
2. "'I'm not anti-Semitic, I'm just anti-Zionist' is the equivalent of 'I'm not anti-American, I just think the United States shouldn't exist.'" (Netanyahu)
3. "Thinking is an experimental dealing with small quantities of energy, just as a general moves miniature figures over a map before setting his troops in action." (Sigmund Freud)
4. "Wittgenstein used to compare thinking with swimming: just as in swimming our bodies have a natural tendency to float on the surface so that it requires great physical exertion to plunge to the bottom, so in thinking it requires great mental exertion to force our minds away from the superficial, down into the depth of a philosophical problem." (George Pitcher, *The Philosophy of Wittgenstein*)

5. "Running a government is like running a ship; we need a strong hand at the tiller." (Thomas Carlyle)

6. "A government run by the people is as impossible as a theater managed by the audience." (G.B. Shaw)

7. "Medicine, to produce health, must examine disease; and music, to create harmony, must investigate discord." (Plutarch, *Demetrius*)

8. "That the universe was formed by a fortuitous concourse of atoms, I will no more believe than that the accidental jumbling of an alphabet would fall into a most ingenious treatise of philosophy." (Jonathan Swift)

9. "'This is a matter of national spirit,' said Marjorie Wilson, coordinator of the Kangaroo Protection Cooperative, an Australian wildlife group. 'We believe here that we have enough meat in this country to satisfy people without them having to eat their national symbol. You Americans don't cook your bald eagles, do you?'" (*New York Times*, 7/10/95)

10. "Just as the bottom of a bucket containing water is pressed more heavily by the weight of the water when it is full than when it is half empty, and the more heavily the deeper the water is, similarly the high places of the earth, such as the summits of mountains, are less heavily pressed than the lowlands are by the weight of the mass of the air. This is because there is more air above the lowlands than above the mountain tops; for all the air along a mountain side presses upon the lowlands but not upon the summit, being above the one but below the other." (Pascal, *Treatise on the Weight of the Mass of the Air*)

11. "What is prudence in the conduct of every private family can scarce be folly in that of a great kingdom. If a foreign country can supply us with a commodity cheaper than we can ourselves make it, better buy it from them with some part of the produce of our own industry." (Adam Smith, *The Wealth of Nations*)

12. "A few dead flies make the perfumer's ointment give off an evil odor; so a little folly outweighs wisdom and honor." (Ecclesiastes 10:1)

13. Baby's implicit reasoning: "Daddy looks a lot like Mommy, so he probably has milk for me too."

14. "The having of the idea of any thing in our mind no more proves the existence of that thing, than the picture of a man evidences his being in the world." (John Locke, *Essay Concerning Human Understanding*)

15. "Compromise makes a good umbrella but a poor roof; it is a temporary expedient." (James Russell Lowell)

16. "By good works a lively faith may be as evidently known as a tree discerned by the fruits." (Anglican *39 Articles of Religion*)

17. "Reason can no more influence the willing than the eyes which show a man his road can enable him to move from place to place, or than a ship with a compass can sail without a wind." (Richard Whately, *Elements of Rhetoric*)

18. "A woman without a man is like a fish without a bicycle." (feminist slogan)

19. "As a wall'd town is more worthier than a village, so is the forehead of a married man more honourable than the bare brow of a bachelor." (Shakespeare, *As You Like It* 3, 3)
20. Judith Jarvis Thompson, defending abortion, used the analogy between a woman who is unwillingly pregnant and a woman who is kidnapped, tied to a hospital bed, and hooked up to a famous violinist, who needs her rare blood type, by continuous intravenous blood transfusion. If she pulls the plug, the violinist will die. But this act is morally legitimate. Therefore so is abortion.

Section 7. *A fortiori* and *a minore* arguments

These are really forms of argument by analogy. The *a fortiori* ("all the stronger") argument reasons that if something is true in one case, it is probably true in a second, similar case in which the reason for it being true is even stronger. For instance, "What father among you, if his son asks for a fish, will instead of a fish give him a serpent; or if he asks for an egg, will give him a scorpion? If you then, who are evil, know how to give good gifts to your children, how much more will the heavenly Father give the Holy Spirit to those who ask him!" (Luke 11:11) (Jesus had a penchant for *a fortiori* arguments.)

The *a minore* ("all the less") argument is simply the negative version of the *a fortiori*, and the two are convertible. For instance, the above *a fortiori* argument could have been transformed into an *a minore* argument if it had concluded, "how much less will the heavenly Father give you evil instead of good?"

Here is an *a minore* argument from the rocket scientist Wernher von Braun: "Scientists now believe that in nature matter cannot be destroyed without being converted to energy. Not even the tiniest particle can disappear without a trace. Nature does not know extinction – only transformation. Would God have less regard for His masterpiece of creation, the human soul?" (*The Miami News*, 8/6/66)

Sometimes a given argument can be interpreted either as an *a fortiori* or *a minore* argument or as a simple argument from analogy. E.g. "Whoever does not bear his own cross and come after me, cannot be my disciple. For which of you, desiring to build a tower, does not first sit down and count the cost, whether he has enough to complete it? Otherwise, when he has laid a foundation, and is not able to finish, all who see it begin to mock him, saying, 'This man began to build and was not able to finish.' Or what king, going to encounter another king in war, will not sit down first and take counsel whether he is able with ten thousand to meet him who comes against him with twenty thousand? And if not, while the other is yet a great way off, he sends an embassy and asks terms of peace. So therefore, whoever of you does not renounce all that he has cannot be my disciple." (Luke 14:27–33)

The criteria for evaluating an *a fortiori* or *a minore* argument are commonsensical and essentially the same as those for evaluating any argument from analogy.

An Exercise on Nearly Everything

The following argumentative dialogue tests your ability to integrate the whole of this book in a practical way: to know which logical tools are needed to evaluate each step of the long argument, and to use them.

The topic is deliberately controversial (feminism, gender, and women's "roles") to test your ability to be objective and logical even about an emotionally volatile issue.

The numbers in the margin are for easy reference. They correspond to distinct steps in the conversation, each requiring its own logical analysis and evaluation, as well as being related to its preceding and following steps.

You may not be able to see how all 71 distinct steps can be explained and evaluated by some specific point in this book, but the more you can do, the better. This would be a good exercise to work on with one or two other students, to multiply the angles of vision and to discuss each point together.

Fatima is a very conservative Iraqi Muslim. Tiffany is a very "liberal" American. Socrates is – well, Socrates. He enters the conversation near the end and produces some consternation in both his dialogue partners, as is his wont.

1	Tiffany:	You know, Fatima, you're a swell person even though you were brought up in an awfully repressive society. I guess that proves free will is stronger than social conditioning.
2	Fatima:	How dare you insult my people by complimenting me! They are part of me. They are my family.
3	Tiffany:	I'm sorry; I didn't mean to insult your people – I mean the individuals. I meant your social system.
4	Fatima:	What's wrong with our social system?
	Tiffany:	All the injustices, of course.
5	Fatima:	Why do you say that?
	Tiffany:	Everybody knows your society is full of injustices.
6	Fatima:	Well, I don't. And I lived there. Did you?
	Tiffany:	No . . .
7	Fatima:	In fact, I believe my society is one of the most just societies on earth.
8	Tiffany:	You sound so certain! Well, I guess that's true for you.
	Fatima:	How can something be "true for you" unless it's *true*?
9	Tiffany:	Look, let's not argue, OK? You love your society, and that's great; because love is always great, even though "love is blind."
10	Fatima:	No it isn't!
	Tiffany:	Of course it is: look at you. Look at what it's done to you: it's made you blind to injustice.
11	Fatima:	Either Iraq is one of the most just societies on Earth or I'm as blind to injustice as a bat is to the sun. And I am *not* that blind.
12	Tiffany:	OK, prove it. Prove Iraq is one of the most just societies on Earth.
	Fatima:	Iraq is an Islamic society. And Islamic society is formed by Islamic law. And Islamic law is the most just law on Earth.

13	Tiffany:	But how can your society be just if it oppresses women?
14	Fatima:	It couldn't possibly oppress women, because oppression is unnatural, and our law, Islamic law, is the true natural law.
15	Tiffany:	Natural? Just? When it doesn't even allow a woman to vote or appear in public without a veil? You gotta be kidding.
16	Fatima:	You don't understand. That's not injustice; it's letting women be in their proper place.
17	Tiffany:	You sound like some male chauvinist pig! Do you really think you should be kept in your "proper place" like a dog in a cage or a baby in a crib?
18	Fatima:	No, like a woman in a family. What's wrong with that? Do you think it's *unjust* to have a proper place?
19	Tiffany:	That's not our definition of justice. We believe justice is equality.
20	Fatima:	If that's so, then you must believe it's unjust that men can't have babies.
21	Tiffany:	So your definition of justice is putting everyone in their so-called proper place? Even if some tyrant defines your 'proper place'?
22	Fatima:	No. That wouldn't be justice. Tyranny can't be justice.
23	Tiffany:	Why not? It fits your definition.
	Fatima:	Because it's disharmony. Justice is *proper* place, and that always means harmony.
24	Tiffany:	But not equality?
	Fatima:	No. Justice is harmonious order among unequals.
	Tiffany:	That's a terrible definition! Slavery could be just then.
25	Fatima:	No. Slavery isn't just because slavery isn't harmony.
26	Tiffany:	But what if it is? What if the slaves are brainwashed into behaving harmoniously and even being contented?
27	Fatima:	No, no. Justice and slavery can't match. Slavery isn't justice because justice isn't slavery.
28	Tiffany:	That doesn't prove anything. I still want to know how you can call your society's oppression of women "harmonious order" *or* "justice." Oppressing *any* people isn't "harmonious order" or "justice." And women are people, you know. Or is that fact news to you, maybe?
29	Fatima:	We don't oppress women; we liberate women. You can't be both oppressed and liberated at the same time.
30	Tiffany:	You still haven't proved anything yet. You're just shifting words around.
31	Fatima:	What's wrong with my argument?
	Tiffany:	I think there's something wrong with the *arguer*. Anyone who defends oppression must be oppressed herself. And you're defending oppression.
32	Fatima:	Then I will show you another argument. Tell me, Tiffany, does oppression make you happy? Can the oppressed by happy?

Tiffany:	Of course not.
Fatima:	But our women are happy. That proves they're not oppressed.
33 Tiffany:	Who says they're happy?
34 Fatima:	They do! We do! And if they say they're happy, then they're happy. How could you be mistaken about that?
35 Tiffany:	You can't be as happy as American women are. Look at all the things we have that you can't have . . .
36 Fatima:	Don't bother listing the things. Things can't make you happy.
37 Tiffany:	Well, we've *got* the happiness and we've got the things; don't you think that shows there's a connection?
38 Fatima:	You *don't* have the happiness. You're not as happy as we are.
39 Tiffany:	Wait a minute. You just said no one could be mistaken about whether she's happy or not. Now you're saying *we're* mistaken about being happy.
40 Fatima:	No, I'm saying you're unhappy and you know it. The polls show it. The statistics show it. The suicides show it.
41 Tiffany:	And does Iraq have polls and statistics? Can we compare?
42 Fatima:	We can compare us, anyway. You are an American woman, aren't you? And I am an Iraqi woman, right?
Tiffany:	Yes.
Fatima:	And which one of us is smiling and which one frowning now?
Tiffany:	But . . .
Fatima:	Please answer my question, and then I will answer yours.
Tiffany:	You're smiling and I'm frowning. But . . .
Fatima:	And do people smile when they're unhappy? And do they frown when they're happy?
Tiffany:	No, but . . .
Fatima:	See? American women are unhappy and Iraqi women are happy.
43	What makes the difference? What's the missing factor in America that's present in Iraq? Islamic law. Islamic law makes us happy. The proof of the pudding is in the eating – isn't that what you
44	say? And may I also tell you why you are unhappy?
Tiffany:	Why?
Fatima:	Because you are oppressed.
Tiffany:	What? *We're* oppressed?
Fatima:	Which one of us is frowning and complaining and unhappy?
Tiffany:	I am. Because . . .
Fatima:	And which one of us is happy?
Tiffany:	You are. Because . . .
Fatima:	And which kind of person is happy: the oppressed or the free?
Tiffany:	The free.
Fatima:	See? We are the free. You are the oppressed.
45 Tiffany:	This is ridiculous. Why are we oppressed, according to your wacky perspective?

Fatima:	I think your unhappiness began after you started insisting on equal rights, defining justice as equality instead of harmonious order. So I think that is the cause of your unhappiness.	
46 Tiffany:	Fatima, you have been brainwashed.	
Fatima:	Well, thank you, Tiffany. I'd rather have a brain that's washed and clean than one that's dirty.	
47 Tiffany:	I guess our minds are just so totally different that we'll just have to agree to disagree about everything.	
48 Fatima	Even that?	
Tiffany:	What do you mean?	
Fatima	Isn't that a self-contradiction?	
49 Tiffany:	Where do you think we are, in a logic book or something?	
Fatima:	So you are giving up on the argument?	
50 Tiffany:	No! It's my turn to cross-examine you now. Tell me, if justice is "harmonious order among *un*equals," does that mean that women are not equal to men?	
51 Fatima:	Of course women are not equal to men. Everyone knows we're different. And if we're different, we're not equal. And it's either "equal" or "unequal." Thus, it's "unequal."	
52 Tiffany:	But unless you're either superior or inferior, you're *not* unequal. So you must think we women are either superior or inferior to men. Do you think we are superior?	
Fatima:	No – not socially.	
Tiffany:	Then we must be inferior to men.	
53 Fatima:	Yes, socially, our nature and our place is to submit to our men. You simply cannot believe that, can you?	
Tiffany:	Absolutely not!	
54 Fatima:	So you must therefore believe that we are by nature equal.	
55 Tiffany:	Of course! Our social inequalities all come from society, from oppressive societies, like yours.	
56 Fatima:	So you are saying that society invented wombs?	
Tiffany:	Of course not. Why would I say that?	
Fatima:	Because our wombs are certainly one of our biggest differences, one of our biggest "social inequalities." If our inequalities come from society, then our wombs come from society, which is absurd.	
57 Socrates:	Excuse me, ladies, but I have been listening to your argument for quite a while now, and I'd like to try to help you both by asking one wee little question. Do you both see that you are assuming the same highly questionable premise?	
Both:	No. What is it?	
58 Socrates:	I'd really rather let you find it. *Answering* questions has always seemed to me a less effective way to train minds than *asking* them. Don't you see it?	

59 Tiffany: All I see is that Fatima here is buying into the old, repressive stereotypes like "a woman's nature" and "a woman's place" and "the feminine mind."

60 Socrates: So you believe there is no such thing as a woman's nature? Doesn't everything we can speak about meaningfully have some sort of nature?

61 Tiffany: Yes, but surely you don't believe there is such a thing as "the feminine mind." Obviously there is a biological difference in our bodies, but "the feminine mind" is a social convention. In fact, "the feminine mind" is a fiction invented by the masculine mind!

62 Socrates: I think you may have a self-contradiction there . . .

63 Tiffany: I was only kidding, not literal.

64 Socrates: Tell me, Tiffany: do you agree with my disciple Plato that a human being is essentially a mind? Or with *his* disciple, Aristotle, that a human is essentially what psychologists call a psychosomatic unity, one substance with two dimensions, material and mental, rather than two substances?

Tiffany: Aristotle, I think. He sounds much more commonsensical.

65 Socrates: And that "psychosomatic unity" – does it mean that any essential and innate quality that pervades all of either of these two dimensions must have some natural effect in the other?

Tiffany: That seems true.

66 Socrates: And are masculinity and femininity essential and innate and all-pervasive qualities of the body? Or does our biological gender come from social convention too, as "the feminine mind" does?

Tiffany: It's by nature. I wouldn't call it "all-pervasive" though. That's sexism.

67 Socrates: I don't know what you mean by "sexism," but our identity as masculine or feminine pervades every cell in our bodies, doesn't it?

Tiffany: Yes.

Socrates: So it seems to follow then that it must have some effect on our other dimension, according to the principle of the psychosomatic unity that you believe.

Tiffany: I guess that follows.

68 Socrates: Does it not also follow, then, that there is some truth to the old idea of a "feminine mind" and a "masculine mind"?

69 Fatima: Congratulations, Socrates. So you agree with me in seeing that women are quite naturally and quite happily inferior.

Socrates: I did not say that, Fatima. Nor do I believe it.

70 Fatima: But you must see that that logically follows, Socrates. You are the father of logic, after all.

71 Socrates: Yes, and you two are the mothers of the same unquestioned assumption from which both of your opposite conclusions follow. Don't you see it? You really should take a logic course some time, and pay close attention to enthymemes!

Texts for Logical Analysis

Here are a few suggestions of philosophical texts for longer, more ambitious, and more advanced logical analysis of philosophical arguments. Some are much longer than others; the longer ones can be divided further and done in part.

I. relatively easy

1. St. Thomas Aquinas, *Summa Theologica* i-ii, 1, 2, "Those Things In Which Happiness Consists," in eight articles (all easy syllogisms but good practice and profoundly practical content)
2. Plato, the part of *Apology of Socrates* that contains Socrates' dialogue with Meletus
3. Peter Kreeft, *Between Heaven and Hell*, the first half (the dialogue between C.S. Lewis and J.F. Kennedy)
4. Kreeft, *The Unaborted Socrates*, the first dialogue
5. Kreeft, *Socrates Meets Jesus*, any of the dialogues, especially "Candy Confessions"
6. Kreeft, *The Best Things in Life*, any of the dialogues, especially #6 or #12
7. Kreeft, *Ecumenical Jihad*, the Luther-Aquinas-C.S. Lewis trialogue
8. Kreeft, *Socrates Meets Machiavelli*, any of the chapters
9. Kreeft, *Socrates Meets Marx*, any of the chapters
10. Kreeft, *Socrates Meets Sartre*, any of the chapters
11. Kreeft, *Socrates Meets Descartes*, any of the chapters
12. Kreeft, *Socrates Meets Hume*, any of the chapters
13. Kreeft, *Socrates Meets Kant*, any of the chapters

II. Intermediate

1. St. Thomas Aquinas, almost any of the articles in the *Summa Theologica*
2. Boethius, *The Consolation of Philosophy*, Book 4
3. Plato, *Republic*, Book 1, the dialogues between Socrates and Cephalus and between Socrates and Polymarchus
4. Plato, *Meno*
5. Plato, *Euthyphro*
6. Plato, *Phaedo*, the three arguments for immortality
7. Plato, *Crito*
8. Plato, *Gorgias*, the first half, the dialogues between Socrates and Gorgias and/or between Socrates and Polus

III. Harder

1. St. Thomas Aquinas, *Summa Theologica* i, 2, 3, the "five ways"
2. C.S. Lewis, *Miracles*, chapter 3
3. Plato, *Republic*, Book 1, last half, the dialogue between Socrates and Thrasymachus
4. Plato, *Gorgias*, second half, the dialogue between Socrates and Callicles
5. Berkeley, *Three Dialogues between Hylas and Philonous*

XV. Some Practical Applications of Socratic Logic

Section 1. How to write a logical essay

Students are required to write essays throughout their educational career. This ability can even determine whether or not you get into a good college or graduate school, or get good enough grades to stay in. The simple, three-acts-of-the-mind structure of Socratic-Aristotelian logic gives us an ideal simplified form for writing an effective, clear, and persuasive essay.

What follows is certainly not the *only* good way to write a persuasive essay. But it is a simple and effective way, and many intelligent students today have never been taught even this simple form. That is why it may seem at first artificial and confining, or "picky" and over-strict. However, following this seven-step guideline in each detail can make a tremendous difference: the difference between a vague, weak, rambling, disordered, confusing, and therefore non-persuasive essay and a sharp, strong, economical, orderly, clear, and convincing one.

It will feel rigid at first, but rigid forms are necessary for beginners in every field. Aspiring poets should first learn to write sonnets before writing free verse. Pianists must master scales and chords and Bach's two-part Inventions. Babies need walkers, and the lame need crutches, and sinners need "organized religion."

The principles below can apply to argumentative essays of any length but especially to a medium length essay in the neighborhood of 3–6 pages.

HOW TO WRITE A LOGICAL (ARGUMENTATIVE) ESSAY

1. **Choose a good topic**. A good topic for a logical essay has all three of the following qualities:
   (a) It is *controversial*, that is, argued-about, not obvious. "War is painful" is not controversial; "all wars are unjust" is. "Man is mortal" is not controversial; "man can be made immortal" is.

(b) It is *specific*. "Philosophers have helped humanity" is not specific; "Aristotle's philosophy helped the progress of science more than Descartes's philosophy did" is specific.

(c) It is *an either/or*: a single question with only two possible answers, as in formal debates. "What is God?" is not a good topic; "Is God unchanging?" is.

2. **Explain the importance of your question**, to motivate the reader's interest. What *difference* is made by answering it in one way vs. the other way?

3. **Give your answer (thesis, conclusion)**. This is the "point" of your whole essay. This tends to come at the end in a Socratic dialogue, but it should usually be "upfront" and come at the beginning in an essay.

4. **Define your terms**. Terms need defining if they are
   (a) *ambiguous* (can be taken in two or more different senses); or
   (b) *obscure or technical* to some readers; or
   (c) *controversial* (i.e. imply a presupposition that not everyone agrees with, like "anti-life" or "anti-choice" in an essay on abortion. Avoid such terms in an essay unless you need them and will defend them).

5. **Prove your thesis**. Give one or more *reasons* (arguments) for it. These reasons will be either *inductive* (from specific examples) or *deductive* (from a general principle) or both.
   If they are deductive, your reasons will be either *linear* (A, therefore B, therefore C, therefore D) or *cumulative* (D is true because of A, and also because of B, and also because of C).
   Each of your arguments should have
   (a) no ambiguous terms,
   (b) no false premises, and
   (c) no logical fallacies (i.e. the conclusion should follow necessarily from the premises)

6. **Summarize and then answer your opponent's arguments**, i.e. the strongest and most commonly given arguments for the opposite position. (Remember, since you formulated your thesis in an either/or, yes-or-no form, there are only two possible answers to your question.)
   To refute an argument, you do not merely find a counter argument to prove the opposite conclusion, but you must
   (a) first summarize the argument honestly and fairly;
   (b) then analyze (take apart) the argument and explain what is wrong with it. That is, you must find and show the presence of one of the only three things that can go wrong with an argument:

(1) a term used ambiguously (Which term? Distinguish its two meanings. Show how it has changed its meaning in the course of your opponent's argument.); or

(2) a false premise (Which premise? Is it stated or implied? If implied, prove that it is *necessarily* implied. Whether stated or implied, show that it is false; give reasons for disagreeing with it.); or

(3) a logical fallacy. (Which fallacy? Use the principles in this book to show that the conclusion does not logically follow from the premises.)

7. **Anticipate and answer objections**. To be maximally complete and fair, add one more step:

(a) imagine the strongest way your opponent would try to refute *your* arguments (that you gave in part 5) in one of the three ways above, and then

(b) defend your argument against these criticisms.

Section 2. How to write a Socratic dialogue

I have written and published about a dozen full-length books of Socratic dialogues, and judging by reader reactions, they are the most successful and appreciated of my 50-odd published books. So I want to spread the secret (which is no secret at all, as far as I can see).

Like most philosophy students, I loved reading Plato and found the dramatic form of dialogue much more engaging than the monologue. A monologue is more likely to commit the one unforgivable sin of any writer, boring the reader, because it has only one voice, it is impersonal, and it usually lacks drama. I wondered why so few other philosophers copied Plato's dialogue form, and why even when they did, the dialogues were not really Socratic. I still don't know. (Augustine's *On the Teacher* and Berkeley's *Three Dialogues Between Hylas and Philonous* are the only two lasting philosophical classics I know in dialogue form, unless you count Boethius's *The Consolation of Philosophy* as a dialogue too).

No one knows how close Plato's Socrates is to the actual historical Socrates, but Plato surely included *some* invented fiction, however closely based on Socrates' historical character; so I could think of no reason why we today could not extend the historical figure of Socrates through our own imagination. I asked many people why we couldn't, but no one gave me an answer. So I tried a simple experiment, with my students as the guinea pigs.

I always introduce students to philosophy first through Socrates, and I encourage original essays, so I suggested that the students write their essays by imitating Plato's form and writing Socratic dialogues. Many tried it, and almost all succeeded, both by their own estimation and by mine. If students can do it, why can't teachers? I couldn't imagine why. So to find out why it can't be done,

I did it. And the answer is simply that there is *no* reason why it can't be done. Furthermore, I think I can even give at least a few pieces of pretty obvious and commonsensical advice to others now about *how* to do it. Here they are:

A. Points of personal advice to the writer:
1. As with most enterprises, the first and necessary step is: "Begin!" "Just do it." "Try." For "well begun is half done" (ancient Greek proverb) and "whatever is worth doing, is worth doing badly" (G.K. Chesterton).
2. Don't be afraid to imitate. Apprenticeship by imitation was the primary method of teaching almost anything (and it worked!) until the modern cult of individuality and originality. You can never be as creative or original by trying to be original as you can by forgetting all about originality and just "doing your thing."
   And if anyone is imitable and worth imitating, it's Socrates.
3. So immerse yourself in Socrates. Read all Plato's earlier dialogues, up to *Republic*, Book I. (After that, the personality of Socrates recedes and Plato the professor emerges. He may be an excellent professor, and a great philosopher, and his system may be a valid extension of Socrates' beginnings, but he's just not Socrates, as St. Paul may be a profoundly wise and great Christian but he's just not Jesus.)
4. Instinctive and inward imitation is better than contrived and external imitation. Let the *spirit* of Socrates get under your skin, so that you can use your imagination and ask yourself: What would the real, historical Socrates have said here? Socrates' method is only partially technical and able to be formulated objectively and impersonally. Learn both parts, but don't neglect the inner spirit.
5. There are two ways to write a Socratic dialogue: (a) You can simply use your imagination, be Socrates and his dialogue partner (let us call him "O" for "other"), and let the argument and the two personalities carry you wherever they naturally go, like a river. (b) Or you can make a logical map of the argument before you begin, and add the dramatic and personal dimension to it as you write. If (b) proves too un-Socratic and artificial, try (a). If (a) proves to be too unstructured, use (b) at least for a while. After some practice with (b) you may be able to transition to (a).
6. Whether you use (a) or (b) above, you must know logic, naturally and instinctively. Don't think you can master this section without mastering the rest of this book.
7. In the process of arguing, use the rules for Socratic debate on pages 348–50. Also see pages 211–14.

B. Points of advice in constructing the dramatic character of Socrates:
1. Confine yourself to only two characters, Socrates and "O." Perhaps later you can add other characters, as Plato does, but even then each should take

his turn: do not put three or more people into the conversation *at once* (except perhaps very briefly). If you do, that will loosen its logical structure, and *argument* will turn into *conversation*.

2. The initial question should arise naturally from an ordinary situation or conversation. It should not be artificial or imposed, but arise from "O's" interests.

3. Like Plato, you might want to add the little trick of placing a veiled clue to the central point of the dialogue in the very first line.

4. Socrates asks the questions rather than giving the answers (except, perhaps, in response to his dialogue partner's questions). Remember, Socrates is not a preacher. (This is easy to understand, but surprisingly hard to obey.)

5. There is always an ironic contrast between Socrates' knowing that he doesn't know and "O's" not knowing that he doesn't know. The one who seems to know, doesn't; and the one who seems not to know, does. The one who seems to be the student (Socrates) is really the teacher, and vice versa.

6. This irony may emerge in the interaction between the characters if "O" is a bit arrogant – in which case Socrates gets a chance to use his (always light and subtle) ironic wit and humor. But "O" should never be unfairly treated, put down, or preached at; and neither should the reader.

7. The personal, psychological struggle is as much a part of the Socratic dialogue as the struggle of ideas. A Socratic dialogue is a form of spiritual warfare, therapy, or doctoring to the spirit of the student. Yet paradoxically, it is for this reason that you must avoid direct personal confrontation and let the *argument* always be the object of attention. Socrates sees himself and "O" not as a winner and a loser but as two scientists mutually seeking the truth by testing two alternative hypotheses. Whichever one finds the truth, both are winners.

8. Socrates' goal is always ultimately somehow moral (though this is not always apparent at first). For he has only one lifetime, and it is too precious to waste on issues that are not somehow connected to the most important purpose of human life, becoming more wise and virtuous.

9. Socrates' aim is not to harm but to help "O." Sometimes, this involves shame, but it never involves a conflict of interests – at least not from Socrates' point of view. "O" may or may not understand this, but Socrates, like Jesus, is altruistic in his very offensiveness. He believes, as Aquinas says, that "there is no greater act of charity one can do to his neighbor than to lead him to the truth." Socratic dialogue is ultimately missionary work.

C. Points of advice about the logical method:
1. The question must be defined early on.
2. The question should be formulated disjunctively, so that it has only two

possible answers. Otherwise, an infinite number of arguments, and of dialogues, will be necessary. In the *Republic*, e.g., the question "What is justice?" quickly becomes "Is justice the interest of the stronger or not?" and "Is justice always more profitable than injustice or not?"

3. Potentially ambiguous terms must be defined by mutual agreement.

4. Like a psychoanalyst, Socrates does not give his opinion unless it is demanded, but asks "O" what *he* believes.

5. Once he gets an answer from "O," Socrates may now use one or more of the following strategies:

   (a) Ask "O" *why* he believes this, and examine "O's" argument, looking for an ambiguous term, a false premise, or a logical fallacy; or

   (b) Trace "O's" premises back to further premises, either by *showing* what missing premises "O's" enthymemes must presuppose or else *asking* "O" to prove his premises, and then examining that proof; or

   (c) Draw out the consequences of "O's" belief, in a (usually multi-step) *reductio ad absurdum*, or

   (d) Construct an argument whose conclusion will be the contradictory of "O's" belief. If Socrates does this, his argument should begin well "upstream" from the falls where "O" will come to grief. It should usually be a long, linear epicheirema, whose first premise "O" will agree to, like a man who puts his boat into a calm, inviting river upstream, and then finds that the river takes him downstream to rapids and waterfalls – and sinking. However, sometimes this argument is short, often an argument by analogy.

6. After the "sinking" the dialogue can end, or begin again with another attempt.

7. Socrates rarely uses cumulative arguments for the same conclusion, preferring one very sure and carefully worked out argument rather than a larger number of weaker arguments that need reinforcements. When he does use a number of cumulative arguments (e.g. in the *Phaedo* to prove the immortality of the soul) they are usually surprisingly unconvincing. (Contrast *Republic* X's more convincing single argument for immortality.)

8. See pages 294, Section 2, and 308, last paragraph, on the use of hypothetical reasoning.

9. The dialogue ends either with closure and proof (as in the *Republic*) or not (as in the *Meno*). If with closure, "O" may accept this (as in the *Republic*) or not (as in the *Gorgias*). If the dialogue does not end with closure, a better answer may be suggested (as in the *Meno*) or it may not (as in the *Euthyphro*).

10. If Socrates interacts with modern people, remember that he is not a typically modern person – in his personality, in his assumptions, in his style of speech, or in his unlimited patience.

Section 3. How to have a Socratic debate

The Middle Ages "institutionalized" two forms of Socratic debate. One was the "Scholastic Disputation," an elaborate, demanding, and (to modern minds) artificial form. The subject was usually a highly technical philosophical or theological question, and the format was confined to strictly labeled syllogistic forms. The other was the written form of the "article" in a *Summa*, a collection of abbreviated summaries of such a disputation, the most famous of which was the *Summa Theologica* of St. Thomas Aquinas.

Neither form is ideal for debate today without revision, for the Scholastic Disputation is too long (they often lasted for half a day), and the *Summa* article too short (it is often only one page or less). But the basic principles that governed such debates can be summarized and used to good effect in a modern, more informal (and thus more Socratic) dialogue.

Some of these rules were explicitly stated, some assumed and implied, by medieval debaters. The reader will notice the similarity of many of the following points to those that we have already listed as governing a Socratic dialogue; for in a sense both the Scholastic Disputation and the *Summa* were systematizations of the Socratic dialogue.

A. Some rules about attitudes and presuppositions:
1. Total honesty is presupposed. This means (a) that the aim of both parties must be simply to seek and find the truth; (b) that this truth is *the* truth, not "my" truth or "your" truth – i.e. objective and universal truth; and (c) that personal victory or defeat should be purely incidental and not the goal aimed at. (This will be difficult. What does that tell you about yourself?)
2. Neither party to the debate should be either a skeptic (who believes that no one can hope to know anything) or a personal dogmatist (who believes that he already knows it all). A skeptic thinks he can't be right and a dogmatist thinks he can't be wrong. Neither has a reason to inquire.
3. Both the fear of reason (which Socrates calls "misology" in the *Phaedo*) and scorn of anything other than pure reason ("rationalism" in the worst sense) are rejected at the outset.

B. Some rules about protocol and procedures:
1. Reasons must always be given when asked for. "Why?" is always a legitimate question.
2. "Follow the argument wherever it goes." Reason is the common master. The two debaters are like rafts, and the argument is like a river.
3. The river has both calm and turbulent parts, and perhaps rocks and waterfalls. But the aim is to find the sea, not to tip your opponent's raft over.
4. Always listen before you respond, so that you respond to what was actually said. In fact, no one has the right to respond to his opponent's argument

until he has first restated that argument, in his own words (to prove that he understands the meaning, not just the words), to his opponent's satisfaction.

5. The order must always be: first data (what, exactly, was actually said?), then interpretation of the data (what the speaker meant, not what the hearer would have meant), then evaluation and argument (is he right or wrong?). This might be called "constructionism," for it is in explicit contradiction to the method that calls itself "Deconstructionism," perhaps the most polar opposite to a Socratic debate in the entire history of philosophy.

6. Two formats are possible. (a) In the formal one, each debater is given a set amount of time to state, and his opponent to try to refute, his argument, turn by turn. E.g. A summarizes his argument in 5 minutes, then B has 5 minutes to respond, then A has 5 minutes to respond to B, then B gets another 5 minutes, etc., either for a pre-set amount of time or until the moderator (or both debaters) decide they are "debated out." (b) In the informal format, pre-set time structures are not imposed.

7. Whether the time is explicitly counted and monitored or not, in both formats each debater must be given approximately equal time, or at least enough time to satisfy him and his need to explain himself.

8. The debate will usually work better with an impartial moderator, but it can sometimes work without one, if both parties adhere conscientiously to all the rules. Any two people can start a debate club, or a "Saint Socrates Society." Try it! You might begin a Quiet Revolution

C. Some rules about arguing logically:
1. Arguments must be stated explicitly, preferably (though not necessarily) in syllogistic form.
2. When confronted by an argument, there are *only* four legitimate responses:
   a. "I do not accept your conclusion because you have used a term ambiguously (and I will point out which term that is and show how you have used it ambiguously)"; or
   b. "I do not accept your conclusion because you have assumed a false premise (and I will show [1] which premise it is, [2] why it is logically necessary for you to assume it, and [3] why it is false)"; or
   c. "I do not accept your conclusion because your argument contains a logical fallacy (and I will point out this fallacy in your argument)"; or
   d. "I can find no ambiguous term, false premise, or logical fallacy in your argument, therefore I must accept your conclusion as true (since I am an honest, intelligent, open-minded seeker of objective truth rather than a dishonest, stupid, closed-minded seeker of personal victory)."
      There is no fifth option, "I can find none of these three errors in your argument; you have proved your conclusion to be true; but I do

not accept it. I will not tell you why. Instead, this conclusion you have proved to be objectively true I will label 'your' truth, as I hug 'my' truth to myself like an auto-erotic intellectual security blanket."

3. When your opponent finds an ambiguously-used term, you must redefine it and reword your argument without ambiguity, or else abandon your argument and find another one. When he claims to find a false premise, you must prove that it is not false, or else that you do not need to assume this premise. When he claims to find a logical fallacy, you must show that he has misunderstood your argument, or else reword your argument to avoid the fallacy.

4. Do not leave arguments "hanging." Do not respond to his argument proving x simply by an argument proving non-x.

5. One long, linear, many-step argument is preferable to many cumulative arguments because this "backs up" the discussion onto more and more fundamental premises, so that even if no one "wins" the debate, both see more clearly the more basic reasons behind their disagreement.

6. Be honest enough to change your mind if your opponent convinces you. Remember, no one loses a Socratic debate except ignorance, and no one wins except truth. If no one finds truth, both lose. If one finds it, both win.

These many points of advice will seem very complex and difficult if you have no experience of reading Socratic dialogues, but quite simple, easy, and obvious if you have – which shows that induction, starting with concrete experience, is a much more effective method of learning than deduction, starting with abstract principles. The same holds for learning ethics as for learning Socratic method, by the way. (Saints teach it more effectively than philosophers.)

Section 4. How to use Socratic method on difficult people

Although *not* effective in dealing with homicidal maniacs or people in a state of panic, the Socratic method is ideally suited for dialogue with "difficult people," or threatening people, people with whom we are not in friendly debate but in confrontation. The method emerged from the confrontations in ancient Athenian law courts, especially the technique of cross-examination, when Socrates began to cross-examine ideas, not just people. It was difficult for these people to realize that Socrates' confrontational arguments were not directed against them, as if they were in court, but against their ideas.

The essence of the Socratic method is this logical cross-examination of an idea, following the argument wherever its inner logic takes it. Thus, the impersonal laws of logic become a "common master" rather than either person mastering the other, and the argument is not "me vs. you" but "us vs. ignorance"; not "we are not together because we differ about what is true" but "let us try to find the truth together." The personal confrontation is thus defused.

But a "difficult person" (let us call him DP) is difficult precisely because he or she *refuses* this attitude of "let us try to find the truth together." Either DP does not believe in objective truth at all, and is a principled subjectivist; or else he cannot or will not believe that he lacks this truth and his opponent has it (i.e. he is an egotist – which is usually a cover-up for a very fragile and threatened ego, as the bully is the cover-up for the coward). The charm of the Socratic method is that it seems tailor-made for such people. For (1) it allows the truth to seep in under their defenses like subterranean water as they are busy erecting walls against the army of opposing ideas on the surface; and (2) it allows DP to be his own corrector, thus saving his ego. When you play Socrates *you* do not define the truth; you only ask questions and let DP define the truth with *his* answers, which then become your teacher which you explore and examine humbly, on the assumption that it is true, not false. (In the course of your examination, of course, you discover that this assumption is questionable, and let us hope that DP discovers this too.)

The art of Socratic dialogue resists being put into a universal and unchangeable formula, since you as Socrates must be flexible enough to follow DP wherever he takes you. And this is one of the keys to its usefulness with difficult people: it is in thus *serving* DP that you become the *master*, or rather allow truth to become the master.

Thus the Socratic method, used with a "difficult person," is an illustration of the irony of Hegel's famous "master-slave dialectic," in which the master is really the slave, enslaved to the slave he needs, while the slave is free and thus is really the master, for he does not need the master while the master needs him.

To say the same thing in a different way and using a different historical reference, it is an illustration of the Taoist principle that the humble, yielding water-like attitude is the one that conquers the proud, "difficult," self-assertive, rock-like one – ultimately because the first attitude corresponds to the nature of ultimate reality, and thus is, ultimately, the most "realistic."

Still another historical reference to the same mysterious principle is the Christian one: he who would be last becomes first and he who would be first becomes last. In the Kingdom, the greatest is the servant of all, since this Kingdom is nothing less than the epiphany or manifestation of the divine King whose eternal and essential nature is revealed by the King's Son to be self-giving love. Thus the Socratic method, like the Taoist and Zen arts, is ultimately rooted in the nature of God, if Christianity is true.

Taoists' favorite symbol for this art is water. By its softness it wears away hard rock. It seeps in under walls and defenses precisely because it seeks the lowest, humblest places. Water has no form itself; that is why it can conform to any form, fill containers of any size and shape.

However, there is an intrinsic structure to water (H_2O), and to the Socratic method even when used with "difficult people." As soon as the "Socrates" and the DP are engaged in conversation about whether some idea is true or not, that conversation must follow certain essential logical principles, even when the topic of the conversation is charged with "personal particles" as a dynamo is charged with electricity. And we can analyze the conversational process into steps and thus prepare its strategy beforehand. Those steps would be the following:

1. From the outset you must establish the Socratic **relationship**: you are the listener, not the teacher; the disciple, not the opponent; the one who needs to be shown the right, *not* the one who is in the right, or knows the right, or has the right while DP is the one who is wrong.

   The next three steps correspond to the three acts of the mind: first, the thesis (proposition), then the definition (terms), then the reasons (argument).

2. First, get clear what DP's basic contentious contention *is*. Find his thesis, or **conclusion**, or "bottom line." ("What, then, are you saying?")

3. Next, be sure you understand it as DP does. Ask for DP's definition of his **terms**. ("What, exactly, do you mean?")

4. Then, find DP's **reasons**, or evidence – not in the spirit of the inquisitor about to pounce on it and refute it, but in the spirit of the apprentice being led and instructed by the master. Ask "why?" in this spirit, like a good psychoanalyst.

5. After DP's thesis, terms, and reasons are clear, be sure to express your understanding of them, repeating them in your own words, so that it is clear to DP that there is at least one other person in the world who understands "where he's coming from." Difficult people often feel lonely and isolated, as if "no one else understands."

6. Once DP sees you are on his "side," you can begin the next step: exploration either "upstream" or "downstream" on the river of DP's original argument, i.e. the exploration either of DP's *premises* (and perhaps also *their* premises) or of the *consequences* of DP's conclusion.

   You have already taken care of the terms; you have "come to terms" with DP, so there is no misunderstanding and no ambiguity.

   You have also seen and stated DP's argument (though informally) to determine that there is no logical fallacy. Even difficult people rarely commit logical fallacies. And you should hope that DP has *not* done so, for it is rather embarrassing and insulting for anyone to be shown that his argument is fallacious; and (more to the point practically) being shown that his argument is fallacious will probably not change or convince DP, for he will still believe his conclusion. Everyone knows, instinctively, that showing that a given argument for a certain conclusion is weak or fallacious does not disprove that argument's conclusion. Everything is still "up for grabs."

   However, if there *is* a fallacy in DP's argument, you may still be able to show DP his fallacy in such a way that it disarms his hold on the conclusion. E.g. "Yes, he said this terrible thing to you yesterday. But it does not necessarily follow that he still feels the same way today; he may be feeling remorse." Or "Yes, he is a cannibal. But he doesn't want to eat *everybody*, so maybe he doesn't want to eat you." Or "Yes, he did a terrible job at X, and it is natural for you to conclude that he just doesn't care about X, or about you; but is it not possible that he cares too *much* about X, and had performance anxiety? Or that he has a mental block, or even a mental defect, that we do not know about? Perhaps it is his mind rather than his will that has the defect. Or perhaps there is some other cause we don't know about. Maybe his dog just died, or his mother-in-law just came back to life. Isn't it true that people sometimes do a terrible job at X even when they care?"

7. Suppose you are now convinced that it is not the *terms* or the *logic* of the argument, but the *propositions* that remain to be investigated. You believe that DP's thesis or conclusion is false, and you want to serve DP and the truth by opening up DP's mind to this possibility in a personally non-threatening way, so that DP sees it for himself. There are two paths, logically: "upstream" or "downstream": (A) to show DP what questionable premises are necessary to prove his thesis, or (B) to show DP what questionable conclusions his thesis necessarily entails when that thesis is taken as a premise. Both investigations can be undertaken nonthreateningly, for DP should be personally *interested* in his thesis, and therefore also in its premises and in its conclusions, or corollaries.

Although the "upstream" strategy (A) may be logically easier and more conclusive, the "downstream" strategy (B) is psychologically preferable. For it is easier to win DP's sympathy and attention with strategy (B), drawing out the further conclusions logically entailed by DP's thesis, because DP is already attached to his thesis and therefore suspicious of investigating its possibly-weak foundations (premises), which is what the "upstream" strategy does. Further, even if you do show DP the falseness of some of his premises, and thus the weakness of his argument, this may not wean him from his conclusion if he is attached to it; he can simply find another argument for it.

The "downstream" strategy is really *reductio ad absurdum*, for you show that if DP's thesis is true, it logically entails a conclusion that is so absurd that even DP must rethink his thesis. If you do this, be sure you do not give DP the impression that you think he believes this absurd conclusion that you deduce from his thesis, but rather that he does *not*. You will insult him if you seem to assume that he is stupid enough to believe an absurdity; you will compliment him if you seem to assume that he is intelligent enough to refuse to believe an absurdity. When you show DP that his wisdom in rejecting the absurd conclusion necessarily entails also rejecting his original thesis which logically entails that absurd conclusion, you enable DP to save face by correcting himself by his own wisdom instead of being corrected by yours.

8. Use options, dialectical (disjunctive) arguments, as much as you can, to give the difficult person a choice.

   Use dilemmas, but constructive rather than destructive dilemmas, so that DP does not feel "destroyed."

9. As a concrete example, watch how Socrates deals with Cephalus, Polemarchus, and above all, Thrasymachus, in Book I of the *Republic*, or with Gorgias, Polus, and Callicles in the *Gorgias*. Five or these six (not Polymarchus) are difficult people in different ways, and Socrates matches his style to their personalities, instinctively.

10. Reflect on the wisdom of Kierkegaard in *The Point of View for my Work as an Author*, in which he reflects upon and interprets all his previous books, and on the Socratic method he has used in them. He speaks here of "dispelling an illusion," which was Socrates' lifelong task.

> . . . A direct attack only strengthens a person in his illusion, and at the same time embitters him. There is nothing that requires such gentle handling as an illusion, if one wishes to dispel it. If anything prompts the prospective captive to set his will in opposition, all is lost. And this is what a direct attack achieves, and it implies moreover the presumption of requiring a man to make to another person, or in his presence, an admission which he can make most profitably to himself privately. This is what is achieved by the indirect method which, loving and serving the truth, arranges everything dialectically for the prospective captive, and then shyly withdraws (for love is always shy), so as not to witness the admission which he makes to himself alone before God – that he has lived hitherto in an illusion.
>
> . . . if real success is to attend the effort to bring a man to a definite position, one must first of all take pains to find him where he is and begin there. This is the secret art of helping others. Anyone who has not mastered this is himself deluded when he proposes to help others. In order to help another effectively I must understand more than he – yet first of all surely I must understand what he understands. If I do not know that, my greater understanding will be of no help to him . . . all true effort to help begins with self-humiliation: the helper must first humble himself under him he would help, and therewith must understand that to help does not mean to be a sovereign but to be a servant, that to help does not mean to be ambitious but to be patient, that to

help means to endure for the time being the imputation that one is in the wrong and does not understand what the other understands.

Take the case of a man who is passionately angry, and let us assume that he is really in the wrong. Unless you can begin with him by making it seem as if it were he that had to instruct you, and unless you can do it in such a way that the angry man, who was too impatient to listen to a word of yours, is glad to discover a complaisant and attentive listener – if you cannot do that, you cannot help him at all . . . if you cannot humble yourself, you are not genuinely serious. Be the amazed listener who sits and hears what the other finds the more delight in telling you because you listen with amazement . . .

If you can do that, if you can find exactly the place where the other is and begin there, you may perhaps have the luck to lead him to the place where you are.

For to be a teacher does not mean simply to affirm that such a thing is so, or to deliver a lecture, etc. No, to be a teacher in the right sense is to be a learner. Instruction begins when you, the teacher, learn from the learner, put yourself in his place so that you may understand what he understands in the way he understands it.

* * * * *

The point is (1) very simple, (2) very obvious, (3) and very rarely practiced. Apparently there are more than just intellectual difficulties in the way of practicing this method, since it is (1) simple to understand and (2) obviously correct. Why then is it (3) rare?

We learn the answer to this question when we learn the identity of the "difficult person." And we learn that by looking into a mirror. This is the most Socratic thing we can do: "know thyself."

Section 5. How to read a book Socratically

This section is basically a *very* short sample and summary of just a *few* of the most important ideas in Mortimer Adler's book *How to Read a Book*. This is an extremely useful book and highly recommended as a supplement to this one.

The following principles apply especially to nonfiction books, especially books designed to convince the reader of something. *How to Read a Book* shows how analogous principles apply to other kinds of books.

A. **Distinguish** *data*, *interpretation*, **and** *criticism*. You cannot intelligently agree or disagree until you have correctly interpreted a book, and you cannot interpret it until you have read it. First listen, then understand, then talk back. Do not interpret any book in light of your beliefs; that is putting these three steps backwards. Interpret a book in light of the author's beliefs. And when you do, base all your interpretations on the data, the text itself. Many misunderstandings come from simply not paying attention to the text.

Data, interpretation, and criticism are like fact, faith, and feeling. As long as faith keeps its eyes on fact, all three move ahead; but if faith takes its eyes off fact and turns around to be guided by feeling, both faith and feeling fall (though fact never does). As long as interpretation keeps its eyes on data, it and the criticism that follows from it will be just; but if interpretation takes its eyes off data and turns to be guided by pre-existing criticism (i.e. ideology), both it and its criticisms will become unjust and ridiculous: in other words, Deconstructionism.

B. **Read actively**. A book is like a ghost: it is almost a person, it talks back to you, you can have a conversation with it. If you have never done this, it may startle you almost as much as a ghost does to find that a book talks back to you and you can talk back to it. A book is not merely an object, it is also something like a subject, a person; it is a person's communication to you. (Authors speak to readers, after all, not to the air.) It asks you questions, and you must respond. After you listen (to the data), you must interpret it by asking it the right questions (see below) and by understanding its answers. Then you must respond to its arguments, evaluate it, agree or disagree with it. It challenges you. It is not like a piece of prerecorded music to listen to passively, but like a piece of sheet music which you must perform yourself. It is directions for some interactive thinking with its author.

C. The **questions** you ask the book are not random, nor are they personal and subjective. They have a common structure. Here are the main questions you should ask about any book:

(1) **Classification**: What kind of book is it? Classify the book. To interpret a book correctly, you must know what kind of book it is, and what the author's intentions were. Interpreting Darwin as religion or Genesis as science has caused immense confusion. So has interpreting Plato's *Republic* as practical politics or Machiavelli's *The Prince* as ethical philosophy.

(2) **Summary**: What is it about? What is its main theme?

(3) **Outline**: How do its subordinate themes or points relate to the main one? Give a basic outline of the book.

(4) **Argument**: What are its contents, its main terms, propositions, and arguments?

(5) **Evaluation**: Is it true or not, and why? Use the principles you have learned in this book to summarize and then evaluate the book's argument.

(6) **Application**: What of it? What follows? What difference does it make? Here we look not just *at* the book but *along* it or *with* it, like a telescope, at the world, at reality, at ourselves and our lives.

Some recommended philosophical classics that reward a Socratic Logical Analysis:
Plato: *Ion, Meno, Republic* Bk. I, *Gorgias*
Aristotle: *Nicomachean Ethics*
St. Augustine: *De Magistro* (On the Teacher); *De Ordine* (On Order)
Boethius: *The Consolation of Philosophy*
St. Anselm: *Proslogium*
St. Thomas: any excerpts, e.g. from *Summa of the Summa* (edited by Peter Kreeft)
Descartes: *Meditations*
Berkeley: *Three Dialogues between Hylas and Philonous*
Hume: *An Enquiry concerning Human Understanding*
Kant: *Grounding for the Metaphysics of Morals*
Kierkegaard: *Philosophical Fragments*
Ayer: *Language, Truth and Logic*

Some examples of Socratic Analysis of Great Books (by the author of this one, all from Ignatius Press):
Philosophy 101 by Socrates (on the *Apology*)
Socrates Meets Machiavelli (on *The Prince*)
Socrates Meets Marx (on *The Communist Manifesto*)
Socrates Meets Sartre (on *Existentialism and Human Emotions*)
Socrates Meets Descartes (on *Discourse on Method*)
Socrates Meets Hume (on *An Enquiry concerning Human Understanding*)
Socrates Meets Kant (on *Grounding for the Metaphysics of Morals*)

XVI. Some Philosophical Applications of Logic

Logic is not philosophy, but it is an excellent preparation for it. Logic is to philosophy what a telescope is to astronomy or a cookbook to a meal. It is an instrument. It is no substitute for the real thing, but it makes "the real thing" work much better.

What follows is the briefest sample of the interface between logic and each of the basic systematic divisions of philosophy: philosophical theology, metaphysics, cosmology, philosophical anthropology, epistemology, and ethics. These divisions correspond to basic questions: about God, or the Ultimate Reality; about reality as such, universally; about the visible universe; about human nature; about how we know; and about good and evil, the good life and the good society. The following is only a sketchy sample of how logic can make a difference to each of these kinds of questions.

Section 1. Logic and theology (P)

In principle, what could possibly be a more important application of logic than its application to the ultimate question, the question about ultimate reality? Whether there is an ultimate being, an absolute reality, and what it is, must make a difference to everything, for it is the ultimate standard or reference point for everything, and also the ultimate end, "meaning of life," *summum bonum*, or greatest good. Even if this is only pleasure or survival or money or sex or power – well, then, that is God and that is the ultimate and everything else is relative to it. Even if it is nothingness, or meaninglessness – well, then, everything else is relative to *that*.

Is it logically provable that there is a God, i.e. a being with at least some of the attributes ascribed to God by the world's religions? An Infinitely Perfect Being? An Uncaused Cause? A Creator? Can the use of the principles of formal logic that must be admitted by everyone plus sensory data available to everyone together supply premises from which the existence of God can be validly deduced in a way that *should* convince everyone? The most famous arguments for the existence of God, such as Aquinas's "five ways," try to show that the answer is yes.

But can any sense data prove or disprove the existence of a God who by definition cannot be sensed? Modern empiricists claim that the answer is no; that God's existence cannot in principle be proved.

Can formal logic alone disprove atheism – i.e., is atheism logically self-contradictory? St. Anselm's famous "ontological argument" answers yes.

Does the existence of evil (which by definition is the opposite of good) disprove an infinitely good God? The most famous argument for atheism answers yes.

Whatever your answer is, it must answer the arguments of the other side. The debate over the existence of God is not merely one about faith, it is one about logic too. It is not just "sharing personal feelings" but a hard look at facts and arguments. In fact, one argument for God (used by thinkers as diverse as Pascal, Chesterton, and C.S. Lewis) argues that logic itself would be worthless if it were not God but mindless chance that caused our minds to be as they are.

A good sample of how contemporary philosophers on both sides argue this issue can be found in *Does God Exist?* by J.P. Moreland & Kai Nielson.

Section 2. Logic and metaphysics (P)

Metaphysics is not "mushy." It is not the occult flakiness you find under that title in California bookstores; it is the study of being as such, i.e. of whatever totally universal laws there may be. An excellent introduction to this subject is *The One and the Many* by W. Norris Clarke.

Many modern philosophers believe that metaphysics is impossible. Most classical philosophers disagree. They hold, commonsensically, that the basic "laws of thought" (page 188) are laws of being, of reality; they tell us not only how we all have to think, but how all being has to be. The universe and everything in it, and also the self, (1) can't ever be what it isn't (the Law of Non-contradiction), (2) always must be what it is (the Law of Identity), and (3) always either is or isn't (the Law of Excluded Middle). Also, (4) all that comes into being – i.e. all changing being – has a cause (the Principle of Causality), and (5) everything that is has a sufficient reason why it is and is what it is (the Principle of Sufficient Reason). If these are laws of being, are there others? E.g. can we say that all that is (6) has some nature or essence, (7) has a unity, (8) *does* something or is in some way active, (9) is in some relation to other things, (10) is in principle intelligible to some mind, (11) desirable to some will, and (12) pleasing to some feeling or sensibility? If so, we have seven universal qualities of all being: something, one, active, related, true, good, and beautiful.

Or are such laws mere words, mere man-made games, mere tautologies? This is the case if Nominalism is true (the position that only individual entities are real, and that universals are mere words, not realities). For "being" and "the laws of all being" are universals. But isn't the very question of Nominalism a metaphysical question? Aren't you doing metaphysics when you deny metaphysics?

Kant argued that metaphysics is impossible because it transcended the possible limits of what we could know, since all we could know was appearances ("phenomena") and not "things-in-themselves" or "noumena" (i.e. objective reality). But this seems to be logically self-contradictory, for Kant seems to be saying that he really knows, as an objective fact, that we cannot really know objective facts. As Wittgenstein put it, "to draw a limit to thought, you must think both sides of the limit."

If metaphysics is legitimate, all the rest of philosophy depends on it, somewhat as an I proposition falls under an A proposition on the Square of Opposition. If x is true of all of reality, then it must be true of each part of reality. Take, e.g., the following dispute among three different philosophical positions. Note how the disagreement in every other field logically follows from the disagreement in metaphysics:

	Platonic Realism (Extreme of excess)	Aristotelian Moderate Realism	Nominalism (Extreme of defect)
Metaphysics	Universals are the supreme realities; the "Forms" are independent entities.	Universals are real (so are individuals); they are the forms of individual entities.	Universals are not objectively real.
Epistemology	Reason, which knows the Forms, knows reality; the senses know shadows.	Reason knows reality – form and matter – by abstracting and inferring from sensation.	Reason is deceptive when it tries to go beyond sensation.
Anthropology	Man = soul	Man = soul/form + body/matter	Man = body with a brain
Ethics	The supreme good for man is knowledge of the Forms.	The supreme good for man is happiness, perfection of soul & body.	The supreme good for man universally is unknowable.
Politics	Priority of the common (universal) good	Balance of the common good with the private good	Priority of the private (individual) good

Section 3. Logic and cosmology (P)

Many of the questions about the cosmos, or material universe, that used to be dealt with by philosophers are now dealt with by modern science, but not all of them. E.g. science's presupposition that the fundamental laws of the universe are the same throughout all time and space (the "uniformity of nature") must be assumed rather than proved by science; can philosophy prove it? Science explains things by causes; can philosophy prove that causality is real rather than merely mental, as is held by some philosophers (like Hume and Kant, in different ways)? Are final causes as real as efficient causes? Is it logically necessary that the universe had a beginning? These are some of the questions about the cosmos that philosophers still argue about, and some of the arguments seem to be able to be settled logically, in principle if not in practice. For instance, take Kant's notion that our concept of causality comes not from the real world and our discovery of it, but from the inherent, necessary structure of our consciousness and our unconscious projection of that concept onto our sensations so as to organize them and make them intelligible – is this not logically self-contradictory? For it claims that on the one hand causality is not real and on the other hand that our unconscious mind *really* causes us to think the way we do, causes our sensations to be orderly.

Section 4. Logic and philosophical anthropology (P)

"Know thyself," said Socrates at the beginning of Western philosophy, echoing the inscription on the Delphic oracle's temple. Is this possible? Can the subject of knowing become its own object without falsifying itself?

And if it can, what does it find? Is the "self" something that stands behind or above all it can know, of both soul and body? Or is it soul and body? Or is it just soul? Or is it just body?

And if it is soul and body, how can these two be one? How can they interact? How can a ghostly spirit push the buttons of a machine-like body?

Are we complex machines, chemical equations, clever apes, ghosts in machines, angels in drag, chunks of God with amnesia, or none of the above? Obviously, much hangs on which way we answer this question. Your self-image influences everything you do and think. What logical evidence stands behind each answer? Could a machine, a chemical, or an ape stand above itself or outside itself and look at itself as an object?

How can *we* do that? If the knowing subject must transcend the known object, how can the self that knows *be* the self that is known? And if it can't, how can I know myself? Is there a logical contradiction whichever way we answer this question?

Another classical question in philosophical anthropology is the question of free will. Most of us have a strong sense of both fate and free will, destiny and choice. All our stories presuppose both. Yet these two ideas seem contradictory. Can logic help sort out and clarify this puzzle?

Still another classical question in this field is the relationship among intellect, will, and feelings. Which rules? Is reasoning really rationalization of desires? Does the will command the mind, or the mind command the will, or both? What is the relationship between "I think," "I•want," and "I feel"?

Section 5. Logic and epistemology (P)

Some questions in epistemology (theory of knowledge) are:

How do we come to know anything? Is sensation inherently deceptive? Is reason? If both reason and the senses know truly, how do they interact? Here more than anywhere else in philosophy the need for logic is obvious.

It is also obvious that epistemology also colors everything else, for it concerns our instrument, knowledge; and your attitude toward and use of your instrument shapes everything you do with that instrument.

What reasons are there for each of the three epistemologies distinguished on page 360? What are the logical consequences of each? What data are left unexplained by each? Compare the *six* alternatives to Aristotle on page 214.

Logic can help explore these questions.

Section 6. Logic and ethics (P)

What the good for man is (ethics) depends on what man is (anthropology). And how we *know* what this good is depends on our epistemology. And what good is, and what man is, and what knowledge is, all depend on what *is* (metaphysics).

Is "the practical syllogism" (page 296) the right way of ethical reasoning? Or is it too pragmatic, implying that "the end justifies the means"?

How can we come to know our true good, our moral duties, or our moral rights? How can we prove them? How can we argue about them? We know how people *do* in fact behave by sense observation (and by its refinement in the sciences of psychology and sociology); but how do we know how people *ought* to behave?

Are moral values objective facts? Are they subjective feelings? What kind of reality might they have if they are neither?

Can man be good without God? Is morality dependent on religion? Is a thing good ultimately because God wills it, or does God will it because it is good?

Ethics is the most important part of philosophy – the only part Socrates ever explored. If logic is irrelevant to ethics, then both logic and ethics become almost trivial: logic because it cannot help us with life's most important questions, and ethics because it cannot be logical and is reduced to being illogical, sentimental, uncritical, subjectivistic, self-deluding, self-justifying, rationalization instead of reason. If logic is to be more than a clever game with words, and if ethics is to be more than a pretty game with rules, then we must do what

Socrates did and take both seriously, subjecting ethical questions to the most demandingly honest logical reasoning.

His example was meant to continue.

THE BEGINNING

Appendix: Problems with Mathematical Logic

BY TRENT DOUGHERTY

1. Basic modern logic

At several points in this book comments have been made about "symbolic" or "mathematical" logic ranging from the suspicious to the downright derogatory. Lest the reader suspect that such negative evaluations stem from ignorance, we set forth here, briefly, what we find objectionable about modern mathematical logic. One reason we feel this is important is that modern logic is quite sophisticated. This can be attractive (but don't forget who the sophists were!). There is a certain lure to the formality of modern logic. It is also so complex that the uninitiated can be intimidated. We hope that there will be no need for the reader to be intimidated by or over-impressed by modern mathematical logic.

The best place to start is usually in the beginning. Modern logic got its real start[1] in the early 20th century when Bertrand Russell and Alfred North Whitehead published their *Principia Mathematica* in three volumes in 1910, 1912, and 1913. The name of their work (*Principia*) is the same as Sir Isaac Newton's famous book in which he set forth his laws of motion. Presumably they thought their book would be pretty important with a title like that. However, some of their thunder was stolen when Albert Einstein published a little paper called "General Relativity" in 1915. At any rate, one effect of the work was to solidify in the minds of "up to date" logicians a certain treatment of conditional (hypothetical) statements.[2] This treatment is usually called the "truth-functional" interpretation.

A truth-functional statement is one whose truth can be calculated from (is a function of) its parts. All you need to know are the values of the parts. For

---

1   Though important work was pioneered by George Boole, Augustus De Morgan, and Gottlob Frege.

2   The conception of conditional to be considered was already present in the literature on the subject, but there was no uniform agreement. For an interesting account of some relevant discussions see *Lewis Carroll's Symbolic Logic*, pp. 444–49.

example, consider the simple mathematical equation $x^2=9$. This is a truth functional statement. All you need to know, to know if it's true, is the value of x. And if you do know the value of x, then you can tell whether the statement is true. So knowing the value of x is both necessary and sufficient to know the truth of the equation. If x=1, then the statement is false; the same goes for x=2. If x=3, however, the statement is true.

Now consider a logical claim that two statements (let's pick two arbitrary statements and call them 'p' and 'q') are true. So the claim is "p and q". All we need to discover to know the truth of "p and q" are the individual truth values of 'p' and 'q'. Clearly, if either 'p' or 'q' are false, then their *conjunction* "p and q" will be false. It will be true only when they both are. This fact about conjunctions is usually represented in a *truth table*.

	p	q	p and q
case 1	T	T	T
case 2	T	F	F
case 3	F	T	F
case 4	F	F	F

The chart represents the four possible cases with respect to the truth value of the constituent parts ('p' and 'q') of the complex expression "p and q". They can both be true, one can be true and the other false, one can be false and the other true, or they can both be false. The only case in which the conjunction is true is the case in which both its parts, its *conjuncts*, are true.

An even simpler truth-functional logical connective is *negation*. Letting '~' represent the word 'not', we get the following truth table for negation.

	p	~p
case 1	T	F
case 2	F	T

Here the atomic statement is p and the compound composed out of '~' and 'p' is "~p". Now if we let 'p' be any meaningful assertion, then p must be either true or false. Whichever it is, we can immediately figure out the value of "~p". It is always the opposite of "p". So negation is also truth functional.

It would be natural at this point to wonder whether all logic is truth-functional. A consideration in favor of an affirmative answer is the fact that other logical expressions can be built out of the previous two (in fact, in most mathematical logic textbooks *all* are). Consider the logical connective 'or'. Taking 'or' in the inclusive sense, that is, as a "weak disjunction" (see page 301), the statement "p or q" is true if either 'p' or 'q' is, that is if either *disjunct* is. The only case in which an inclusive disjunction is false is that in which both its disjuncts are. Now we might represent that with the table following on page 366.

But there is no need to take 'or' as atomic. It can be built out of 'and' and 'not'. To say that at least one of 'p' or 'q' is true is to say that it's not the case

	p	q	p or q
case 1	T	T	T
case 2	T	F	T
case 3	F	T	T
case 4	F	F	F

that both are false. Let's represent that last statement in a truth table, building its parts progressively.

	(1)	(2)	(3)	(4)	(5)	(6)
	p	q	~p	~q	~p & ~q	~(~p & ~q)
case 1	T	T	F	F	F	T
case 2	T	F	F	T	F	T
case 3	F	T	T	F	F	T
case 4	F	F	T	T	T	F

The expression we are interested in is at the top of column six. It reads, "It is not the case that p is false and q is false," or in more natural English, "p and q are not both false." This is obviously equivalent to "either p or q is true," which was represented in the previous truth table. Note that the two expressions are true in exactly the same cases. They can both be true in every case except number four in which both p and q are false. Thus we can define 'or' in terms of 'not' and 'and'.[3]

This seems so promising for logical atomism that it leads philosophers to try to represent 'if...then...' statements in truth tables. As we will see, this creates problems, problems which seem to us insurmountable for logical atomism.

One fact about any universally true 'if...then...' statement is that the presence of the item following the 'if' is always followed by the item following 'then'. The 'if' clause is called the *antecedent* and the 'then' clause is called the *consequent*. In ordinary English, if we say "If it rains, then I'll get wet" we imply that there's no way, given present circumstances, for it to rain without my getting wet. We can represent this implication, letting 'p' be "It will rain" and 'q' be "I will get wet" as ~(p & ~q). So according to modern logic, which presupposes logical atomism, the ordinary English conditional can be reduced to the elements 'not' and 'and'. Here is where the problems begin.

2. The paradoxes of material implication

The above treatment of the conditional results in what is called the *material con-*

---

3 To follow the truth table fully, notice that column three is calculated from column one in accordance with the truth table definition of negation. Likewise for columns four and two. Then column five is calculated from columns three and four in accordance with the truth table definition of conjunction. Finally, column six is calculated from column five in accordance with the truth table definition of negation.

ditional. The problems that result are called the *paradoxes of material implica-tion.* They are easy to see once we represent material implication with a truth table (we will use '→' to represent the conditional, so p → q reads "If p, then q").[4]

	p	q	p → q
case 1	T	T	T
case 2	T	F	F
case 3	F	T	T
case 4	F	F	T

Notice that the only case in which the material conditional is false is where the antecedent is true and the consequent false. This case is certainly correct, but each of the other cases reveals problems with this treatment of conditional state-ments.[5]

In case one, we see that any two true statements can be linked in a condi-tional. Take any two true statements you want and according to the theory of material implication they will imply one another. Thus, according to this theory, "Grass is green" implies that "Snow is white." So the conditional "If grass is green, then snow is white" comes out true. Again, "Abe Lincoln was the 16th president" implies that "The Sun is a star." Case four has it the other way: any two false statements imply one another. So "Fire is cold" implies "The Earth is flat," and "All rocks are soft" implies "The Moon is made of green cheese." Similar implications result from case three.

Looking at the cases in pairs we see that cases one and three have the result that every true statement is implied by any statement at all, regardless of truth value. So "1+1=3" implies "1+1=2," i.e. according to logical atomism the statement "If 1+1=3, then 1+1=2" is true! Similarly, cases three and four have the result that a false statement implies any statement. Finally, the modern treat-ment of conditionals has the surprising result that for *any* two statements, one of them implies the other. That is, regardless of whether either is true or false, it will turn out that one of them implies the other. This will hold for a pair of true statements, a pair of false statements, or a mixed pair. We'll leave it to you to come up with your own examples in each variety.

3. Responses to the paradoxes of material implication

There have been two main ways of responding to the paradoxes of material implication. One, as might be anticipated, is to stubbornly refuse to admit that there is a real problem and defend the system at all costs. The other, more rea-

4   To see that this is the truth table for material implication, construct the truth table for '~p & ~q)' using the methods exemplified earlier in the appendix. I leave this as homework.

5   One of the very first to express dissatisfaction with the mathematical treatment of con-ditionals due primarily to Boole was Scottish logician Hugh MacColl. See his "Symbolical Reasoning," published in the journal *Mind* volume five, 1880.

sonable but ambitious approach, has been to try and keep the baby while dumping the bath water.

This strategy involves either strengthening or weakening the basic logical system. Modal logics pioneered by MacColl in the 19th century and extensively developed in early to mid 20th century by C.I. Lewis[6] take the problem with the basic logic to be one of weakness. That is, the connection between statements in a conditional is stronger than the material conditional implies; the connection should be necessary. So modal logic adds operators for necessity and possibility, the two *modes* a statement can be in. When a necessity operator is attached to a material conditional, the new conditional is called *strict implication*. The good news for modal logic is that the paradoxes of material implication tend to go away. The bad news is that they reappear in most systems as the *paradoxes of strict implication*. For example, an impossible statement implies any statement. Also, any statement implies a necessary statement. This does not seem to be much of an improvement. There are replies that interpret strict implication as a deducibility relation, which some think neutralizes the paradoxes. This debate, however, is far beyond the scope of this book.

We will end our discussion of modal logic with two observations. First, whether or not modal logic is burdened by similar paradoxes, it is clearly a departure from the attempt to have a purely truth functional logic. You cannot necessarily infer the truth value of "p is necessary" from knowing whether p is true or false. For example, "You are now reading a logic book," is true, but it didn't have to be. You could have gone on a walk instead (and perhaps should have).[7]

Secondly, modal logic turns out to support the basis of traditional logic. Modal logician Alvin Plantinga, considering W.V.O. Quine's accusation that modal logic implies "Aristotelian essentialism," the view that things actually have essences, says that "Quine seems to be right ... [it] clearly does imply the truth of that ancient doctrine."[8]

The second way of responding to the paradoxes involves weakening the standard logic. It removes certain principles from basic modern logic, insisting that there must be some relevant connection between the antecedent and the consequent. This family of logics are thus called *relevance logics*. Like modal logics, relevance logics are not purely truth functional.

There are many other kinds of systems of intensional logic: temporal logic, epistemic logic, deontic logic, intuitionist logic *et al*. It is important to point out that whenever philosophers use advanced logical techniques to attempt to solve complex philosophical problems they always use one or more of these intensional systems. For every proposed solution on the basis of a system of inten-

---

6   That's the C.I. Lewis with whom C.S. Lewis was once confused (see page 12).

7   There is also ineliminable intensionality in the semantics of modal logic.

8   Alvin Plantinga, *The Nature of Necessity* (Oxford: Oxford University Press, 1979), last page.

sional symbolic logic there is a philosophical dispute over its basic principles. Though making extensive use of symbols and formal procedures, they are not truly systems of mathematical logic in that they are not purely truth-functional. The literature on these logical systems is vast and highly technical. One thing is sure: the attempts on the part of some modern logicians to remove substantive metaphysical content from logic has failed. Aristotelian logic not only recognizes the contribution of metaphysics to logic, it is based on it. Once again, modern man, through his greatest intellectual and "scientific" endeavors, has confirmed ancient truth.

Answers to Even-Numbered Exercises

(NB: Teachers seeking answers to odd-numbered exercises should e-mail St. Augustine's Press at benjamin@staugustine.net)

Page 34

A
  2: term
  4: argument
  6: proposition
  8: not a proposition; an imperative sentence
10: term
12: argument ("so" = "therefore")
14: term

B
  2: false
  4: false
  6: false
  8: true

Page 49
  2: analogical (moral evil vs. physical evil; sin vs. suffering; doing harm vs. suffering harm)
  4: univocal (numbers are the most univocal language there is)
  6: analogical
  8: analogical
10: analogical
12: univocal (or perhaps analogical, since death is not an accidental change but a substantial [essential] change)
14: analogical (ask a theologian to explain this)
16. equivocal

Page 51
  2: universal
  4: singular
  6: universal
  8: particular

Page 52
2: collective
4: collective
6: collective
8: ambiguously used: first collective, then divisive

Page 53
2: "Human" is used ambiguously, first as an adjective and then as a noun. Parts or products of human beings are "human" but they are not humans.
4: Guilt feelings, like all feelings, are subjective. Courts try to judge real guilt, objective and impersonal truth about whether the accused is guilty in fact of violating a law. Judges deal with real guilt, by punishment; psychologists deal with guilt feelings, by therapy.
6: "Good" is used ambiguously. Self-esteem may be *psychologically* good, in aiding happiness; but a judge's verdict is *legally and morally* good if it is legally and morally just. Was it "good" that Hitler had so much self-esteem?
8: "Love" is analogical. Love of wisdom is not the same kind of love as sexual love. (However, Socrates would probably still press the point that the two have some principles in common, one of which is that pure love of any kind should not "sell itself" for money.) He would probably call professional philosophers prostitutes.
10: "Ambiguity" is ambiguous: first it is used nominally, then really; it refers first to the *word* 'ambiguity' and then to real ambiguity.

Page 55
2: "Near" = relation; "blasted" = passion; "heath" = substance (or "near the blasted heath" = place); "midnight" = time; "three" = quantity; "Weird" = quality; "Sisters" = substance (but in relation); "stood" = posture; "gleefully" = quality; "stirring" = action; "round" = quality; "black" = quality; "witches'" = possession; "pot" = substance; "filled" = passion; "three" = quantity; "tiny" = quantity (even though not mathematically measured); "broken" = passion; "frogs" = substance.
4: "Pooping" = action; "on" = relation; "pieces" = quantity (fraction); "pork" = substance; "in the park" = place; "is" = no category but a copula (see page 149); "proper" = quality; "performance" = action; "perky" = quality; "pelicans" = substance.
6. "Categories" = substance; "are" = a copula (page 149); "used" = passion; "classify" = action; "things" = substance.

Page 61
2: genus
4: genus
6: property (or accident if "temper" is taken to mean "an unusually hot temper")
8: genus
10: property
12: species
14: accident
16: genus

Page 64

2: OK (although it is a matter of degree)

4: OK

6: Not exclusive (some totalitarians are very popular); *and* not exhaustive (it omits unpopular non-totalitarian regimes); *and* two different standards (popularity and power)

8: OK

10: OK (if "man" is included in "animals")

12: OK

14: OK

16: Not exhaustive; not only are there other "excesses" but even if the class to be divided is taken to be "excesses *concerning equality*," there could be other excesses concerning equality.

18: OK

20: Uses two standards at once: how many and how qualified the rulers are; compare #21. Also not exhaustive.

22: OK logically, though some would find it controversial religiously; a good division to outline as an exercise.

Page 72

2: "The most hungry" is temporally ambiguous: those who are the most hungry before they eat, will usually then eat the most, but those who are the most hungry after they eat, have usually eaten the least.

4: There are two ambiguities: Sam interprets "bored to death" literally, while his father means it figuratively, and Sam interprets "the service" as "the church service" while the minister means "the military service."

6: The question can mean "who's the (offensive) baserunner on first?" or "who's the (defensive) first baseman?" And in the Abbot & Costello routine, "Who" is also the player's last name.

8: "Premises" can mean "logical assumptions" or "living quarters."

10: "Sound" can mean "logical valid" or "physical noise."

12: "Pronounce your sentence" can mean "utter your proposition" or decree your punishment.

14: "Cares for" can man "physically takes care of" or "is emotionally attached to."

16: "Right" can mean the opposite of "left" or the opposite of "wrong."

18: To "love" violence is to enjoy it, even though it harms persons. To "love" in the religious sense (charity, *agape*) is to will good, not harm, to other persons.

20: "Is" can be multiply equivocal: e.g. a copula ("Socrates is mortal"), an equation ("2+2 is 4"), a tautology ("x is not non-x"), a timeless truth ("justice is more profitable than injustice"), a temporal truth ("Bush is President"), an assertion of existence ("Though he died, he still is"), a fictional identity ("Hamlet is the Prince of Denmark"), and many more.

22: The first "nothing" means "There is no thing that is . . ." The second "nothing" means "nothingness" or "nothing at all." The first "nothing" begins a universal negative proposition, the second "nothing" is a term.

Page 83
  2: dogmatic
  4: uncritical and unreliable
  6: uncritical appeal to the "expert"
  8: reasonable if not dogmatic
  10: reasonable on Islamic premises

Page 130, I (These are not, of course, the only possible good definitions, but samples.)
  2: "an ordered body of knowledge through causes"; or "systematic, rational explanation through evidence"
  4: "reasoning from a universal premise to a conclusion that necessarily follows"
  6: "the logical expression of judgment"; or "a statement with a subject and predicate which can be true or false"
  8: "an object of knowledge which in reality is an aspect of things rather than a thing, but is considered by the mind apart from the real things in which it inheres"
  10: as a category, "that which that exists only in a substance (thing) and not in itself"; as a predicable, "any predicate which is not the essence of its subject or a necessary property of it"
  12: "a statement of what a thing is, which distinguishes it from everything else"
  14: "the mind's conformity to reality"
  16: "the universal nature of a thing"
  18: "a created spirit without a body"
  20: "a large natural satellite of a star"
  22: "part of speech designating a person, place or thing"; or "the subject of predication"
  24: "the cessation of life"
  26: "an artificial means of exchange of goods and services"

Page 131, II
A
  2: essential, good
  4: circular: "episcopal" is simply the adjective formed from "bishop"
  6: negative and far too broad
  8: negative
  10: no genus (never define by "is when") and too narrow (some living things don't breathe)
  12: metaphorical
  14: nominal, but too narrow (some people, though really secure, do not feel content) and too broad (some people feel content without being secure)
  16: metaphorical (literally, anyone can pronounce those two words) and too narrow (is that all personality is? Is that all character is?). Clever, though.
  18: too broad
  20: circular ("round" means "circular" and "circular" means "round"), no genus (should be "geometrical figure"), and too broad (wheels are not circles but are round)
  22: nominal; OK

24: OK; it distinguishes plants from animals, as the lack of reason distinguishes brutes from humans

26: nominal; OK

28: OK (Is it essential or by final cause? Or both? Is its final cause an artifact's essence?)

30: nominal; OK

32: metaphorical

34: no genus, negative, and too broad (also too narrow)

36: too broad

38: OK by property, since insanity is a disease of *reason*, which is proper to man alone. However, animal psychologists speak of "psychosis" and "insanity" also in higher animals using these words more broadly; and in this sense the definition is too broad.

40: too narrow; only one virtue (temperance, self-control, or moderation) does that

42: OK, by material cause

44: too broad (are there no bad laws from bad lawmakers?), too narrow (there are some goods that bad lawmakers do not find acceptable, and some goods that are irrelevant to lawmakers), and no genus

46: much too narrow (unless you are God)

48: a joke

50: nominal; OK

B (Page 132)

2: metaphorical

4: metaphorical

6: too narrow, also too broad (is addiction *love*?)

8: OK (by both efficient and final cause)

10: metaphorical and too broad (but it is probably not meant as a definition)

12: circular

14: within the context already defined in the *Republic*, OK; out of that context, too broad

16: too broad and too narrow: the idea that there is a tunnel under the prison may be true but quite inexpedient to the jailer; the idea that "everything is going to be all right" may be expedient to a worried man yet untrue

18: too narrow; it excludes *partial* happiness ("*all* our desires"?), *undesired* happiness ("surprised by joy"), and objectively real but not subjectively experienced blessedness (like the wisdom that comes through suffering)

20: needlessly complex, long, and obscure

22: metaphorical

24: nominal

26: Too narrow, for nothing except God has liberty by this definition. If "impediment" is taken to mean "*harmful* impediment," the definition is too broad, for it applies even to planets, raindrops, and fingernails.

28: Too broad: corpses, wimps, and hermits may also not inflict pain. Also too narrow: does it not inflict emotional pain to be told in a discreet and gentlemanly way, "Excuse me sir, but your fly is open"?

30: OK; but "knowledge" is also sometimes *distinguished* from "opinion" by Plato himself (e.g. in the *Meno*).

32: Not, as it seems, nominal but real and even essential, if we use Einsteinian rather than Newtonian physics. If gases and liquids are also "bodies," OK.

34: circular, also too narrow

36: too broad in principle but accurate in practice in America in 1992

38: if serious, too broad *and* too narrow (unless the colleagues in his department consist of the Father, the Son, and the Holy Spirit)

40: obscure and complex and also too broad, since evolution applies only to *living* matter

C (page 135)

2: The first definition is rightly rejected as too broad (is it bigotry to be certain that 2 + 2 = 4?); the second gives a property of bigotry but is probably too broad, since it also covers a weak imagination.

4: This is similar to 2 and seems too broad because it also is true of intellectual weakness, and even is true of certainty about self-evident propositions.

6: If this is a critique of a popular definition of humility, it is on target: humility is a moral virtue, not an intellectual weakness (skepticism, or doubt about truth). The popular notion of humility has the wrong *genus*, and confuses a moral virtue with the lack of an intellectual virtue. However, "doubt about oneself" is too broad to be a good definition of humility. Some self-doubt is extreme and pathological: an emotional disorder at the opposite extreme from bigotry or arrogance.

8: GKC shows that "limitation" is a property of art, and that "freedom" is ambiguous: freedom from external, alien laws is compatible with art but "freedom" from intrinsic, essential laws is not. But it is not a *definition*. No one of the three concepts discussed (limitation, freedom, art) is a genus or a specific difference of any other one.

10: In differentiating suicide and martyrdom by motive, this seems accurate. However, if they are meant as definitions, the second seems too broad; for care about someone outside himself may motivate a man to suicide, however foolishly: e.g. the desire that his family get rich from his life insurance.

12: A valid critique of the attempt to conceive a "peasant" individualistically, but this is not usually an error in *definition* but in sociology.

Pages 156–63

A (Page 156)

2: not a proposition, only one long term (no predicate)

4: All [Socrates] is [tw was a philosopher] We need to add the "tw" ("that which") only because we need to include the past tense in the predicate; ordinarily we do not need to add "tw" or a "twi" (that which is") if we already have a noun.

6: All [I] am [tw itches]

8: All [things which are not the observer of every thing in the universe] are [things in the universe] and No [observer of every thing in the universe] is [a thing in the universe]

10: Some [gamblers] are [tw are just lucky] and Some [gamblers] are not [tw are lucky]
12: All [Alexander the Great] is [tw was Aristotle's student]
14: All [tw know that everyone is a fraud] are [frauds]

B (Page 156)
   2: All [charity] is [tw begins at home]
   4: not a proposition; a performative sentence
   6: not a proposition: an imperative followed by an interrogative
   8: If all [you] are [tw continues to turn the crank of that torture rack], then all [you] are [tw will in all probability detach all four of my limbs from their sockets]. The next-to-last words of the Stoic philosopher; his words were "See? I told you so."
  10: All [he who jest at scars] is [he who never felt a wound]
  12: All [men] are [good judges of their own interests]
  14: All [loose lips] are [tw sink ships]
  16: All [tw this country needs] is [a good five cent cigar]
  18: No [history] is [tw ever repeats itself]
  20: not a proposition; a performative sentence
  22: All [tw man has done] is [tw man can do]
  24: All [he who laughs last] is [he who laughs best]
  26: No [tw is morally wrong] is [tw can be politically right]

C (Page 157)
   2: All [a good talker] is [tw implies a good audience even more than a good orator does]
   4: If All [we] are [tw trample our vices underfoot] then All [we] are [tw make a ladder of our vices]
   6: No [tw do not complain] are [tw are ever pitied] OR:
      All [tw do not complain] are [tw are never pitied]
   8: All [the world] is [a looking glass] and All [the world] is [tw gives back to every man the reflection of his own face]
  10: All [tw can understand the greatness of the past] are [the adventurous] OR:
      No [tw are not adventurous] are [tw can understand the greatness of the past]
  12: All [they] are [tw were born of the sun] and All [they] are [tw traveled a brief while toward the sun] and All [they] are [tw left the vivid air singed with their honor]
  14: All [work] is [the curse of the drinking class]
  16: Some [books] are [tw is to be tasted] and Some [books] are [tw is to be swallowed] and Some [books] are [tw is to be chewed and digested]
  18: If All [Cleopatra's nose] is [tw had been longer] then All [the history of the world] is [tw would have been changed]
  20: All [happy families] are [tw resemble one another] and All [unhappy families] are [tw are unhappy in their own fashion]
  22: No [running when you are on the wrong road] is [tw is of use] (This is a rhetorical question, which is really a proposition, a declaration, not an interrogative.)

24: Either All [death] is [a state of nothingness and utter unconsciousness) or All [a change and migration of the soul from this world to another] is [twi real]. (Existential proposition; no predicate, unless we add 'real.')

26: All [it] is [tw was brillig] and All [the slithy toves] are [tw did gyre and gimble in the wabe] and All [the borogoves] are [tw were mimsy] and All [the mome raths] are [tw were outgrabe]

28: All [tw is necessary for the triumph of evil] is [for good men to do nothing]

30: No propositions; all imperatives (commands), except the last: All [tw can procure future Honor] is [Virtue and Wisdom]

32. All [the silken, sad, uncertain rustling of each purple curtain] is [tw thrilled me]

34: All [I] am [tw never had a job] and All [I] am [tw just always played baseball]

36: All [man] is [tw was created a little lower than the angels] and All [man] is [tw has been getting a little lower ever since]

38: No [time before this time] is [one in which so much has been owed by so many to so few]

D (Page 159)

2: All [tw speak or act with an impure mind] are [tw are followed by trouble as the ox that draws the cart is followed by the wheel] and All [tw speak or act with a pure mind] are [tw are followed by happiness as you are followed by your shadow] OR:
If All [you] are [tw speak or act with an impure mind] then All [you] are [tw will be followed by trouble as the ox that draw the cart is followed by the wheel] and if All [you] are [tw speak or act with a pure mind] then All [you] are [tw will be followed by happiness as you are followed by your shadow]

4: All [the fool who knows he is a fool] is [tw is that much wiser] and All [the fool who thinks he is wise] is [a fool indeed]

6: All [tw are slow to do good] are [tw are caught by the mind delighting in mischief] OR:
If All [you] are [twi slow to do good] then All [the mind, delighting in mischief] is [tw will catch you] "Be quick to be good" is am imperative.

8: All [hurt] is [tw rebounds]

10: All [ignorant men] are [oxen]; All [ignorant men] are [tw grow in size, not wisdom] (This is two propositions connected not by "if" or "either" or "and" but by an implied "because." It is an abbreviated form of argument, called an enthymeme, which you will learn to evaluate later.)

12: If All [you] are [tw let go of winning and losing] then All [you] are [tw will find joy] OR:
All [tw let go of winning] are [tw will find joy]

14: No [the way] is [twi in the sky] and All [the way] is [twi in the heart] OR:
All [the way] is [twi not in the sky] and All [the way] is [twi in the heart] OR:
All [the way] is [twi not in the sky but in the heart]

E (Page 159)

2: All [the uses of adversity] are [twi sweet]

4: All [cowards] are [tw die many times before their deaths] and All [the valiant]

are [tw never taste of death but once] OR:
All [cowards] are [tw die many times before their deaths] and No [the valiant] are [tw die many times before their deaths]

6: All [twi fair] is [twi foul] and All [twi foul] is [twi fair] OR:
All [fairness] is [foulness] and All [foulness] is [fairness]

8: If All [you] are [twi true to yourself] then All [you] are [tw cannot then be false to any man] OR:
All [tw are true to themselves] are [tw cannot be false to any man]

10: All [golden lads] are [tw must come to dust, as chimney sweepers] and All [golden girls] are [tw must come to dust, as chimney sweepers] OR [All golden lads and girls] are [tw must come to dust, as chimney sweepers]

12: Some [remedies which we ascribe to heaven] are [tw lie in ourselves]

14: All [these mortals] are [fools]

16: No [course of true love] is [tw ever ran smooth]

18: All [the things in heaven and earth] are [twi more than are dreamed of in your philosophy]

20: All [men that have no music in themselves and are not moved with concord of sweet sounds] are [tw are fit for treasons, stratagems and spoils]

22: not a proposition: a command, wish, exclamation, or imprecation

24: All [tw steal my purse] are [tw steal trash]

26: not a proposition; a command

28: not a proposition; a wish

30: All [the serpent that did sting thy father's life] is [tw now wears his crown]

32: All [sweetest things] are [tw turn sourest by their deeds]; All [lilies that fester] are [tw smell far worse than weeds] (The second proposition is an example of, or evidence for, the first, so they are logically connected, but not by "if," "either," or "and.")

34: not a *logical* proposition but a *proposal* "proposition."

36: If All [it] is [twi now] then No [it] is [twi to come] and if No [it] is [twi to come] then All [it] is [tw will be now] and if No [it] is [twi now] then All [it] is [tw will come]

38: All [gilding refined gold, painting the lily] is [wasteful and ridiculous excess]

40: No [the water in the rough rude sea] is [tw can wash the balm off from an anointed king]

42: All [the hungry lion] is [tw now roars] and All [the wolf] is [tw now behowls the moon] OR:
All [now] is [the time when the hungry lion roars and the wolf behowls the moon]

44: All [to be or not to be] is [the question]

46: not a proposition; an exclamation

48: All [I] am [twi dead] (But this is an existentially self-contradictory proposition; if you can say you're dead, you're *not* dead! Cf. Descartes's proof that he exists: "I think, therefore I am." His point is that "I AM" is existentially [or practically or psychologically] self-evident, for its contradictory "I am not," or "I am dead," is existentially [or practically or psychologically] self-contradictory. "I AM" is not, however, a *logically* self-evident proposition, a tautology, since the predicate is not essential to the subject unless the subject is God. Perhaps Descartes harbored this minor confusion!)

F (Page 161)
2. No [thoroughly worldly people] are [those who ever understand the world]
4. No [men] are [those who loved Rome because she was great] and All [Rome] is [tw was great because they had loved her]
6. All [great classics] are [tw one can praise without having read]
8. All [logic is [a machine of the mind] and if All [logic] is [twi used honestly], then All [logic] is [tw ought to bring out an honest conclusion]

G (Page 162)
2. All [the poor in spirit] are [tw are blessed]
4. If All [God] is [tw so clothes the grass of the field . . .]
   then All [God] is [tw will much more clothe you]
   (The proposition is a "rhetorical question.")
6. All [tw a man sows] is [tw he shall also reap]
8. All [tw are not with me] are [tw are against me]
10. No [good tree] is [tw can bring forth evil fruit]
12. If all [I] am [tw speak with tongues of men and of angels but have not love]
    then All [I] am [a noisy gong or a clanging cymbal]
14. This interrogative sentence is not a proposition, but it contains a proposition:
    All [she] is [tw looketh forth as the morning, etc.]
16. not a propositon; a wish
18. All [things] are [tw work together for good for them who love God], OR
    All [tw love God] are [those for whom all things work together for good]

Page 164
2: c
4: d
6: b
8: a

Pages 171–72
A
2: Some [tw eat little fish] are [bigger fish]
4: No [hero to his valet] is [a man]
6: You can't validly convert an O.
8: No [tw ends] is [love]

B
2: No [bigger fish] are [tw do not eat little fish]
4: All [men] are [non-heroes to their valets]
6: Some [tw glitters] is [non-gold]

8: All [love] is [tw never ends] OR, if this was your original form, No [love] is [tw ever ends]

C

2. Partial contrapositive: No [tw do not eat little fish] are [bigger fish]; Full contrapositive: All [tw do not eat little fish] are [twi not bigger fish]. Partial inverse: Some [tw eat little fish] are not [twi not bigger fish]; Full inverse: O does not convert.

4. Partial contrapositive: Some [twi not heroes to their valets] are [men]; Full contrapositive: Some [twi not heroes to their valets] are not [non-men]. Partial inverse: All [heroes to their valets] are [non-men]; Full inverse: Some [non-men] are [heroes to their valets].

6. Partial contrapositive: Some [non-gold] is [tw glitters]; Full contrapositive: Some [non-gold] is not [tw does not glitter]. No inverses; O does not convert.

8. Partial contrapositive: No [tw ever ends] is [love]; Full contrapositive: All [tw ever ends] is [non-love]. Partial inverse: Some [tw never ends] is not [non-love]; no full inverse; O does not convert.

E

2: valid: first an obversion, then a conversion (thus a partial contraposition)

4: invalid conversion of an O

6: valid conversion of an I

Page 174

2: Some [flowers] are [twi born to bloom unseen] vs. No [flowers] are [twi born to bloom unseen]

4: All [things of beauty] are [a joy forever] vs. Some [things of beauty] are not [a joy forever]

6: Some [fair faces] are [tw may be a foul bargain] vs. No [fair faces] are [tw may be a foul bargain]

8: Some [slips between the cup and the lip] are [twi real] vs. No [slips between the cup and the lip] are [twi real] (Existential propositions can also contradict each other.)

10: all [tw deserve the fair] are [tw are brave] vs. some [tw are non-brave] are [tw deserve the fair].

12: All [tw deserve the fair] are [twi brave] vs. Some [tw deserve the fair] are not [twi brave].

Pages 178–79

A

2: Some [thing new under the sun] is [twi real] OR: Some [thing under the sun] is [twi new]

4: No [men] are [those who hate by morning what they love by night]

B

2: valid

4: valid

6: invalid

C

2: false

4: true
6: false
8: unknown (not an opposition; an illicit conversion)

Page 199
2: false
4: false
6: false
8: false
10: false
12: false
14: false
16: true (for in a valid argument, true premises necessitate a true conclusion)
18: true
20: false

Page 205
2: formal (argument *or* explanation)
4: efficient (explanation)
6: material (argument)
8: material (explanation)
10: material or efficient (explanation)
12: final (explanation)
14: final (explanation) [a magnet does not push but pulls, by attraction]
16: formal (argument)

Page 219
2: true
4: false
6: true
8: true
10: false (only 2 terms and 2 propositions)

Page 234
A
2: invalid
4 valid
6: valid
8: invalid
10: invalid

Page 235
B
2: Some great men are political nonconformists.
   No political nonconformists are patriotic.
   Therefore some great men are not patriotic.
4: Somebody passed wind.
   All who passed wind, farted.
   Therefore somebody farted.

6: Whatever has color, has molecules.
Whatever has molecules, has size.
Therefore whatever has color, has size.
8: All who by nature need to know, by nature desire to know.
All men by nature need to know.
Therefore all men by nature desire to know.

Page 236

C

2 Whatever can be created by our imagination is subjective.
Beauty can be created by our imagination.
Therefore beauty is subjective.

What is argued about is not subjective.
Beauty is argued about.
Therefore beauty is not subjective.

4: Whatever is defined differently by different societies, changes with time and place.
Moral rightness is defined differently by different societies.
Therefore moral rightness changes with time and place

What flows from man's essence does not change with time and place.
Moral rightness flows from man's essence.
Therefore moral rightness does not change with time and place.

6: Man is created by God
Whatever is created by God is essentially good
Therefore man is essentially good

Man is naturally selfish.
What is naturally selfish is not essentially good.
Therefore man is not essentially good.

8: Capital punishment is a practice of justice
Whatever is a practice of justice is morally right
Therefore capital punishment is morally right

Capital punishment harms its victims.
Whatever harms its victims is not morally right.
Therefore capital punishment is not morally right.

Page 253

A

2: valid
4: invalid: Illicit Major
6: valid (if you obvert one of the premises to avoid two negative premises)
8: valid
10: valid (translate the second premise as an A, not an E, both to avoid two negative premises and to get a common term with the first premise)
12: valid
14: invalid: Illicit Minor
16: invalid: Undistributed Middle
18: invalid: four terms (Jill, John, tw loves John, and tw loves Jesus)

Page 254
B
2: All [mercy] is [sorrow]
No [sorrow] is [twi in God]
Therefore no [mercy] is [twi in God] : valid
"But 'sorrow'·is used ambiguously: there is the *act* of sorrow (a *will*) in mercy, but here is no *passive* sorrow (a passion, or emotion)·in God," Aquinas explains.
4: Some [subjects that tend to withdraw the mind from pursuits of a low nature] are [twi useful]
No [classical learning] is [a subject that tends to withdraw the mind . . . etc.]
Therefore no [classical learning] is [twi useful] : invalid; Illicit Major
6: All [happiness] is [twi desired as an end and never as a means]
All [pleasure] is [twi desired as an end and never as a means]
Therefore all [happiness] is [pleasure] : invalid: Undistributed Middle
8: No [apes] are [angels]
No [philosophers] are [apes]
Therefore no [philosophers] are [angels] : invalid: two negative premises
10: All [animals] are [bodies]
All [you] are [an animal]
Therefore All [you] are [a body] : valid

All [you] are [a body]
And all [stones] are [bodies] (first premise mentioned)
Therefore all [you] are [a stone] : invalid; Undistributed Middle
12: All [rational beings] are [responsible beings]
No [brute animals] are [responsible beings]
Therefore no [brute animals] are [rational beings] : valid
14: All [knowledge] is [tw comes from sensory impressions]
No [sensory impression] is [twi of substance itself]
Therefore no [knowledge] is [twi of substance itself] : invalid : four terms ("That which comes from sensory impressions" is not the same as "sensory impressions.")
16: All [fighting against neighbors] is [twi evil]
All [fighting against the Thebans] is [fighting against neighbors]
All [fighting against the Thebans] is [twi evil] : valid
18: No [after-image] is [twi in physical space]
All [the brain process] is [twi in physical space]
Therefore no [the after-image] is [the brain process] : valid
20: All [rhapsodes] are [those who interpret the mind of the poet to their hearers]
No [man who does not understand the meaning of a poet] is [a man who interprets the mind of the poet to his hearers]
Therefore no [man who does not understand the meaning of the poet] is [a rhapsode] : valid
22: All [morals] are [tw have an influence on the actions and affections]
No [reason alone] is [tw has an influence on the actions and affections]

Therefore no [morals] are [twi derived from reason] : Invalid: four terms (That which is *derived from* reason is not the same as reason alone.)

24: No [metaphysical sentence] is [either a tautology or an empirical hypothesis]
All [significant, meaningful propositions] are [either tautologies or empirical hypotheses]
Therefore no [metaphysical sentences] are [significant, meaningful propositions] : valid
(But this "verification principle" of "Logical Positivism" is self-contradictory, for it itself is neither a tautology nor an empirical hypothesis, therefore it is by its own criterion meaningless and insignificant.)

26: All [friendship] is [love]
All [love] is [tw has three objects]
Therefore all [friendship] is [tw is of three kinds] : Invalid, four terms as it stands.
However, it is an enthymeme with the implied premise "Whatever has three objects, is of three kinds," and when this is added, we have two valid syllogisms.

28: All [existence] is [a perfection]
No [perfections] are [twi lacking in God]
Therefore no [existence] is [twi lacking in God] : valid
OR:
All [God] is [tw lacks no perfection]
All [tw lacks no perfection] is [tw does not lack existence]
Therefore all [God] is [tw does not lack existence] : valid
However, the argument merely proves that if the concept, or nature, or definition, of God is to lack no perfection, and therefore not to lack existence either, then we can conclude only that the concept of God cannot lack existence; we cannot conclude that God in fact exists. If we begin only with a concept ('God'), we end only with a concept ('God'); if we want to end with more than a concept (God without the quotation marks), we must begin with more than a concept (God without the quotation marks), but that would be begging the question in assuming a real God. You cannot prove God from 'God' without committing the fallacy of four terms. You need other facts to prove the fact of God. A second problem with the argument is the confusion of existence with essence: perfections are qualities of an essence. Existence is not a perfection but the precondition for or actualization of all perfections.

30: Some [twi south] is [twi west]
And some [twi west] is [twi north]
Therefore some [twi south] is [twi north] : invalid, Undistributed Middle and two particular premises. ("*Can* be" means "*Some* is.")

Page 271
2: All [tw makes the world go round] is [tw does not make it go flat] ◄
All [love] is [tw makes the world go round]
Therefore all [love] is [tw does not make it go flat] : valid

OR:

No [tw makes the world go round] is [tw makes it go flat] ◄—
All [love] is [tw makes the world go round]
Therefore no [love] is [tw makes it go flat] : valid

4: No [act of will] is [an emotion] ◄—
All [love] is [an act of will]
Therefore no [love] is [an emotion] : valid

6: No [tw has no wheels] is [tw can be moved] ◄—
All [mountains] are [tw have no wheels]
Therefore no [mountains] are [tw can be moved] : valid

8: All [tw deserve the fair] are [twi brave]
No [you] are [twi brave]
Therefore no [you] are [twi deserve the fair] ◄—: valid (third order enthymeme)

10: No [tw did not have enough food to fulfill the needs of a warm blooded animal] is [a warm blooded animal] ◄—
All [dinosaurs] are [tw did not have enough food to fulfill the needs of a warm blooded animal]
Therefore no [dinosaurs] are [warm blooded animals] : valid

12: All [those whose views were always incompatible with those of the existing societies which they wanted to overthrow] are [those who have always been social radicals] ◄—
All [Marxists] are [those whose views were always incompatible with those of the existing societies which they wanted to overthrow]
Therefore all [Marxists] are [those who have always been social radicals] : valid

14: All [Bull-friendly sets] are [conclusions of Bull's equation] ◄—
No [null sets] are [Bull-friendly sets]
Therefore all [conclusions of Bull's equation] are [null sets] : invalid; affirmative conclusion from negative premise, whichever implied premise we add

16: All [the one to whom the center is hiking the ball] is [the quarterback] ◄—
All [Bub] is [the one to whom the center is hiking the ball]
Therefore all [Bub] is [the quarterback] : valid

18: All [I] am [twi loved by God]
No [twi loved by God] is [junk] ◄—
No [I] am [junk] : valid

20: All [restrictions on abortion] are [restrictions on a woman's right to control her own body] ◄—
All [restrictions on a woman's right to control her own body] are [twi wrong]
Therefore all [restrictions on abortion] are [twi wrong] : valid
(NB most of these arguments can be put into valid form; the main practical use of doing so is not find fallacies, since these are relatively rare, but to smoke out the logically necessary assumptions. The first premise here implies that abortion is controlling the mother's body, not the baby's.)

22: No [tw commit suicide] are [twi happy] ◄—
Some [twi rich] are [tw commit suicide]
Therefore some [twi rich] are not [twi happy] : valid

24: No [twi given by Moses] is [twi given by God] ◄—
All [the 10 Commandments] are [twi given by Moses]
Therefore no [the 10 Commandments] are [twi given by God] : valid, but only
with this questionable premise.

26: All [pines] are [trees] ◄—
All [conifers] are [trees]
Therefore all [pines] are [conifers] : invalid, Undistributed Middle, OR, with
another premise,

All [trees] are [pines] ◄—
All [conifers] are [trees]
Therefore all [pines] are [conifers] : invalid, Illicit Minor. No missing premise
can make it valid.

28: All [green things] are [snakes] ◄—
Some [green things] are not [tw slithers]
Therefore some [snakes] are not [tw slithers] : valid, but only with this obviously false premise. If we use "all snakes are green things" as our premise instead,
we have Undistributed Middle.

30: All [those who are loved by me] are [those who loved God] ◄—
All [St. Thomas] is [one who is loved by me]
Therefore all [St. Thomas] is [one who loved God] : valid

32: As it stands, it is not a syllogism, since the "conclusion" is an imperative.
However,
All [sinners] are [tw should forbear to judge] ◄—
All [we] are [sinners]
Therefore all [we] are [tw should forbear to judge] : valid

34: All [the principal thing] is [tw should be gotten] ◄—
All [wisdom] is [the principal thing]
Therefore all [wisdom] is [tw should be gotten] : valid, cf. #32

36: All [matters which are the subject of one's own free exercise of will] are [mat-
ters in which it is impossible to bind oneself]
All [the king's own laws] are [matters which are the subject of one's own free
exercise of will] ◄—
Therefore all [the king's own laws] are [matters in which it is impossible to bind
oneself] : valid

38: All [flesh] are [twi passive, the plaything, etc.]
All [man] is [flesh]
Therefore all [man] is [passive, the plaything, etc.] : valid

40: No [one who would not take the crown] is [one who was ambitious] ◄—
All [he] is [one who would not take the crown]
Therefore no [he] is [one who was ambitious] : valid

42: All [nations without consciences] are [nations without souls]
All [nations without souls] are [nations which cannot live]
Therefore all [nations without consciences] are [nations which cannot live] ◄— :
valid (third order Enthymeme)

44: All [tw we can explain] is [tw we can reduce to laws whose object can be given in some possible experience]

No [freedom] is [tw we can reduce to laws whose object can be given in some possible experience]

Therefore no [freedom] is [tw we can explain] ◄—: valid

46: All [tw occurs] is [tw God wills to occur] ◄—

All [evil] is [tw occurs]

Therefore all [evil] is [tw God wills to occur] : valid (But which term is ambiguous?)

48: All [those with whom Thou art] are [ones who will fear no evil] ◄—

All [I] am [one with whom Thou art]

Therefore all [I] am [one who will fear no evil] : valid

50: All [tw should be invited to international conferences] are [tw have legions] ◄—

No [the Pope] is [tw has legions]

Therefore no [the Pope] is [tw should be invited to international conferences] : valid

Or, more simply (nearly every syllogism can be recast into an AAA syllogism):

All [tw have no legions] are [tw should not be invited to international conferences]

All [the Pope] is [tw has no legions]

Therefore all [the Pope] is [tw should not be invited to international conferences] : valid

52: All [tw copies nothing] is [tw copies life] ◄—

All [art] is [tw copies nothing]

Therefore all [art] is [tw copies life] : the main syllogism is valid

It is, however, very difficult to put the rest of the argument into a syllogism. Clearly, the fact that "life copies nothing" is the reason why "That which copies nothing, copies life." And the point seems right. But if we put it into a syllogism it will come out fallacious.

All [life] is [tw copies nothing]

Therefore all [tw copies nothing] is [tw copies life]

We already have an illicit minor. We also need to connect the two terms "life" and "tw copies life" in the implied premise. But Chesterton's point is that life does not copy life. It is a clever logical paradox that will apparently not go into a valid syllogism. Can you make it do so?

54: All [tw are at the head of something with which she can do as she likes] are [tw are in the more powerful position] ◄—

All [women] are [tw are at the head of something with which she can do as she likes]

Therefore all [women] are [tw are in the more powerful position] : valid

56: All [things that are never presented otherwise than as a phenomenon] are [things I know not] ◄—

All [things in themselves] are [things that are never presented otherwise than as a phenomenon]

Therefore all [things in themselves] are [things I know not] : valid

58: All [tw assert nothing] are [twi neither true nor false] ◄─
All [metaphysical propositions] are [tw assert nothing]
Therefore all [metaphysical propositions] are [twi neither true nor false] : valid
(NB in this case it is the expressed premise rather than the implied premise that
is false.)

60: This is not a syllogism but an immediate inference, a contraposition (assuming
that 'belonging to no one' and 'not property' are the same term) :
No [twi untouched by human work] is [property]
Therefore all [property] is [twi is touched by human work]

62: All [tw gives you the chance to love, etc.] is [tw you should be glad of] ◄─
All [life] is [tw gives you the chance to love, etc.]
Therefore all [life] is [tw you should be glad of] : valid (Literally, the conclusion
is an imperative, not a declarative, sentence. But it is argued for: it is *followed*
by the premise indicator 'because.')

64: All [tw God has made for Himself] are [those whose hearts are restless until they
rest in God] ◄─
All [we] are [tw God has made for Himself]
Therefore all [we] are [those whose hearts are restless until they rest in God] :
valid, but explanation not argument (like #57)

66: All [animals that laugh and weep] are [animals that are struck by the difference
between what things are and what things ought to be] ◄─
All [animals that are struck by the difference between what things are and what
things ought to be] are [men]
Therefore all [animals that laugh and weep] are [men] : valid; explanation by
efficient cause (being struck by this difference *moves* us to laugh and weep)

68: All [pleasure and pain] are [tw we cease from at the same time]
No [good and evil] are [tw we case from at the same time]
Therefore no [pleasure and pain] are [good and evil] : valid

70: All [tw made many plain people] is [tw loves plain people] ◄─
All [God] is [tw made many plain people]
Therefore all [God] is [tw loves plain people] : valid; OR:

All [twi many] is [twi loved by God] ◄─
All [plain people] are [twi many]
Therefore all [plain people] are [twi loved by God] : valid

Page 282
2. Some [lizards] are not [tw bite]
All [lizards are [reptiles]
Therefore Some [reptiles] are not [tw bite]
And All [reptiles] are [snakes]
Therefore Some [snakes] are not [tw bite]
Valid, but only with the circled premise, which is false.
4. All [tw laugh at my bad puns] are [tw love me]
All [she] is [tw laughed at my bad puns]
Therefore all [she] is [tw loves me]

(Re-word this to:) All [I] am [twi loved by her]
All [twi loved by her] are [those whose lives are meaningful]
Therefore All [I] am [one of those whose lives are meaningful]
Valid, but only with the two circled premises.
6. All [angels] are [pure spirits]
   All [pure spirits] are [twi not composed of atoms]
   Therefore All [angels] are [twi not composed of atoms]
   All [twi not composed of atoms] are [tw does not occupy space]
   Therefore All [angels] are [tw does not occupy space]
   All [tw does not occupy space] are [tw cannot be confined in prisons]
   Therefore All [angels] are [tw cannot be confined in prisons]
   Valid.

Page 285
2:

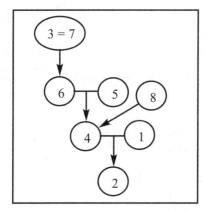

4:

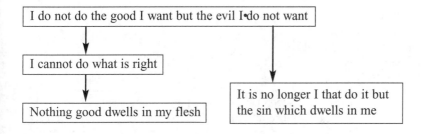

6:

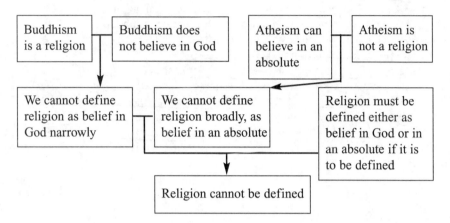

8:

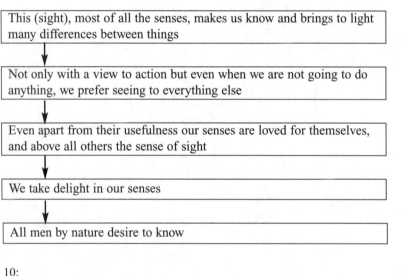

10:

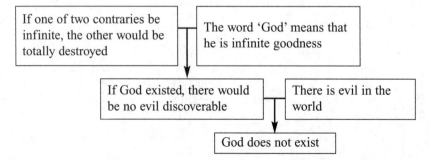

12:

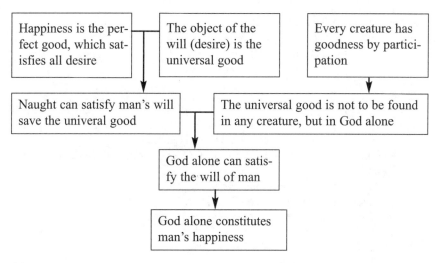

14:

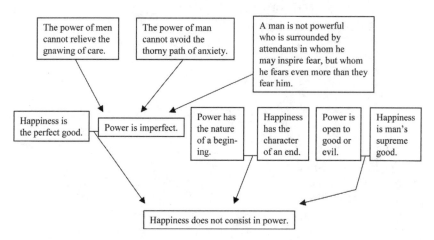

Page 299

2: Denying the Consequent; a valid enthymeme, with the implied premise "light does not possess momentum"

4: An enthymeme with the second premise *and* the conclusion implied. Valid, Denying the Consequent:

If [the objective of marriage were contentment then the discontent of either party would be a sufficient reason for ending it

But it is not true that the discontent of either party is a sufficient reason for ending it

Therefore it is not true that the objective of marriage is contentment

6: p = you are deceived
    q = you exist
    r = you can be certain you exist
    s = you can be certain of something
    t = you are not a skeptic

$p \supset q$	$q \supset r$	$r \supset s$	$s \supset t$
p	q	r	s
$\therefore$ q	$\therefore$ r	$\therefore$ s	$\therefore$ t

8: If [everyone followed total pacifism] then [total pacifism is a good principle]
    But it is not true that [everyone follows total pacifism]
    Therefore it is not true that [total pacifism is a good principle] : invalid: Denying
    the Antecedent

10: p = a man is morally responsible for an act
    q = a man is a legitimate object of moral praise or blame for an act
    r = a man is in some important sense a free agent

    $p \supset q$
    $q \supset r$
    $\therefore p \supset r$ valid: a pure hypothetical syllogism

12: p = Beauty is an objective reality
    q = Beauty is in the eye of the beholder

    $p \supset {\sim}q$
    q
    $\therefore {\sim}p$ valid: Denying the Consequent

14: p = God does not exist
    q = we feel so alone that we are unable to endure a universe without Him

    $p \supset q$
    q
    $\therefore$ p invalid: Affirming the Consequent

16: p = I eat chocolates
    q = I get migraines

    $p \supset q$
    q
    $\therefore$ p invalid: Affirming the Consequent

18: p = there is confidence in promises
    q = the greatest part of our conduct proceeds upon chance
    r = men are obliged to perform their promises

    ${\sim}p \supset q$
    ${\sim}r \supset {\sim}p$
    $\therefore {\sim}r \supset q$ valid: pure hypothetical syllogism

20: p = mankind understands the power of love
    q = man builds noble temples and altars and offers solemn sacrifices in his honor

p ⊃ q

~q

∴ ~p valid: Denying the Consequent

22: p = I am great

q = I am misunderstood

p ⊃ q

q

∴ p invalid: Affirming the Consequent

NB this can also be put into a categorical syllogism as follows:

All [twi great] are [twi misunderstood]

All [I] am [twi misunderstood]

Therefore all [I] am [twi great] invalid: Undistributed Middle

24: p = men are angels

q = no government is necessary

p ⊃ q

~p

∴ ~q invalid: Denying the Antecedent (But perhaps it is not meant as an enthymeme, i.e. not an <u>argument</u> at all, but as an <u>explanation</u> of why government is necessary by contrasting the real situation and an ideal situation, in which men are angels).

26: p = I cherished iniquity in my heart

q = God listened to my prayer

p ⊃ ~q

q

∴ ~p valid: Denying the Consequent

Page 302

2: p = the professor's Theory of General Insanity is true

q = I am insane

p v q

~p

∴ ~q (invalid)

4: p = human authority is natural

q = human authority is conventional

p v q

~p

∴ q (valid)

6: p = a tail is there

q = a tail isn't there

p v q

~p

∴ q (valid)

Page 305

2: p = vampires are undead
   q = vampires are dead
   r = vampires are alive

~[p & q]
p
∴ ~q (valid)

~[q & r]
~q
∴ r (invalid) "Dead" and "alive" may not be the only two possibilities.

4: p = Plato is objectively reasoning about love
   q = Plato is subjectively experiencing love
   r = Plato has a right to philosophize about love

~[p & q]
p
∴ ~q (valid)

~q ⊃ ~r (You could argue that this is a false premise.)
~q
∴ ~r (valid: Affirming the Antecedent)

6: No [disjunction] is [conjunction]
   All [disjunction] is [twi exclusive]
   No [conjunction] is [twi exclusive] invalid: illicit major

Page 311

2: p = culture is profound and noble
   q = culture remains rare
   r = culture is common
   s = culture becomes mean

(p ⊃ q) & (r ⊃ s)
p v r (implied premise of the enthymeme)
∴ q v s (implied conclusion)

Answer: One could take it by the horns and deny that common culture must become mean. Or one could escape between the horns and embrace a sort of compromise culture just common enough to escape rarity and just noble enough to escape meanness.

4: p = a man knows what he is inquiring about
   q = a man has need to inquire
   r = a man can inquire

(p ⊃ ~q) & (~p ⊃ ~r)
p v ~p
∴ ~q v ~r

Plato himself escapes between the horns of this dilemma in the *Meno* by con-
tending that a man can inquire by "remembering" what he has forgotten. We
might call this making implicit knowledge explicit, or raising unconscious
knowledge to the level of consciousness. "Know" is ambiguous.

6: p = these books agree with the Qur'an
q = these books are superfluous
r = these books are heretical
s = these books should be burned

$(p \supset q)$ & $(\sim p \supset r)$
$p \vee \sim p$
$\therefore q \vee r$

$(q \supset s)$ & $(r \supset s)$
$q \vee r$
$\therefore s$

One could take it by a horn: a book can "agree with" the Qur'an without being
superfluous: e.g. helpful commentaries on it. One can also escape between the
horns: a book of geography, e.g. neither agrees nor disagrees with the Qur'an.
Finally, one can take the *second* dilemma by the horns and say that there are better things to do with superfluous or heretical books than burning them: e.g.
heretical books can be argued against and refuted. Muhammad would not have
approved Omar's act or his reason for it.

8: p = the reader knows how to read a book before reading *How to Read a Book*
q = *How to Read a Book* is superfluous
r = *How to Read a Book* is unreadable

$(p \supset q)$ & $(\sim p \supset r)$
$p \vee \sim p$
$\therefore q \vee r$

Adler himself would escape between these horns. His book is not for those who
cannot read at all, nor is it for those who can read as well as he can, but for those
in the middle. In other words, the term 'read' is used ambiguously.

10: p = the conclusion of a deduction contains something new that is not in the
premises
q = the deduction is useless
r = the deduction is logically invalid

$(\sim p \supset q)$ & $(p \supset r)$
$\sim p \vee p$
$\therefore q \vee r$

One could escape between the horns since a conclusion can be validly implied
by the premises but not explicitly known until deduction shows it. It can be psychologically new without being logically new. See also pages 222–30.

12: p = freedom of speech is restricted
q = we will cease to be a democracy
r = we will be at the mercy of demagogues and fanatics

$(p \supset q)$ & $(\sim p \supset r)$
p v $\sim$p
$\therefore$ q v r

Either horn can be denied. Every democracy restricts *some* speech. (This "some" means, in effect, escaping between the horns.) And if speech is not restricted, demagogues and fanatics will speak but we need not be at their mercy.

14: p = a thing moves
q = a thing moves where it is
r = a thing moves where it isn't

$p \supset [q \, v \, r]$
$\sim[q \, v \, r]$
$\therefore \sim p$

This is really a hypothetical syllogism, Denying the Consequent. We can answer it by denying the first (hypothetical) premise, for a thing moves *from* one place *to* another, not either *where* it is or *where* it isn't.

16: p = the citizens are good
q = laws are unnecessary to prevent evil
r = laws are impotent to prevent evil

$(p \supset q)$ & $(\sim p \supset r)$
p v $\sim$p
$\therefore$ q v r

The second horn seems weak and "takeable." Laws obviously make a potent difference and deter many evil men from many evil deeds by threat of punishment.

Page 317
2: Descartes's data base for his generalization is extremely tiny: only one example!
4: First, it is not at all clear, or agreed, that these are relevant examples of oppression. Most individuals in these relationships did not feel oppressed. Second, they are only professional and economic relationships: there are many other kinds.
6: The inductive generalization can be corroborated by ordinary experience. Its conclusion is put in the sentence beginning with "It looks, in fact, very much as if . . ." The following hypothetical syllogism beginning with "And there would be no sense . . ." is illustrated, in the same sentence, by the analogy of football, and the analogy specifies the common principle: agreement about the rules. This too seems corroborated by experience.

Page 333
2: Relevant differences include the following: 1) "Semitic" is a racial adjective; "American" is not. 2) "Anti-Zionism" does not always seek the abolition of Israel: sometimes it seeks only equal sovereignty for Palestine. 3) No one makes any

important distinction between "America" and "the United States," as they do between Zionism and Israel. Relevant similarities include the following: 1) Both nations came into existence through military force against another nation's will and territory. 2) Both were based on beliefs or ideology. 3) Precisely because there is no parallel here to people who want the U.S. to not exist, the analogy is powerful in opening American's eyes to how Israelis feel: "how would you feel if you . . . ?"

4: This is not an argument but an illuminating illustration. Both the experience of difficulty and the objective reason for it seem similar. By the way, all or nearly all thought about immaterial things rests on analogies with material things. Wittgenstein also said, startlingly, that "the best picture of a human soul that we can imagine is a human body."

6: Obviously, the former has worked many times, while the latter has not. A theater is a specialty that requires specialized competence, while a democratic government governs not some specialty but human life as a whole in its public domain; so the analogy seems superficial.

8: This is a very common and commonsensical argument from analogy. A text, composed of different letters, and a universe, composed of different things, are both diverse matter formed into a unified order (a *uni*-verse), things of different natures working together for a common result. This can be done only by a planning intelligence. This analogy is one form of the most popular of all arguments for a God, the "argument from design," and the version given here seems intuitively convincing, especially because its conclusion is not bold but claims very little, and its claim is negative, not positive: it does not claim to know who or what the intelligence behind the universe is, only that it is not just blind chance.

10: If water and air are in all relevant ways similar, this is a convincing analogy. It is also verifiable by experiment and measurement.

12: This is probably not an *argument* but an explanation showing how in both cases, physical and mental, a tiny amount of evil can corrupt a large amount of good.

14: The analogy holds only on the questionable assumption that ideas are pictures.

16: A fruitful analogy ("by their fruits you shall know them"), based on the common principle that "action follows being" (*operatio sequitur esse*); i.e. the activity, or work, of any thing reveals its nature.

18: The fact that the analogy strikes one as ridiculous does not disqualify it, for that is precisely its point: that the thought that women need men is ridiculous, that there is no natural or necessary relation between women and men, that women have no more need or use for men than fish have for bicycles. The point, of course, is simply false: no fish ever used a bicycle to become happy, pregnant, protected, loved, honored, or even sexually stimulated. A piece of ideological fantasy, not a real analogy.

20: If you think this is a fair analogy for pregnancy, you probably believe in the stork. The only abortion thiis analogy could possibly justify is the abortion of a baby whose conception was due to violence and rape. Even there, the violinist is not the woman's child: surely a relevant consideration. And it is questionable whether even in this strange case it is justifiable to kill the violinist if he is innocent. Almost as bizarre as the fish and the bicycle.

Pages 336–341
Sample of Logical Analysis of the "Exercise on Nearly Everything"

1. T's conclusion ("I guess that proves . . .") is a *non sequitur* and a *hasty generalization* (look them up).

2. The implied syllogism here is:

   All (part of me) is (my people).
   All (my people) are (insulted by your complimenting me).
   Therefore all (part of me) is (insulted by your complimenting me).

3. T distinguishes individuals from the "system"; and implicitly accuses F of the fallacy of division (predicating of individuals what is said of a group); but a "system" is not a group of individuals but a set of laws and customs.

4. This is simply a direct question and a direct answer. It might be accused of *begging the question* though.

5. T's "everybody knows" is an *argumentum ad populam.*

6. F's reply is an *ad hominem.*

7. This is F's thesis, or conclusion, which F and T will argue about.

8. "True for you" is meaningless patronizing, as F shows with her argument:

   If something is not true, it cannot be true for you.
   And this is not true.
   Therefore it cannot be "true for you."

9. T's syllogism is: All love is great;
   All your love for your society is love;
   Therefore all your love for your society is great.

   Perhaps implied is also:
   Some love is blind;
   All love is great;
   Therefore some of what is blind is great.

10. F disagrees with T's "love is blind" premise.
    T tries to prove it with the following sylloism:

    Whatever makes you blind to injustice, is blind.
    Your love of your society makes you blind to injustice.
    Therefore your love of your society is blind.
    And your love of your society is love.
    Therefore some love is blind.

11. F uses a disjunctive syllogism.

    p = Iraq is one of the most just societies on Earth.
    q = I'm as blind to injustice as a bat is to the sun.
    p v q
    not q
    therefore p

12. To T's challenge to prove p, T responds with a sorites:

All (Iraq) is (an Islamic society).
All (Islamic societies) are (societies formed by Islamic law).
All (societies formed by Islamic law) are (societies formed by the most just law on Earth).
All (societies formed by the most just law on Earth) are (one of the most just societies on Earth).
Therefore all (Iraq) is (one of the most just societies on Earth).

13. T's rhetorical question is the premise of an enthymeme:

No (society that oppresses women) is (one of the most just societies on Earth).
All (Iraq) is (a society that oppresses women).
Therefore no (Iraq) is (one of the most just societies on Earth).

14. F tries to disprove the second premise of T's syllogism with the following enthymemic epicheirema:

All (Iraq) is (a society formed by Islamic law).
All (societies formed by Islamic law) are (societies formed by the true natural law).
Therefore (Iraq) is (a society formed by the true natural law).
No (society formed by the true natural law) is (an oppressive society).
Therefore no (Iraq) is (an oppressive society).

15. T disputes the second premise of the above argument and tries to refute it thusly:

All (Iraq) is (a society that doesn't even allow a woman to vote or appear in public without a veil).
No (society that doesn't even allow a woman to vote or appear in public without a veil) is (a society formed by the true natural law).
Therefore no (Iraq) is (a society formed by the true natural law).

Index of Principal Names